The Meadow of the Bull

A history of Clontarf

Best Wishes
Dennis McIntyre

Dennis McIntyre

Dedication

To Clontarf

and

Its people.

Published by:

The Shara Press

"Glenbeigh"

32 Howth Road,

Clontarf, Dublin 3, Ireland.

Email: dracdennis@hotmail.com

© Dennis McIntyre

ISBN no: 978-0-9527311-2-2

First Published April 1987

Second Edition April 2014

The Material in this publication is protected by copyright law. No part of the material included may be reproduced, printed, copied, stored in a
retrieval system or transmitted in any form or by any means, electronic, mechanical, photocopying, recording or otherwise (now known or hereafter invented) or adapted, rented or lent without the written permission of the author as copyright owner.

Layout, Design & Printing by

www.printsourcesolutions.ie

Contacting Clontarf Tourism
(incorporating the Stoker Dracula Gothic Organisation)

All correspondence, enquiries etc with regard to:

1) the above organisation eg tours, walks, talks, powerpoint presentations, film shows etc

2) Book Orders for "The Meadow of the Bull" - A history of Clontarf" and "Bram Stoker and the Irishness of Dracula"

3) Other publications and souvenirs/merchandise issued/supplied under the auspices of "Clontarf Tourism" should be directed to:

Clontarf Tourism
Glenbeigh,
32 Howth Road,
Clontarf,
Dublin 3,
Ireland.
E-mail: clontarfestival@gmail.com or
dracdennis@hotmail.com
Websites: www.thebramstokerorganisation.com

Contents

Preface to First edition
Preface to Second edition

Chapter One: 1
Where is Clontarf?
Clontarf - Origin of Name
Ancient Names associated with Clontarf
Clontarf and the Sea
Fishing in Clontarf - The Sheds
Clontarf in the nineteenth century - Greenlanes
The approach to Clontarf
Character of Clontarf and her people
Today's Clontarf

Chapter Two: 19
Christianity in Clontarf
The Early days
Vikings
Norman's and Knights
History of the Catholic Church in Clontarf since the Reformation
340 Years of Clontarf Parish Priests 1620 - 1966
Clontarf's three Catholic Parishes
History of the Church of Ireland in Clontarf
All Saints Church of Ireland, St. Annes Park, Raheny
Clontarf Presbyterian Church and Parish
Clontarf Methodist Church
Clontarf Graveyard, Castle Avenue
Convent House

Chapter Three: 52
Earliest Settlers
Brian Boru and the Battle of Clontarf

Brian Boru's Well
The Brian Boru Harp
The Brian Boru Tree
Brian Boru's Skull
Legacy

Chapter Four: 76
Clontarf in the Middle Ages
Various Occurrences
The Crown takes the Castle
The 1641 Rebellion in Clontarf
The Vernon Family and Clontarf Castle
The Castle Building

Chapter Five: 86
Daniel O'Connell and Repeal
James Stephens and the I.R.B
The Howth Gun-Running
Clontarf Town Hall and the 1916 Rising

Chapter Six: 96
Clontarf Island
The North Bull Island
History of the Growth of the North Bull Island
Geography of the North Bull Island
Ownership of and Buildings on the North Bull Island
Conserving the Island
Wildlife and Vegetation on the North Bull Island
The North Bull Island as a Biosphere Reserve
The North Bull Island Interpretive Centre
The Causeway Road
Uses of the Bull Island
Curleys Hole
Statue of our Lady of the Port of Dublin
Bull Island
Shooting Competition on Bull Island

Chapter Seven: 126
St. Annes Park
The Guinness Family
The Making of Lord Ardilaun
Lady Ardilaun
St.Annes Rose Garden

Chapter Eight: 143
Lord Charlemont and Marino
The Casino
Furry Park House

Chapter Nine: 153
Origin of the Place Names in Clontarf
Clontarf - Street by Street, Road by Road
Periphery Roads and St Anne's Housing Estate Roads

Chapter Ten: 170
Famous Clontarfites - Past and Present
Politicians
Literary Figures
Others
The Infamous Sham Squire

Chapter Eleven: 186
Schools in Clontarf
Clontarf Royal Charter School
Mount Temple Comprehensive School
The Hibernian Marine School
Greenlanes School
Clontarf Presbyterian School
St Pauls College
Holy Faith Convent
Clontarf Traffic School for Children
Clontarf National Schools
Belgrove Schools are Born
Belgrove House (St Johns House)

Chapter Twelve: 201
Health Service in Clontarf
The Central Remedial Clinic
The Incorporated Orthopedic Hospital of Ireland
The Irish Wheelchair Association
Verville Retreat
Nursing Homes
Clontarf Community Affairs
Clontarf Residents Association
Clontarf Community Festival
Éigse agus Pobal Chluain Tarbh
Clontarf Community Information Centre
Clontarf Garda Station
Scouts in Clontarf
Public Transport in Clontarf
Clontarf's Licensed Premises
Clontarf Baths
Clontarf's Blue Lagoon
Clontarf Lead Mine
Clontarf's Rivers
Crab Lake

Chapter Thirteen: 227
The Sports Clubs of Clontarf
Gaelic Football in Clontarf
Soccer in Clontarf
Clontarf Rugby Football Club
Golf Clubs
Swimming
Clontarf Yacht and Boat Club
Clontarf Cricket Club
Tennis

Appendixes:

1. From Dublin Directory 1870
2. From Dublin Directory 1910
3. From Porter's guide and Directory for North County Dublin. 1912
4. Address of King Brian Boru to his Army prior to the Battle of Clontarf, Good Friday 1014.
5. A song of defeat.
6. Brien the Brave.
7. Suppression of 1843 "Monster Meeting"
8. Captain Weldon's hand written account of the escape of James Stephens.
9. Addendum.
10. Clontarf Shops of Yore.

Nota Bene:
Where small reference numbers eg, 1,2,3,4 etc appear in the text corresponding numbers with relevant information can be consulted at the end of the chapter.

PREFACE TO FIRST EDITION

"If a man is worth knowing at all, he is worth knowing well" **Alexander Smith**

A good knowledge of our locality or district can give us a sense of identity within our surroundings. A local history can be socially helpful by making life more meaningful. It can even generate patriotism. Besides, ignorance is sad. A local history can be a kind of historical anchor in the parish and surrounds.

Today, in a vastly changing and fast moving world, it is perhaps more important than ever to be familiar with one's roots and one's heritage. Yet, sadly, so many young people are deprived of this sense of identity and belonging.

While writing local history can be something of a passion for some people, most of us are fascinated by relics from the past. We find details of the past precious and although we cannot recreate or buy back old times, we love tracing the development of past generations and recording that development. The more we find out about the past, the more we feel we have an insight into life's line of development. The past is precious to us; we patronise it. We believe we are more sophisticated and consequently feel superior. But in may aspects we can be surprised - our forefathers weren't so backward at all in many ways. Moreover, while the future is a mystery to us all we can look at the past critically. And surely understanding the past - especially mistakes that were made can lead to more understanding and tolerance. A local history shows up the noble and ignoble moments of any parish. In this way it can be a valuable contribution to the future of the local community.

"To be able to enjoy ones past life is to live twice"
Marcus Valerius Martialis

When we think of history, generally, we tend to assemble visions of round towers, St Patrick, the Norman's and events which always seemed to happen elsewhere. With local history we must realise that history is on our immediate doorstep, and that we ourselves are part of the process that is history. Thus local history is more meaningful than the more abstract general history. And a knowledge of local history can enable the student to progress from the particular to the general.

I have many reasons for attempting to produce a history of Clontarf. First of all I like history as a subject - especially local history, and being something of a collector and recorder by nature it seemed a logical avenue to follow if only to fulfill personal curiosity. Since I first heard of Brian Boru, and his great triumph in 1014, the name Clontarf has always had a magical ring for me. When I came to live and work in Clontarf I became somewhat enchanted with the area. In a sense my Clontarf local history is a thank you to a place which, in the past number of years, I have come to call home.

Another reason for my attempt to collect and compile Clontarf's saga is the fact that during the 1970's and 1980's many of Clontarf's sporting clubs (rugby, cricket, swimming, golf) have celebrated their centenaries. Thus one can state that "social Clontarf" is a centenarian about now so it seemed a ripe time to record her story. I have always wanted to separate myth and legend concerning Clontarf from fact and reality. Being so historically rich, the vicinity of Clontarf I feel, has a longstanding need of recording and preserving her store of historical data and eradicating at least some conflicting accounts of many events. But above all perhaps the real reason I embarked on the perilous voyage towards a history of Clontarf is the fact that I realised that there was a practical need for such a production as it simply had not been previously produced. As a teacher I felt that a comprehensive reference book documenting the history of the area would be most useful for many aspects of classroom work on the locality... indeed since the introduction of the "new curriculum" at primary school level in the early 1970's it is urged that particular attention be given to studying local history- so that studying history's effect on their own locality might help pupils understand a wider scale of historical study later. In Clontarf's case, it is hard to imagine a more practical starting point for a study of any period of our national history as so many phases, events and personalities in our country's story have a Clontarf dimension.

In attempting to capture Clontarf's story in the form of a local history publication, I have no pretentions to produce a critical or analytical work. Nor have I had illusions of compiling a literary masterpiece - indeed by its very nature local history leads to some meandering and even repetition. In any case this work is aimed to be a collection and presentation of available data on Clontarf. It is meant to be purely and simply the tale of Clontarf's history past and present. It attempts to compile the story of Clontarf today and yesterday - some of it a Clontarf you may not know. It is the result of a detailed process of research over the past few years and whatever its shortcomings, I think you will agree that it is fairly comprehensive. At least it has taken me into Clontarf's forgotten catacombs; it has led me through her threadbare diaries and sent me foraging among the files of her dusty archives.

Compiling Clontarf's life file has caused me some moments of agony, frustration and even despair. However the joys and compensations too have been plentiful- such as eventually managing to eke out that date, or name from an avalanche of references and cross references. But above all I must record and give due appreciation to the solid support I received from a cross-section of Clontarfites - who were always a refuge for me when morale might be at a low ebb! One can say that the greatest asset any locality has, its best heritage, is the quality of its people, especially the youth, the adults of tomorrow. Having close contact with 'growing up' Clontarf (through Belgrove School and through many sporting involvements) it is evident to me that Clontarf's youth will safeguard her future. I hope my meagre 'labour of love' on Clontarf will help preserve her heritage for future generations.

The bulk of this work was written during the course of 1986, but I have made every effort to include information and relevant facts up to the time of publication. Readers will understand that, with a work such as this, certain information 'dates'. This is a hazard which simply cannot be avoided. If I have omitted any aspect of 'Clontarf's History', it is purely accidental.

ACKNOWLEDGEMENTS

I wish to acknowledge my deep and sincere thanks to everybody who contributed in any way to the compilation of this volume on the history of Clontarf. My fondest recollections of the sometimes difficult writing period will be of the positive suggestions and the general encouragement I received from so many people. I wish to offer my deep gratitude to all those who gave of their valuable time to jog their memories for me. I wish to warmly thank everybody who lent me private materials - books, pamphlets, articles, magazines, maps, photographs and other memorabilia. Indeed if the hallmarks of greatness are co-operation, kindness and helpfulness then Clontarfites qualify with something to spare. The people I refer to are the general people of Clontarf. They include club leaders - past and present - local historians, retired teachers, church leaders and many of my colleagues on the teaching staff of Belgrove Schools as well as teachers in other Clontarf Schools. They also include members of staffs of many public offices, institutions and bodies. They include various manuscript readers, photographers, artist and the typist. I hope that this volume in some ways repays everyone for their trust and help..

Dennis McIntyre
April 1987

Preface to second edition

As I began the work of updating "The Meadow of the Bull" (Clontarf's historical story), I was genuinely shocked to realise that the twenty seventh Springtime had come upon me since that auspicious publication date back in 1987.
Tempus Fugit! Indeed. Constant demand for copies of the book, as much as any other factor, led me down the road of a fresh edition. The second shock for me was realising the rate and extent of the changes in those years.

"There is music in my heart all day
I hear it late and early
It comes from fields far far away
The wind that shakes the barley"   **J.C Mangan**

Every age changed and changes because things new and better were and are invented. The Bronze Age didn't come to an end because of the lack of bronze! In the aforementioned 27 years, the very heart of society and the way we live has changed, as has our tolerance, values and attitudes - only maybe not enough. We have begun to dismantle the Irish world of dishonesty, corruption, hypocracy (and collusion there-in), the "nod and wink" mentality, lack of transparency, nonaccountability and nepotism. Many "Sacred Cows" have been removed, many of the "smug", choked with sheer avarice, have been exposed and humiliated and some of the meek are at last getting a taste of life's sweet wine. A certain amount of openness and a better sense of proportion and equality has fallen upon us and the "Golden Circle" in the "Hallowed Halls" at least challenged as competition emerged in fields for so long labelled "Closed Shop"

While the great"Mammon" may never really be challenged its good to feel that traditional values will always stand the test of time and that today's Clontarf is part of an Ireland somewhat cleansing itself, awakening and breaking free from the repressive chains of such as authoritarianism, repression, conformity, conservatism, provincialism, double standards, the cover-up mentality and the yoke and badge of begrudgery.

Surely nepotism/cronyism/favouritism is one of our most henoius of practices, indeed a practice we have just about patented. Instead of despising this activity, which is rampant at all levels in our incestuous society, we appear to be happy that what counts in this state is not what you know but who. It can be observed at all levels of society from the corrupt vainglorious or alcoholic (or all three) Parish Priest inflicting a favourite/nepot teacher as principal (though totally incompetent and unsuitable to the position) on a school staff to a state minister rewarding "the boys" (or indeed "the girls") who "delivered" in the election campaign. Another to be despised operator in our midst is the Brathadóir (the informer or the traitor). A type vilified throughout our torturous history, the Brathadóir is still at large. Its simply gut-wrenching to observe someone so blinded/mesmerised/indoctrinated by an individual or an institution or more likely promotion or a "position" as to inform on or betray a colleague. Nepotism and brathadorism must be ruthlessly gutted out of our society.

We await a government that isn't obsessed with the tax, fines, interest and penalties (and the Most High between us and austerity) but rather lead from the front in reawakening throughout our land traits we used to abound in such as imagination and creativity. Employment and jobs must always be our priority.

So much has changed. So many small businesses, and especially shops, have gone reflecting changes in lifestyles such as fast food replacing the traditional family meal.

Twenty seven years ago modern amenities such as cash dispensing machines and mobile phones were unheard of for the masses while the personal computer was in its infancy. Who foresaw the major decline in the role and the status of the Public House - once the hub of the social circuit? Suffice it is to say that in Clontarf that well known establishment, Dollymount House, has come and gone. And of the once three once great players in Irish Life - the Catholic Church, the

Fianna Fáil political party and the Gaelic Athletic Association (GAA), only the latter has (despite emigration problems, especially in rural Ireland) weathered the tsunami of change we experienced and are experiencing.

One of the most striking (and shameful) episodes of thirty years ago (late 1970's and early 1980's) was the way Dublin allowed the world-class irreplaceable heritage site that was the Viking settlements of Wood Quay, in the heart of Dublin, to be brutally demolished and destroyed. This was surely a pivotal time when Dublin undeniably blighted its soul, character and very dignity. I hope that our youth - grown and growing - in a world almost engulfed by technology and consumed by greed will never repeat such an appalling occurrence. In Clontarf, the history of which is surely a microcosm of Irish History generally, we must be wary of the speculator / developer/builder and the bulldozer a combination that can do (and has done) more damage in a few hours than vandals do in a lifetime. And Clontarf arms must always especially protectively cuddle its three great natural amenities - the sea (Dublin Bay, Clontarf Bay) the Bull Island and St.Annes Park. We must never confuse conservatism with conservation.

While over the years many are the good Clontarfites who have shuffled off this mortal coil, and I salute them, there is one aspect of Clontarf that hasn't changed for me and that is the genuiness of the people of Clontarf I have met and Deo Volento will continue to meet. I feel charmed to have wonderful friends throughout the locality and I hereby acknowledge and treasure their friendships. And Clontarf itself surely remains an iconic part of Ireland's capital city of Dublin.

The author L.P. Hartley in the first sentence of his book "The Go-Between" wrote "the past is a foreign country; they do things differently there"

How relevant is that observation now?

Dennis McIntyre
April 2014

CHAPTER ONE

Where is Clontarf?

For the purposes of this study when I refer to Clontarf I am speaking of that part of coastal north-east Dublin surrounded by the areas known as Fairview, Marino, Donnycarney, Killester, Artane and Raheny. Dublin Bay embraces the remainder of Clontarf's boundary and the area includes Dollymount and part of the offshore island known as the North Bull Island. Clontarf is within the Dublin 3 postal area and for general election purposes lies in the constituency of Dublin Bay North. If the reader looks at a street map of Dublin City North, Clontarf is essentially that suburban area enclosed by the Howth Road, and the sea, and the area lies in the old barony of Coolock. But it is physically, geographically and historically impossible to divorce Clontarf and her story from the broader history of her hinterland and indeed from that of the country in general. As we shall see Clontarf had a vital part to play in the circumstances surrounding many major events central to the creating of our national story.

Basically Clontarf comprises of three distinct districts:
i) The medieval village of Clontarf represented today by Clontarf Castle and the Castle Avenue area.
ii) The eighteenth century fishing village known as Clontarf Sheds which was centered where today we have the modern Clontarf village at the junction of Vernon Avenue and Clontarf Road.
iii) The 'newest' area of Clontarf, Dollymount.
But many aspects of Clontarf's history will bring us straying far beyond these boundaries-for example the 1014 battle of Clontarf will have us 'broadcasting' from places such as Cashel and Bruree. Local historical sites and characters not within the Clontarf precinct but which, because of their proximity and historical significance, will be dealt with in considerable detail. These include Lord Ardilaun and St. Anne's Park (which has a Raheny Dublin 5 postal address), Lord Charlemont and his Marino Estate and Furry Park House. Indeed in parts we will find ourselves stretching the Clontarf boundary to the Malahide Road to include 'traditional' Clontarf roads such as The Crescent, Charlemont Road and the Copelands. Many residents regard the Dublin Belfast railway line as Clontarf's 'western frontier', but in truth there is no strict demarcation line and it is impossible to say, for example, where Clontarf ends and Killester begins. And even where there are fairly clear boundaries we sometimes have to stray outside

in order to include a place or a building that is vital to our mental picture of the area we are discussing.

Clontarf - Origin of the Name

"When mingling with the wreckful wail
From low Clontarf's wave trampled floor,
Comes booming up the burdened gale,
The angry sand-bull's roar" **Sir Samuel Ferguson**

Clontarf[1] is often mentioned in the Annals and various other Irish manuscripts from the eight century martyrology of Tallaght down to the renowned seventeenth century history of Ireland, penned by Doctor Geoffrey Ketting. The spelling of the name is consistently 'Cluain Tarbh', e.g " Comhfoigsí do ChluainTarbh" (annals of Ulster iii, 594); " i gCluain Tarbh" (annals of the four masters A.D 1013); " Cluain Tarbh i Magh Ealta Eadair" (Wars of the Gael and Gall 176). In two manuscripts only the 'tarbh' is recorded with an 'i' - 'Tairbh'. The Book of Lecan, 115 has "Aodan Cluana Tairbh". The Book of Ballymote records both forms- "siol nDodharcon Cluana Tarbh"(124A) and "Clan Cluana Tairbh"(12B). Thus the authentic 'Cluain Tarbh' an ancient proud and honourable name has been handed down in writing for twelve hundred years. Direct translation gives us The Meadow (Cluain) of the Bull or Bulls (Tarbh). It has been suggested that Cluain Tarbh could originally have been Cuan Tarbh, i.e The Bay of the Bull. It would seem fitting considering Clontarf's position in the eye of Dublin Bay but we must trust the ancient manuscripts. Cluain Tarbh has also been translated as the field of the bull or the plain of the bull, where in early agricultural times cows were brought to be served by the bull.

Tradition holds that the noise the waves of the sea created as they beat along the shingle and sands of the Clontarf coastline resembled the bellowing of a bull. And in the misty past the lush meadow that was the Clontarf plain tranquilised the roar of the waves. To our own day the bull is alleged to roar whenever a storm throws the foaming breakers over Clontarf's sandbanks. Our earliest settlers could always hear the roar of the tide on the sand banks which filled Dublin Bay. It sounded like the bellowing of a bull and thus the North Bull and the South Bull got their names. Then the nearest ground above the sand on the north side of the bay was called Cluain Tarbh, 'The Meadow of the Bull'. Some commentators have tried to connect Clontarf's historic name with the large sandbank known as North Bull Island. Is it quite ridiculous to suggest that Clontarf derived her name from it as the sand island is but a modern phenomenon and the district has had her name centuries before the island appeared.

From my research I have found that Clontarf shares its name with four other Clontarf's worldwide, all named after our subject by Irish immigrants who took the name with them to their new worlds. There are two places called Clontarf in Australia. One is a suburb of Sydney, the second a suburb of the city of Redcliffe some 35 kilometres north of Brisbane. From studying maps of both Australian cities our two namesakes are situated in remarkable similar positions in relation to their cities as Clontarf is to Dublin, i.e. on the north-eastern side of the harbour. In America, in the north central state of Minnesota there is a small town named Clontarf. In Canada, in the Orillia-Pembroke-Kingston area of southern Ontario there is an unincorporated place (name approved) called Clontarf. This one is in good 'Irish' company as it is surrounded by a host of places with Irish names, e.g. Letterkenny, Tramore, Connaught and even Fairview! And for good measure the nineteenth century county Meath poet Thomas O' Brien chose the pseudonym 'Clontarf!'[2]

Ancient Names Associated with Clontarf

Placing Clontarf historically involves recalling from the archives some long forgotten place names and territorial boundaries.

Moynalty

The late Mr. B Bowen in an article read to the Old Dublin Society in the early 1960's stated: "If one stands on the top of Shielmartin in Howth on a clear day and looks to the north-west, the plain known as Moynalty is spread like a carpet before one." Moynalty, meaning the plain of the flocks, acquired its name from the numerous flocks of birds that used to gather there. Apparently it was an area in which a wood never grew. We know that it certainly was without trees about 2,000 B.C. because Nin, son of Bel landed here and recorded the fact. Doctor Geoffrey Keating's well known "Foras Feasa ar Eirinn" informs us that 'Magh an Ealta' is the first known recorded name of any district in Ireland. In referring to the death of Partholon about 600 years later Keating's history again refers to the plain as "Sean Mhagh Ealta Eadar" (the old plain of the bird flocks of Eadair). Of the exact extension of the plain we cannot be sure but it did include most of the area which was later to become Fingal. It included Clontarf but some accounts have taken it, incorrectly, to specifically apply to the Clontarf area. Generally speaking Moynalty, or more correctly Magh nEalta, can be regarded as the plain lying between Howth and Tallaght.

Bregia and Ard Cianachta

As history ushered in the Christian era the expanse of country between the rivers Liffey and Boyne was named Bregia-from Bregia the son of Brogha one of the Parthalonian chieftains. The Irish form of the name, Magh Bhreagha, signifies the magnificent plain. All of Fingal would have been within Bregia including Clontarf. After the Battle of Crinna, which was fought in 226 A.D the sept known as Cianachta over-ran the territory from which the Desi tribe had been removed. (Waterford students will know that part of the Desi tribe, when defeated, marched south and settled in that part of County Waterford known as 'The Decies'.) This area was the southern part of Bregia between the Liffey and Devlin rivers again encompassing Clontarf. Through time the area was given the name Ard-Cianachta from the Milesian leader Cian son of Olioll(or Oluim).

Meath

In Celtic times the present County Dublin extended into two provinces. The Southern half (Cualann) formed part of Laighin or Leinster. The Northern half, including Clontarf, stretched into the above mentioned Bregia, part of Midhe or Meath. This Meath is not to be confused with the present day county Meath. It was the country's fifth province created in the second century by Tuathal the legitimate King of Ireland by cutting off a portion of each of the other provinces round the hill of Usnagh. This new province was to be the special demesne of the High King. In time it was to disappear again and the original four remained- Leinster, Munster, Connaught and Ulster.

Fingal

The name Fingal is one that any student doing research work on practically any part of north County Dublin will encounter on many occasions. Fingal is sometimes written with two 'l's - Fingall. The original race of foreigners (white or fair) who first settled in Dublin were Fin Gall or 'white strangers' from Norway. They seized the rich land of North Dublin. Then came the Dubh Gall or 'black strangers' from Denmark. They fought each other but eventually united under Olaf the White. (An old Irish march "The Return from Fingal" - not to be confused with "Brian Boru's March" - commemorates the triumphant return of Brian Boru's Delcassian warriors to their native Clare from Fingal (after the Battle of Clontarf.) The name itself is derived from the Irish 'fine' for land or territory and 'gall' for stranger or foreigner. Thus Fingal means the territory of the foreigners, who were of course the Scandinavians who conquered the area in the ninth century and settled down there (before their misunderstanding with Brian Boru at Clontarf!)

Where exactly is Fingal?
From south to north, Fingal stretches from the Tolka river to the Delvin river with the sea as its eastern boundary. The western boundary of Fingal is not so easily defined. However most authorities now agree that the point on its course towards the sea where the Delvin river turns from its easterly route to flow northwards is the north west corner of the territory. And if we draw a line southwards from that point on the river until we reach the Tolka river (close to Blanchardstown) we have laid out Fingal's western border. The line is in fact marked by a serious of nine hills, some natural elevations, some artificial. The names of these hills are (from south to north - the first four west of Ashbourne Road, the rest to the east of it) (1) Knockbrush, (2) The Hill of Broughan, (3) The Moat of Kilshane,(4) The Hill of the island, (5) The Moath of Coolatrath, (6) The Rath of Kilsallaghan, (7) The Moat of Palmerstown, (8) The Moat of Knockineek and, (9) The Moat of Knocklyon. Thus Fingal includes all of Dublin City North of the Tolka including Clontarf. Most of north county Dublin lies in Fingal and places such as Swords, Lusk, Rush and Skerries are generally regarded as the heart of Fingal. It is roughly nineteen miles long and thirteen miles wide and the whole Fingal plain slopes slightly eastwards to the sea. Not a huge area but a place of which few, if any, areas of comparable size in Ireland have so many historical associations - religious and political. The name 'Fingallian' is commonly applied to all people who live in this defined region.

Originally the name would have applied to the settlers themselves but then it applied to the coastal strip they occupied in the ninth century. As they gradually pushed further inland the Fingal frontier expanded accordingly. Fingal was granted to the Norman Hugh de Lacy by King Henry II and was then known as 'the English land'. It remained a distinct and separate district until 1210 A.D when King John assigned it to the county of Dublin. But even after this, the name continued in use as the official designation of the district until it ceased to be used officially at the close of the sixteenth century. But to this day inhabitants like to recall the name, with a certain pride, which gives them a distinct origin. The north County Dublin Gaelic football competitions run under the title 'Fingal League' recall the old name of the district as do the G.A.A clubs Fingallians and Fingal Ravens. A host of North Dublin businesses have, over the years, adopted Fingal as their name. In general Fingal's history rings with echoes all too familiar in Irish history-battles, smuggling, priest's secret hideouts, churches, castles, lords and ladies. And since January 1994 Fingal County Council is one of four local authorities that manage the affairs of the entire county of Dublin.

The Maraton of Ireland

Many readers, when browsing through various accounts concerning Clontarf, are puzzled to sometimes find it referred to under another name, the Marathon of Ireland or the Plains of Marathon. This has nothing to do with the fact that since the birth of the Dublin City Marathon in 1980 the green promenade along the seafront at Clontarf has become practically the ' marathon' training and jogging centre of Dublin if not Ireland. Rather the name recalls the 'marathon' gathering of forces here in 1014 and the ensuing 'marathon' battle fought between Brian Boru and the Norsemen. Other sources which suggest the name comes from the ' marathon' travelling for Daniel O'Connell's famous non-meeting in 1843 would appear to be misguided as the name has been recorded in writing long before 1843.

Clontarf and the Sea

"I must go down to the seas again, to the lonely sea and the sky,
And all I ask is a tall ship and a star to steer her by,
And the wheel's kick and the wind's song and the white sail's shaking,
And a grey mist on the sea's face and grey dawn breaking."

Clontarf is today, a stable mature, desirable suburb. It has an ideal setting picturesquely sleeping by the sea and yet quite close to Dublin City centre. It is a tranquil residential area on the road to Howth. Clontarf is low and flat- no part more than 100 feet above sea level. Clontarf's climate has the moderating influence of the sea. Much like the rest of the country, the coldest months are January and February with an average temperature of 5 Celsius. July and August are the warmest months with temperatures averaging at 15 Celsius. The wettest months are December and January. And if you are a regular walker along the seafront in Clontarf or the Bull Wall embankment you won't have to be told that Clontarf gets her share of 'fresh' to 'strong' and 'gusty' sea breezes. Indeed, when in operation, if you looked across the bay and observed the smoke ejecting in a straight line skywards from the twin towers of the E.S.B's Ringsend generating station, you could indeed say it was a calm day. Clontarf has habitually been subject to heavy fogs.

The identity of the Clontarf area is inseparable from the sea. Indeed much of it is physically cushioned from the dancing briny waves, only by the familiar green promenade stretching from the 'Skew' railway bridge to the North Bull Wall. Clontarf's essential charm and its real character lie in its proximity to the sea which appears to cloak the whole region in an atmosphere of tranquillity and smoothness. The sea gives the entire district an aura of tolerance and peace. It was the sea that created a harbour in Clontarf and in turn established the area as a fishing village and a holiday resort. And yet, once in a while, the great sea, strong, proud and defiant can show Clontarfites how insecure life can be. Clontarf throughout her history has witnessed the sea in some of its worst moods. When it becomes angry, in full tide, it turns into a raging monster and proceeds to trespass inland and rock Clontarf on her sand dunes. The sea threatens the stability and permanence of the region hinting at reclaiming its own as it renders roads impassable and forces house evacuations and can strike at the least likely time. In the last century serious high tides flooded Clontarf in 1949, 1967 and 1981. Later dangerous incursions by the sea have occurred, and keep occurring when the tearaway giant again threatens to engulf homes, reminding Clontarfites that the sea can be cruel and totally unforgiving- and the briny eye is forever watching. After the 1981 storm, local residents were left to foot their own damage bills accumulated by sea flooding. Local public representative, the late Sean Dublin Bay Loftus, at the time, asked the Dublin Port and Docks Board and Dublin Corporation to accept responsibility. They refused saying they were not responsible for such a storm which was 'an act of nature'. Loftus however maintained that if the Bull Island Causeway Road had a bridge incorporated into it much of the huge volume of sea storm water could have escaped instead of flooding so many homes. Many local people continue to clamour for the aforementioned Causeway Road to be breached to allow the sea to circle the Island as was the original situation.

"I must go down to the seas again, for the call of the running tide,
Is a wild call and a clear call that may not be denied;
And all I ask is a windy day with the white clouds flying,
And the flung spray and the blown spume, and the sea-gulls crying."

The sea in question is that part of the Irish sea which meets the land in Clontarf as Dublin Bay. It is a part of the great North Atlantic Ocean. Clontarf has always been an excellent vantage point from which to view around Dublin. (See appendix nine). We can view the Clontarf section of Dublin Bay itself which when adorned with colourful sailing boats in summertime is in full bloom and can be quite spectacular and beautiful- like a radiant bride dressed for her wedding! On the subject of water travel one can see the great ferry boats, as they begin and end their journeys to and from Liverpool and Holyhead. On the north side of the bay we can view the Howth peninsula with its rugged little peaks; towards the city are the chimneys and spires of the metropolis. To the south we can see the long South Wall, Poolbeg lighthouse and the ranging Dublin and

Wicklow mountains. However the immediate vision or seascape which Clontarf Road residents faced daily across the bay was one of oil tanks, silos, warehouses and cranes, a rather uninspiring view! but the Dublin Port company have coaxed some trees and shrubs to grow landward of the docks area to form a green "screen".

The sea has also been good to Clontarfites. Clontarf folk appear to be inspired by the mood of the sea- if only in reaction to it. The vibrant, powerful and healthy sea is in Clontarf veins- and the strength of the sea is great. From the earliest times locals have had an income from the sea. Clontarf was lucky to have the larger of Dublin harbour's two deep pools (the other was at Poolbeg). Long before the days of the South and North Bull Walls, in such a wide bay as Dublin, the tide ebbed rapidly and much of the bay silted up-leaving the North and South"Bulls"[3] or sloblands hazardous to ships. Thus many ships anchored in Clontarf Pool and a useful source of income was to be had by providing ferrying services for men and merchandise to and from the shore. Of course it also provided opportunities for smuggling contraband cargo as a useful nixer! Smuggling appears to have a long history with coastal dwellers in north County Dublin and Clontarf is no exception. Indeed smuggling was an intrinsic part of the lives of these coastal dwellers in the eighteenth century. In fact a coastal area somewhat barren and bleak easily conjures up images of shipwrecks and smuggling. Smugglers ran the gauntlet of the exise men. In Clontarf, while the savage battles fought between between revenue officers and the smugglers of nearby Mud Island (Ballybough) were not repeated, there were many nasty skirmishes. Smugglers broke the law and the penalties were quite stiff. However the locals were loyal and tight-lipped and were also glad of the illicit crates, casks and kegs smuggled ashore. Tea, brandy and butts of wine were scarce locally. Then with the outbreak of the Napoleanic wars smuggling became impossible. And Clontarf traditionally had its longshoremen who were always ready to collect and trade any items lost from passing ships.

"I must go down to the seas again, to the vagrant gipsy life,
To the gull's way and the whale's way, where the wind's like a whetted knife;
And all I ask is a merry yarn from a laughing fellow-rover,
And quiet sleep and a sweet dream when the long trick's over."
John Masefield

The sea has always provided Clontarf with ample fishing grounds. In the eighteenth century fishing became a major activity in Clontarf with particular rich oyster beds situated off the seafront end of the present Vernon Avenue. Around this oyster bank the new fishing village called Clontarf Sheds or Clontarf

Herring Sheds grew up and 'Herring Sheds' is clearly marked on Captain Perry's map of Dublin Bay and Harbour drawn up in 1728. A certain romantic mystique appears to accompany the subject of this quaint habitat (The medieval village of Clontarf had been centred around Clontarf Castle and Castle Avenue) The Clontarf Sheds village acquired its name from the Sheds or wooden buildings erected there in the eighteenth century for the use of people employed in curing and preserving fish. The sheds were somewhat haphazard along the waterfront where Vernon Avenue converges onto the seafront. We must picture a very different seafront - with no wall, no promenade and no front road proper. In fact at one time a small promontory projected from this point towards Clontarf Island.

This was named "The Furlong' or sometimes Clontarf Head and Clontarf Pool was just off it. The growth of the fishing industry shifted the centre of Clontarf from Castle Avenue to the seafront. Vernon Avenue now became the main street in Clontarf.

The Sheds were Clontarf's new or second village and are marked on the maps of Dublin from 1728 on. One account tells us:

"On the edge of the water are numerous and small buildings termed "The Sheds of Clontarf" which appelation they acquire from the former residence of fishermen who erected there many wooden fabrics for the purpose of drying fish" In other pieces The Sheds are referred to as 'pent-houses or 'stages'. These sheds were the heart of the fishing village. During the eighteenth century, Clontarf had a high reputation for fishing and the area became a major supplier to the Dublin City market. Older clontarfites would have inherited a sea-faring tradition from their Scandinavian ancestors. Indeed it became customary for many city citizens to frequently visit The Sheds to buy supplies of herrings, mackerel, oysters, whiting, turbot and lobsters. The colony of fishermen in the area was 'considerable' As early as 1718 a Humphrey French petitioned the Corporation for a lease of a portion of Crab Lough. He was duly granted his licence for 61 years to "take up oysters on that part of the strand commonly called Crab Lough for an annual rent of £70." The other conditions were that he had to supply the Lord Mayor of Dublin with ten thousand lobsters annually, and each city Sheriff with two thousand. He also had to allow the Lord Mayor, Sheriffs, Aldermen and their ladies to go to his area and pick lobsters from the site for one day each year.

The fishermen themselves lived in dilapidated cottages, which despite outward appearances were quite appallingly insanitary and unhygenic inside. We can deduce that hardy lives were led by fishermen from a passage such as this.

"There is filth and a foul smell in Clontarf. The natives are very hardy. They live a life of fatigue. After days of incessant toil they snatch a few hours rest in their wet clothes, in which they are drenched, recover their spirits with fish, potatoes and whiskey their only diet, and proceed again to the dangers and toils of fishing. Till very lately they were noted smugglers and added the dangers of this illegal calling to their ordinary life. Yet they live to a great age"

Due to their (quite misleading) appealing and picturesque appearance both The Sheds and its fishermens cottages were the subject of numerous etchings, drawings and paintings. Not all the inhabitants of Clontarf Sheds village were fishermen. Many of the residents engaged in farming. Indeed farming was very central to life in The Sheds. The vast majority of the farmers were tenants with plots rented from local landlords - the Vernons of Clontarf Castle, whose property Clontarf was. There were specially constructed slipways to the sea in order to facilitate farmers taking seaweed in their carts as fertiliser.

In 1787 a local resident, Charles Weekes, at his own expense, organised a water supply from a local stream into a reservoir for the public use. From then on the Sheds are recorded as having a bountiful supply of fresh water. Weekes also built a wharf extending several hundred feet into the sea. It carried a water supply used by ships at anchor in Clontarf Pool. "Weekes Wharf" became a very popular promenade for Dubliners taking summer evening strolls. It even provided seating on a platform toward the open sea end of the Wharf. This provided a panoramic view around Dublin Bay. Rocque's map of 1756 shows Clontarf oyster bed and the two Clontarf villages. Incidentally just down the road - towards the city -other maps show a slight promontory, beside the present Haddon Road, as Cockle Point. As we know the Clontarf shore also abounded with muscles so the noted 'cockles and mussels' of the famous Dublin song might indeed have been sung by the Clontarf ladies- who 'cried' the fish through the Dublin streets carrying them in baskets or sieves on their heads.

Writing in 1818 Rev James Whitelaw described The Sheds as "Whitewashed houses, a picturesque promontory very conspicuous, floating as it were on the dark-green water". Like that other Dublin folk song ("Dublin In the Rare Oul Times") says Clontarf Sheds have long since "given way to progress". In this case, considering their filthy state, it's perhaps just as well that "nothing seems the same". Donnelly, writing in about 1910, has this to say regarding the Sheds when giving an account of Father Callinan's struggle to build the present St John the Baptist Church in the 1830's: "Where upon he (Fr. Callinan) addressed himself to Colonel Vernon to get a site for a commodious Church. The site he selected adjoined his own house and at the time was covered by a fisher settlement popularly known as 'The Sheds'. It comprised some 200 families who lived in wretched mud cabins built by themselves with small laneways meandering through them. The landlord was most anxious to get rid of them and offered Fr. Callinan a lease for 99 years on condition that he would do away with those unsightly and unsanitary habitations. Behind the P.P's house and behind the present Church of St John the Baptist there was a considerable plot of ground included in this lease. On this plot he allowed some of the fishermen to build cottages and promised them leases. In this way was originated what is still known as 'Snugboro', (nowadays called St Josephs Square). To the remaining fishermen he made compensation in money. Thus the famous Sheds came to an end". In an issue of the "Irish Builder" in the 1860's Snugboro itself is described thus "...the rookeries termed Snugboro ... are almost reprehensible in their sanitary arrangements, the human kind living promiscuously in cabins with pigs and horses and all revelling, as it were, in squalid filth." In the same issue-having referred to the "antiquated mud and thatched structures" around Clontarf and other structures "for years tottering and nodding obeisance to mother earth" the Irish Builder states: "we sincerely trust that Mr. Vernon ... raze those abominable eye sores that present themselves on his property and also afford something like reasonable encouragements to capitalists to build suitable substitutes."

In any case, towards the end, the fishermens', farmers' and labourers' cottages of The Sheds became totally dilapidated. Of their exact extent we are not sure but they most likely stretched as far as what was later the tram sheds (present Dublin Bus garage). The last of them were probably demolished during the construction of the tram line. But the nostalgia of the Sheds lives on in tradition, and memories of them appear to have been handed down through Clontarf generations with a particular fondness. Now the name is immortalised as the name of the well known public house, Connolly's 'The Sheds'.

In the Clontarf area generally the majority of the people were labourers and the quality of their lives was of the subsistence variety- this was common at the time all over the country. Their homes were thatched mud cabins, very meagerly furnished. Overcrowding was quite common with two or more families often sharing one cabin. Clothing tended to be ragged and the stable diet was milk and potatoes. In his submissions(for the Clontarf area) to the 1835 commission of inquiry into the state of the poor Fr. William Walsh C.C. Clontarf observed: "The public houses (in the area) are highly injurious to the morality and domestic comfort of the lower orders. . .I think the facilities for procuring ardent spirits are too numerous. The law should diminish rather than increase them; intemperance is the besetting sin of the lower classes." The commission also heard that "only half the poor in the area had constant work" . . . "those who are clothed wear grey frieze(but) a great number are only half clothed"... " Their food was potatoes and milk with bread occasionally".... "Women were paid eight(old) pence per day and children six(old) pence when employed picking potatoes." The result of this inquiry was the passing of an "Act for the more effectual relief of the destitute poor in Ireland" and the only result it produced was the setting up of the notorious workhouse system.

Clontarf in the Nineteenth Century - Greenlanes

"Dear old Clontarf!... Your lanes are the greenest of green leafydom, your rows of little cottages are unchanged; so too the more ambitious Crescent where the houses are mostly to let; your straggling seaboard where the tide is nearly always out ... And yet, despite the sadness of the grey sky, and the general stillness of the surroundings, there is a certain charm in the absence from all the stir and turmoil of busy life, which is restful." **Frances Gerard 1898**

Samuel Lewis in his 1837 Topographical Dictionary tells us of Clontarf. "It was formerly a fishing town of some importance, and along the waters edge are still many wooden buildings, called the Clontarf Sheds, formerly used for the purpose of curing fish taken here. Several neat lodging-houses have been erected and numerous pleasant villas and ornamented cottages have been built in detached situations." The appearance of Clontarf was changing and it was to change drastically in the course of the nineteenth century. The change came about mainly because of ever improving communications-better and more roads and improved transport featuring the coming of the bicycle and the tram. A new emphasis saw people begin to "harness" the seaside as a source of income Let us examine the approach to Clontarf in the period up to the building of Annesley Bridge (in 1797) which helped in no small way to 'open up' the Clontarf area.

The Approach to Clontarf

Up to and including much of the eighteenth century the sea was not confined by embankments and the strand extended from Ballybough Bridge citywards to Beresford Place. John Decer (or le Decer) erected the first bridge over the river Tolka at Ballybough in 1308. This joined Ballybough 'to the causeway of the mill-pool of Clontarf, which before was a dangerous charge'. The sea then and for a long time afterwards ran from Clontarf coastline to Ballybough and along the present North Strand Road to Amiens Street. Turning round by Beresford Place it continued by Strand Street to Essex Bridge (now Grattan Bridge). The construction of Decer's bridge over the Tolka (at this shallow point) opened up a thoroughfare from the city (which was then centred around Church Street and

Christchurch through the present Parnell Street, Summerhill and Ballybough to Clontarf, Howth and Malahide. Decer's bridge was swept away in 1313 and it was 1488 before it was replaced by a solid structure which was to last for over 400 years. A large white stone near Ballybough Bridge marked the then city boundary. The bridge itself had a large gate which was locked at night[4]. Ballybough Bridge was widened and strengthened in 1985 and renamed Luke Kelly Bridge after the folk singer. But this approach road to Clontarf was anything but inviting. The area between Ballybough Bridge and the North Strand became quite notorious in the eighteenth century as a haven for robbers, brigands and thieves, and was known as Mud Island[5]. In this age of smuggling, cargoes of dutiable goods were taken ashore at night on Fairview Strand, and quickly escorted to be hidden in the mudflats where even the most job conscious revenue officers dared not penetrate. But tussles between the two sides often had fatal consequences. Thus Ballybough gained an unenviable evil reputation and only a daring person would venture through in daylight never mind at night. At times gallows were erected beside Ballybough bridge and used. The corpses of male factors were sometimes left to hang for days as a warning to outlaws that crime would not pay. And there was also the rather chilling presence of a plot of ground at the Ballybough end of Clonliffe Road specially reserved for burying suicide victims. Thus it was quite understandable why city folk and south Dubliners were reluctant to venture north to the seaside at Clontarf. And if the 'suicide plot' and the 'bridge gallows' weren't daunting enough there was later to be added the chance of an encounter with the 'phantom horseman' who allegedly used todays Clonliffe Road area as his nightly stamping ground. This was the 'ghost' of one Frederick 'Buck' Jones, a magistrate, a gambler and a theatre operator. He resided in the one house on what is now Clonliffe Road[6]. Also the existence of Lord Charlemont's turnpike gate at Fairview effectively gave him control over the entrance to Clontarf.

But the building of Annesley Bridge in 1797 began to change all that. It was a landmark in the history of the whole coastal area to the north - Fairview, Clontarf and along to Howth in that it opened up a new road via Amiens Street and the North Strand Road. The old Ballybough Bridge was no longer of such importance, as the only connection with the city, (Annesley Bridge was named after the first Lord Annesley whose town house was acquired by Dr. Troy Archbishop of Dublin to build the Pro-Cathedral which opened in 1825.) Fairview of course was still practically non-existent. What is now Fairview Park is marked on early maps of Dublin simply as 'mud'. But locals referred to it as the 'sloblands'. Up to 1800 the sea fringed Fairview Strand. Between 1900-25 Fairview Park was reclaimed from the sea, with the bulk of the work completed by 1920. Much of it was filled in by city refuse. By 1938 map makers were naming it Fairview Park. Situated literally on the gateway to Clontarf it is an elegant sprawling park always magnificently landscaped.

A regular spot for Dubliners at this time was a stretch of sand and shingle emanating from Fairview Strand towards Clontarf. It became known as 'the Strand' and was a very popular recreation centre. Here the lords and ladies promenaded and regular citizens came to admire the style and indeed to criticize the grandeur of the carriages and horses. The great satirist Dean Swift loved to ride on the Strand on his way to Howth. Quite large numbers must have come to watch the pageantry and a verse of the time (referring to this place) ends: . . .

"The Strand to view the conquests you have won
Where oft those eyes supply the missing sun"

By the mid nineteenth century Clontarf had developed into a very popular bathing area for northsiders. Many people began to find Clontarf a convenient and healthy environment, especially after the arrival of the trams in 1880 and later the buses. The invention of the bicycle which came into common use in the late 19th and early 20th centuries also made Clontarf a very accessible region, as did the gradual arrival of the motor car (first invented in 1886) in the same period, although the quality of the roadways still left much to be desired. Clontarf began to turn into an area of stately mansions with an affluent people. (Movement to the suburbs in general did not begin until the early nineteenth century. Until then merchants lived over their city premises while the landed gentry had their own town houses in the fashionable streets and squares.) As the area began to earn a reputation as a bathing centre the main activities of fishing and agriculture, together with some mining, continued. But a new trend was being established in Clontarf. More and more people saw the sea with new eyes and as a source of revenue from a new angle. Their livelihood began to centre around letting lodgings and bathing machines to summer and early autumn visitors. As bathing became ever more popular from the beginning of the nineteenth century more and more boarding houses opened up. Many visitors arrived by boat from Ringsend. Locals gained more income by carrying passengers backwards and forwards during summer months on cars, jingles and shadrydans-even conveying people from the city. Thus at the end of Clontarf's era as a fishing centre, the vicinity began to adopt the air of a 'secluded' bathing place enhanced by pleasant local country walks. Her position made the precinct an ideal out of town seaside resort. Even in their later years we find the old wooden sheds interspersed with neat dwellings erected specially as lodgings for sea bathers-used in the main during the summer.

But apart from the people attracted to Clontarf by the lure of the place as a seaside resort, Clontarf was establishing herself as a very desirable residential suburb. As the nineteenth century progressed people generally began to move steadily to new developing spacious areas like Rathmines and Donnybrook. Clontarf fell into this category. Once a good roadway was opened up the big obstacle of crossing the Tolka mouth (which blocked easy access to Clontarf) was overcome and Clontarf was open for bathers, visitors and residents. Slowly the population increased and the two villages of Clontarf merged. However most of the development would have been along the established roads and especially the seafront. Much of inland Clontarf remained green and beautiful-in fact an enchanting and romantic area. Only an occasional house interrupted the vista of green fields and lanes. The hamlet got quite a reputation in the later nineteenth century- clean, healthy and enticing, famous for pretty sylvan scenery which especially attracted many prominent and wealthy citizens. We have some interesting accounts of Clontarf as she then stood.

"The green and devious lanes of the town form a series of pleasant walks and command from various points, exquisite views of the scenery of the bay. The avenue called Greenlanes in particular is a favourite resort of visitors and the whole countryside is luscious with cultivation and warm with sheltering wood".

An 1825 account sees Clontarf as follows:

"Neat dwellings used as lodging houses are now interspersed among the relics of those humble Sheds; but the most pleasing parts of this retired and agreeable village are scattered with an unstudied diversity of site, through shaded and rural lanes. Several of the buildings, thus widely spaced, are villas of some extent. Others are cottages of a soft embellished character, and well adapted to the occupation of persons who seek, on the tranquil shore, a summer or autumnal residence for the advantage of bathing. The whole district is adorned with sheltering wood; and prospects of considerable beauty are obtained at several points of green and devious lanes"

The centre of the Greenlanes area or townland (which at the time covered a sizeable portion of Clontarf) would have been the east side of the part of Castle Avenue backboned by Seafield Road and Vernon Avenue. Two avenues entered the Greenlanes-Seafield Avenue (now Seafield Road) and Verville which led to Vernon Avenue. The Greenlanes name is today preserved as that of the Clontarf Church of Ireland National School on Seafield Avenue.

Character of Clontarf and her People

Clontarfites are Fingallians and Fingallians are a mixed race with Gaelic and

Anglo-Norman the chief components. There remains also segments of Scandinavian and Danish blood due to many Fionn-Gall and Dubh-Gall who settled in Fingal up to and after 1014. Indeed specialist studies undertaken in this field suggest that many of the characteristics of Fingallians resemble those of Viking people-features of build, temperament and voice. Also it is a fact that a great number of surnames with Scandinavian origins survive in Fingal e.g. Seagrove, Sweetman, Dowdall, Harfort, Plunkett etc. (see chapter three below) However it must be stated that, within the area of North County Dublin that Fingal occupies no group or class of people betray any real evidence of an origin different from their neighbours. Fingallians (and this includes Clontarfites or at least 'Old Clontarf Stock') are traditionally accepted as a mixed race, perhaps not as 'fiery' as their northern neighbours. They are in general a solid, balanced, honest and even-tempered people. Fingallians tend to be emotionally placid-sentiment and feeling are not traditionally expressed in trivial matters. The phrase 'don't wear your heart on your sleeve' has been used to describe the Fingallian[7]. But Anglo-Norman-Scandinavian blood or not, Fingallians are thoroughly Irish. Indeed the history of Fingal bears ample testimony to their love of country and their patriotic fervour.

Fellow Dubliners would regard Clontarf people as traditional Dublin sea-folk with a great loyalty to the city. Clontarf people, together with residents of Howth, have had the very pleasant distinction of having the lowest death-rate in Dublin. Clontarf folk have traditionally been called 'seasiders' and also 'cockle pickers' from the Sheds fishing era!

TODAY'S CLONTARF

Today's Clontarf is a much changed area from the Clontarf of the early to middle twentieth century. Then Clontarf could be described as richly wooded and finely cultivated countryside. Intensive farming was carried on in Clontarf, with a particular emphasis on dairying. Some of the last dairy farms were Davitts of Crab Lake, Guerins of Dollymount, Ryans of Seafield Road, Mackeys opposite the Bull Wall, Geoghans of Mount Prospect and Keoghs of Seafield Avenue. The last Clontarf farm was Mc Mullans of Vernon Avenue. While farming was widespread in the area the built up section of Clontarf was a mere strip along the coast. Today Clontarf has become a fully built up and mature suburban area-indeed it is one of Dublin's most desirable suburban residential areas with demand for houses (new and old) usually exceeding supply in the vicinity. Much of the older streets of Clontarf are red bricked and Victorian with some house styles from the Georgian period. The newer estates and residential areas represent all the various modern styles. The green fields of Clontarf really began to disappear during the building boom in the post World War Two years. Clontarf developed and expanded rapidly and by the 1950's was a heavily populated suburb as thousands of families came to reside in the precinct. Most of the villas of Clontarf's past have long since given way to progress via the bulldozer. Those that do remain proved simply too expensive for any family to maintain and have long since been converted into and let as smaller units of accommodation-flats and bedsitters. In many cases only the outer facade and perhaps the presence of a big garden betray the original grandeur of a residence. However some samples of elegance still exist in Clontarf's older and bigger houses in the form of ornate insides-for example delicately carved edging boards along ceilings. Outside the odd remaining sample of beautifully carved railings, are well worth preserving to show that Clontarf has a bountiful legacy of architectural excellence. Even if much of her grandeur was inherited from ascendancy days and colonialism it is part of what Clontarf is and nothing can ever alter that. The 'good old days' smacked of snobbery and elitism is not unknown in today's Clontarf. The fact is that Clontarf, sadly, has never fully eradicated snobbery.

Developers in particular have much to answer for in Clontarf. They wreck and have wrecked- through unadulterated greed - more in one day than vandals would in a lifetime. For some time now the ever increasing demand for residences in Clontarf and the lack of available development land has led to a trend where practically all accommodation being erected in Clontarf is in the form of town houses or luxury apartments. These are very economical on space. All the new apartments that have dramatically sprung up in the Clontarf region can only be described as of a very high quality with original and distinctive designs. Modern and comfortable, prestigious, secluded and invariably brilliantly landscaped with sophisticated television monitoring, intercom and audio security systems they are very attractive as living quarters for single and retired people or 'professional' couples. They do not, perhaps, augur well for the building up of a large young population as they are simply too small and unsuitable for families. But, sadly, for many young couples with aspirations to live in the area the question is not "will we live in Clontarf?" but rather "can we afford to set up home in Clontarf?" What is so appealing about Clontarf as a locality in which to live? The answer is that Clontarf's charm and appeal is manifold. A very convenient three miles from Dublin City Centre, Clontarf is a quiet settled, pleasant district with an enviable character. It is set amid a plethora of pleasure and leisure amenities and facilities. These include a fine beach at Dollymount, a fabulous bird sanctuary on the Bull Island and acres of green parkland at St.Annes Park, Clontarf has excellent schools, six churches, a post office, good bus and local train (Dart) services and has adequate shopping facilities. The whole area is essentially cocooned by the dominating influence of the sea while the broad green seafront promenade-now as essentially part of Clontarf as the sea itself-gives the area a peaceful and select setting. Thus Clontarf is indeed a haven of tranquillity-but is not, unfortunately, free from the modern era of larcenies, muggings, drug offences and such crimes. Of course the healthy sea air and the scenery of the bay always enticed people to live in Clontarf as did the wealth of clubs and organisations in the area. The sporting clubs are dealt with in a separate chapter but here it is necessary to mention that in the fields of culture, art, history and heritage, residents are more than catered for by the activities of a myriad of societies and organisations.

Clontarfites have varying backgrounds and identify with different aspects of the area. Thus it is very difficult to state what Clontarf culture is. But according to each individual's traditions it should include some of the following -a walk on the Bull Island especially into a south easterly gale, a yacht trip on Dublin Bay, a view of the visiting Brent Geese in December, the Christmas Morning plunge into the sea off the Bull Wall, a good read of a stirring account of the Battle of Clontarf, a visit to Clontarf's oldest church- St.John the Baptist's on the seafront, waiting for a 130 bus, a tour around Clontarf Castle and the old graveyard, and a piece of reminiscing on the 'deeds' of the Brian Boru G.A.A team while sipping your favourite tipple in The Sheds! Clontarf's colours have traditionally been red and blue. The origin of the association of these colours with Clontarf is steeped in history. Viking sagas refer to blue and red banners at the famous 1014 Battle. While the blue is also associated with the wife of Brian Boru. Her name was Gormliath which means 'the blue one'. The Clontarf emblem has always-and not surprisingly-been the bull.

Footnotes

(1) Many different spellings of the English form of the word can be found in literature down through the years Clandaf, Cluntarf, Clantarff, Clumtorf, Clontarfe, Clantarf, and Henry II's gem, Clemthorp.

(2) Thomas O'Brien of Elm Grove Co Meath wrote under the fictitious name of 'Clontarf'. One of his well known works is the lengthy ode entitled "The Mountain Spirit". In the twelve years up to 1889 he composed his volume of ballad poems with somewhat nationalistic themes entitled "Songs of Liberty". The volume contains such popularly known ones as "The Raparees", "The Men of Ninety Eight", "The Flag of Innisfail", "Robert Emmet" and "A Song of Freedom".

(3) The bulls referred to here are not the bull walls or the North Bull Island but the North

and South Dublin Harbour strands so referred to on early maps of Dublin Harbour. They are strands which are dry at low water for a considerable distance seawards. Bull Island eventually grew on the North Strand.

(4) The Monks of St.Mary's Abbey then owned lands at Ballybough. The reformation changes were to later destroy the abbey. There are some fascinating accounts of this area available, including the work of the monks and the abbey itself.

(5) The name Mud Island came literally from the mud at the mouth of the Tolka river. Like the area further south at the mouth of the Liffey it was filthy with oozing slobby mud.

(6) Jones died in 1834. Holy Cross College is built on the site of his house. (Jones became manager of Dublin's Crow Street Theatre in 1798 but was very unpopular with his associates. Jones Road- where the Gaelic Athletic Associations headquarters, Croke Park are located, is named after him). Although much of this 'fear' and 'smuggling' era belonged to the eighteenth century I came across a possible connection much later. Clontarf Swimming Club (founded 1884) had to fight long and hard to have the normal half of their water polo fixtures played at Clontarf. As most of the Dublin Swimming Clubs were based on the south side Clontarf Swimming Club tradition holds that they refused to travel to Clontarf because of the reputation of the 'gateway area' to Clontarf!

(7) This is not a sociological or demographical study but we must bear in mind that the typical Clontarfite today might not be as typically Fingal as someone from say, Rush, Skerries or Lusk. By its very position, ie .a north Dublin suburb, Clontarf over the years, has experienced quite an influx of people with extremely diverse backgrounds. Through these she has expanded and accepted new ideas, values, traditions and attitudes.

Old Clontarf by the sea

Sheds of Clontarf by J.A O'Connor

Cabin at Clontarf c. 1817. C.M.Campbell

Another representation of the Sheds by B McAdam from the 1785 drawing by F. Wheatley

Jonathan Swift

CHAPTER TWO

Christianity in Clontarf

"What matter that at different shrines?
We pray unto one God?
What matter that at different times
Our fathers won this sod?
In fortune and in name we're bound
By stronger links than steel;
And neither can be safe or sound
But in the other's weal"   **Thomas Davis**

The Early Days
The mantle of Father of Christianity in Clontarf falls on the shoulders of the abbot St. Comgall (517-603). The first church in Clontarf is traditionally accepted as the one founded in the year 550, by Comgall and his followers. Later on the little church was dedicated to the saint and he came to be revered as Clontarf's patron saint. We do not know how much time Comgall spent in Clontarf, or how many of his monks laboured there. Even the site of that first simple little church of 'oak beams and wattles' is uncertain but quite likely was the spot now occupied by Clontarf cemetery where there are ruins of a later church. No doubt the little establishment at Clontarf was similar in appearance to the many others founded by the saint. (A strict rigid disciplinarian his greatest achievement was founding the famous monastery at Bangor near Belfast about the year 555.) As well as the little church, it would have consisted of a few cells of 'wood, mud and wattles' covered with thatch or even maybe with skins. It would have had its own gardens which provided a sustenance for the monks. Over the years the principal lands in the Clontarf area became vested in Comgall's Clontarf centre.

We must fit Comgall's Clontarf foundation into the general pattern of early Irish small monasteries, and the work carried on there would have been of a similar nature to all monasteries of the period. It must be remembered that, since the (Irish) Christian era began with St. Patrick in the year 432, the monastic institutions were the chief agencies in civilizing and evangelizing the people. Indeed the importance of the monasteries needs no further emphasis than to state that under the old Celtic monastery system the church had no organised dioceses or parishes. Each monastery spread the gospel in the surrounding countryside. Chapels were built gradually and haphazardly and monks from the monasteries ministered to the people of an undefined area in the vicinity. The monasteries were centres of Christian life and the monks maintained themselves by voluntary endowments, contributions, and labour. Their work centered on (1) lecturing and generally preparing students who travelled abroad, (2) manufacturing various articles, (3) cultivating the profession of scribes, (4) giving employment to the poor. The life of a monk had, as a basis, constant and regular prayer and they spent much time instructing the ignorant. Indeed their houses provided shelter and refuge for the oppressed and alms for the needy.

Comgall and his disciples stated aims in Clontarf were (1) to care for and to turn to Christianity the heathen Celts, a pastoral people dwelling in their simple huts in Moynalty and (2) to train and sent forth messengers of the gospel to different parts of Europe. No doubt their work at Clontarf helped gain Ireland the later title of 'Island of Saints and Scholars'[1]. Comgall's monastic influence spread among the local people and his missionary messengers were also active spreading the gospel abroad. Local Clontarfites accepted the monks as leaders on account of the reverent lives they led and because of their moral practices. They would also have taught 'scientific' agriculture to the local peasants. However if we judge Comgall's mission to Clontarf as one to build a centre like those of say St. Mobhi at Glasnevin and St. Canice at Finglas, we can judge that he was unsuccessful. This failure can be attributed to a number of factors. First of all he wasn't in Clontarf in person for very long. In fact it is really only presumed that Comgall himself actually worked in Clontarf. No records of any significance have been preserved of any activity at Comgall's Clontarf establishment between its foundation and the Anglo-Norman invasion. Secondly he was a complete stranger to the district which is possibly the real reason why his efforts did not flourish. We must understand that a famous monastery is not erected in one night, but the Clontarf foundation did have over two centuries to establish itself before the arrival of the Danes. Comgall[2] remained Clontarf's patron saint until the 14th century when the Knight's Hospitallers of St. John of Jerusalem established St. John the Baptist as patron.

Vikings

Some very strong arguments (supplemented by local tradition) state that a very early Celtic church at Donnycarney may have been founded by St. Patrick himself. Thus it could be argued that the people of Clontarf might have been brought in touch with Christianity through this Donnycarney influence. However the monastery of monks founded by Mobhi at Glasnevin-where

Comgall studied - would have helped more firmly to influence the Clontarf area and establish Christianity there. (St. Mobhi and his cohorts were almost certainly disciples of St. Patrick himself.) In any case the work of Comgall gave Christianity lasting root in Clontarf. But it wasn't very long before the work of this little community was severely disrupted by the raids, marauding, and plundering of the Vikings. These invading warriors from Scandinavia first began to appear on our shores in the closing years of the 8th century. Some lines from a ninth century manuscript written by a monk, reminds us of the fear in which they lived;

"Fierce and wild is the wind tonight,
It tosses the tresses of the sea to white;
On such a night as this I take my ease,
Fierce Northern only course the quiet seas."

Also, at the time, a regular petition included in the litany read: "From the fury of the Northmen, good Lord deliver us." The sacking and plundering of the Vikings went on for over 200 years. They raided monasteries, churches and the homes of the people. Howth was ravished in 819 and later the great monasteries including those at Swords, Finglas, and Glasnevin. No doubt Clontarf's little church and collection of monks' cells met the same fate as so many others did. Clontarf's church history at this time is not recorded. In the many accounts we have of Brian Boru's great victory over the Vikings at the Battle of Clontarf there is no reference to the church or local clergy. But tradition strongly holds that Comgall's church existed both before and after the battle. Brian Boru's victory gave a period of more stability and peace to the harassed Christians of the Celtic church. Many of the Danes, who continued to find a livelihood in north Dublin after the battle, accepted Christianity. (see chapter three below)

Norman's AND KNIGHTS

In 1169 the next 'tourists' to arrive were the Norman's. In 1171 when Strongbow succeeded Dermot Mc Murrough as King of Leinster, the church's monastic system came to an end, and a network of parochial districts with separate pastors came into force. Fingal was divided into more than forty parishes subject to the archbishop of Dublin. A decree by Pope Alexander III confirmed this new arrangement. The large number of parishes need not suggest a huge population. In creating a parish, population was only one of a number of factors considered- the tithable capacity of the area, and the pre-existence of a church building being of more importance. These forty or so Fingal parishes formed by this 12th century changeover from the Monastic system to the Diocesan/Parochial system remained up to the Reformation.

After the Reformation the parishes continued intact in the state church established by Queen Elizabeth I until it was disestablished by Queen Victoria in 1869. It must be stated that the monarchal episcopate common to all Christendom would have been the system introduced originally by St. Patrick. But the influence of abbots and their monasteries appealed very strongly to early Irish Christians and the monastic system overran that of the bishops and the dioceses. Further confusion was added when Danes, who settled in Ireland as Christians after 1014, embraced only the authority of the archbishop of Canterbury. Indeed the extraordinary situation arose in Dublin for some years after 1028 when the city had its own bishop and the rest of the county was included in the sea of Glendalough. Before the arrival of the Norman's, several Irish synods were well on the way to introducing the orderly and efficient Roman system of dioceses and parishes the Norman's did in fact introduce. The synods were at Cashel in 1101, Rathbreasil in 1118, Inispatrick in 1148 and Kells in 1156. In 1171 King Henry II appointed Hugh de Lacy as Justiciar or Kings Deputy in Ireland and granted him the lands of the province of Meath which consisted of today's counties of Meath and Westmeath and parts of counties Cavan, Louth and Dublin including Clontarf. The lands of Clontarf were granted to Adam de Phepoe by Hugh de Lacy. A strong castle was erected by de Phepoe in 1172. (Some scholars of this period argue that de Lacy built the castle and, on its completion, granted it to de Phepoe.) As part of his penance for his involvement in the murder of St. Thomas a Becket, Henry II had vowed to make a pilgrimage to Jerusalem and provide for the support of 200 Knights Templars. Consequently when Henry was in Dublin in 1172 (to satisfy himself as to his authority over Strongbow and the other early Norman leaders in Ireland) he founded a branch of the Templars granting them estates in Ireland for their upkeep. Parts of the lands assigned to them by Royal Charter, was 'a villa near Dublin called Clemthorp'. The Clontarf Manor was then valued in goods at £125-15-7, and £32-10-0 in yearly value of lands. Henry II's granting of Clontarf to the Templars was confirmed by Henry III in 1226. It is probable that Adam de Phopoe had no difficulty handing over his acquired property to the church. As a Norman he would have been proud of the castle as a building and Norman's were traditionally very generous towards the church. The castle had been built close to Comgall's old church ruins. Now those ruins completely disappeared and the Templars built a new church most likely on the exact site of the present old ruins which was to be Clontarf's Parish Church up to the Reformation. We assume they dedicated this church to Comgall. In the 'Crede Mihi' (the oldest existing record of the state of parishes in the Dublin diocese) dated 1275, the Templars church at Clontarf is listed as one of the thirty seven churches then in use in Fingal. When Strongbow established himself in Dublin after his arrival in 1170, he founded a priory of the Knights of St. John of Jerusalem (or Knights Hospitallers) at Kilmainham[3].

Various Popes wished that these two orders (Templars and Hospitallers) would unite, but the Templars always declined. By the early 14th century however, with the Crusades long over, the Templars had lost, somewhat, the original purpose of their foundation. They had become very powerful and rich, not unlike a rich corporation with rumour attributing quite unbecoming activities- including heresy and idolatry- to them across Europe. In 1307 Pope Clement V, perhaps somewhat stage managed by Philip le Bel, King of France (who owed them a large sum of money) suppressed the order[4]. He sent a Papal Bull to Edward II King of England ordering their suppression and the confiscation of Templars property. The consequent Writ for Ireland came to the Justiciar John Wogan (or Wigan) on the 25th of January 1308 and on February the 3rd all the Knights Templars in Ireland were rounded up and imprisoned in Dublin Castle. The inquiry into their case did not take place until 1310 and was held in St. Patrick's Cathedral. One of the charges made against them was that of being inattentive at Mass in their Clontarf Church! The order's master, Henry de Anet (or de Tanet) with 13 other Knights maintained their innocence of any crime. We do not know what the final court of enquiry verdict was, but in 1312 the Pope issued another Bull formally dissolving the order. By the power of a further Bull, he transferred all the property of the Templars to their kindred order, the Hospitallers. On their arrival in Clontarf, the Hospitallers established a Commander of their order in the Castle, began to farm the grounds and dedicated the church to St.John the Baptist who from now on replaced St. Comgall as Clontarf's patron saint. It is not clear in exactly what year after 1312 the Hospitallers took control of Clontarf Castle. It appears to have taken them a few years to get peaceful possession of the castle and grounds. The Hospitallers were to administer Clontarf Church and Manor, in the same way as the Templars did before them, until the Reformation-in fact until 1541 when the crown took possession of their property. The Hospitallers themselves were disbanded in 1542. When the Reformation did take place the last Prior of the Knights, Sir John Rawson was granted a peerage- which he timidly accepted. He was created Viscount Clontarf with an annual pension of 500 marks and a seat in Parliament. He was allowed occupy 'Clontarf Manor House' until his death. Being an old man at the time, he died, in fact, as soon as 1547.

History of the Catholic Church in Clontarf since the Reformation.

The Reformation comes to Clontarf

Thus far as we have traced Christian worship in Clontarf from 550 through the change whereby Norman clergy replaced the native, and the Roman diocesan system was firmly established. But now, Clontarf, in common with much of the rest of the country was to experience the 'New Order' as the Reformation was termed. It was to be a black age for Clontarf Catholics, and the sad aspect of the whole changeover was that its basis lay in greed- the greed of the monarchy, or more precisely the greed of the Tudors, for absolute power.

"Such as do build their faith upon
the holy text of pike and gun"

The follow through effects were both the shameful and disgraceful looting of monasteries and church property in general. In Clontarf's case, as in many others, the work and legacy of centuries was devastated in a few short years. The Reformation also added a new dimension- the religious issue- to the struggle against Anglo-Norman power in Ireland. In 1534 the English parliament, in passing the Act of Supremacy, declared Henry VIII head of the church. Even before a similar act was passed through the Irish parliament in 1536, the religious houses of the Pale began to disappear. In 1535 the Reformation first came to Fingal. Urged on by Thomas Cromwell (a top advisor to Henry VIII who received the nickname 'Malleus Monarchorum' or persecutor of monks and monasteries) Henry had the monasteries robbed or their sacred vessels, bells and all precious ornaments. Altars were broken and religious books torn and burned. Monks themselves were murdered or banished. It was robbery enough to confiscate land from the religious, but to strip roofs of their lead and allow splendid edifices to rot away was simply vandalism. The pillaging of monasteries must be recorded as perhaps the most obnoxious period in English history.
 In 1538 the prior of the Knights Hospitallers-probably anticipating closure- had leased the Clontarf estate to Matthew King most likely with arrangements agreed for Sir Rawson's welfare. King was a staunch Catholic and the Clontarf parish church managed to remain in Catholic hands, and with full Catholic, services through the reigns of Henry VIII, Edward VI and Mary I. But shortly after Elizabeth I ascended the throne in 1558 Clontarf was to feel the full brunt of the New Order. Clontarf parish church was handed over to the Protestant service and allowed fall into the ruin. For the first time since 550 Clontarf was without

a Catholic church and Catholics had to provide for their spiritual needs as best they could as they had no regular pastor. As all Catholic churches were confiscated the old parish system was destroyed. This state of affairs lasted until early in the 17th century when the Catholic Church responded and reorganized itself for a fight back. A new era began in 1614 with the Synod of Leinster ecclesiastics at Kilkenny where an attempt was made to form some sort of parish system again. (Some sources quote the year of the Synod as 1618.) By now the number of priests was drastically reduced through death, banishments, imprisonments, and martydoms and the laity impoverished. The new parochial system formed at Killkenny mapped out vast parishes instead of the former compact ones. A priest was to be in charge of each- and he was no longer to be called Rector or Vicar, but simply Parish Priest. Under the new system Clontarf parish was expanded to include a huge area of no fewer than eight of the forty old parishes that made up the Fingal area. The eight were Clontarf itself, Raheny, Coolock, Drumcondra (or Conturk), Santry, Glasnevin, Killester and Artane. It was really a union or district of parishes and was to last unbroken until 1879. Each of these eight parishes had its own church originally, but they were confiscated and allowed fall into ruin by the Reformers. In 1630 the Protestant Archbishop of Dublin reported that all but one of these churches were in ruins.

340 Years of Clontarf Parish Priests, 1620 - 1966

Since the Reformation down until three Clontarf parishes were constituted in 1966, seventeen (recorded) Parish Priests have administered to the Catholic parish of Clontarf (including the A.N other listed) in its various sizes. Their pastorates ranged in length from the shortest- a one month stint in 1805 by Canon Murray- to the extremely long reign of nearly forty years by Canon Andrew Tuite in the eighteenth century. As we will see the parish had the distinction of having quite a few priests who later became bishops.

Father James Drake , A.N Other	1620 -1680
Father Richard Cahill	1680-1703
Father Cormac Cassidy	1704-1720
Father Nicholas Gernon	1720-1733
Canon Terence McLoughlin	1771-1785
Canon John Larkin	1785-1797
Conon Patrick Ryan	1797-1805

Canon Daniel Murphy	March 24th, 1805-April 25th 1805
Dr. Paul Long	1805-1829
Canon James Callinan	1829-1846
Canon Cornelius Rooney	1846-November, 1878
Archdeacon Patrick O'Neill	April 1879-1909
Very Rev. James Hickey	1909-1923
Canon James Dempsey	1923-1936
Archdeacon Matthew Mc Mahon	1936-1949
Canon Patrick Carton	1949-1966 (cont. as P.P of St.John The Baptist Parish)

(Dates listed up to 1733 are necessarily only approximate):

The first parish priest appointed to the new sprawling parish was Rev. James Drake who must have come early in the reign of Charles I, even as early as 1612. He made Artane his headquarters- no doubt mindful of the protection offered by the Hollywood family of Catholic stock who resided in Artane Castle. Fr. Drake offered mass at Hollywood's residence or in the homes of the people, as there was no Catholic church in the entire parish. It was strictly forbidden to attend mass during the worst of the Penal Law days under Elizabeth I and James I. We have to thank the Protestant Archbishop Bulkeley for information on Fr.Drake. Making notes on Clontarf in 1630 the bishop wrote: "There is one James Drake, a Mass-priest resident at Artane and commonly saith Mass there. There is likewise his brother Patrick Drake a papish schoolmaster, to whom the children thereabouts go to school." It is impossible from existing records to say just how long Father Drake, that initial Father of the massive Clontarf Parish, administered. Most sources agree that he was there for about thirty years. He certainly was ministering when the dreaded Cromwellian Puritan period was ushered in.

"No more the cuckoo hails the spring;
No more the woods with staunch hounds ring;
The sun scarce lights the sorrowing day,
Since the rightful prince is far away." **Caltanan (Translation from Irish form)**

The next parish priest we have on record for the parish of Clontarf is Rev. Richard Cahill. There almost certainly was another 'guide' between Fr.Drake and Fr. Cahill but we have no means of determining who. Fr. Cahill was a very young priest when he came to Clontarf. He was ordained on St.Patrick's Day in 1674 by the Bishop of Meath Dr.Plunkett. He probably took up his duties in Clontarf in 1680. Taking advantage of the 'lull' in the anti-Catholic campaign during the brief reign of James II he opened the first Catholic church in the reorganised parish. Choosing Coolock as fairly central to the whole area under his care he had the little wooden chapel of St.Brendan with its thatched roof, erected there in about the year 1689. This was as for many years the only chapel in the entire parish. But after the defeat of James at the debacle that was the sham Battle of the Boyne in 1690 Catholics were to again experience the severest religious persecution and Fr.Cahill's little Coolock church was often closed down.

To help us appreciate the hardship endured by Catholics during those penal days, it might be appropriate to quote some extracts from the state papers of June 17th, 1714. "Co. Dublin. The examination of John Mitchell of Drumree in the said county, farmer, taken before the Right Honourable the Lord of Santry, Thomas Stepeny, Foliott Sheringley, Laurence Grace, John Jackson and Daniel Wybrarts, six of her Majesty's justices of the peace for the said county. Who (Mitchell) being duly sworn and examined said that the last time he heard mass was a Sunday last in the town of Coolock but by whom it was said or celebrated he did not know. (Many Catholics, like John Mitchell could honestly swear that they did not know the identity of the priest celebrating mass as it was quite common to drop a screen in front of the altar during mass in the worst days of persecution. Catholics who refused to attend heretical services were termed 'Recusants'.) Saith that he had a son called James Mitchell and that he said James Mitchell teaches the children of Michael O' Hara who lives in Kinsealy in the said county as schoolmaster, and that the said James was beyond the seas for some time and returned into this Kingdom about Christmas last past. Saith that he had not known of any parish bishop or regular Romish clergyman in this Kingdom (bound to prosecute in the sum of £40). James Fottrell of the Grange, Baldoyle heard mass on Sunday last at Coolock. Priests name was Father Cassidy living at Mrs. Hollywood's Artane. Darby Ward of Kilmore and James Walker of Coolock were present. Heard of Mitchell keeping a school in Kinsealy. Patrick Dodd of Balgriffen confirms the same and adds that his son went to school to Mitchell these eight days. £40. James Cunihan of Rathhenny (Raheny) being duly sworn and examined said that he heard mass said or celebrated on Sunday at Kilmore (house of Darby Ward)in the said county. Saith that Darby Ward of the same and John Byrne of the same, Christopher Saver of Clontarf were all present when the said mass was said or celebrated. John Wade of Rathkenny bore testimony for a Sunday later and testified that he heard mass said or celebrated at Rathkenny by Father Charles alias Cormac Cassidy and that James Smith and James Erwin of RathKenny were present. Bound to prosecute in the sum of £48."

From this we can deduce that the Coolock church did indeed serve just about the whole parish and that the priests moved about offering mass in people's houses where possible. We also notice that Fr. Cahill had a curate called Fr. Cormac Cassidy who most likely succeeded him as Parish Priest of Clontarf, but at what date we are not sure. Father Cassidy is listed in the Government Register of 1704, for the parish of Coolock and lived in the residence of Mrs. Hollywood of Artane. The Catholic tradition in Clontarf- indeed in all southern Fingal- must never forget the staunch solidarity and patronage shown at this time by the Artane family of Hollywood. One of the first Irish members of the Society of Jesus (Jesuits) was Fr. Christopher Hollywood, a member of the Artane family. Born at Artane Castle in 1559 he guided the Jesuit missions in Ireland from 1603 to 1626, twenty three of the most severe years of religious persecution. Many other powerful and influential families of the time went over to the 'new thinking' for reward, for greed, or indeed by eventually bowing to persecution. Not so the Hollywoods, and there is no doubt that except for their presence a priest could not have survived in the area. It is beyond the scope of this work to study how the Hollywood family managed to hold their property as well as their Catholicism in this black period. Their old castle of Artane stood until 1825 when the Christian Brothers erected a house there.

A father Nicholas Gernon succeeded Fr. Cassidy as parish priest in about 1720. We have absolutely no data on this period or on his work with his flock. Indeed his very name would probably have been erased from the memory were it not for the fact that it is recorded in the Deed of Institution of his successor. We know Fr. Gernon died in 1733 and Rev. (later Canon) Andrew Tuite was appointed parish priest in his stead. From here on (1733) church records are quite good and in tracing the history of the Catholic parish of Clontarf we are working from firm historical data.

Second Church and oldest Records

Canon Tuite was to serve as P.P until 1770. By now the government was realising that the Penal Laws were not successful in 'eradicating papish superstition'. In 1731 the House of Lords had ordered a religious census to be conducted particularly to enumerate the papists, but the returns for the union of Clontarf are not on record. One statement concerning the area recorded under "Raheny" which reads "One priest at Coolock and chapel; several itinerant priests." However in 1766 the returns of another such inquiry or religious census were published. These returns showed a big increase in population over the entire Clontarf parish, although the Drumcondra and Glasnevin areas of the parish were predominantly Protestant. (These two areas were at the time particularly fashionable suburbs where many Protestant nobility had residences.) Under

"Clontarf and Killester" the parish priest and curate are named as "Andrew Tuite and James Murray and two papish chapels." This is the first record of the parish having a second church. It had been erected by Canon Tuite to help administer to the sprawling parish. It is difficult to pinpoint the exact site of this church. But it is almost certain that it was on Yellow Lane near the present traffic lights at the junction of Collins Avenue and the Swords Road. This meant that it was reasonably convenient to Ballymun, Glasnevin, Drumcondra and Santry. Father Murray most likely operated from here while living at Black Bull, Drumcondra. On the death of Canon Tuite in 1771 he was succeeded as P.P by Canon Terence McLoughlin who had been a curate in Liffey Street for many years. To show that Penal times were still very much alive the Catholic Archbishop of Dublin Dr.John Carpenter in 1782 accepted the 'Test' or Oath of Allegiance in order to gain small measures of relief in conditions for Catholics. Canon McLoughlin lived at Coolock, thus ending the 'established' tradition of the P.P residing in Artane (which dated back to the first P.P. Fr.Drake) and making Coolock the centre of his parish. Canon McLoughlin had a Fr. William Green as curate. The Canon is credited with establishing the procedure of documenting proper parochial registers- at least no exising register reaches further back. His registers were begun in that little Coolock church. They are the oldest such records in the country and remain remarkably clear and legible. Canon McLoughln died in 1785 and Canon John Larkin, who had been a curate in Francis Street replaced him as P.P. Father Green remained as curate. As a team these two priests must have had a very harmonious understanding for each, in his will, left a legacy to the other.

By now the worst of the Penal sanctions against Catholics were relaxed or removed, especially after the 1793 Catholic Relief Act (although 1829, Daniel O'Connell and full emancipation were still a considerable distance away). Certainly the time had come for something of a real Catholic revival in the parish- especially in the areas of providing churches and schools. However the ordinary parishioner was very poor. Before his death in 1797 Canon Larkin (who lived in Donnycarney) had a new church built in Ballymun (with a schoolhouse beside it) to replace the now dilapidated one on Yellow Lane which ceased to exist. The building was one of rough stone with a thatched roof. It was in the townland of Balcurris and was to last exactly fifty years.

The next P.P of Clontarf was a former brilliant student of the Irish College in Rome, Canon Patrick Ryan. He was a man of quite outstanding talent who was to remain for only eight years in Clontarf when he became coadjutor to Dr. Caulfield bishop of Ferns and succeeded him as bishop in 1814. As a curate in the parish he had Fr. Strong, a Dominican. In the Castlereagh Correspondence we find Canon Ryan mentioned in 1800 for the "Coolock, Santry, ect. Parish" with an income of £100 per annum. The appointment of Canon Ryan to the Bishopric of Ferns meant that the Vatican would have to appoint his successor. But due to a mix up or misunderstanding between Dr.Troy, the Archbishop of Dublin and the Holy See the man chosen in 1805 was the saintly Rev. Daniel Murray as P.P of Coolock and Clontarf. (Although the entire Parish had always been accepted as the Clontarf Parish this is the first official mention of Clontarf in an appointment. Now however it became the official name of the parish until the first redivision came in 1879.) Apparently Dr. Troy forwarded the wrong name for ratification, which should have been of that of Dr. Paul Long. Rev. Murray, aware of the circumstances, asked the Archbishop to allow him to resign. This was done and then Dr. Long took over as Clontarf P.P in 1805. Very Rev. Canon Murray was later to become arguably Dublin's greatest Archbishop from 1823-1852. His duration as P.P of Clontarf was the shortest on record- just one month from 24th March, 1805-25th April, 1805. Dr. Long was destined to spend much of his term of office abroad, in France, active in the cause of the many Irish colleges as he was 'au fait' with the French scene- he had been educated in France and had served for some years as curé in the diocese of Laon. It was with great difficulty that he had escaped to Dublin in 1792 during the "Reign of Terror" in France. Now, when Napoleon eventually made a concordat with the Pope the Irish bishops rushed Dr. Long to France as their agent[5].

Curates- the parish now had two in the absence of the P.P. - and administrators carried on the parochial work in Clontarf while Dr. Long was away. Father Ham, Fr. Cunningham, Fr Lawlor and Fr. Charles Boyle (who served in the parish for 25 years as curate and later administrator starting in 1814) all worked diligently throughout the parish. Later Fr. Ryan, Fr Nugent and the legendary Fr. Harold served Clontarf faithfully[6]. Between 1814 and 1819 a Father Cruise O.P chaplain to the Dominican nuns (who had a house on Vernon Avenue since 1808) allowed many Clontarfites attend mass at this residence. This was most convenient to the locals- saving them the trek across fields and pathways to Coolock on Sundays and Holy Days. Thus Fr. Cruise's house was the first step towards a chapel for Clontarf. A pious merchant named James Younge, in conjunction with the Carmelites, opened a branch monastery on Fairview Strand with a chapel at the back which came to be known as Brophy's chapel. Dr. Troy, Archbishop of Dublin, officially opened and blessed the chapel in 1819 for use by the faithful. Two masses were celebrated here each Sunday and the locals naturally found it most convenient. Like Clontarfites, it was difficult for people to get from Fairview to Coolock for mass. The long trudge on stony badly kept roads, especially in winter in the mud, was nothing short of hardship. As most

Catholics couldn't afford a donkey let alone a horse it was "Shank's Mare" all the way. Part of Brophy's chapel building was on the site of the old cinema in Fairview. With some intervals this was to be Fairview's church until the new Church of the Visitation was opened in 1855. On his death in 1826 Mr. Younge willed the place to his niece Mrs. Brophy to whom rent was paid. Hence the name 'Brophy's Chapel'. It was also referred to as 'the monastery church'.

A Church for Clontarf
In 1824 the P.P Dr. Long finally returned, to stay, from his administrative duties in France. Immediately realising that Clontarf was now something more than a fishing village and should have its own church Dr. Long had 'a plain rectangular edifice, without any pretentions to distinction' erected on a strip of ground 'running west to east behind a short modern terrace of houses adjoining the residence known as Summerville.' This church was opened in 1825. It was quite close to the site of the present St. John the Baptist Church. A local businessman, Mr. Edmund Keary had contributed £1,000 for the provision of a Clontarf chapel. In 1829, Catholic emancipation year, Dr. Long was transferred to Meath Street were he died in1837. His place as P.P in Clontarf was taken by Canon James Callinan who had been P.P in Celbridge for some years. He immediately decided to increase the capacity of the Clontarf chapel, so he had a wing or porch added which extended the church "by seventeen feet at the south-eastern end." With a balcony this extension did add greatly to the ever increasing population of Clontarf. The Canon bought, from his own resources, a suitable residence, on the site now occupied by Holy Faith Convent Clontarf. (This was personal property, and when dying he bequeathed it to his sister who sold it to the Royal Irish Constabulary. Later it was to be acquired by the Holy Faith Convent.) He then approached Colonel Vernon of Clontarf Castle with a view to securing a good site, adjoining the Canon's own house, but it was occupied at the time by a settlement of fishermen and popularly known as 'The Sheds'. Part of the agreement for the church plot was the removal of these 'Sheds'. (See chapter 1 above).
The lease was secured and the site cleared so the Archbishop of Dublin Dr. Murray solemnly laid and blessed the first stone of the present St. John the Baptist Church on Jun 16th, 1835. Three years later, in 1838 the church was opened for Sunday masses and public worship. Thus it is by far Clontarf's oldest church. Father Charles Boyle, by then curate in the Fairview end of the parish had accumulated a considerable amount of materials- stones, timber, ect.- to build a new church in Fairview, on the corner of what is now Fairview Park beside Annesley Bridge. However the site was reclaimed land and deemed too unstable

to support a church. Instead the building materials he had accumulated were transferred to Clontarf and worked into the earlier portion of St. John the Baptist's Church. Fr. Boyle was made P.P of Skerries in 1839. A curate in Clontarf at that time was Father William Walsh. He was a very close friend of Cardinal Paul Cullen and he was later to become Archbishop of Halifax, Nova Scotia. It was Father Walsh who was deputed by the P.P to draw up answers to the 'Poor Inquiry (Ireland) Commission' in 1835. Some of his observations are a great insight into the social history of the period and are referred to in Chapter one (above). Another curate appointed to Clontarf in 1839, Fr. Edward McCabe was to become Archbishop of Dublin and later Cardinal. In 1842 the Foreign Missionary College of All Hallows was opened in the parish of Clontarf. Indeed it proved to be the first of many religious and educational establishments that found a home within the limits of the old parish frontiers. Some of these were St. Patrick's Teacher Training College, St.Joseph' Male Blind Centre, High Park Convent, The Christian Brothers Noviciate and the Holy Faith Convents at Glasnevin and Clontarf. The problem of schools for Fairview was solved when the Presentation nuns opened their school on Convent Avenue, off Richmond Road. Canon Callinan died, in February 1846 and Canon Rooney was appointed to replace him.

The way back - re-division begins
Canon Cornelius Rooney was to be the last P.P to rule over the huge Clontarf parish which had been formed at the synod of Kilkenny in 1614. Apparently Canon Rooney was a refined man of great charm, who won admiration from all classes and persuasions by his kindness and amiability. His birthplace was Glenarm in Co. Antrim but he attended school in Dublin. (On his way to school he witnessed the execution of Robert Emmet on Thomas Street in 1803.) But the fact that he had to obtain his baptismal certificate from the parson at Glenarm when he first went to Maynooth was a reminder of just how close we still were to the Penal days. In 1848 he had the pleasure of seeing the new St. Papan's Church in Ballymun opened. Canon Callinan had completed the groundwork for this church before his death. It was built at the height of the Great Famine. A local man Mr. James Coughlan was a very generous benefactor towards the building. Father Boyle, though now in Skerries, was also very involved. Canon Rooney then concentrated on providing Fairview with a church suitable to its ever growing needs - he in fact secured the site of the present Church of the Visitation in 1847. In 1859 Canon Rooney asked the Archbishop to provide the parish with a third curate. This was agreed, and in 1854 with the arrival of Father Purcell at Glasnevin as chaplain to the Sacred Heart Sisters there were four

curates assisting the P.P. - each based respectively in Clontarf, Fairview, Glasnevin and Coolock. In 1885 the new Church of the Visitation in Fairview was opened and the old 'Brophy's chapel' closed. This brought the number of churches in the parish to four and the population of the vast parish was 6,000 people. Canon Rooney added a fifth church when in 1864 he invited the Archbishop, Cardinal Cullen, to bless and open the handsome new church of St. Assam in Raheny. The number of Catholics in the Raheny part of the parish was small but the building of this little church made the practising of their religion much more comfortable. In his 82nd year and his 32nd as P.P. in Clontarf - Canon Rooney, that man of likeable qualities, died in November, 1878.

He left the parish with five churches (four of them new) and a number of schools and all parochial property was secured by long leases. During his term the Carmelite brothers had come to Grace Park Road and the Sacred Heart nuns had settled into their Glasnevin home. The French Sisters of Charity opened a psychiatric home on the grounds of the Presentation nuns establishment, on Convent Avenue Fairview (the Presentation sisters moved to Terenure in 1866). A new school was built on Philipsburgh Avenue to replace their school. As early as 1847 Clontarf National Schools were opened on Vernon Avenue. Also in 1842 the Loreto nuns of Rathfarnham opened a young ladies school in Baymount Castle(now Manresa House). However after a fire gutted their premises in 1851 they left. A tragic memory from this period was the death of one of the curates, Fr. Gaffney, who had come to the parish in 1864. He died in a freak accident at Sutton in 1875, when he was killed instantly after being thrown off a car. Canon Rooney's death occurred during a vacancy of the Dublin See - Cardinal Cullen died a month before Canon Rooney and his successor, Archbishop McCabe, was not appointed until April 1879. During the six month interval the parish was administered to by its five curates. With a growing population the large parish was now beginning to burst at the seams. The Kilkenny divisions of more than 250 years before could no longer endure and redivision time had clearly come. The new Archbishop was quite familiar with the parish having served from 1839 until 1853 as a curate in Clontarf. He considered the parish much too large a unit with its ever expanding population. This became of almost chronic proportions in the Clontarf area alone after the completion of the Bull Wall in 1823. Thousands of holiday makers converged there in Summertime as the Bull Wall added enormously to Clontarf's reputation for amenities.

Using the Malahide Road as the dividing line Archbishop McCabe made two moieties of the parish. The old parish of Clontarf (the northern section) would now comprise Clontarf (including Killester), Coolock and Raheny. The Southern section was constituted as the new parish of Fairview comprising Fairview,

Glasnevin, Santry, Drumcondra, and Artane (including Donnycarney and Marino). This division became effective as and from the beginning of 1879. William Keown became the first P.P. of the new Fairview parish of the Visitation. The first P.P. of the new dimidiated Clontarf parish of St. John The Baptist was Canon Patrick O'Neill. Coming from the Clonmel area of County Tipperary, Canon O'Neill had been taught Greek and Latin at one of the 'hedge' schools then predominant in the south of Ireland. The early years of Canon O'Neills ministry might be described as years of quiet usefulness. However in 1890 St. John the Baptist must have been exercising considerable control behind the 'Golden Gates' because in that year a serious of benefactions to the Clontarf Church and parish began, that were remarkable by any circumstances. Indeed all future parishioners would have good reason to remember the name of the local family Allingham of Seafield Road with respect. First Miss Allingham secured a house to act as a convent for the Holy Faith Sisters (in 1890). This was on part of the grounds where the convent stands today. The nuns opened a school for girls with a junior boys' school attached. In the next few years the sisters extended their premises by acquiring Canon Callinan's old house from the R.I.C - which was also on the site where the convent and schools stand today. On part of the ground at the rear of their premises, the convent erected enough two-storey cottages to accommodate forty families. Miss Allingham then donated £600 to decorate the interior of St. John's Church. She also gave a further £2,000 to enlarge and equip Clontarf male and female national schools on Vernon Avenue. Miss Allingham's generosity was in similar vein to that of her brother Mr. Owison T. Allingham. In 1895 he spent £6,000 renovating the present church. This included extending it at the chancel end and providing a new 'high' altar, an apse, a pulpit, the altar rails, a sacristy bell and belfry and some church seats.

Canon O'Neill became Vicar- Forane of the Deanery and in 1897 he was made Archdeacon of Dublin. In the early 1900's his age began to incapacitate him severely and indeed for a few years before his death, in July 1909 at 84 years of age (in some church records this date is wrongly stated as 1912), he ceased to take any active part in parish work. While Canon Rooney had lived in the local house known as Summerville Archdeacon O'Neill resided at Number 1, St. John's Terrace, In fact, before his death, he bought numbers 1 and 2 St John's Terrace - from his private recourses for £1,000 and willed them to the parish as future residencies for the clergy. Also, in his will, he acknowledged a gift of yet another £1,000 for the poor of the parish from the previously mentioned Miss Allingham. The porch of today's St. John the Baptist Church was erected by parishioners and friends in memory of the venerable Archdeacon, who had thirty years of a pastorate in Clontarf.

In 1909 the Diocesan authorities, realising that the Clontarf area had grown out of all proportions decided to divide it from Raheny and Coolock and make it a separate parish. The first P.P appointed to the now restricted parish of Clontarf was Rev. James Hickey. He served the parish until his death in 1923 and then Canon James Dempsey was appointed. Before long it became clear to Canon Dempsey that one church simply couldn't serve the ever growing demands of a rapidly increasing parish population. Thus in 1927 he bought the Old Clontarf Town Hall on Clontarf Road from Dublin Corporation and opened it up as the chapel-of-ease of St.Anthony of Padua. Thus it began to serve the population of the western portion of the parish.

In 1936 on the death of Canon Dempsey, Archdeacon Matthew McMahon became P.P. of Clontarf. Once again, towards the end of his tenure of office, it became obvious that Clontarf's two churches were not sufficient to serve the needs of the parish especially on the eastern or Dollymount end which was rapidly expanding in population. Before he died Archdeacon McMahon acquired a site for a new church on the present St. Gabriel's road. On his death in 1949 Canon Patrick Carton acceded to the 'see' of Clontarf. (He was, in fact, to be the last P.P. to administer all three Clontarf parishes). In 1956 the church of St. Gabriel the Archangel was opened by the Archbishop of Dublin Dr. John McQuaid to answer the needs of the faithful in Dollymount. In 1966 Archbishop House decided that the Clontarf area would be more easily and efficiently administered in smaller units. Consequently it was split into the three parishes of St. John the Baptist, St. Anthony of Padua and St. Gabriel the Archangel.

Clontarf's Three Catholic Parishes 1966- 2007
The three Catholic parishes organised for Clontarf in 1966 represent the three distinct areas or villages of which Clontarf is comprised.

I. Clontarf - the old medieval village centered around Clontarf Castle and Castle Avenue is represented, in the main, by St. Anthony's parish. (Upper Clontarf)
II. Clontarf Sheds - the eighteenth century fishing village centered at the foot of Vernon Avenue is represented by the area's 'mother' parish - the parish of St.John the Baptist. (Middle Clontarf)
III. Dollymount - the 'youngest' part of Clontarf. It eventually merged with Clontarf due to expansion and is represented by St. Gabriel's Parish. (Lower Clontarf)

PARISH PRIESTS

St. John the Baptist Parish

Canon Patrick Carton	1966 -1973
Monsignor Liam Martin	1973- 1981
Father Donal O'Leary	1981 - 1990
Father Ciaran Holahan	1990 - 1998
Father Patrick Molony	1998 - 2001
Father Gabriel Slattery	2001 - 2007

Moderator and Co-PP took over

St. Anthony's Parish

Father Laurence Brophy	1966 - 1971
Father John Gunning	1971 - 1984
Father Patrick Devine	1984 - 2007

Moderator and Co-PP took over

St. Gabriel's Parish

Father Michael Murphy	1966 - 1971
Father Joseph Newth	1971 - 1983
Father Cornelius O'Dowd	1983 - 1994
Father Michael Hastings	1994 - 2009

Moderator and Co-PP took over

" Everyone must have sentiment and love for their native country, but one's native parish has an even stronger attraction. After the home itself there is no unit that effects our lives so much as our parish; in our parochial church we receive the sacraments of Baptism and Confirmation and make our First Communion, and in our parish school we receive our first instructions in religion and virtue. Is it any wonder that we love and reverence our parish church and are proud of the parish we belong to?"

John Kingston (Rev.)

All three Clontarf parishes are in the Fingal South East Deanery of the Dublin archdiocese of which the spiritual leader is the Archbishop of Dublin.

PARISH AND CHURCH OF ST. JOHN THE BAPTIST, CLONTARF

We have earlier in this chapter traced the building of this 'mother' church which in 2013 celebrated the 175th anniversary of its opening for public worship. Canon Callinan had to clear 200 families from The Sheds to please Colonel

Vernon and secure a 99 year lease for the site. The Canon managed to rehouse most of the fishermen on a vacant plot behind his own house (while others were compensated) and the new dwelling place came to be known as 'Snugboro'.(see chapter one above) The church was not fully completed or decorated when it was first opened in 1838 and it was only used for Sunday Mass. It was however, fully furnished, before Canon Callinan died in 1846.

The church was designed by the Architectural firm P. Byrne and Son. It is a spacious and elegant structure in the later style of English Architecture. The site of the church will always be linked with the romantic and nostalgic memories which surround the old fishing village that was The Sheds. The church's position is a picturesque one on Clontarf Road by the seafront on the city side of Vernon Avenue. In 1895 the building was elongated at the chancel end and the present sacristy was built with the other items - mentioned earlier in this chapter - installed due to the munificence of Mr. Owison Allignham, a wine merchant who also traded in mineral water and lived at Seafield House, on Seafield Road. When the church first opened it had to cater for an estimated 500-600 people at Mass on Sunday - the number ever increasing. The church, dedicated to the 'Herald of Advent', has a representation of St. John The Baptist baptising Jesus in the river Jordan, at the Baptismal font. The church seal, crest or symbol is the head of St. John The Baptist on a plate with St. John The Baptist's cross. The church has a parish resource centre on its grounds.

PARISH AND CHURCH OF ST. ANTHONY OF PADUA, CLONTARF

Up to the year 1900 Clontarf was a separate township from the city of Dublin, with its own town hall and Urban District Council. In 1900 the Boundaries Act brought the Clontarf precinct into the city proper in common with other Dublin Urban districts. The town hall was built on that part of the Clontarf Road known as Strandville. The hall served as a concert and dance hall, a public assembly hall as well as a cinema and library. After 1900 the corporation let the premises for various purposes - dances, meetings, ect. but in reality found it something of a liability. In 1925 the hall, complete with court-house and other offices, was bought by Canon Dempsey P.P. of Clontarf. He extended the building, added a cut stone frontage and skillfully and happily transformed it into a church to serve the western end of his bulging parish. It was blessed, officially opened and dedicated to St. Anthony of Padua by the Archbishop of Dublin Dr. Byrne on August 28th, 1927. Up to then it was still known as Clontarf town hall.

First opened as a chapel-of-ease to St. John the Baptist's, it was to become a parish church on July 1st, 1966 when St. Anthony's parish was constituted from St. John

The Baptist's. Now a solid mature parish, the church played a central role in fostering its own community spirit and character within the new parish which is back boned by part of Kincora Estate with Castle Avenue, The Stiles Road, St. Lawrence's Road and the Holly-brooks. This self same old building still stands and is now used for various community activities. The hall's '1916' connection is dealt with in chapter five below. Many people, parishioners, Clontarfites and others have a genuine fondness for the old building which in any case is a strong and structurally sound edifice. Therefore hopes are high that in any future development of the area around the new St. Anthony's Church some way will be found to preserve and maintain this, one of the last of Clontarf's genuinely historic buildings. In 1975 a modest, modern, intimate and beautifully comfortable new church of St. Anthony was built just landward of the old church. Perfectly designed, it can seat about 750 people and its total cost including all furnishing was £172,000. The foundation stone for the church was belatedly laid by Archbishop of Dublin Dr. Dermot Ryan on the 12th May 1975. On November 23rd of that year Dr. Ryan officially opened and blessed the church.

PARISH AND CHURCH OF ST. GABRIEL THE ARCHANGEL, DOLLYMOUNT
As development and building in Clontarf and Dollymount continued in the last decades of the 19th century, Dollymount ceased to be a separate village and merged with Clontarf. As a large population settled in the new building schemes around Dollymount in the 20th century it became obvious that Clontarf's two existing churches couldn't cope and that the Dollymount area should have its own centre of worship. Accordingly the P.P. Archdeacon McMahon acquired the site of the present church on the grounds of the local St. Vincent de Paul convent. The sisters kindly donated it free of charge. Archdeacon McMahon's successor, Canon Carton, took on the sizeable task of the construction of the church. The church was completed in 1956 and on the feast of Christ the King October 28th of that year it was blessed and officially opened by his Grace the Archbishop of Dublin John. C. McQuaid as the church of St. Gabriel the Archangel. (Dr. McQuaid blessed and laid the foundation stone for the church three years earlier - on August 30th, 1953.)
Built on St. Gabriel's Road, Clontarf, it was to serve as Clontarf's second chapel-of -ease. St. Gabriel's became a full parish on July 1st, 1966 when it was constituted, like St. Anthony's, from the St. John The Baptist Parish. Serving mainly the Dollymount area the local enthusiasm for the church project, soon generated an identity, spirit and character special to St. Gabriel's. The church building is mainly of concrete and is designed in the Hiberno Romanesque style.

The architects were Hugh Duffy and Louis Peppard. It is an imposing building and a Clontarf landmark. A magnificently spacious church it can accommodate about 1,800 people. The interior is adorned with art work in two mediums - mosaic and stained glass. The figure of St. Gabriel in the large stained glass window being very eye-catching, while it is well worth visiting the church for the sole purpose of viewing the stations of the cross which are beautifully executed in Italian mosaic frieze. St Gabriel's parish (or community) self-financing centre was opened in 1969. Since then it has been a hive of activity, catering for a flood of organisations, clubs, committees, teams, crèches, ect. The premises has certainly proved to be most useful providing facilities for parishioners who in St. Gabriel's parish have a very high degree of involvement in parish activities.

Perhaps the church's proudest day was January 1st, 1980 when it was chosen to host the Archdiocesan annual Peace Day Mass. The chief celebrant was the Apostolic Nuncio Dr. Alibrandi. His Grace Archbishop Ryan presided and in all, seven bishops were present. Dignitaries who attended included the then President Of Ireland Dr. Hillery and Mrs. Hillery, the Taoiseach Mr. Haughey, his Tánaiste Mr. Colley and the then leader of Fine Gael Dr. Garrett Fitzgerald. A host of civic and political representatives also attended and the presidents of numerous professional societies were present. Ordinary parishioners, other Clontarfites and outsiders packed the church. A true parochial team effort saw the very successful and happy occasion end with a reception in the parish centre. A distinguished visitor on one occasion to St. Gabriel's church was the late Pope Paul VI. He visited the building, in the company of Archbishop McQuaid, during a visit to Dublin. This was when he was Cardinal Montini and before he was elected Pope.

. . . .

Today the wheel has come full circle (from 1966) for Clontarf's three Catholic Parishes, and in a new arrangement they have been reunited or clustered as one under a Moderator Parish Priest. They are, however, administered separately with Co-Parish Priests. This arrangement began at the term of office of the last Parish Priest in each parish (as listed above) came to an end.

Immaculate Conception House
Beside St. Gabriel's church is the convent of the aforementioned sisters (daughters) of Charity of St. Vincent de Paul (or daughters of Charity also commonly known as the 'White Bonnets') who donated the original site for the church. The sisters acquired this property, which was the site of the old Mount

Prospect House, in 1873. It was established as a rest home for poor children and a holiday home for orphans , then called the St. Vincent de Paul Female Orphanage. In the 1950's the convent was extended to provide a home for old retired sisters who had worked for the poor in various parts of Ireland, England and Scotland. Before St. Gabriel's church was built, the sisters, with the permission of Canon Carton P.P., were delighted to accommodate people of the district with young families for Sunday Mass in their tiny private Oratory. The sisters regarded it as a great privilege to give part of their ground for another church to the glory of God. The convent is officially named 'Immaculate Conception House' (see chapter nine below).

Manresa House
Within the confines of St. Gabriel's parish and standing on its private grounds just off the seafront in Dollymount - between Dollymount Avenue and Mount Prospect Avenue - is the building known as Manresa House. Originally part of Vernon Estate, first named Granby Hall and then Baymount House and Castle, it became in 1775 the residence of Dr. Traill, a Protestant bishop of Down and Connor. Baymount Castle, described as 'a handsome castellated suburban house', was owned by a John Kiely who ran a short lived seminary there before selling it in 1838 to Robert Warren. Warren spent over £2,000 in renovating the residence and in 1847 disposed of it to Mother Ball, foundress of the Irish Loreto nuns. The Loreto order transferred some pupils from their Rathfarnham Abbey Girls School premises to Baymount Castle and organised a school there. Mother Ball, somewhat ahead of her time, had a swimming pool built in the grounds which was filled with sea water at every high tide by means of pipes direct from the sea. However, all this water didn't prevent the building being ruined by fire in 1854. The nuns moved their school to Balbriggan, spent £4,000 rebuilding and restoring the premises and then disposed of it to George Tickell who had a furniture and auctioneering business in Mary Street. Tickell's widow sold the estate in 1898 to Lord Ardilaun of St. Anne's. In 1904 with William Lucas Scott as headmaster it opened as a preparatory school for protestant boys which continued until 1936. In that year it was acquired by Mr. John T. Gwynn (of the well known literary family) who became headmaster. The school closed in 1946. In 1948 Baymount Castle became the property of the Society of Jesus. They (the Jesuits) renamed the building Manresa House - after the Spanish Cave of that name where the founder of the Jesuits, Ignatius Loyola, composed his famous 'Spiritual Exercises'. They opened the premises as a retreat house for laymen and dedicated it to Our Lady. Later Manresa House was extended to cater for

students studying to become Jesuits. They spent the two first years of their noviceship at Manresa. This ceased in 1991. Then becoming a simple retreat house for men Manresa has blossomed into a rigorous and vibrant centre of spirituality which offers priests, religious and laity guidance in prayer and christian living through retreats and workshops.

The original entrance to the Baymount estate was from Mount Prospect Avenue but this entrance has been replaced by Park Lawn building estate, The castellated Gate Lodge, sold independently in 1977, is still there. The entrance to Manresa is now directly from Clontarf Road. The establishment also commemorates the memory of the famous Irish Jesuit Chaplain of World War 1 - Father William Doyle.

HISTORY OF THE CHURCH OF IRELAND IN CLONTARF

In 1558 Elizabeth I acceded to the English throne. The following year Clontarf Parish Church - the one built by the Knights Templars and dedicated to St. John The Baptist by the Knights Hospitallers - was handed over to the "New Order". Thus it is from then - the Reformation - that we can trace the history of the Protestant Church in Clontarf. The church building was allowed fall into ruin for many years. Then in 1609 the first Protestant church was built on the ruins of the old church. All records of the time recall the church as "a small rectangular, very plain and unimportant edifice, about 75 feet by 25 feet with west gable and one arched bell turret of ungraceful proportions". The new church building was in line with reformation concepts of simplicity and austerity in church design and architecture. The church, dedicated to St. John The Baptist, was to serve for 257 years as Clontarf's church of Ireland parish church and the ruins of this church stand to this day in Clontarf graveyard on Castle Avenue beside Clontarf Castle. The Protestant Church of Killester seems to have been united to the Clontarf parish in 1686.

From about 1850 on, Church of Ireland parishioners appear to have been preoccupied with the need for a new parish Church. Extracts from parish magazine files of the time tell us that "the parish commences at Marino Crescent and extends along the sea for three and a quarter miles and contains 1190 acres." 750 non- Catholics resided in the parish with a big influx in the summer. "The Manor Church is supposed to accommodate 350 people" but the average summer attendance was put at 400 while in winter about 250 attended. With the Clontarf population expanding a magazine line from that time states "Clontarf church is quite inadequate to meet the requirements of the parish ... the ministers are frequently told by the residents in the parish that they would gladly attend Divine

Worship if they could obtain church accommodation." A meeting held on December 6th, 1859 attended by the "Trustees of Clontarf New Church 1860" - including Mr. B.L Guinness and Mr. J.E.V Vernon - decided to erect a new church at the Dollymount end of the parish. All members of the parish seemed happy to support and go ahead with this idea. The Archbishop was agreeable but the Rector, Rev. Mr. Kempston, was totally against the idea of building in Dollymount - he was particularly hostile to the notion of removing the centre of the parish from Castle Avenue. He felt that if the existing church was renovated, it would suffice while keeping the heart of the parish where it always was. The matter was then dropped.

In 1862 a new Rector, Rev. James Pratt, was appointed. Now the 'New Church Project' was resurrected, this time with a view to building close to the existing church. Plans progressed quickly. John E.V. Vernon of Clontarf Castle presented a suitable site for the church on what is now Seafield Road. On August 10th, 1864 the foundation stone was laid by Mr. Vernon. "The stone having been placed in a convenient position there was inserted within the cavity a bottle containing several of the current coins of the realm, also a copy of the "Daily Express" of 9th of August, 1864". (From the Daily Express August 11th, 1864.) The whole structure was to cost £6,000 and the capacity would be 550 persons. It was formerly consecrated and opened on May 14th, 1866.

The church, which is built from granite, is comfortable, elegant and neat with Gothic windows. It was designed by Mr. Welland. Two features in particular stand out. The first, is its 150- foot high spire. It is a local landmark, very conspicuous - even from far out in Dublin Bay. In 1899 the spire was stuck by lightning and the wrought iron seven - foot cross at the top was badly bent and much of the stonework shattered. The cross was gilded when it was straightened, and a lightning conductor was installed from top to base along the spire. The other outstanding feature is the east window behind the altar. Its stained glass representation of the twelve apostles being an outstanding work of art, with Matthias replacing Judas as the twelfth apostle.

The original Glebe House beside it was built in 1878 and the Parish Hall further along Seafield Road, opposite Belgrove Boys School, was built in 1880. The Chancel, at a cost of £2,000 was added to the church in 1899. In 1966 St. John The Baptist Church proudly celebrated its centenary. In the churchyard is a war memorial honouring all those parishioners who served and died during the First World War. Over the years, the church has had the good fortune to have excellent men appointed as rectors, who, with their curates, have served the parish with loyalty and zeal. In 2007, the select vestry of the parish decided to centralise the community around the church so they disposed of the old parish hall and sexton's house and a new hall and parish centre was opened in the church grounds on Seafield Road West.

IMPROPRIATE CURATES AND RECTORS

CURATES
1545/'70	John Quyn
1591	William Savage (Curate)
1615	Timon Thelwell (Curate)
1630	Richard St. Laurence (Curate)
1637	Randolph Dymocke (Curate)
1642	William Tedder (Curate)

RECTORS
1669/'70	Henry Bereton	1862	James Pratt
1680	Adam Ussher	1875	Macnevin Bradshaw
1713	Frederick Ussher	1894	Frederick Mervyn
1766	John Usser	1904	John Neligan
1811	Charles Mulloy	1936	John McCullum
1829	William Handcock	1962	Robert McCullum
1840	Thomas Huddart	1989	Thomas Haskins
1841	James Reid	2003	Derek Sargeant
1855	William Kempston	2013	Lesley Robinson

ALL Saint's Church of Ireland, St. Anne's Park, Raheny
The lovely little Protestant church of All Saints, Raheny, has a beautiful setting in the groves of St. Anne's Park along the Howth Road. In the 1880's when the old Protestant parish church of Raheny - St. Assams, the ruin in the graveyard dominating the centre of Raheny village - became unsuitable for further use, the Rector (Canon Hayes) approached Lord Ardilaun of St. Anne's regarding the provision of a new church. The old building became quite dangerous with the roof literally caving in. The Canon put a proposition to Lord Ardilaun to build a new church on his estate stressing how convenient it would be for Ardilaun's own estate workers. Ardilaun agreed and as a Raheny parishioner, he presented the site and built All Saint's Church in 1889 at his own expense, which became the new Protestant Parish Church of Raheny.

Lord Ardilaun's architect for the building of this church was George Coppinger Ashlin. The style is a very elaborate Victorian Gothic type - the church, especially the tower and steeple, is allegedly modelled on the famous Salisbury Cathedral

(Salisbury Cathedral is in Salisbury, Wiltshire, England.) The entire cost of building the church, (built of Wicklow granite) was £9,000. The church is cruciform in structure and the octagonal spire is 110 feet high. The beautiful stained glass windows are dedicated to previous residents of St. Anne's. The transept windows were erected by Lady Ardilaun in memory of her husband. In the porch, a tablet states that the bell in the tower was erected to proclaim the glory of God in memory of Lady Ardilaun, but the outstanding feature of the interior, (generally decorated with both Irish oak and Irish marble) is the font.

The Ardilauns are buried in the mortuary chapel in the church, where in 1987 the parish set up a columberium where parishioners may leave the ashes of deceased family members in their own niche. Lord Ardiluan controlled the appointment of Rectors to the church, as did his wife after him until 1925. Then Bishop Plunkett inherited control from the Ardilauns with their direction that "under no circumstances is an Englishman to be appointed as Rector. . .any such Rector must be Irish by birth and parentage." In 1941 the appointment of Rectors eventually came under the direct control of the Church of Ireland itself. The present Rector's house beside the church, was built in 1950 when the old residence on the other side of the Howth Road (in Ennafort) was sold to the Belton building firm.

THE RECTORS IN RAHENY HAVE BEEN:

1873-1918	Canon F.C. Hayes
1918-1950	Canon T.W.E. Drury
1950-1970	Canon T.J. Johnson
1970-1975	Rev W.R. Kelly
1975-1992	Rev C. Wilson
1992-2013	Rev J. Carroll
2013->>>`	Rev N. Mc Causland

Clontarf Presbyterian Church and Parish

The Presbyterian congregation in Clontarf have a very interesting history dating back to the arrival in Dublin of the Reverend William Wilson of Drumbo in Co. Down. He came in December 1836 to take permanent charge of a Presbyterian Mission which had occupied several premises in Dublin south of the Liffey during 1835. The Mission, up to then, had been supplied with ministers sent by the Secession Presbytery of Down. Installed as minister, early in 1837, Wilson obtained a regular meeting house known as the Ebenezer Chapel on D'Olier Street and the group were established as the Second Secession Congregation. In 1845 D'Olier Street Presbyterian congregation sold the Ebenezer Church for

£1,000. They 'crossed the Liffey' to Lower Gloucester Street and established themselves in what came to be known as 'The Scots Church'. The Doric structure complete with basement session room cost £1,800, and an accompanying manse was built on Great Charles Street in1864. (Lower Gloucester Street is now Sean Mc Dermott Street). The "Scots Church" built in 1846 became famous as one of only two churches in Dublin bearing a Greek inscription on the facade - the other being St. George's Church in Hardwicke Place.)

Reverend Wilson retired in 1854 due to ill health (but remained as Senior Minister of the Congregation until his death in 1865). Rev. James Edgar replaced him but died also in 1865. Edgar was succeeded by Reverend Robert Watts who remained only two years when he was appointed to the chair of systematic Philosophy in Assembly's College. Rev. Robert Hanna took up duty then and remained until he was removed to England in 1880. In that same year Reverend William Moore took Reverend Hanna's place and he ministered to the community until 1883 when he was appointed superintendent of a Theological Training College in Spain.

The year 1884 brought Reverend J.L. Morrow as minister to the Gloucester Street congregation. He quickly realised the need for a Presbyterian church in Clontarf. After obtaining permission from the Presbytery, the congregation decided to move to the site in Clontarf, at the junction of the Howth Road with the Clontarf Road, where it still remains today.

"Until at last they found a spot where two great highways tend,
Where Dollymount and distant Howth their varied products blend,
As sinful human nature with reforming grace doth close,
This wilderness our fathers made to blossom as the rose."

(These lines referring to the congregation's move from the city to Clontarf were written by Rev. Morrow's assistant, Rev. Tom Barry.)

On July 26th, 1889 the foundation stone for the Clontarf Presbyterian Church, which is built of granite stone, was laid by Mrs. Blyth wife of the Sessian clerk. The architect was Thomas Drew and the nave and trancept were completed and officially opened in 1890. The tower was added in 1897-98 and the vestry in 1932. The emblem of the church is 'The Burning Bush'.

The outstanding feature of the church apart from its picturesque tower is without any doubt, the fantastic 1914/18 Great War memorial stained glass window which was designed and made in 1918/19 by Harry Clarke R.H.A who was one of Ireland's most notable stained glass artists. Known simply as 'the memorial window' it was unveiled and dedicated (to the Presbyterian church's members who lost their lives in the first world war) on March 7th, 1920 by Right Rev.

Major General J. Morrow Simms D.D. The main subjects in the work, in the central portion, are the Death and Resurrection of Christ. The uppermost or tracery part of the window symbolises victory, fame and honour and has a martyr's crown. At the bottom are the names of congregation members who died in the first world war with the coats of arms of the regiments in which they served. Generally the minute detail quite expertly portrays the various scenes and the use of the rich colours - especially that of deep blue which is a Clarke hallmark - makes this window a quite beautifully brilliant work.

A manse for the presiding minister was built in 1990 on the seafront end of Haddon Road. In 1967 the manse and its grounds were sold for redevelopment and the minister's residence moved to Kincora Grove. The old manse is incorporated into Hadden Court Apartments.

The City Centre based Scottish Presbyterian Community amalgamated with the Clontarf Presbyterian Community in 2003.

MINISTERS

Rev. William Wilson	1836-1854
Rev. James Edgar	1854-1865
Rev. Robert Watts	1865-1867
Rev. Robert Hanna	1867-1880
Rev. William Moore	1880-1883
Rev. J.L Morrow	1884-1940
Rev. J. Murray Moore	1940-1962
Rev. McCollum	1962-1966
Rev. McKillen	1966-1972
Rev. John Wynne	1972-`1987
Rev. David Bruce	1987-1992
Rev. James Brogan	1992-2003
Vacant	2003-2007
Rev. Lorraine Kennedy-Richie	2007->>>

The outstanding personality in the history of Clontarf Presbyterian congregation was without any doubt Rev. (and later Dr.) John Love Morrow. Born near Clough in Co. Antrim he was ordained by the Dublin Presbyterian Presbytery in April 1884 and his first (except for a short period in London) appointment was to be the spiritual leadership of the congregation then based in Gloucester Street. A man of commanding presence of courtly address kindly disposition he became attached and devoted to the parish he was to serve until his death at 87 in April, 1940 - a ministry of almost 56 years. He oversaw the congregation's move to Clontarf and stablized it in its new base. In 1929 he had the honour of being elected Moderator of the General Assembly of the Presbyterian Church of Ireland. Rev. Tom Barry recalled the event in these lines:

"For here was no mean pedagogue,
No mere pedantic prater
At last the Assembly stirred itself
And made him Moderator."

Dr. Morrow a 'larger than life' figure was well known in golfing circles. He was honary secretary of the golfing union of Ireland for twenty years and later vice-president. A Bronze tablet to his memory was placed in the north wall of the Clontarf Church.

Clontarf Methodist Church

A real turning point came in the life of John Wesley, the father of Methodism, in 1738 when his passion for an effective religious life was deepened into a real compassion for the ordinary people of his day - agriculture workers and those earning a sustenance from emerging industry - the majority of whom, he felt, were untouched by the somewhat self-satisfied established church. Wesley, with no thoughts of forming a separate church, began to set up religious ' societies' wherever he travelled and it was only after his death in 1791 that a new denomination came into being. Prior to 1738, Wesley and his friends at Oxford had been nicknamed 'Methodists' because of their endeavour to develop a methodical prayer life and service to the poor.

John Wesley spent seven years of his life travelling the roads of Ireland on horseback, preaching his method to all who would listen. His first sermon in Dublin was preached in the city centre on August 9th, 1747 in the still existing St. Mary's Church. Wesley came to love Ireland and her people.

As Dublin expanded in the second half of the nineteenth century so too did Methodism grow in the city. Quite a number of new churches were erected in suburban areas - such as Rathmines and Rathgar on the south side and Clonliffe and Clontarf on the north side. Clontarf's first Methodist Church, designed by Edward Tarleton and sometimes known as "The Wesley Church" was first built in 1867 on a site acquired at the seafront end of St. Lawrence Road. It was a modest church and really not suitable for its purpose. In 1881 this inadequate structure was enlarged but the renovated building also proved to be unsatisfactory in many ways. New plans were laid and in 1906 an almost entirely new suite of premises was constructed by Collen Brothers, contractors, of East Wall. The handsome granite stone church - adorned with the familiar clock in the gable end - has been a landmark on the seafront for successive generations of passers-by-ever since 1906. The church itself, complete with minister's vestry, originally could seat close to 500 people and contains a splendid pipe organ which was built by George Benson of Manchester.

The trowel used in the stone laying work on the church in 1906 came to light in an unusual way. It was found among a collection of items (belonging to someone who had died) and sent for sale to a Dublin auction room. It was returned to the relatives of the deceased person, and from there it was passed on to the Minister of Dun Laoghaire Methodist church who returned it to Clontarf - almost eighty years after its use. The trowel has now been lodged for safe keeping in the Wesley Historical Society archives at University Road, Belfast.

Over the years the Clontarf Methodist congregation has been, at different times, linked with the Methodist Church in Lower Abbey Street - (which is now part of the base of operations of the Dublin Central Mission of the Methodist Church), and has support from many Clontarf members. The Clontarf Church has also been, in the past, linked with Clonliffe Methodist Church. Today Clontarf, Sutton and Skerries form the one Methodist Church circuit.

The continuing expansion of Dublin in the past generation has seen most of the younger families moving to the suburbs. This shifted the balance of numbers away from churches like Clontarf. Thus Sutton, once the poor relation (in the circuit) is now the stronger base of Methodist activity.

Methodist children in Clontarf would mostly have attended Howth Road (Presbyterian) or Green Lanes (Church of Ireland) National Schools. The choice of secondary school would almost automatically have been the renowned Wesley College, when it was conveniently located in St. Stephen's Green. However since Wesley College was re-established in Ballinteer in 1969, most Methodist students are educated in Mount Temple Comprehensive School on the Malahide Road.

While numbers attending Clontarf Methodist Church are small in comparison with its heyday, the congregation is in good heart and actively seeks ways of adapting and using its buildings and other resources, under God, for a new generation in an ecumenical age.

Ministers of Clontarf Methodist Church, since it was separated from Abbey Street and constituted a Circuit at the Conference of 1902:

1902-1905	Rev.John O.Park	1917-1921	Rev.T.E. Gibson
1905-1908	Rev.Pierce Martin	1921-1924	Rev.W.W. Hutchinson
1908-1911	Rev.B. Lumely	1924-1926	Rev. J.W Carrothers
1911-1913	Rev.W.A. Bracken	1926-1929	Rev.C.H McClayton
1913	Rev.W.L. Borthridge	1929-1930	Rev.R.C. Phillips
1913-1914	Rev.W.H. Green	1930-1933	Rev B.B Morton
1914-1917	Rev.Alex McCrea	1933-1938	Rev.Johnstone Hunter

1938-1943	Rev. H.M. Watson	1970-1978	Rev. Alan Meara
1943-1948	Rev.J. Lynam Cairns	1978-1982	Rev.W.Kenneth Bradley
1948-1953	Rev.Herbert Irvine	1982-1990	Rev.Kenneth H. Thompson
1953-1958	Rev.J.Aubrey West	1990-1995	Rev.Buckley,Levinstone Cooney
1958-1963	Rev.Albert W.Gamble	1995-2003	Rev. Noel Fallows
1963-1964	Rev.George W. Ferguson	2003-2012	Rev's Conrad & Sonia Hicks
1964-1970	Rev.N.Cyril Haire	2012->>>	Rev.David Nixon

Clontarf Graveyard, Castle Avenue

This far we have detailed seven active Clontarf churches. The Old Clontarf Graveyard contains the ruins of an eight church which, as we have stated earlier, is the ruin of the 1609 Protestant church and probably the original site of Comgall's little monastery church. The cemetery itself was vested in the poor Law Guardians of Dublin North Union in 1874 by the Irish Church Temporalities Commission under the powers vested in them by the Irish Church Act of 1869. The cemetery came under the control of Dublin Corporation by the extension of the city boundary in 1900. Clontarf cemetery is not officially closed, but no new graves are available. It is interesting to note that there is no record of the graveyard ever having been dedicated to St. Comgall or St. John The Baptist - it has traditionally been known simply as Clontarf Graveyard. Existing registers of burials for the cemetery date back to 1876, but the burials there go back much further, as many inscriptions on tombs from the beginning of the 1700's can be identified. Famous and Old Clontarf family names can be located all over the cemetery. The family vault of the Vernon's and the Oultons group being very conspicuous.

In accepting that Comgall's little church of 550A.D on this site was the 'birthplace' of Clontarf, it is surely fitting that it should provide the final resting place for so many of Clontarf's sons and daughters. To the right of the old graveyard (looking from Castle Avenue) is the site of a Carmelite Monastery. It was occupied by Carmelite Monks or Brothers who worked as carpenters, shoe markers and various other trades to support their institution. They also had an extensive bakery which Samuel Lewis (1837) notes "supplies the neighbourhood and part of Dublin with excellent bread."

Convent House

Where Duncan court block of apartments now stands on Vernon Avenue there once was a house known as Convent House. Between 1808 and 1819 it was occupied by some Dominican nuns who ran a school there for a while. The nuns came from their premises in Chanel Row (now North Brunswick Street) where they had been since about 1700, but a renewal of their lease was refused in 1808. From Clontarf they moved to a permanent residence in Cabra.

Footnotes

(1) The translation by J.C Mangan of a poem attributed to Prince Alfrid of Northumbria who came to Ireland to be educated about the year 684 gives us an idea of what the 'Island of Saints and Scholar's' was like.

"I found in Innisfail fair,
In Ireland, when in exile there
Piety, learning, fond affection,
Holy welcome and kind protection

I travelled its fruitful provinces round,
And in every one of the five I found,
Alike in church and in palace hall
Abundant apparel and food for all."

(2) Various spellings of the saint's name can be unearthed - Comgall, Comgal, Comghal, Comgell, Comgallus, Comgellus. The seven other framers of monastic rules were St. Patrick, St. Brigid, St. Brendan, St. Kieran, St. Columkille, St. Molassius and St. Adaman.

(3) The Knights Templars were a military order of monks founded about the year 1118. They wore a white habit with a red cross sewed on. Their name 'Templars' was adopted from Solomen's Temple of Jerusalem. They played a major role during the Crusades of the 12th and 13th centuries protecting pilgrims travelling to the Holy Land, especially from attacks by the Moslems. Like the Templars, the Knights of St. John were also an order of military monks. Founded in 1099, their patron, from whom they adopted their name, was St. John The Baptist. Arising from the Crusades the order concentrated on helping poor and sick pilgrims on their way to Jerusalem. They wore a black habit with a white cross on their breasts.

(4) It will be recalled that Clement V was the first of the Avignon Popes. Philip le Bel himself ordered the imprisonment of all the Knights Templars in France and the confiscation of their property - mindful no doubt of the effect this action would have on his exchequer! The grand master of the order, James de Mola, was burned at Paris while loudly protesting his order's orthodoxy and innocence.

(5) In 1794 Britain and all her subjects lost their property in France. In 1818 the French Government, by way of a general settlement, placed at England's disposal a sum producing an annual income of three million francs- leaving England the duty of

adjudicating on the claims of her subjects such as Ireland. However, English bigotry did not allow the money due to the Irish colleges to be ever paid over, using it instead for futile purposes such as building the Marble Arch at Tyburn.

(6) The Harold's were an old Danish family who had played their role in Dublin history and development for about 1,000 years. Father James Harold (later Canon) had been P.P of Saggart since 1794 and being sympathetic to the United Irishmen he gave shelter to a local wounded "united" leader in 1798- Felix O' Rourke. A local parishioner named Walsh is alleged to have betrayed him and Fr. Harold received the rather harsh sentence of ten years transportation to Botany Bay. O'Rourke escaped again and took part in Robert Emmet's attempted uprising in 1803. This time he was executed by shooting and hanged from the rafters of Fr. Harold's house. Fr. Harold, may, quite possibly, have been the first priest to arrive in Australia. He endured great hardship in the Penal colony and was for quite a while strictly forbidden to exercise his priestly office. In 1810 the government allowed him to leave New South Wales. The long years in the penal settlement and the testing voyage home took their toll on Fr. Harold's health. He was a delicate and failing man when he was appointed administrator to the Clontarf parish in 1818. Not being strong enough to carry out his duty, he resigned the following year (1819). He died in 1830.

Old Church Ruin Clontarf Graveyard Castle Ave

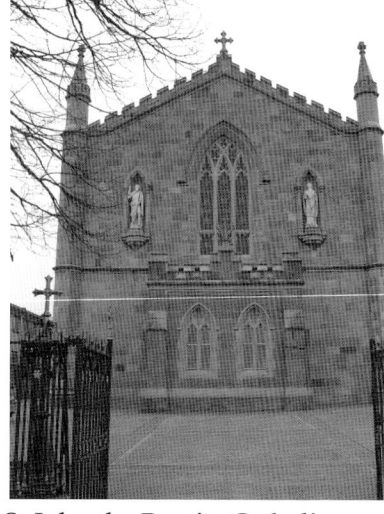

St John the Baptist Catholic Church

Old St Anthonys Church

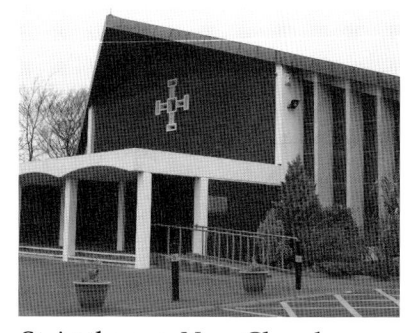

St Anthonys New Church

St Gabriels Church Dollymount

St John the Baptist Church of Ireland    All Saints Church

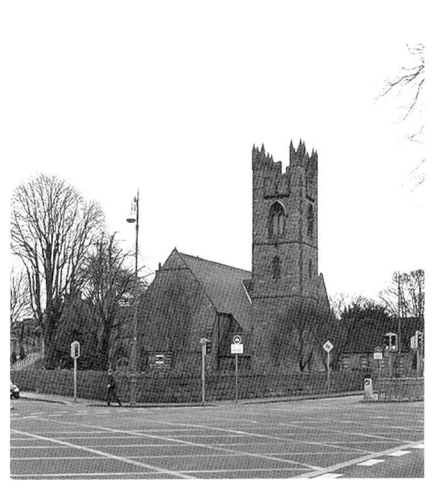

Clontarf Presbyterian Church    Clontarf Methodist Church,

CHAPTER THREE

Clontarf's history is typical of Irish history in general -full of strife, turmoil, war, murder, intrigue, invasion and oppression. Just about every episode in our national history, right down to the Civil War and modern times, had particular relevance to Clontarf. As we shall see many of the most famous people and events in Irish history had the Clontarf name associated with them in some way.

Earliest Settlers

"Long long ago, beyond the misty space
Of twice a thousand years,
In Erin old there dwelt a mighty race
Taller than Roman spears;
Like oaks and towers they had a giant grace,
Were fleet as deers.
With winds and waves they made their 'biding place
These western shepherd seers.

Great were their deeds, their passions and their sports;
With clay and stone
They piled on strath and shore those mystic forts
Not yet o' erthrown:
On cairn-crown d hills they held their council-courts;
While youths alone
With giant dogs explored the elk resorts,
And brought them down."   **Thomas D'Arcy McGee**

When speaking of early settlers in Ireland, in general, we are really dealing with a grey area defined by words like legend, tradition and folklore. Dates are consequently quite fanciful. Indeed many historians place little credence in what legend tells us about the people of the Stone and Bronze Ages in Ireland. However it is certain that the country was inhabited during these periods. Many authorities claim that it was on Clontarf's then barren shore in Moynalty that the country's first invaders, the Parthalonians, led by Parthalon (or Partholanus) arrived in Ireland. They made settlements but a plague stuck them about 20 years later and some 9,000 people fell victim to its ravages and were buried in Tallaght. Clontarf would have been a good choice as a landing place for invaders, being strategically placed in the eye of Dublin Bay. She also possessed one of the bay's two anchorage pools, Clontarf Pool, which had particular significance in the later Danish and Norman invasions. Clontarf was then commandeered and ruled by the next wave of invaders for 217 years as Keating tell us. These were the Nemedians. They were haunted by continual attacks by Formorians, a race of sea pirates centered around Tory Island. Then the Firblogs, originally from Greece, arrived. They were a pastoral people led by the five sons of Dela. Thirty six years after their arrival Moynalty was once more overrun by yet another tribe (also originally from Greece) called the Tuatha De Danann, or Children of the Goddess Danu. They were a tribe of considerable culture, being something of a manufacturing, commercial and merchant people. They allegedly had in their possession the famous Lia Fáil (the stone of destiny, now on the Hill of Tara) - the stone upon which (according to the biblical story) Joseph reputedly rested his head when he experienced the vision of angels. They were also regarded as a somewhat mystical and magical race and remained in occupation of Clontarf for almost 200 years. They were held in high esteem by later inhabitants. In subsequent ages they were in fact mystified as the 'sidhe' or fairies.

"They came from a land beyond the sea,
And now o'er the western main
Set sail in the good ships gallantly,
from the sunny land of spain,
Oh where's the Isle we've seen in dreams,
Our desin'd home or grave?
Thus sung they as, by the morning's beams,
They swept the Atlantic wave."

(The Milesians on their way to Ireland as commemorated in Moore's Melodies.)

The fifth wave of invaders to set foot in Clontarf were the very war-inclined Milesians. This eastern clan first migrated to Egypt where they sojourned at the time Pharaoh and his entourage were lost in the Red Sea. Indeed their 'Sacred Banner' depicted a dead serpent and the rod of Moses. They defeated The Tuatha De Dannan when they arrived about 1,000 B.C and ruled undisputed for a considerable period. The Milesians have become identified with the Celts. They were known as the 'wee soldiers' and were a dominant ruling type. The Irish people are often referred to as Milesians.
The Irish National Museum in Kildare Street, Dublin, houses about 20 items of antiquity found in Clontarf consisting of a neolithic flint blade, some axeheads,

a bronze age dagger, bronze age axeheads, a 9th/10th century iron sword and an 11th century bronze ring pin.

The Celts arrive

The last wave of early invaders to arrive were the pagan Celts or Gaels, who ushered in a period of pagan, bardic and legendary fame in Ireland. We believe they came about 300 years before Christ. They were to stay permanently and Ireland has been a predominantly Celtic nation since their arrival. They were to imprint the design of what Irishness was going to be like - giving us our characteristics including our language. They were an agricultural and pastoral race.

Little 'concrete' history is available about any of the tribes prior to the Milesians. Even from their era on, materials are scant, for some time. The most ancient historical record we have tells of the expulsion of the Desi tribes from Moynalty, having being defeated by Cormac Mac Art in seven battles. (See chapter one above). This was in the 3rd century. Some of the Desi migrated to Wales while the remainder settled in that part of the County Waterford since known as 'The Decies'. In the 3rd century Fionn MacCumhaill and his band of Fianna Eireann warriors would have passed through Clontarf on their way to their look-out headquarters in Howth Head from their favourite hunting ground, Glen Na Smol in County Wicklow[1].

The earliest settlers depended on native wildlife for their existence and sustenance. People ate small animals, fruit and berries as well as fish from the sea. Deer were particularly valuable, providing hides for clothing as well as food. Gradually tillage of the land brought a bigger variety of dishes as agriculture evolved. Clontarf would have been tilled and farmed in the early centuries by her Celtic inhabitants and Clontarf shared the Celtic world of tribal kingdoms, the Brehon Laws and a tradition of oral poetry and music as well as the Celtic Gaelic language. (The Brehon Laws, modified from time to time, remained in force right up to the Tudor conquest.) When St. Patrick's Christianity bonded brilliantly with the Gaelic - Celtic world a new Ireland was spawned. The Island of Saints and Scholars was in the making. (Clontarf, as detailed in Chapter Two, openly embraced Christianity as preached by St. Comgall.) This created Ireland's famous 'Golden Era' in the 7th and 8th centuries when she became the most learned country in Europe. Her monasteries produced numerous outstanding men of learning who travelled throughout Europe teaching the ignorant and illiterate - as most of Europe was then.

VIKINGS

"Purple wings our ships expand
O'er the fleckt and flowing wave;
Mid the masts the champions stand
Fit for foray, mild and brave."

Towards the close of the 8th century and early in the 9th the peace and tranquillity in Clontarf was once again interrupted by a new and fierce menace in the form of raiders and plunderers sailing west over the sea. (See chapter two above) These new invaders came from the modern areas of Norway, Sweden, Denmark and in general from the islands and coasts of the Baltic Sea. They first raided the western coasts of Europe and when they forayed as far as Ireland, Clontarf, because of her position, was always in the front line of battle. The early sighting of their oaken warships with serpent-type heads must have been quite frightening to local defenceless farmers and fishermen. Our records distinguish two separate races of Galls or Northmen. First were the Lochlanns, the Norwegians and Swedes. They were fair-haired and the Irish nick-named them the Finn-Galls or white strangers. The second group were the Danars or Danes of Denmark, who were pet-named Duv-Galls or black strangers by the Irish. In modern history we collectively refer to them as Danes, Norsemen or Vikings. The romantic aspect of their history reveals that they regarded piracy as the most worthy and noble of careers in which a chief could involve himself. They certainly were daring and desperate sailing west over the sea as pagans and killers bringing plunder, pillage, rape and murder. However we wonder, in hindsight, if this romantic image is a myth. Perhaps behind the buccaneering lifestyle were the wants of normal emigrants who had a burning urge to check just how green were the faraway hills while leaving behind a subsistent way of life. When their swords clashed with those of the Irish it was the clash of two polar worlds - the wild and materialistic Scandinavian civilisation trying to overpower the more mature and spiritually cultivated Gaelic world. After all their fighting and plundering the Vikings were to be finally defeated. Some chose to settle down and remain part of the Irish Christian world while others returned to their ancestral home with strange tales of the White Christ who was stranger than Odin himself.

The invaders' first "Irish experience" was at Lambay Island (then named Rechro) in 795. In their early raids they sailed into the small harbours on the east coast and marauded coastline towns, ravaged churches and monasteries and sailed off with what bounty they could while clearing the coastal water of all opposition shipping. Then they switched tactics and instead of appearing as robbers they began to establish permanent settlements with a view to eventually conquering the whole country. The renowned Turgesius (or Thorgils), after his arrival in 832, directed their strategy towards this goal of subjugation. Thus Clontarf's tranquil existence was violated as the sea spewed up wave after wave of Danes. As they usually landed along Clontarf strand (which was suitable for mooring their long ships) the local coast-dwellers suffered most as the Vikings wiped out all vessels that might threaten the dominance they were determined to establish. They didn't find the sand bank of the North Bull much of an inconvenience as their shallow-draught vessels could manoeuvre in shallow water. Clontarf's deep sea water pool would have been strategically important as an anchorage point and a base. Very quickly they devasted southern Fingal.

Brian Boru and The Battle of Clontarf

The name of the High King Brian Boru and the famous battle of Clontarf on Good Friday April 23rd, 1014 will always be associated with, and indeed, is central to any history of the Clontarf area. But before dealing with the events of that fateful day it is necessary to look at the state of the country then and at the rise to power of Brian Boru himself.

State of the Country
Since they first 'docked' in 795 the Norsemen were by now well established in the country. They had occupied the then tiny trading post that Dublin was in 836[2] and established themselves at other strategic coastal points around the country - like Dundalk, Limerick and Waterford. From these pivotal strongholds they would go 'a - Viking' inland berserking and leaving a desert of destruction in their wake. The Irish were no match for the Norsemen for two reasons. First of all their weapons and methods were not as professional as their foes, although many local chiefs had laudable successes against the invaders and inflicted numerous heavy losses on the Vikings. But here in lies the second reason - local was the word, as Irish chiefs tended to defend their own specific territory when it was attacked, and such attacks came from rival Irish chiefs as well as from the Danes. Indeed the wars among the Irish themselves, in the best tradition of Irish infighting, were often more serious than the conflict with what should have been identified as a common enemy. A litany of Irish High Kings from the first coming of the Vikings up to the Battle of Clontarf were rulers in name only, in that they had no absolute power over many regional chiefs throughout the country. Nobody, including the High Kings saw the national issue and there was,

consequently, no unity of purpose. However, this was about to change. After 219 years creating havoc throughout the country, the hour produced the leader who was to call the Vikings' high noon.

Brian Boru

Brian Boru was to have the distinction at the Battle of Clontarf of presenting quite a united Irish front - Irishmen fighting a common cause. It was one of those rare occasions when the country presented such a unified front. It is to his credit, that, even living as he did in such primitive times, he is spoken of and regarded by many international historians as one of the world's outstanding leaders[3]. He was an Irishman who won a battle that really mattered, and indeed changed the course of history.

Brian was born Brian Ó Cinnéide about the year 941 most likely at the fortress called Kincora in County Clare[4]. He was sent as a student to the monastery of Inisfallen near Killarney - but after receiving his education Brian left as he was not interested in proceeding to take religious vows. Kincora was part of the Dalgcais Kingdom, itself part of Thomand. Brian Boru was a Dalcassian, a race of fiercesome warriors. The traditional and great ruling family in Munster at the time were the Owenaghts (or Eugnians) of Desmond. The Owenaghts were however unable to check the growing strength of the Danes in Munster and as Brian grew to manhood the Danes held the chief ports of the province - particularly Limerick, Cork and Waterford. From these bases they frequently ravished the countryside - sending 'berserkers' to 'Viking' the land. (The Danes were proud of these raids as they believed that if they created the maximum destruction the 'Valkyries' would look on them favourably and come for their spirits after death.)

In 964 Mahon (Mathghamain) older brother of Brian became King of Munster and for a while together with Brian carried on a relentless series of attacks on the Vikings. Then, Mahon made a truce with the foreigners but the more warlike young Brian would have no part of it. Instead he maintained the war from the mountains beyond Kincora against tremendous odds with a party of fighting men whom he himself trained. At length Brian coaxed Mahon to resume hostilities and in 968 at Sulcoit (near where Tipperary town stands today) they won a resounding victory over the forces of the redoubtable Ivor, Danish King of Limerick. The treachery and disunity of the Irish among themselves was never more clearly exposed than it was during the Sulcoit battle and its aftermath. During the fighting Mahon's great rival Molloy the King of Desmond (forever jealous of the Dalcais) and Donovan King of the Hy Carbery area of County Limerick actually sided and fought with the Danes. In 976 these same rivals lured Mahon to a 'friendly' meeting at Bruree, the Donovan residence. On his arrival, however, Mahon was seized and Molloy had him callously murdered at the Pass of Barnaderg. Brian, whose loyalty to, and affection for, his brother were unequalled now (976) assumed the kingship of Thomond with his headquarters at Kincora. He immediately set forth to avenge Mahon's murder. At Scattery (an island off Kilrush in County Clare) he defeated the Danes and killed Ivor. In 977 he routed Bruree and Donovan met his end. In 978 he marched south and at Barnaderg, the very scene of his brother's brutal murder, he inflicted a heavy defeat on Molloy, killing 1,200 men. Molloy himself was slain by Brian's young son Murrough. After this battle Brian became king of all Munster.

Brian Boru, or Brian of the Tribute, wasn't the totally ferocious fighting King these latter battles might indicate[5]. But he was terribly ambitious. He probably realised - especially after Mahon's murder - that he would have to command a regular, solid and strong army, and subdue local rival short-sighted princes, to have any hope of realising a united kingdom with a common cause. This appears to have been his ambition after claiming the Munster throne at Cashel which ended 'phase one' of his career. From now on his military expertise, his reputation and influence assumed and all-Ireland dimension.

Brian directed much wealth into the church's 'safe' as king of Munster and later High King of Ireland. His regime saw the building of many schools and chapels and provided chalices and other religious vessels and ornaments for the clergy. He laid specific amounts of resources aside for the upkeep of monasteries and erected many monuments to the glory of God. His period as High King was to mark an era of general restoration in the country for the arts and for learning. A literary revival began and law and order were re-established.

When Brian's many successes against the Vikings are recalled it is often forgotten that from his youth he studied their weapons and tactics. Among his own troops he instilled a code of discipline then unheard of in Ireland. Perhaps one of our first ' nationalists' unlike other Irish chief's and kings, he didn't stop at local success and revel in the glory of usurping power from a weaker prince, It is fair to say that his vision was the creation of a nation harnessing the many positive aspects each tribe, race and tradition had to offer. He never let a local win in a little battle overshadow the real war, in which he rightly stated that taking the initiative against the invader was a better policy than reacting to their deeds. Above all he realised the need for a strong permanent force to have lasting peace.

As his dealings with Malachy (Mór) were to show Brian didn't necessarily believe in tradition. Malachy was High King by inheritance because of his rank in the Ui Neill tribe - as the High King was always an Ui Neill. But Brian believed in the best man for the job - irrespective of tribe. For this attitude he was regarded by many as something of a 'unsurper' and many chiefs, as a result, refused him men and aid in his campaigns.

Malachy Mór or Malachy (Maolseachlainn) II became High King of Ireland in 980 and he exhibited some fine qualities of leadership in his many battles with the Danes. But in the closing years of the 10th century it became clear that Malachy's jealousy of Brian's growing power was matched only by Brian's own resolution to seize the royal seat at Tara. Malachy began to fear the increasingly over-shadowing presence and influence of Brian who had a special appeal to so many people. A very tall (as tall as the tallest of the Vikings) kingly figure of a man with huge hands, Brian was a great diplomat as well as a great general. He knew that in order to drive the Vikings from the country it was first necessary to control and enjoy the support of all of the country, and he sensed that Malachy would never achieve this. They became involved in a bitter 'civil war' and the struggle between them lasted almost 20 years. Indeed their feud allowed the Danes the opportunity to re-establish themselves firmly all over the country. In 997 an uneasy truce or alliance was agreed between them. Malachy was to rule the northern half of the country (Leth Conn or Leath Chuinn) and Brian the southern half (Leth Mow or Leath Mhogha). Leath Mhogha contained the kingdom of Leinster including Dublin and the Danish settlements in its vicinity. With this arrangement Mailmora (Maolmordha) King of Leinster became a tributary King of Brian Boru, a position he detested as he had always detested Brian. In 999 he joined forces with the Danes of Dublin (who were led by Harold son of Norse Chief Olaf Cuaran) and revolted. Brian marched north and Malachy joined forces with him to rout Mailmora and Harold at Glenmama (near Dunlavin, County Wicklow) killing 4,000 Danes and Leinstermen.

Brian Boru now determined that the 'supreme crown' of High King should be his. To strengthen his position he made many alliances with chiefs and tributary kings around the country who had been his enemies. He also got many church leaders to back his claim. He married Gormlaith mother of the Danish King of Dublin (Sitric Olafson of the Silken beard) and sister of his bitter enemy Mailmora[6]. Brian also gave his own daughter (Sláine), in marriage to Sitric. These arrangements created at least temporary peace with both Sitric and Mailmora.

In the year 1002 after skirmishes between the forces of Brian and Malachy, Brian and his entire Leath Mhogha army marched on Royal Tara. Brian demanded that Malachy offer battle or unconditionally surrender. Realising he was outnumbered Malachy submitted. Brian was then crowned High King of Ireland at Tara with the traditional ceremony involving the stone of Fáil. He had the distinction of being Ireland's first Christian King not descended from the ancient

O'Neill Tribe - or more specifically from Niall of the Nine Hostages, and he came as close as any Irishman ever has to uniting the country. Malachy agreed to rule as sub-king in Meath. Brian knew that he could then march and overwhelm the Danes in Dublin, Wexford, Waterford, Cork and Limerick. But he felt it would be a more prudent and beneficial policy for the country generally to control them and allow them operate from those coastal points and encourage their seafaring nature to cultivate trade and traffic.

For almost 10 years following Brian Boru's accession to the throne in 1002, Ireland was closer to unity than ever before. During this time the peace that Brian had dreamed of fell over the country. Only some rebellious northern chiefs sporadically challenged his authority. It is from this period that we are handed down the legend that so peaceful was the country that a beautiful maiden laden with jewels travelled throughout the land alone, on foot and was unmolested! It was at this time (1005) during a trip to Armagh that the title "Imperator Scotorum" (Emperor of Ireland) was bestowed upon Brian by his confessor, the scribe Máel Suthain and recorded in the Book of Armagh.

THE BATTLE OF CLONTARF 1014

Brian Boru realised that there were almost as many Norsemen in certain areas of Ireland as there were Irish. Some belonged to families established in the country for more than 100 years. He understood that their contribution to life in the country, especially as experienced and traditional seafarers, was substantial and accepted that their many talents could enhance the prosperity of the country. But he clearly intended that their continued involvement in the country could only be accepted if they forgot the notion of being overlords and instead became one with the native Irish.

In the first years of the 11th century the Norsemen were again making notable advances all over Europe. They established a firm Kingdom in Normandy in France, and in England their efforts led to the Danish prince Canute being crowned King in 1017. In these years they began to renew their efforts to conquer Ireland and they deeply resented paying tribute to Brian Boru. From time to time Danish warships appeared off the Irish coast in various locations, but were always driven back. Yet it was as if they were organising for one supreme effort to subjugate the country once and for all and place a Danish King on the throne. They had been peaceful since the crushing defeat at the Battle of Glenmama, as they simply hadn't the power and means to exert themselves. But it was uneasy - a forced submission - and any plot to overthrow Brian Boru would attract their instant support. Such an opportunity was about to present itself.

The confederacy that hatched the battle of Clontarf originated not among the

Norsemen but in the heart of Brian's old enemy, Mailmora King of Leinster. The actual incident which sparked off the momentum which culminated in the famous battle occurred far away from Clontarf - in remote Kincora in fact, at Brian's Royal residence. Mailmora decided to pay a visit to Brian's palace at Kincora. (Brian was his brother-in-law now of course.) The King was absent on business in Cashel and while awaiting his return Mailmora watched a game of chess between Murrough and an opponent called Conaing[7]. During the course of the game Mailmora offered advice to Murrough as to how he might win the match. The advice cost Murrough the game and he immediately castigated Mailmora for his bad advice. With much annoyance he suggested that he could well do without the advice of a man who gave the Danes such bad advice in tactics and strategy at the Battle of Glenmama. Mailmora flew into rage and in reply promised Murrough that the next time he would make sure his advice to the Vikings was sound enough to end the days and the rule of Brian Boru. With that he stormed out of the Kincora residence and, feeling gravely insulted, set off for his own headquarters in Naas.

When Brian returned to Kincora and was informed of the event he sent a favourite from his entourage, the diplomatic Corc, to pursue Mailmora and persuade him to return to the hospitality at Kincora. However Mailmora murdered Corc, which outraged Brian. He now realised that Gormlaith too, like her brother Mailmora, was an instigator of trouble so he sent her back to her son Sitric in Dublin. She had been a constant embarrassment to Brian being forever planning and scheming, seeking revenge and counter revenge. Meanwhile Mailmora arrived back in Leinster determined to revolt.

We can be certain of one thing. It was the scheming of Gormlaith and her brother Mailmora that really instigated the Battle of Clontarf. And that scheming and planning was the result of their mutual hatred towards, and jealousy of, the Ard Rí Brian Boru. Gormlaith is very much the scarlet one and added a domestic feud as an extra angle to the hostilities A beautiful and clever woman, but unprincipled and subject to extremes of temper, she had been married to a previous Viking King of Dublin Olaf Cuaran (945 -980) and to Ard Rí Malachy II. She was the mother of the present Danish King, Sitric Silkenbeard. Mailmora began to form an alliance of Irish subchiefs and concerted and plotted also with Sitric and other Danish leaders. 'The last field-day of Christianity and Paganism on Irish Soil', as the Battle of Clontarf has been styled, was in the making.

First Mailmora's and Sitric forces attacked Malachy's Kingdom of Meath and defeated Malachy at Drinan (near Swords). Malachy sent to Brian for help. Brian was in any case becoming alarmed by the movements of the Leinstermen and the Danes. He and his Son Murrough immediately marched north with separate armies and by different routes. They suppressed all Leinster and Danish territories. In September 1013 they both camped at Kilmainham in an effort to take Dublin by blockade. The Norsemen remained inside the walls of Dublin and at Christmas Brian returned to Kincora but now each side knew that there was no avoiding a final confrontation. The die had been cast and the Rubicon well and truly crossed. Both sides began to prepare for a winner-take-all contest. And Brian fully realised that his high Kingship was at stake.

Mailmora and Sitric with the help of Gormlaith began to assemble their forces. (Gormlaith was once again burning with the proverbial wrath of a woman scorned. It could truly be said that Hell had no fury like Gormlaith discarded!) Sitric spent a long time overseas enlisting Viking help. In their confederacy they enlisted the help of Sigurd Hlodvisson (Sigurd the Stout) chief of the Orkney Islands with his vast fleets. Brodir, who operated from the Isle of Man, eagerly enlisted his support[8]. However Ospak his brother did not join the fast accumulating forces to do battle against Brian Boru. (Also based in the Isle of Man, Ospak instead sailed around Ireland to Kincora and informed Brian of the conspiracies being formed and of Brodir's intentions.) Amlaff of Denmark pledged a large contingent of troops to help Sitric as did Canuteson, the Earl of Denmark. Norse help set sail for Ireland from Norse bases in Scotland, and the Shetland Islands and the Herbrides. Sitric's agents collected more and more help from bases all over Western Europe including France, Germany and Scandinavia as well as from Wales and Cornwall. Overseas Norse help was readily forthcoming because it was important for them to have the Irish Sea to themselves for trading purposes with Dublin as a trading post. This was to be the final onslaught, the ultimate trial. Palm Sunday April 18th, 1014, was the date chosen for all to rendezvous in Dublin. Meanwhile at home in Dublin the traitor Mailmora was busy. While Dublin Bay was being bedecked with black Norse ships he rounded up all the allies he could muster in Leinster and organised them for battle. It was as if a mighty thunderstorm gathered over Ireland. The magnitude of the effort to once and for all conquer Ireland was frightening. It was the supreme moment for the High King to prove himself - a real hour of trial. (The Viking longships in Dublin Bay would have been quite eye - catching, warlike, even frightening. Made from planks of oak and some 70 feet long, the front or prow of each was carved to resemble the head of a dragon of serpent.) Brian Boru rose gloriously to the challenge and proved equal to what was a real emergency. And with rigour and pride the tributary princes and kings answered his clarion call from all over the country. All prepared their troops during January, February and early March of 1014. In truth many Irish and Viking local kings, sub-kings, princes and lords had little allegiance to either Brian Boru of Sitric. It was their own interests they had at heart. Right up to the beginning of the battle many of them lingered and pondered long and hard at the possible outcome. They wanted to be on the winning side for security and to hold onto their territory and positions.... after all they would have to live under whoever the victor was.

Losing no time Brian ordered all to march towards Dublin on March 17th, 1014. On spy Wednesday they encamped at Kilmainham where they were joined by the army of Malachy of Meath. (Kilmainham their chosen site for encamping, was the district north and south of the river Liffey covering the present day Phoenix Park, Kilmainham, Inchicore and Chapelizod, and tradition maintains that part of their encampment occupied the area covered by Bully's Acre Graveyard.) With the exception of the northern O'Neill and Mailmora's Leinstermen, just about all Ireland was represented in Brian's army. He also had Ospak's sturdy troop of Norsemen. (Some Danish accounts of the battle claim that Brian also had the help of groups of Norsemen based in Ireland who had always been friendly with him.) Two Scottish Thanes - the Great Stewart of Mar and the Great Stewart of Lennox- realising they had a common cause in resisting the aggression of the Northmen brought two companies of fighting men across the Irish Sea to stand with Brian. From Kilmainham Brian's troops ravished and burned the Danish districts throughout Fingal, as the invaders watched from the walls of Dublin. Brian's youngest son Donnchadh (who was born to Brian and Gormlaith) would be pitted in the forthcoming battle against his half brother Sitric who was married to his half sister Emer and against his uncle, Mailmora. Realising this Brian dispatched him to Waterford with a garrison of men in case of any Norse scheme to attack the south-east while his troops were occupied in Dublin. Brian made it clear to all beneath his standard that a grave clash lay before them. It was a clash that wasn't simply a matter of Christianity against Pagan or Irish against Lochlannach. With many from each side fighting against his own countrymen, self interests were a high priority - for political, trade or power reasons.

Plotting and scheming on both sides continued during Easter week with the Norse beseeching their pagan Gods for victory and apparently being convinced by one of their oracles that if the battle were fought on Good Friday they would be the victors and Brian Boru would die. Brian himself used superstition to upset the Norse - arranging a false image of their God Odin portraying death and destruction on them. Malachy in fact had some differences with Brian regarding his schemes and tactics, and withdrew his men from the camp. On Holy Thursday April 22nd Brian realised that the Norse meant battle the next day.

According to his own Christian tradition he would not normally enter battle on Good Friday. However on Holy Thursday night he announced that he would lead his troops at dawn against the invaders. Thus on Good Friday morning April 23rd 1014, at sunrise, the venerable monarch Brian Boru now in his 73rd year (or more) rode at the head of his army from Kilmainham to the place of conflict. There they halted. Holding aloft a crucifix in one hand and his sword in the other Brian then strode through the ranks on his grey horse and urged his forces to fight bravely and well for 'faith, fatherland and liberty.' As he gave the final signal for battle his sons and friends prevailed upon him to return to his tent and take no part in the action because of his age. He agreed and left the chief command to his son Murrough. He himself retreated to pray for victory in his tent.

The precise site of the Battle of Clontarf has become the centre of much debate over the years. Generally speaking much of the battle was fought between Dublin's Liffey and Tolka rivers, bounded on the west by Tomar's Wood and on the east by the sea. Action did occur along the coast in todays Fairview area and in the area until recently known as "Bloody Fields" in Marino, then part of Clontarf. Indeed bones and remains of military weapons, dating from this period, discovered in excavations in many areas in north east Dublin are believed to be relics of the famous day.

It is almost certain that none of the battle action took place in the area we know as Clontarf today. Indeed most of the shore area of today's Clontarf is in fact reclaimed land and an 11th century map would be quite different from the reclaimed and well drained coastal Clontarf we know today. But Clontarf has had changing boundaries over the years and at one time Clontarf territory stretched to the Tolka river, and as stated above much of modern day Marino was once part of Clontarf.

The main strength of Brian's army would have been concentrated in front of Tomar's Wood (named after the Viking Tomar) in todays Phibsborough, and from here, on both sides of the Tolka, and between the Tolka and the Liffey, to the sea, the thick of the fighting took place. There has also been much speculation as to the exact spot where Brian Boru's tent was pitched on that Good Friday. The truth is we don't know. Local tales associate it with places as diverse as Kilmainham, Griffith Avenue, St. Lawrence Road and Castle Avenue. It was most likely located in or close to Tomar's Wood on the elevated ground of present day Glasnevin and Phibsborough. Local folklore that associates it with Cross Guns Bridge and the site of a nearby public house on Prospect Road (The Brian Boru) bearing the monarch's name, appears to carry considerable weight. (Tomar's Wood was a remnant of an ancient forest, with 'thick undergrowth and majestic oaks'.)

Tactics for the battle would appear to be no more than three large divisions of each army fighting a series of hand to hand encounters, with the leaders fighting side by side with their men. The Viking troops, lined along the coast facing inland, from Dublin City to the mouth of the Tolka river.

The Viking three divisions consisted of 1) Sigurd, Brodir and the Vikings from overseas including the infamous 1000 "invincibles" specially brought over from Norway. 2) Dubgail Mac Amlaíb and the Dublin Vikings (Sitric himself, only interested in protecting Dublin city remained inside the city walls and took no part in the fighting). 3) Mailmora and the Leinstermen. Opposing them the three Irish divisions had their right flank between todays Glasnevin and the city, their centre on todays Drumcondra and their left wing towards the Tolka estuary and Clontarf. They comprised of 1) Murrough and the Dalgcais, 2) The Munstermen led by Dessi Kings and 3) The men of Connaught under Tadc Ua Cellaig.

Many accounts allege that the battle began with an individual combat between a champion from each side - Plat for the Danes and Domhnall, Stewart of Mar, for the Irish. Both warriors fell fatally wounded. The first divisions to meet were the Dalcassions (the Irish Invincibles) and the Dublin and foreign Danes including the famed 1,000 Norwegians. But the fighting soon became general with little or no order. The battle raged long and hard from dawn until sunset with fierce and furious exchanges. In fact there must have been total and utter confusion with the din of battle, the thud of war and the shouting and screaming. Both sides acquitted themselves valorously with battle axe, sword, dagger and spear.

But the vikings were outfought in the bloody, noisy and fierce contest The Dalgcais were once again to the fore-as they had been in so many of Brians battles to become Ard Ri. If there was a turning point in the course of the battle, it was their earmarking of the 1000 "Invincibles" from Norway, for "special attention" These seemingly indestructible and impregnable warriors clad in their coats of iron from head to toe were simply hacked to pieces by an unstoppable marauding Dalgcais army - not one of the 1,000 surviving the onslaught.

The issue appears to have been in doubt until about 3 or 4 o clock in the afternoon when the Irish made a last desperate attack, and the Danes - now without most of their slain leaders - began to retreat. They began to flee the city to their ships along the Clontarf coastline in total dissaray. It has been calculated that the tide was at flood at about 5 or 6 o'clock that evening and the mouth of the tolka river was swollen with this high tide. (Some accounts state that the tide was at flood at precisely five fifty five). As the Vikings tried to cross the Tolka at the fishing weir of Clontarf, in their frenzy to escape, the greatest destruction of their troops took place and great numbers of them were drowned in the sea as well as those slaughtered by the Irish. It was after events at this weir that the battle derives its name. Many old accounts actually name the battle as 'The Battle of The Fishing-Weir of Clontarf'. The weir in question, which thus saw the thickest of the action, must have been at the mouth of the Tolka, but bearing in mind the fact that the sea stretched much further inland than it does today, the site of the weir can never really be pin pointed with scientific accuracy. Many authorities suggest that it was where Ballybough Bridge stands today. However one might be closer to the truth to suggest that it was further upstream as there is evidence to conclude that the wide estuary of the Tolka allowed the sea to come well inland, so that the weir may have been as far up the present river as Tolka Park and the grounds of the residence of the Archbishop of Dublin.

The Danes were totally routed with large parties of their troops utterly annihilated as they tried to retreat from the death and destruction being inflicted on them. Both sides lost most of their leaders. Many chronicles of the event give accounts of particularly heroic fighting by Murrough. Among his victims were Sigurd and two other Danish leaders, Carolus and Conmael. But in his encounter with another Dane, Anrud (or Anrad) he was mortally wounded with a dagger. As victory went to the Irish they paid a high price. Murrough's son Turlough was found drowned in the Tolka estuary reputedly with his hands still gripping the hair of a Dane whom had pursued into the tide during their fight. But worse was still to come. Towards the close of the battle the guards around the aged King Brian's tent, thinking all was well, joined in the pursuit of the fleeing Danes, leaving only a single attendant, Laiten (or Laidin) with the King. At that very time, Brodir, who had fled the battle, came upon the tent by chance and murdered Brian Boru. Thus the greatest disaster, as a result of the battle of Clontarf, was the destruction of three generations of the reigning Irish ruling family - Brian, his son Murrough and his grandson Turlough.

"Low the dauntless earl is laid,
Gor d with many a gasping wound;
Fate demands a nobler head;
Soon a king shall bite the ground

Long his loss shall Erin weep,
Ne er again his likeness see;
Long her strains in sorrow steep,
Strains of of immortality.

There are various accounts of the last moments of Brian Boru's life. Some declare that he fought Brodir and mortally wounded him before Brodir split the King's skull open with an axe. Other say Brodir killed Brian but was captured by the returning guards who hung him from a tree in the same Tomar's wood. Still other accounts allege that Brian attacked a number of Danes, killed three of them before he died.

The battle was a sanguinary one. The site was covered by a mass of bodies and a tangle of broken weapons. Indeed some accounts tell us that after a half an hour of fighting neither army could discern each other. Nobody could know his father or brother unless he recognised his voice as the whole scene splashed with blood and also with the locks of hair cut off by swords in the fighting. As well as Brian Boru's dynasty being cut down, the Irish lost most of the leaders of Munster and Connaught. Leinster lost the direct conspirator and incitor of the battle, Mailmora. (Mailmora Mac Murrough was an ancestor of the later Dermot Mac Murrough who was to instigate the Norman invasion of Ireland). After the Battle of Clontarf Mailmora's corpse is said to have been indignantly cast into the sea. Estimates of the numbers killed in both sides vary. However it is probable that the fierce hand to hand battle resulted in about 4,000 of Brians's troops losing their lives while as many as 15,000 Danes were killed, including 3,000 of Mailmoras Leinstermen.

The Battle of Clontarf will always be recalled as a great epoch in Irish history. The fame of the event spread throughout Europe (though the fame of Brian was already widespread) and gave heart to others fighting the tyranny of the Vikings. Danish power in Ireland was decisively broken once and for all. One of the most glorious victories in the annals of Ireland's long and torturous history, it terminated the last attempt by the Danes to conquer Ireland, a country they saw as a "land of milk and honey with great wealth, twelve cities and great bishoprics". In winning, the Irish not only won the battle but the war, concluding 219 years of Norse oppression. The battle also represents the last great struggle in Ireland between Christianity and Heathenism. The battle proved that the Irish could unify at a crucial time especially if the leader was of the right calibre. This Brian Boru was, and probably his greatest asset was his diplomacy in that he preferred to make lasting friendships with fellow Irish leaders rather than subjugating them in battle. This battle was something of a pyrrhic victory in that it ended the reign of an outstanding intelligent leader with no apparent successor, at least no one with his unifying power.

The annals state that both Brian and Murrough (who is said to have lived until the morning after the conflict) received the last rites of the church and their remains were conveyed by some monks to their abbey in Swords and thence to the cathedral at Armagh. Their obsequies of prayer and devotions were celebrated for twelve days and then both their bodies were interred at the cathedral. Turlough and many other fallen Irish leaders were buried in the Old Kilmainham churchyard known as Bullys Acre near the church of Maighnenn, beside the surviving shell of an ancient cross to the left of the main entrance. The conduct of Malachy (Brian Boru's predecessor and successor as High King of Ireland) at the Battle of Clontarf is somewhat confused. It is certain that he withdrew his troops from the Irish camp prior to the encounter. Accounts offer conflicting views then as to whether he rejoined at the start of the battle or distanced himself with his Meathmen and watched from a vantage point, joining it later. It is also certain that he was part of the Irish army in the final rout as the fleeing Danes were destroyed at the fishing weir of Clontarf. Malachy was re-inaugurated high king of Ireland after Brian's death at Clontarf and ruled until his own death in 1022.

Not all of the Danes were killed at Clontarf and neither did they all leave the country afterwards. The Howth Peninsula became a place of refuge for fugitives in the immediate aftermath of the battle. Here they defended themselves until the vessels of their countrymen could rescue them. But many remained on the peninsula permanently and Sitric himself eventually became a Christian and is said to have erected a church in Howth. Many Vikings remained in other parts of the country, especially in the cities, where they settled down to trading and became totally integrated with the natives. But their raiding and sacking was over forever and they never again threatened to become dominant in the country.

"Pagan power is over,
False its fair devotion
God rules, Lord and lover,
Earth and Sky and Ocean."

The Battle of Clontarf featured many colourful battle standards, banners and flags. The famous 'Black Raven' banner allegedly woven and embroidered for Sigurd "The Stout" Earl of Orkney by his mother, was captured from the Vikings at the Battle of Clontarf. The Black Raven symbol, years later, was adopted by the then Dublin County Council as its emblem with the Fianna motto 'Beart de réir ár mBriathar.' (Be true to your word)

The Battle of Clontarf is remembered in Irish and Norse annals and folklore. Typical would be "Njáls Saga" (the story of Burnt Njéll, a very important Icelandic saga)

When swords screamed in Ireland
and men struggled, I was there.
Many a weapon was shattered
When shields met in battle.
The attack, I hear was daring.
Sigurd died in the din of helmets
After meeting bloody wounds;
Brian fell too, but won.

In many Norse sources the Battle of Clontarf is referred to as 'Brjánsorrosta' (Brian's Battle). The author of the Gaelic work "Aonar dhuit a Bhriáin Bana" (written in Brian's lifetime) adulates him as a member of Ireland's "greatest quartet" the other three being the God Lugh, Fianna Éireann leader Fionn Mac Cumhaill and Saint Patrick.

To many Brian Boru ranks as Ireland's greatest King having, over his long years, overcome all opposition in the form of Irish rivals and would be Viking rulers.

Brian Boru's Well

On the east side of Castle Avenue in the wall adjoining the house known as 'Moyville' is a large cast iron plate carrying the inscription "Erected over Brian Boroimh's Well by Subscription A.D 1850." This marks the spot where there once was a spring well which helped supply the old medieval village of Clontarf with water. However with development and drainage the well has long since dried up and it was enclosed as it is at present (the actual well is situated in a small house behind the wall), in the 19th century by a hygiene - conscious community with a pumping mechanism. The well was sentimentally named the 'Brian Boru' well (in the interests of tourism) but it is certain that the great King never wet his lips from its waters. The well is sometimes mistakenly identified as the one referred to in the ancient annals in relation to the Battle of Clontarf. A story allegedly concerning this well or brook tells us that Sigurd observed during the battle that Murrough and other Irish chiefs and warriors retired from the thick of battle a number of times to slake their thirst and cool their hands which were swollen from the violent and constant use of sword and battle axe. The nearby well they used had a guard of twelve men and each time they returned from the well everyone seemed to be completely refreshed and doubly vigorous. The Vikings then destroyed the well. After this Sigurd attempted a fresh attack on the Dalcassians. But Murrough singled him out and with a blow of his battle axe divided his body in two through his armour.

The Brian Boru Harp

In the famous 'Long Room' at Dublin's Trinity college in a glass case the historical so - called 'Brian Boru' harp can be viewed. The 15th or 16th century harp has been traditionally, but alas mistakenly, associated with the venerable monarch Brian Boru. Although Brian was something of a harpist he never touched the strings of this particular instrument as it is expertly judged to be 'only' about 500 years old. It evidently dates from the later middle ages as it is consistent in every way with the type then in use. The harp came to light in Limerick in the 18th century (where it was last played in 1760 by Arthur O'Neill) and William Burton Conyngham presented it to the college. The wood of the harp is willow and it has twenty nine strings. It is a very beautiful ornamental harp richly etched with various engravings and carvings. The 'Brian Boru' harp was adopted in 1876 as the Guinness dark ale emblem or trademark by the then head of the firm Sir Benjamin Lee Guinness. The harp is the oldest and finest surviving Irish harp. It was restored and re-restrung and its sound recorded in 1961. In 1922 the newly formed Irish Free State adopted the harp as the national symbol, and the Irish Presidential flag features the harp in gold. In 1945 the harp was registered as Ireland's national coat of arms. Also since Ireland's first coinage came into circulation in 1928 the reverse side of all coins have borne the harp. On the death of his brother Mahon, Brian's anger comes flashing through in a sad lament which he played on his harp. Traditional lines from the verse are:

"My heart shall burst within my breast,
Unless I avenge this great King.
They shall forfeit life for this foul deed,
Or I must perish by a violent death."

The Brian Boru Tree

A large and obviously ancient yew tree in a Castle Avenue garden has been romantically, nostalgically and historically linked with many episodes of Clontarf's history. Yew trees, as we know, lack a graceful appearance but compensate somewhat by 'outstaying' most other trees with their air of strength and endurance. The Castle Avenue yew tree, was locally and affectionately known as the 'Brian Boru Tree' which eventually became little more than a massive ivy-covered bole with large patches of its bark flaked off and rotted away. Standing before this dilapidated but obviously once proud specimen, one realised that its huge girth represented the growth of many centuries. It has been stated that beneath the tree Brian Boru pitched his tent before that fatal encounter with

Brodir on Good Friday, 1014. Another tale tells us that the tree grew on the site of Comgall's little church of 550. Still another yarn connected it with the Commandery of the Knight's Templars and later their successors, the Hospitallers or that it was at least planted by them. Some ancient historians have recorded it as a mulberry tree. The fact is that it is merely the nature of its wood - hard, compact, elastic and very durable - that kept it alive so long to enable an aura of mystery and protection to grow around it. No doubt, if yew trees could talk this defiant specimen was capable of unfolding many stories and much drama concerning the Clontarf hinterland. While its older, higher and heavier branches were long since broken off by the effects of storms - even lightening I would suggest - the tree constantly sprouted new shoots from the lower part of its bole which had (as is the nature of the yew) intertwined with the old bole, giving the effect of not one trunk but several. Obviously the tree did give its name to the former serene house and estate at the junction of Seafield Road and Castle Avenue - known as Yew Park or Yew Lodge. And when the estate was later being developed for housing much controversy arose over the proposed uprooting of the infamous tree - in the event it survived for many years but today no trace of it exists. Much has been said and written as to the toxic qualities of the leaves of the yew tree. It appears that if eaten in large quantities they will kill man, cattle, horses and sheep and perhaps other animals. However even if His Highness Brian Boru did rest beneath the yew it is extremely doubtful that he would have resorted to devouring yew leaves and leave himself in a somewhat dazed state for the arrival of that man Brodir!

Brian Boru's Skull
The American couple on their first holiday to Ireland had a marvellous time. Everything went right. Weather lovely. Food good. No interrupting workers strikes. At Shannon airport, on their way home, they both swore to return again when family funds would allow. Just as they were heading for their flight gate a souvenir seller approached them. Would they be interested in a real Irish souvenir? He was offering them the genuine skull of Brian Boru (he nearly let "last one" slip out!) . "Oh darling"! the wife turned to her husband "wouldn't that be just marvellous! Imagine having the skull of the Irish King who beat off those terrible Vikings?" The husband agreed and duly brought the souvenir (forgetting to examine it for the track of Brodir's axe!)
Several years later the couple did manage to rise to another Irish holiday. Again they had a wonderful holiday and headed for Shannon airport somewhat lonely to be leaving such an honest country. Again they were about to head for their flight when our souvenir friend approached them (uncharacteristically not

remembering them from the last occasion). Would they like to buy the authentic skull of Brian Boru? "Hey" they reproached him "didn't we buy his skull from you on our last holiday?" "Ah but", replied our friend hiding the twinkle in his eye, "sure this is Brian Boru's skull when he was a boy!!"

LEGACY

Part of the legacy of the Vikings, and the Brian Boru era, is the wealth of place and family names left to us from those days. Examples of Viking place names from around the country are Waterford (from Vadrefjord meaning "weather haven"), Wexford (from Waesfjord meaning "harbour of the mud flats), Wicklow (from Wyking meaning "Viking meadow") and Limerick (from Laemrich meaning "rich land").

In Dublin we have such as Baldoyle (town of the dark strangers), Fingal (land of the fair strangers), Howth (from the Danish 'Haved' meaning head), Lambay (from the old norse Lambay meaning lamb Island) and Skerries (from the Norse word 'Skere').

Place names that recall Viking days in Dublin include Dane Road (Ballymun), Danes Court and Danesfort (Clontarf) Daneswell Road (Drumcondra), Norseman Court, Norseman Place, Ostman Place, Oxmanstown Lane, Oxmantown Road, Viking Place and Viking Road all in the Dublin 7 area. Dublin area 6W (close to Greenhills) has Osprey Avenue, Drive, Lawn, Park and Road while in the East Wall district we find Ossory Road and Ostman Place.

Family surnames of Viking origin are found all over Ireland. Concentrating on Dublin, in the Howth/Baldoyle area we find Harford, Waldron, Rickard and Thunder while in north Dublin generally names of Viking origins include Derham, Dowdall, Doyle, Drumgoole, Plunkett, Seaver, Seagrove and Sweetman (Swedeman). The name McLoughlin comes directly from "Loclamach"

From Brian Boru (born Brian O' Cinnéide) the two biggies in terms of surnames he "bequeated" to us are (O) Brien and (O) Kennedy. Concentrating on Dublin, in placenames Brian himself is recalled in Clontarf in particular by Brian Boru Avenue, and Brian Boru Street, and by Brian Road, and Brian Terrace in Marino. His palace at Kincora (Killaloe County Clare) is recalled by Kincora Avenue, Court, Drive, Grove, Park, Road and Walk in Clontarf. Keen "beady eyed" students of this subject will have observed a Kincora Terrace now incorporated into Botanic Road in Glasnevin. Also in Glasnevin the Dalcassian Downs housing estate is named after Brians Dálgcais clan. Boru is remembered by the Boroimhe housing estate on the left before you enter Swords coming from Dublin city and airport. Murrough Terrace in Marino is so named in memory of Brians son Murrough while Torlough Gardens and Torlough Parade (both also in Marino) commemorate Murrough's son and Brian's grandson Turlough. The aftermath of the Battle and the timespan since has also given us a wealth of battle stimulated music, song and dance, a litany of stories and plays as well as a library of books, pamphlets, theses, essays and articles.

Footnotes

(1) Áine Ní Cheannain in her primary school book "Dosaen Scéal" states in the story "Cochall Chaoilte" that on the occasion when Fionn was held prisoner by the High King at Tara his close friend Caoilte could only secure his release on bringing the King two pairs of every kind of bird and animal in Ireland. Caoilte travelled the country making his collection and secured "dhá chorr igCluain Tarbh!" (two herring birds in Clontarf.) The chief residence of the Fianna was the Hill of Allen in County Kildare. They flourished chiefly in the reign of Cormac Mac Art and Fionn was in fact Cormac's son in law. Clontarf woods would have echoed to their hunting and hound yelps. But Caoilte may have had the sense to collect his 'dhá corr' closer to Tara than Clontarf!

(2) The old Dublin - (Baile) Atha Cliath, the city of the ford hurdles - was so named when a group of emissaries led by Atharna were sent by King Conor Mac Nessa of Ulster to take spoils from the king of Leinster. On their return journey they found the River Liffey swollen with rain so they made some large hurdles and set them across the river. Over the hurdles they laid a causeway of boughs so that cattle and other spoils could be taken across safely. According to tradition St Patrick crossed over these hurdles. When the Danes captured Ath Cliath they laid the foundations of the 'new' city of Dublin - calling it Dubh Linn - the city of the Black Pool.

(3) In his book on the great leaders of the world, John Canning honours Brian Boru by listing him alongside such greats as Charlemagne, Alfred the Great, Lawrence of Arabia and Gandhi. Brian is listed in many catalogues of early saints and martyrs.

(4) His date of birth is very much disputed. Some authorities claim he was born as early as 930 or even 926. His mother was Bebinn and his father Cinnedie, Cennedi or Cineidi (Kennedy). The site of the Kincora fortress today lies somewhere under the town of Killaloe. In the older versions his name is written, Bien, or Brien, Boiroimh(e) or, Boromha.

(5) Brian Boru got the name of the 'tribute' when, after he eventually established himself as Árd Rí, he successfully had all subordinate kings pay him annual tributes or spoils to acknowledge his supremacy. This was simply implementing the law that the previous kings had been unable to enforce. We are told that one of his favourite pastimes was playing the harp - something we might find surprising in that the axe-wielding hands of a huge man are not the delicate type we normally associate with the plucking of harp

strings. It however helps portray the touching sensitivity and caring nature that was an integral part of the true character of Brian Boru.

(6) Gormlaith 'the blue one' a very clever if somewhat unprincipled woman had been married previously to Olaf Cuaran (Sitirc's father) who had earlier been King of Dublin. She had also been married to Malachy Mór who had dispensed with her, leaving her hot for revenge.

(7) Murrough (Murchadh or Morough), was Brian's oldest son by his first beloved wife Deirdre who died at a very young age. He was now grown up, a capable and fierce warrior and proved his ability as a first class fighter in many battles. He had met Mailmora face to face at the Battle of Glenmamra and would have killed him instantly were it not for the fact that Brian himself was at hand and intervened to save Mailmora. Murrough was somewhat rash and hot headed. He was forever urging his father to crush all his enemies, especially Mailmora.

(8) Brodar (Brodir, Broder or Bruadar) was a tall powerfully built and fiercely intimidating man with a reputation to match. He had once been a Christian but reverted to the worship of the Norse God Odin. He always wore 'a coat of mail on which no steel could bite'. His black locks were so long that he tucked them under his belt. Apparently it was he who became convinced, by a pagan oracle, that if the Battle of Clontarf was fought on Good Friday his side would win.

(9) These two verses are from Gray's poem "The Fatal Sisters" the subject of which is the Battle of Clontarf. The poem is imitated from the Norse tongue. The earl in line one refers to Sigurd, Earl of Orkney and the king in line four is Brian Boru. The original poem is preserved in the Orcades of Thermodus Torfaeus, and also in Batholinus. Gray's is merely a paraphrase which is (according to many experts) far inferior to the original.

....

Not everyone agrees that Brian Boru was buried in Armagh, in fact it is greatly disputed. In all 36 Irish chieftains died at the battle of Clontarf and all were taken home for burial by their clansmen. (No Viking of importance or rank who partook in the battle escaped with his life. Sitric did not engage in the encounter and he died a normal death in 1028). A story tells us that it was the same for the High King himself – that his Dalcassians took him on the shortest route home (to Clare) by way of Banagher on the river Shannon in County Offaly. There they acquired a boat and went downstream on the Shannon to Portumna in County Galway. They headed on for Killaloe 30 miles away but by now – especially due to the good weather experienced after the Battle of Clontarf – Brian's body was decaying and stinking to such an extent that they stopped at the island in the river Shannon known as the Oileán Mór (Big or High Island) – Irelands largest inland island – and buried him there.
A high stone – which was cleared and whitewashed every year up to 1991 – allegedly marks the grave of the great warrior King, Brian Boru.

Early Clontarf Finds

Flint Scraper and Flint Axehead, Neolithic Finds at Clontarf.

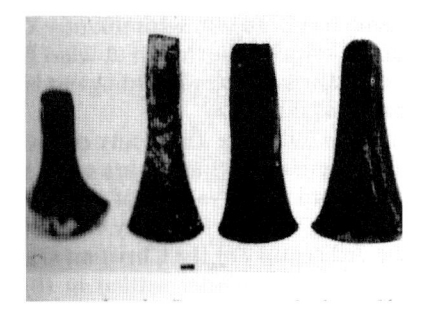

Bronze Axeheads, Bronze Age finds at Clontarf.

Bronze Ring Pin. 11th Century find at Clontarf

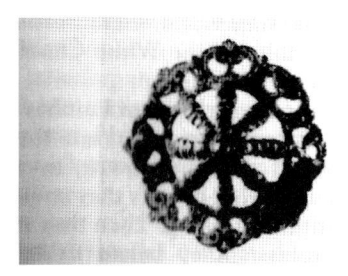

Harness Pendant 17th Century find at Clontarf.

Viking Ship

The Young Brian Boru

Brian Boru Addresses His Troops Before Battle

Boru's Son Morrough (right) in action at Clontarf

Battle of Clontarf by Hugh Frazer

Brian Boru Well, Castle Avenue

Brian Boru Harp

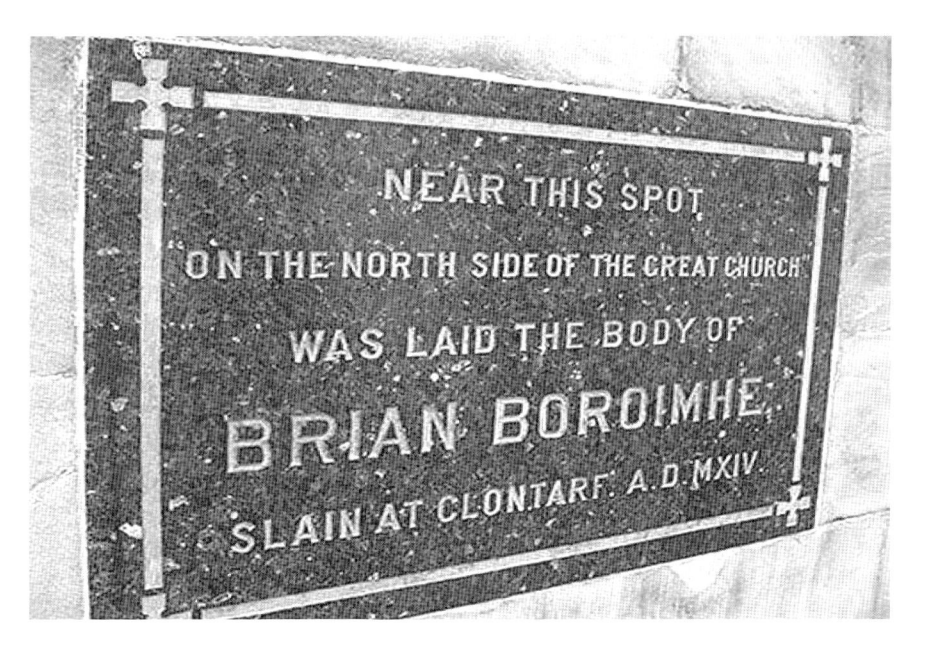

Memorial Plaque, Church of Ireland Cathedral, Armagh

CHAPTER FOUR

Clontarf in the Middle Ages

It would appear that after the Battle of Clontarf in 1014 many Vikings remained settled in Fingal. However time and again native hostility to them manifested itself from various parts of the country. From their geographic proximity the Meathmen almost considered it their duty to devastate and plunder Fingal regularly. The real sufferers, here were the native Irish who were scourged in turn by the foreigners and their fellow countrymen. But after 1016 any aggression from the Danes ceased totally as they applied themselves to commercial activities at the ports and to farming and pastoral pursuits on the excellent land of Fingal. In pre-Norman times the southern portion of Fingal was occupied by the McGillcolman (Mac Gillamaocholmog) and O'Donoghue clans. The McGillcolman territory extended from Clontarf to the boundary of the area around Balbriggan owned by the O'Casey sept. But soon the Anglo-Norman adventurers were to become the new masters of Fingal. They came in 1169 at the invitation of Dermot McMurrough, Maelmora's descendent. In 1170 the Norman's took Dublin. In 1171 with a small army, Strongbow surprised and routed the numerically superior forces of the Ard Rí Ruaidhrí O'Connor that had laid siege to Dublin. Very quickly Strongbow and Hugh de Lacy, in 1172, swept through Fingal with such a devastating campaign that all opposition ceased. McGillcolman's territory was in fact the first district north of Dublin city to be conquered by Strongbow. Each area of Fingal was allocated to various officers of the invading forces. Clontarf was granted to Adam de Pheope (one of his vessels) by Hugh de Lacy who himself became Lord of Meath.

The Norman's brought the feudal system with them. They had little difficulty in over - powering the Irish as they had better weapons, were better trained and were more united. They were a virile and strong race with a genius for building. They erected strong fortified castles - usually at strategic points along rivers and on the coastline - and majestic churches. In common with this policy Clontarf got its castle in 1172, and the history of Clontarf for the next few centuries is synonymous with the history of the castle. Dublin itself, the Norman stronghold, and the area immediately around it came to be known for the first 100 years of their occupation as 'The English Land'. As this territory expanded to cover a wide area - with varying boundaries - it came to be identified as "The Pale'. (It has been pointed out to me that 'new' Clontarf areas such as the Bull Island and areas reclaimed from the sea in modern times cannot be regarded as ever having being part of the pale!) Close to the castle a commandery(as religious houses attached to military orders were called) was established for the Knights Templars (as recounted in chapter two above) and the castle in time became a preceptory for them. They took over the manor lands from de Phepoe and ran it as grounds attached to a regular monastery. When the Templars were suppressed the Clontarf premises fell to the Knights of St. John of Jerusalem or Knights Hospitallers whose Irish headquarters were at Kilmainham. They were to run the affairs of the castle until the Reformation. In typical medieval style a little village began to grow around the castle or manor house - an English style compact village quite distinct from Irish villages which tended to be loosely spread over a large area. The grounds attached to the castle now represented a sizeable farm and had a little church also. And thus when we read old accounts of Clontarf we are reading about the medieval village with the castle as its centre. An avenue led from the seafront to the castle. Clontarf residents in these medieval times led a quiet rural life. Clontarf was in the heart of the Pale and the numerous Norman fortresses throughout the Pale quickly subdued Irish chiefs who tried to expel the Norman's.

Various Occurrences
Dublin began to expand under the Norman's. It spread north towards Clontarf. In 1308 the Provost (a post roughly corresponding to that of the present office of Lord Mayor) of Dublin, John Decer, built a causeway across the Tolka. This was the first Ballybough bridge and it joined Ballybough 'to the causeway of the mill-pool of Clontarf'. Before Decer's bridge the Tolka was crossed by the 'fishing weir of Clontarf' which had become renowned as the central point of the Battle of Clontarf. But now Clontarf was properly and formally attached to Dublin.
In 1317 Edward Bruce ravaged Fingal and disturbed the peaceful life around Clontarf. Later that century the terrible outbreak of 'Black Death' would have taken its toll on Clontarf. This deadly disease was spread by black rats carrying bacterium bacillus which inflicted Bubonic Plague.
In 1377 the king ordered that several books, the property of certain clergyman who were deemed hostile to his crown, should be seized in Clontarf harbour where they had been shipped. In 1395 a state warrant was issued under the laws against absenteeism to commandeer and detain ships in the water of Clontarf" which were ferrying passengers to England. Legislation against landlords who came to Ireland only for the purpose of collecting their rent had been in operation for about 100 years.
In 1413 King Henry V landed at Clontarf and in the same year Sir John Stanley also docked in Clontarf harbour with a mandate 'to implement severe direct government' on the Irish. However he died within a few months.

In 1440 William and James Fitzgerald, two brothers of Thomas Fitzgerald the Grand Master of the Knights Hospitallers attacked the Lord Deputy's entourage near Kilcock. They took the Lord Deputy prisoner and killed a number of his party. The king immediately confiscated the Clontarf estate until Thomas could prove he was innocent of association with this crime.

In 1527 an inquisition found 'Clontarf and Manor' to be valued at £20. It was consisted of '140 acres with 20 cottages, a hall, two towers, some barns, and four pence (4d) tax on every ship in Clontarf pool'. In the cottages lived artisans and labourers who worked plots of land.

The Crown takes the Castle

In 1529 Henry VIII broke all religious ties with the Roman Catholic Church and appointed Thomas Cranmer as Archbishop of Canterbury. The parliament of 1529-1536 was used as an instrument for enforcing religious change. In 1534 the Act of Supremacy declared Henry head of the church in England. A close friend of Henry and of chancellor Cardinal Wolsey, John Allen (or Alan) was appointed Archbishop of Dublin. Although previously sacked from office in England he held powerful influence in the administration of English government in Ireland, and bitterly resented the power of the then leading Anglo-Irish ruling family of Fitzgerald. In 1533 Gearóid Óg Fitzgerald was summoned to London to answer charges regarding his conduct of Irish affairs. Fearing a lengthy absence he left his government in the hands of his oldest son Thomas, Earl of Offaly, better known as 'Silken Thomas'. Allen saw this as an ideal opportunity to create trouble. He and his associates spread a rumour that Gearóid Óg had been executed in the Tower of London. The brash, youthful and inexperienced 'Silken Lord' immediately flew into rebellion. During his rebellion Allen became 'obnoxious' to Silken Thomas so it was decided to get rid of the Archbishop. The prelate was advised of Thomas's intention so he prepared to flee out of Dublin. He sailed from Wood Quay in a small vessel for an unknown destination- probably England. However unfavourable winds drove his vessel ashore at Clontarf and he decided to head to the renowned Hollywood family at Artane Castle for protection. After making his way up Castle Avenue which led to Artane, he was given protection but the followers of Silken Thomas trailed him and murdered him in front of Artane Castle on July 28th, 1534. As they returned to the city after this murder Silken Thomas' troops fought a small but bitter battle at Ballybough Bridge. No one won this confrontation but Thomas' men ravaged the land on both sides of the Tolka river. Silken Thomas' forces did have some success against English bases throughout Fingal but later his rising was suppressed and he was hanged in London. The greedy Tudors, after the overthrow of the powerful Fitzgeralds, saw an ideal opening to implement the king's break with the church in Ireland. The extravagant Henry also realised the enormous wealth of the church with its monasteries and became bent on confiscation.

On 22nd November, 1540 the Knights of St. John were forced to surrender their great priory at Kilmainham and all their property to the Crown. This included Clontarf Castle and estate. However two years previously the prior of the order - probably anticipating this move - had leased 'the town and Lordship of Clontarf, with the appurtenances, the pool, the rectory and the tithes' to Matthew King. King had to promise to repair the castle and maintain a minister to administer the sacraments to the parishioners. The prior also granted to King and the inhabitants of Clontarf a licence to fish with their boats 'within the liberty and bounds of Carlingford' without payment to the vicar of Carlingford. The last prior of the Knights of St. John in Ireland was an Englishman named John Rawson, who had been at all times a supporter of the English government and had served as Lord Treasurer of Ireland. On completion of the Surrender of the Castle estate - on June 20th, 1541 - Henry VIII returned the lands and property to Rawson with the title Lord or Viscount Clontarf. Rawson converted to Protestantism and received a pension of 500 marks together with a seat in Parliament. He was allowed live in Clontarf Castle for the rest of his life, apparently coming to an understanding with Matthew King who remained a staunch Catholic. These arrangements were carried out by the Lord Deputy Sir Anthony St. Ledger under the 'surrender and re-grant policy'. The Act of Supremacy was acknowledged in the transfer. Rawson was then an old man and he died in 1547.

In 1600 the 'Manor territory tithes, town and lordships' of Clontarf were granted by Queen Elizabeth I to Sir Geoffrey Fenton, the principal secretary of state. He died in 1608 and he was succeeded by his son Sir William and the manor of Clontarf was confirmed on him in 1637. Sir Maurice Fenton, son of Sir William, was made a baronet by Oliver Cromwell, but died unmarried and the estate was bestowed on their Aunt Catherine who had married a John King. John, and later George King, were a different family to that of the earlier Matthew King.

The 1641 Rebellion in Clontarf

On December 8th, 1641 Luke Netherville of Corballis (near Donabate) raised an army of 12,000 men to take the field in defence of their religious liberty. Netherville himself was a leader as were other 'gentlemen' of the Pale such as George King of Clontarf and Christopher Hollywood of Artane. The army marched south to Artane Castle and village. Netherville left a garrison there and proceeded with the rest of the army to Clontarf. Here they seized a vessel in Clontarf harbour and plundered its cargo. The nationality and nature of the ship and her cargo or why Netherville should consider it worthy of plunder is not recorded - probably deliberately. We must assume that George King knew it contained the weapons and ammunition of the enemy. After the raid on the vessel in Clontarf Pool Netherville and his men, including the Artane garrison, returned to Swords. Many Clontarf farmers and fishermen had followed the example of George King and joined Netherville's rebellious army, as did many from neighbouring areas. Their behaviour brought the wrath of the English administration down on them and a special proclamation was issued from Dublin Castle stating "the inhabitants of Clontarf, Raheny and Kilbarrack had declared themselves rebels and that, having robbed and spoiled some of His Majesty's good subjects they had assembled thereabouts (at Clontarf) in arms in great numbers mustering and training their rebellious multitudes as well at land as at sea". The inhabitants of this rebel district were declared "turbulent and unruly". The Puritan Republican General Sir Charles Coote was ordered to lead a troop of soldiers into Clontarf to quell rebel activities. On December 15th, 1641 he burned the fishermen's boats in Clontarf harbour and also most of the houses in the village. He is alleged to have found much of the plundered ships cargo in George King's Clontarf Castle. A price of £400 was put on King's head and all his Clontarf property confiscated - 'the manor, Hollybrooks and Clontarf Island' which in all now amounted to 961 statute acres. This marked the end of the road for the King family in Clontarf. Coote's troops then followed the rebellious army of Netherville to Swords were he defeated them, killing 200 in a spot traditionally known as 'Bloody Hallow'. Netherville and the rest escaped but their resistance petered out. In Clontarf many inhabitants who were incensed with the burnings of Coote continued to offer resistance by robbing houses and interfering with estates of people loyal to the crown. A loyalist - Evers the miller - who offered resistance was fatally wounded. But very soon the normal pattern of life returned to Clontarf.

On 14th of August, 1649 the Puritan 'Protector' Oliver Cromwell landed at Ringsend with 10,000 picked men. Cromwell marched through Fingal on his way to the notorious slaughter at Drogheda. He granted the confiscated King estate in Clontarf to John Blackwell, a favourite of his. Captain Blackwell, one of the parliamentary officers, sold or bestowed the estate to John Vernon who was the quartermaster general of Cromwell's army in Ireland. The Vernons were to remain in possession of Clontarf Castle and estate for over 300 years.

"Ill fares the land, to hast'ning ills a prey,
Where wealth accumulates, and men decay;
Princess and Lords may flourish or may fade;
A breath can make them, as a breath hath made;
But a bold pensantry, their country's pride,
When once destroy's, can never be supplied." **Oliver Goldsmith.**

Repression rightly describes the government's policy for the latter half of the 17th century and into the 18th. The people were deprived of their religious and civil rights. And the darkest days of the Penal Laws arrived. In 1690 Irish hopes disappeared at the Battle of the Boyne leaving an underground nation. There was a concentrated effort to wipe out the Irish character and culture even the language was being uprooted as a new ascendancy class appeared. Clontarf would have felt all the winds of change. The people lived in their huts, and religion had to be practiced in secret. Later the building of the Royal Charter School at Clontarf in 1749 was a means of securing Catholic children for the Protestant Church. (see chapter eleven below)

The Vernon Family and Clontarf Castle
Elsewhere we have traced the history of Clontarf Castle from 1172 to the coming of Cromwell. Indeed references to it will be found throughout this work as its history is woven into, and is inseparable from, that of Clontarf as a whole.
Clontarf Castle is alleged to occupy the same site as the old church of St. Comgall. But this is unlikely as that was probably where the old ruin in Clontarf Graveyard now stands, In any case both sites are in close proximity. The original castle or manor house built in 1172 by Adam de Phopoe or Hugh de Lacy, was one of the first fortifications built by the Norman's in Fingal, or indeed within the area which later came to be known as 'The Pale'. (De Phepoe is to be found in various accounts of the time as de Pepoe, de Pephoe, de Pheypo, de Fespo and de Frepo). Hugh de Lacy, the Norman Baron, was created Lord of the then province of Meath by King Henry II. To secure Dublin and the river basins of the Boyne and the Liffey - the fair plains of Meath and Bregia - he built an outer ring of castles represented by a line including the old castles of Slane, Ardbraccon, Trim and Kinegad. There was also a second line – an inner line of defence - and to this group Clontarf Castle belonged. With Clontarf, forming a strong semi-circle of defence, were the castles of Santry and Castleknock. Clontarf Castle would have had its garrison of Norman mail-clad soldiers.
Since Oliver Cromwell's notorious pillaging of the country in the years after 1649, with his "to hell or to Connaught" message, the name Vernon is the one

associated with Clontarf Castle - indeed the area occupied by the castle land was virtually synonymous with the area known as Clontarf. John Edward Venables Vernon, the quartermaster general of Cromwell's army in Ireland was the founder of the Vernon dynasty at Clontarf. Thus the Vernons came, basically as Cromwellian settlers or planters. (John was born in 1813 and was head of the family from 1833-90).

The Vernon family were originally of French origin. Their family tree can be followed back to Squire William de Vernon. In 1052 William in fact assumed the name 'Vernon' from the town and area of France of which he was proprietor. In 1052 he also erected the Notre Dame Church in Vernon - which is situated in a lovely valley beside the river Seine north west of Paris "within the diocese of Evreux and Bailiwick of Gisor's" in Normandy. The name is thus very ancient and is a very respectable French name. William had two sons Walter and Richard who both came to England with William the Conqueror. Walter died without issue. The de Vernon family flourished into many branches from the descendants of Richard de Vernon. Those branches spread throughout about twenty five English shires attaining a wealth of property and estates. Members from different sections of the family held various public offices from time to time in different counties - sheriffs, justices, ect. One de Vernon, a member of parliament for London, was appointed Secretary of State in 1697 - a post he held for the remainder of the reign of King William III. A William de Vernon was chief justice of Chester and he is considered to be the ancestor of all legitimate lines of the family since then. The 'de' before Vernon was dropped in later years.

The Vernons always had a staunch record for giving military service - being people of property. They established a pattern, generation after generation, of heirs becoming church ministers and lawyers as well as soldiers. So it was no surprise to find John Vernon arriving in Ireland with the rank of quarter master general in Cromwell's army in 1649. When Cromwell granted the estate to John Blackwell, John Vernon acquired it from him and established the name in Clontarf. It is likely that John was able to lay the fine solid financial foundation, that the Vernons subsequently enjoyed, by way of rake-offs from army suppliers which in those days were handsome for a quarter master general. He consolidated the substantial property around Clontarf Castle as a strong family base about the year 1660. When one considers that the family held their 'Clontarf seat' for over 300 years one realises that the family motto "Vernon semper viret" was no empty boast. Translated into English the motto reads "Vernon always flourishes". (A latin Scholar and wit came up with a punning variation on the motto which read "Ver non semper viret" - "spring does not always flourish").

The Vernon motto complete with boars head emblem can be seen on the outside of the arched ornamented entrance (a former gate house) to Clontarf Castle grounds at the junction of Kincora Avenue and Castle Avenue. The name given to the house is Vernon Lodge and the date is 1885.

In 1660 John Vernon passed the estate on to his son Colonel Edward Vernon. Some accounts list Colonel Edward (the Cavalier) as John's brother and not his son. Indeed while he definitely served Charles II he has been listed also as serving Charles I. The Vernons might with some justification be regarded as Restoration two-timers as it will be recalled that the original man from whom John Vernon acquired the Clontarf estate - Captain Blackwell - was a Cromwellian parliamentary officer who had been closely involved in the execution of Charles I with the 'Regicides'. Edward, who died in 1684, had two daughters - Eliza and Maria - but no male issue. Colonel Edward had served King Charles II on the battle-field, and in 1661 he was a parliamentary representative for the borough of Carlingford. At this time the Clontarf Vernons also had estates in Derbyshire and Staffordshire in England.

In 1675 the King further enlarged the Clontarf estate.... "its jurisdiction, tenures, and courts with a grant of royalties, power to embark 300 acres, with free warren, privilege of holding two fairs (one on the 10th April and the other on the 6th October) with customs, etc". 'Between 1684 and 1695 the estate was held by a female Vernon, but in 1695 a first cousin of Colonel Edward, another John Vernon, a merchant, claimed the manor and lands of Clontarf 'together with the Hollybrooks, the islands and appurtenances'. His claim was successful and the castle and estate were granted to him by an act of parliament in 1698.

Early in the 18th Century a row broke out between the Vernons and Dublin Corporation because the Corporation were claiming title to a 195 acre portion of the strand described as "the pool and island of Clontarf". (Colonel Edward, in his time had disputes with the Corporation regarding their 'interfering' with the manor.) When he obtained the estate Captain John Vernon in 1731 vigorously opposed the corporation on the issue and forbade city officials to enter any part of his Clontarf estate as a result of the 'boundaries' row. In a speech made in 1731 Vernon stoutly asserted his right to the Island (Clontarf Island) and pointed out to Dublin Corporation that the liberties of the city on the north were bounded according to the charter (de libertatibus) of the second of King John 'by the lands of Clonliffe, by the Tolka, and by the Church of St. Mary Oxmanstown' (St. Mary's Abbey). He won his case and all seems to have been settled most amicably because five years later, in 1762 the first Lord Vernon was created when a great-grand-nephew of the original John received that title from King George III.

About 100 years ago the Vernons land in Clontarf was recorded as 753 acres in area, which meant almost the entire Clontarf locality. The boundary of the Vernon estate with the sea territory under the jurisdiction of the Port and Docks Board was marked by tall concrete bollards starting at today's Clontarf Road Railway embankment.

Biographically speaking the Vernons were a dull dynasty in that they didn't throw up any colourful geniuses in the course of their long and unchequered family records. They didn't have a flamboyant style, rather a solid workmanlike lifestyle that left a deep impression on the Clontarf area and stabilised the castle as the centre of the affairs of Clontarf. They kept up their English connections with great care, generally choosing English girls as brides for their church, army or law employed sons and heirs, and English husbands for their daughters.

At the end of their stay in Clontarf the male line of the Vernons failed and the estate passed through marriage to the Oulton family in 1934. George Oulton was a solicitor for the Vernons and married a Vernon - Sybil Mona Vernon Calverey. In 1952 Mr. Oulton died and two years later the last of the Oulton family left Clontarf Castle forever. Sybil Mona had actually lived her last years in a castle gate lodge with her consort Mrs Murphy, with the castle derelict and empty for a few years. It is now quite alarming to realise that a demolition bulldozer actually arrived at the building to raise it to the ground at one stage.

The Castle Building

The structure erected by the Norman Adam de Phopoe in 1172 was considerably altered over the long years by various repairs, extensions and refurbishments and consequently Clontarf Castle lost much of its original character. But up to the end of the era of the Old Castle the building still had its Gothic windows with an overall ecclesiastical cum military character - one would not argue against the fact that it was at various times the residence of knights and monks. By 1835, due to many alterations on the earlier structure only the square tower was left of the original, and this was preserved as a residence for the proprietor who was at the time T.C.V. Vernon. In that year the whole building had become shaky and decidedly unsafe. The Vernons called in a very distinguished Irish architect of the time - William Vetruvius Morrison - to survey the premises and recommend a course of action. At first Morrison hoped to preserve a good part of the old building. However he soon perceived that the real problem was one of sinking foundations and that there was a very real danger of the structure collapsing totally. Therefore he had no option but to propose demolishing the entire building including the ancient square tower. This was duly done in 1835 and a rebuilding process began which gave us the striking noble building we know today, completed in 1837. Since then, silently concealing its observation of so many Clontarf changes, the castle has stood like a fortress against the elements. It was re-erected in a mixture of styles - Norman, Gothic and Tudor - to represent its long history and can only be regarded as a 19th century imitation of a 12th century castle. The Gothic windows depicted the Vernon family history. The grand feature of the new 1835 building is the tower in which Morrison retained the Norman style of architecture. The tower contains two interesting rooms with deeply recessed windows. The lower room was the study, the upper one the nursery. The main building to the west of the Tower has a Tudor style architecture. Writing in 1838, D'alton, in his 'History of County Dublin' tells us 'His (Mr. Vernon's) lands are chiefly let in ornamented or building lots, with the reservation of an acreable rent of £10 per annum; inferior portions, or such as do not suit for building, at about £7 while cabins without land produce from £4 to £5.' The matching gatehouse or lodge house (now offices) at the end of the main avenue leading up to the castle features a small mock Irish Round Tower and it greatly embellishes the approach to the castle. An extra gateway to the castle - off Castle Avenue at its junction with Kincora Avenue - was added in 1885.

Today's Castle is very much hemmed in and just about all of its land have been "gobbled up", for building purposes. The premises was first officially opened as the North Dublin Hostelry by the acting Lord Mayor of Dublin Alderman Lorcain Bourke on the 10th of May 1957. The first licensee was Mrs Egan who sold it to the Regan family in the 1960's. They developed it to cater for weddings. The castle was acquired by the Houlihan family in 1972 and it became one of Ireland's best and biggest cabaret venues until that ceased in 1997. A board of directors, opened the venue as a luxurious four star hotel and in 2007 it was further upgraded to the magnificent standards enjoyed by patrons today. It exubes a superb baronial atmosphere and with its castellated exterior it has been transformed into a new world of luxury in an old world setting. Fittingly the proprietors have preserved, wherever possible, the characteristics of the 1835 mansion. Its grey and historic turrets still dominate western Clontarf just as the castle once dominated the old Medieval village. It is a building with a sense of occasion and every room is beautifully and comfortably furnished and splendidly maintained. Carved oak canopies, black marble, panelled walls and period style decorations are to be found throughout the entire edifice.

The Castle's famous 'haunted room' once a guest bedroom and later an upstairs kitchen is apparently free of its ghost! The room appears to have achieved its "ghostly presence" from a certain painting hanging on one of its walls of Colonel J. Vernon which possessed 'moving eyes'. However when the painting was removed to another premises it appears the ghost also moved residence!

Marriage of Strongbow to Aoife

Old Clontarf Castle by G. Beranger 1772

Modern Clontarf Castle Hotel

Castle Gate Lodge

A View Inside Clontarf Castle Hotel

Mrs Murphy, Mrs Oulton's Escort with the Picture of the Vernon Castle Ghost

CHAPTER FIVE

Daniel O'Connell and Repeal

Popularly known as 'the Liberator' Daniel O'Connell, after winning the famous 1828 Clare election, proved in 1829 that his methods of popular agitation were successful when he finally won Catholic emancipation. From his early manhood he had denounced the Act of Union of 1800 as an obstacle to the Catholic cause and throughout his life remained an avowed repealer. The Act of Union guided into law by Prime Minister William Pitt, it will be remembered, abolished the independent Irish Parliament and purported to unite Ireland and Britain under the title 'The United Kingdom of Great Britain and Ireland'. Now O'Connell bent his energies on agitation for repeal of the Act, believing that Irish claims were slighted in that 'alien assembly' (the British Parliament). O'Connell's methods were totally peaceful and he had nothing in common with Irish revolutionists who were openly prepared to use physical force to achieve separation from England. He declared that 'Irish liberty is not worth the shedding of one drop of blood'.

From 1840 on, O'Connell really began to mobilise the millions of Irish Catholics behind him in one mass movement for repeal of the Union Act (pre famine Ireland had over eight million people). Using various organisational names such as the 'Catholic Committee', the 'Catholic Board', the Catholic Association', and the 'Repeal Association', all Catholics throughout the country felt part of the 'political scene' by paying their monthly penny (which also acted as a recruitment process) to O'Connell's organisation. The penny was usually collected after Sunday masses. Earlier it had been called the 'Catholic Rent' but later it became the 'Repeal Rent'.

On November 1st, 1841, O'Connell was elected Lord Mayor of Dublin and thereby chairman of the City Council. But on returning to the mainstream of politics in 1842 with the new weapon of 'monster meetings' he appears to have assumed the ultimate success of the repeal movement to be certain. During 1841-43 his Catholic organisation brilliantly convened enormous mass meetings or demonstrations, which were orchestrated by the clergy and controlled by O'Connell. Throughout 1843, which became known as repeal year, about forty of these monster meetings were held throughout the country, with everyone clamouring for repeal. Where possible, sites famous in Irish history were chosen as venues. The biggest of these gatherings was held at Tara, County Meath on the 15th August, 1843 where estimates numbered the crowd at between half and three quarters of a million people. Estimates of the attendance at other meetings were; Mullingar 100,000, Cork 500,000, Kilkenny 300,000 and Donnybrook 200,000.

THE CLONTARF 'MONSTER MEETING' THAT NEVER WAS

O'Connell was now at the zenith of his power and as the momentum of the repeal movement built towards a climax the largest and last of all the monster meetings was planned for Clontarf on Sunday the 8th of October, 1843. The site was picked by O'Connell mindful of its significance and he intended to emulate Brian Boru at Clontarf. Among those who called for the meeting were 24 Fingal clergymen one of them been Canon James Callinan P.P. of Clontarf. The actual site for the meeting in Clontarf was the Conquer Hill area. Various other sites have been suggested as the proposed meeting place, especially the grounds of what is now Clontarf Golf Club. However most accounts favour Conquer Hill. The British Prime Minister of the time, Robert Peel was an openly avowed enemy of Daniel O'Connell and he resolved to terminate the repeal movement. His government proclaimed the Clontarf meeting. At 10 a.m on Saturday 7th, the day before the meeting the Lord Lieutenant and Privy Council met specially in Dublin Castle and issued a draft proclamation 'cautioning all persons from attending an unlawful meeting to be held at Clontarf on Sunday the 8th day of October instant, for the alleged purpose of petitioning for a repeal of the legislative Union between Great Britain and Ireland'. This proclamation was posted on walls all around Dublin and published in the "Dublin Gazette". O'Connell was truly in a dilemma. For him it was a moment of high drama, a crisis. The Clontarf meeting was to be his show piece - it would make Tara look like a caucus! At Clontarf he meant his repealers to force Europe to sit up and take notice of the Irish peoples' solidarity in their demand for liberty! All Clontarf was agog with frenzy and excitement for one of her greatest moments - except the very wealthy who viewed proceedings with contempt.

From all over the country, the crowds were already pouring towards Dublin on horseback, in carriages and walking, complete with banners and bands. Crowds travelled by boat from England. But O'Connell also noticed warships in Dublin Bay, off Clontarf, and regiments of horse and foot troops with artillery pouring into the area. The Pigeon House Fort across the bay had its guns trained on Conquer Hill - this was the only military purpose the fort ever served, to stifle what was, after all, a perfectly democratic demonstration. O'Connell had to decide whether or not to defy the order forbidding the meeting. In the final analysis being a man who believed in peaceful methods his decision was to call off the meeting, as he feared a physical confrontation if the somewhat "business like" troop movements in Clontarf were a reliable yardstick. Nobody will ever know if the troops would have intervened and used force to disband the meeting on the Sunday although it is probable that some kind of collision was inevitable. Should O'Connell have called the governments' bluff? In the event his own decision has come to be known as O'Connells' bluff'.

O'Connell had public notices and messengers dispatched to Dublin outposts to intercept and prevent people from surrounding counties completing the now fruitless journey to Clontarf. O'Connell himself and about twelve of his close associates were arrested and charged with seditious conspiracy. O'Connell was convicted in February 1844 and received a one year prison term and a fine of £2,000. Both were, however, reversed by the house of Lords in September 1844. Two of those arrested with him were his son John O'Connell and Charles Gavin Duffy, of 'the Nation', newspaper who was later to become Prime Minister of Victoria, Australia. Clontarf on that Sunday morning, instead of hosting about a million people was dormant and quiet with only an odd soldier moving around Conquer Hill and warships sleeping at anchor in the bay. Clontarf was not the end of the road for O'Connell's political career, but the spell of his unrivalled power and influence over the people vanished. And the repeal movement died at the Clontarf fiasco. Famine and the young Ireland Movement were about to sweep the countryside.

Many Clontarf people hold a tradition that Daniel O'Connell had a residence in Clontarf or at least came to Baymount House, Danesfield House or another of Clontarf's 'big houses' on vacations. Having contacted some descendants of Daniel, especially one member of the dynasty who keeps accurate family records I can state that O'Connell had no such Clontarf connections. He had two Dublin residences, one at number 58, Merrion Square and the other at Glencullen in South County Dublin. He had, nevertheless, a great, great grand daughter who was born, reared and lived in Clontarf. She was a descendant of Daniel's oldest daughter Ellen O'Connell.

A peal of bells, alleged to be the first bells of Irish manufacture, were to be joyfully sounded at the Clontarf meeting. Made by a Mr. Murphy of St. James Ward the bells, mounted on a portable stage and embellished with the harp of Brian Boru and the shamrock, were actually on their way to Clontarf when the prohibitory proclamation was made public. Thus the chimes of the 'joy bells' did not after all celebrate a victory.

James Stephens and the I.R.B.

The Irish Republican Brotherhood, more commonly known as 'The Fenian Movement' was launched on St. Patrick's Day, 1858, thus initiating another attempt to organise an armed rebellion in Ireland. The leaders of the new conspiracy were, however, almost without exception, completely unsuited to the organisation of an insurrection. They were writers, thinkers and scholars rather than the hard-headed men of action which the task required. James Stephens, a native of Kilkenny who liked to be referred to as the C.O.I.R. - the Central Organiser of the Irish Republic - the organisational genius behind this new underground revolutionary movement was such a man. All his life Stephens remained a somewhat mysterious figure to whom the term 'masterly inactivity' could well be applied.

His masterly inactivity was to a certain degree wise and successful in creating unease among the authorities and keeping them guessing. But Stephens obviously missed his best chance of a rising which was late in 1865, or early in 1866, especially after the ending of the American Civil War in 1865 after which thousands of Irish American soldiers enrolled as Fenians and a steady flow of them poured into Ireland. As leader of the Fenians he became more famous for threats of an uprising than for any real action. Few people knew how or where to contact him and fewer still knew what he looked like. Carrying the totally flattering tag of being a ruthless bloodthirsty leader Stephens was eventually arrested in Fairfield House, Newbridge Avenue, Sandymount on Saturday, November 14th, 1865. He was remanded in her Majesty's Richmond Bridewell Penitentiary on Dublin's South Circular Road (now Griffith College) awaiting trial for conspiracy to organise revolution on November the 27th. However, in the early hours of Saturday morning, November 25th, Stephens was daringly sprung from jail by a team of rescuers organised by John Devoy. (One block of Griffith College buildings is named in his memory.) Devoy (1842-1928) was later to become the dominant voice of Irish Americans. His career seems to span an endless age - from the beginning of the Fenian movement right up until the fledgling independent Irish state emerged. He was later to accuse Stephens of cowardice and play a leading role in deposing him. Stephen's sensational escape threw the authorities into consternation and confusion and put a halo around him in the eyes of supporters. The most desperate efforts were made to recapture Stephens. Cavalry scoured the countryside. Police ransacked suspected neighbourhoods all over the city. Gunboats put to the sea and overhauled and searched steamers, fishing-smacks and coasters. Flaming placards offered no less than £3,000 reward for his re-arrest. Stephens was, in fact, secreted in the house of a Mrs. Butler in Summerhill, on the northside of the city, a woman of humble means, where he remained for some months.

Clontarf's Captain Weldon to the rescue
Most histories of the period then record that Stephens was escorted, dressed as a woman, in a carriage-and-four to Balbriggan where he was placed on board a lugger and set sail for France. He escaped to France sure enough, and from there went to America but he did not leave in a lugger from Balbriggan. He was smuggled out of Dublin by a Captain Weldon of (the then) St. John's Terrace, Clontarf, from under the noses of the authorities at Bachelors Walk in early March, 1866.

The Weldon family of Clontarf (they also lived for some time in Marino) were noted as a household with sympathetic nationalist feelings. The Captain Weldon in question had schooners importing coal from Cardiff to Dublin. Although not a tall man, he was apparently a carbon copy of the accepted model of a daring sea captain. He was bearded, stern and authoritarian. Yet he had a flamboyant swashbuckling style and the romantic appeal of smuggling a man of James Stephen's calibre out of the country appealed to his buccaneering nature. Captain Weldon left a stylish hand written account of the escape and his efforts to get Stephens to a port in the north of France on his brigantine named 'Concord'. His account of the episode portrays a character who liked to dare the odds and who wasn't easily unnerved. After all, who would fancy escorting the dubious Stephens to safety with all the available Crown forces baying for his recapture? And wouldn't it be very enticing to take the £3,000? They had some luck in getting out of Dublin harbour, but after that the elements gave them a stormy and uncomfortable passage to say the least. He didn't quite make France, but left Stephens safely at Ardrossan in Scotland.

The episode was recalled for me with considerable pride, by Weldon's grandson Mr. Daniel O'Connor, then a retired man living on Maryville Road, Raheny. He lent me the authentic original manuscript written by the Captain in beautiful 'cooper-plate' style writing. James Stephens was eventually allowed return to Ireland and lived for some time at Sutton. During his last years he lived at at George's Avenue, Blackrock, where he died.

The Howth Gun-Running

Ever since the Irish Volunteers were founded on November 25th, 1913 they felt something of a token army or an army in name only, as they had no real arms and used wooden guns or hurley sticks for training. The Volunteers drilled openly on Marino's (Dublin north city) green spaces.

On the night of April 24th, 1914, the Ulster Volunteers - formed in January, 1913 - imported 20,000 rifles and 3,000,000 rounds of ammunition at Larne. Nationalist Irish Volunteer leaders, with Bulmer Hobson the orchestrator, hatched a daring and flamboyant plan to get in on the 'gun-running' act. Firstly, they wanted to prove that the Ulster Volunteers weren't the only ones who could outwit the authorities and illegally import arms. Secondly, the publicity their plan - if successful - would get, would enormously help their recruiting campaign. Both these aims were brilliantly achieved and indeed the limelight was stolen from the Ulster Volunteers in that Hobson's plan was carried out in broad daylight.

The plan had three stages. (1) To buy guns to arm the Volunteers, (2) To take these guns to Ireland (3) To take the guns ashore and hand them out to the Volunteers.

The rifles and ammunition were bought secretly in Hambury in Germany. On the 3rd July, 1914 Erskine Childers, captain of the white yacht "Asgard" (now on permanent exhibit at the National Museum, Collins Barracks along the Quays on Benburb Street), sailed from Conway in North Wales and as arranged, picked up the rifles from a tug off the Belgian coast on July 12th. On Sunday 26th July, 1914, by what amounted to something of a timing miracle the Asgard reached Howth at the appointed hour with its cargo of arms, to be met by the Volunteers and the Fianna, who marched to Howth from a meeting point in Fairview (north Dublin). (The Fianna was founded by Countess Markievicz in August 1909 after the model of the 'Fianna Éireann' formed in 1902 by Bulmer Hobson, in Belfast, for Ulster boys. The Fianna was really a boy-scout type body to train boys for military action in later life - and to be prepared to fight for the liberation of their country.) About 1,000 men, 100 of them Fianna, marched back towards Dublin armed with rifles amid acclamation and cheering - the first time in 600 years, that an Irish army paraded openly armed and in defiance of British authorities - through the streets of the city. It was on this journey back to the city that Clontarf was to be the stage for an historic confrontation with the authorities.

They marched from Howth via Sutton, Raheny and Killester. It was when they approached the junction of the Howth Road and Clontarf Road that the problem arose; their path was blocked by police and soldiers in a phalanx with fixed bayonets. Arthur Griffith described the scene. "At ten minutes past four the head of the column had come in sight of Fairview and at that moment it was seen that the road was held by military with constabulary with carbines and, on the flanks of the military, bodies of the Dublin Metropolitan police. The column swung aside through Charlemont Road in order to reach the Malahide Road which on its west side affords cover for a fight. The enemy moved at the same time and the two forces came face to face on the Malahide Road. Darrell Figgis wrote: "Those at the head of the column, seeing the end of Howth Road barred by a double rank of bayonets turned to the right down Marino Crescent into the Malahide

Road. At once we saw the military break and turn at the double down the tram (Clontarf) Road so as to confront the column again." Figgis, (1882-1925), was a Volunteer leader who played a big part in the whole gun-running saga, including the purchase of the arms in Hamburg. He was a writer who became honorary secretary of Sinn Fein from 1917-1919. He was a T.D. for Co. Dublin in 1922. Bulmer Hobson, the main architect of the gun-running wrote of the challenge from the authorities: "When we approached Clontarf we saw the soldiers drawn across the road, and, in order to avoid them and to give them an opportunity of avoiding us, we turned sharply to the right on to the Malahide Road. The police and soldiers came at the double round to the Malahide Road and confronted us again."

A melee cum free for all took place at the seafront end of the Malahide Road between Volunteers and soldiers. In the scuffles which followed clubbed rifles, batons, truncheons and clubs were freely used. Bayonet charges occurred and some revolver shots rang out and a few on each side were wounded. The fighting subsided and the Volunteer leaders outwitted the authorities by engaging them in long debate, argument and general parley regarding the whole scene, while their orders back to the rank and file in the Volunteer column to disperse and melt away, were quickly carried out. They disappeared through hedges and over walls with the rifles, many through the grounds of the Christian Brothers establishment in Marino towards Drumcondra and Glasnevin. The rifles were hidden in 'safe' houses and other places all over the north city and were collected again at a chosen rendezvous twenty four hours later. Of the 900 guns and 26,000 rounds of ammunition landed in Howth, only nineteen guns were lost to the police - and these were broken in the 'Malahide Road struggle.' The actual guns were 11mm Mauser rifles, old fashioned and heavy, but were in perfect working order. They were the rifles with which the German army were re-armed after the Franco-Prussian war.

The 'Clontarf confrontation' on that July Sunday in 1914 was much more than a colourful incident. The guns so boldly landed at Howth, made possible the 1916 Easter Rising and the emergence of a separate Irish Free State. It was a major event in our history. It gave the Volunteers self confidence, courage, a new determination and a fresh impetus. Its timing against a background of high feelings on the then most prominent Home Rule issue between H. Asquith, John Redmond and Sir Edward Carson, gave a powerful fillip to the Volunteers. Their numbers increased rapidly and so did their funds. Among those directly involved on the day, or associated with the organisation of the gun-running, were most of the names that were to become household ones during and after the 1916 Rising. Among these were Tom Clarke, Arthur Griffith, Sir Roger Casement, Eoin

MacNeill, The O'Rahilly, Cathal Brugha, Séan Mac Diarmada, Padraic Pearse, Eamon De Valera, Bulmer Hobson, Erskine Childers, Eamon Ceannt and Thomas Mc Donagh. Many of the principal figures involved have left diaries, letters or papers that document the event very well. Unfortunately the Volunteers triumph was tinged with tragedy later that evening. As the troops involved (The Kings Own Scottish Borderers) were marching back to their barracks along Bachelors Walk in the city centre they were jeered and baited by an unarmed crowd on the pavement. The soldiers retaliated by using their bayonets and by firing into the crowd. Three people were killed (one woman and two men) and thirty eight wounded. However the only immediate impact of this unfortunate occurrence was to harden nationalist leaders against any compromise. The whole incident occurred exactly 900 years after Brian Boru had banished the Scandinavian invaders at Clontarf. A 'second phase' or 'twin' of the Howth gun-running was successfully completed when a further cargo of 600 rifles and ammunition were safely brought ashore at Kilcoole Co. Wicklow in the early hours of Sunday morning, August 2nd, 1914 a week after the Howth landing.

Clontarf Town Hall and the 1916 Rising

Clontarf town hall was to play a central role in providing a fermenting ground for hatching the plot that produced the 1916 Rising. Because revolutionary leaders had long memories of the failure of just about every previous effort at organising an uprising against British rule in Ireland due to 'leaks' of details and informers, much secrecy surrounded the lead up to the 1916 Rising - secrecy to the point of confusion in the end. Centre stage in the revolutionary movements at the time were the Irish Republican Brotherhood (I.R.B.), the Irish Volunteers and James Connolly with his Citizen Army.

As far back as 1914 the Supreme Council of the I.R.B. had decided to effect a rising before the end of World War 1. A Military Council (first called a committee) was set up by the Executive Council of the I.R.B. in May, 1915 to plan the rising. This Military Council consisted at first of Padraic Pearse, Joseph Plunkett and Eamon Ceannt but gradually expanded as planning progressed until, in April 1916, it consisted of seven men - the seven who signed the Proclamation of the Irish Republic - Clarke, Mac Diarmada, Mac Donagh, Pearse, Ceannt, Connolly and Plunkett. Their job was to proceed with drawing up plans and to secure arms for the Rising. Such secrecy surrounded the affairs of the I.R.B. that the Supreme Council of the organisation did not know of the existence of the Military Council for a considerable time. The Executive Council was comprised of only three members and had constitutional control over the entire I.R.B. when the Supreme Council was not in session.

A newly elected Supreme Council first met in September, 1915. Denis McCullough was elected president - it should be noted that he was president of the 'Irish Republic' virtually established by the I.R.B. While the I.R.B. had decided in principle on going ahead with the insurrection the speeches and writings of James Connelly were influencing the rank-and-file of the Volunteers, and the Supreme Council of the I.R.B. felt it was essential to meet with and consult Connolly with a view to streamlining their approaches and ideals. One of the I.R.B. 'havens' for secret meetings in those years was Clontarf town hall which also doubled as a library and cinema. Caretakers and librarians of the hall at the time were the McGinn family. Michael McGinn from Dungannon, Co. Tyrone the town that Tom Clarke lived in for much of his youth - had been a Fenian organiser in that county. The whole family were I.R.B. sympathisers and had a 'secret' or 'committee' room available in the hall for various revolutionary meetings - often held on Sundays - and as librarians then worked on Sundays, this was the perfect cover. Many and varied were the meetings held there and the room heard the voices of all the leading political figures of the 1916 era, including that of Eamon De Valera - indeed the room was often referred to by locals as the 'De Valera Room'. De Valera did join the I.R.B. but later resigned as he never really approved of secret organisations. In his declining years De Valera had a nostalgic return to the same building, then St. Anthony's Church, for a funeral. Many present, saw him revisit the famous room and heard him recall incidents where he and colleagues had to 'hightail' via the back-door from various 'proscribed' or 'secret' meetings on a pre-arranged signal that the authorities were 'paying a visit'. Mr. McGinn's sons, Conway and Ronnie, were both active in the 1916 rebellion and later War of Independence.

A vital meeting of the I.R.B. Supreme Council took place in Clontarf Town Hall on Sunday January 16th, 1916. At that meeting the I.R.B. - being a democratic body - voted to change its decision on the Rising in 1916 from one in principal to one in fact. After this Clontarf meeting the Rubicon had been crossed and there could be no going back. It is notable that just six years later also on January 16th, 1922 Dublin Castle was handed over to the new native Irish Government. The decision of the Council was 'to fight at the earliest possible moment'. The names of the I.R.B. eleven man Supreme Council who met at Clontarf on that historic January day in 1916 were - Denis McCullough (President and Ulster representative), Séan Mac Diarmada (secretary), Tom Clarke (treasurer), Séan Tobin (Leinster), Diarmuid Lynch (Munster), Alex McCabe (Connaught), Dick Connolly (South of England), Joseph Gleeson (North of England), Pat McCormick (Scotland), and two co-opted members, Padraic Pearse and Doctor Patrick McCarton. The first three named were at this time also the three man Executive Council.

At the meeting Clarke, Mac Diarmada and Pearse (members of the Military Council) were reported to be very quiet and somewhat slow to report the full extent of their 'progress towards a rebellion'. However this was totally accepted by their colleagues and appreciated as necessary - for ultimate success it was deemed essential to keep the plans and decisions of the military council within as close a circle as possible. Sean Mac Diarmada, it was, who proposed the motion adopted by the meeting - 'to fight at the earliest possible moment'. Contrary to some detractors' allegations, the motion was carried unanimously even though one member suggested that the formula 'should await the opportune time to fight', might give the organisation more time to mobilise properly.

A second and vitally important aspect of the Clontarf meeting was that it opened the door for the I.R.B. to blend James Connolly's path with their own. It led, a few days later, to direct talks with Connolly and the so called 'January Agreement', by giving the go ahead for delegations to meet other 'committees or councils' and constitutionally fix the date for the proposed rising.

Connolly had been pressing for some time for a rebellion to go ahead. He had been quite outspoken with regard to lone action by the Citizen Army - which the I.R.B. leaders felt would be premature and bring disaster on their overall strategy. In the event Connelly 'disappeared' under 'arrest' on January 19th, 1916. He was back at Surrey House (Liberty Hall) on January 22nd. Much speculation surrounded his 'term in exile' but events transpired that he was deliberately 'detained' by the I.R.B. Military Council. He spent the few days in lengthy discussion with the Military Council, especially Pearse. The venue was the Brickworks in Crumlin and the talks themselves are wrapped in mystery. Pearse explained the I.R.B. position to Connelly who was happy to row in with I.R.B. plans and in fact he was co-opted as a member of the Military Council later in the month. Also, the form of the 1916 Rising was decided upon, if not the date. This coming together was called the 'January Agreement' and it was brought about as a direct result of the Supreme Council's meeting at Clontarf Town Hall. From now on the two sides worked together with a common approach towards the historic day that was to be Easter Monday, the 24th April, 1916. Citizen army and volunteers would drill side by side. The Supreme Council of the I.R.B. never met again after the Clontarf meeting.

Daniel O'Connell

James Stephens

Bulmer Hobson

Padraig Pearse

John Devoy

Erskine Childers

Asgard Ship

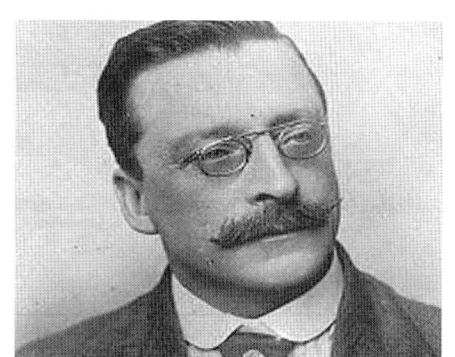

Arthur Griffith

1916 Figures most of whom were part of the Howth gun running and the IRB meetings in Clontarf Town Hall

CHAPTER SIX

Clontarf Island

Today's Dubliner, and anyone unfamiliar with the changing image of the Dublin Bay shoreline, will be somewhat surprised to realise that Clontarf once had an offshore Island. This is not to be confused with today's North Bull Island as it existed centuries before the Bull Island was born. The Island was situated in deep water beside Clontarf Pool at the mouth of the Tolka River about 140 metres from the most easterly point of the present East Wall Road. The Island was called Clontarf Island as Clontarf was the nearest point of the shore to it. It was also commonly known as the 'Old Mud Island' and later called 'Cromwell's' Island - this latter name adopted from an Island resident of that name. From the very earliest records the island was always part of the Clontarf Castle estate. In former times (before the North Lotts[1] were reclaimed) when the coastline ran from Ballybough Bridge by what are now the North Strand Road, Amiens Street and Beresford Place, the island lay quite a distance out to sea. It was in fact a most conspicuous object, indeed a prominent landmark, in Dublin Bay. The island is clearly shown on old maps of Dublin and Dublin Bay. Its existence can be verified by checking the very interesting map of Dublin in Haliday's "History of the Scandinavian Kingdom of Dublin" published in 1673. Rocque's map of Dublin, completed in 1753 also clearly shows the island. On some early maps the island is marked as "Clontarf Hard". Gradually the reclamation of lands close to the shore on the northern side of the Liffey estuary and the general silting in the estuary enabled the island (in the later years) to be easily reached from the shore.

Clontarf Island was, most likely, originally formed in the same way as the modern Bull Island was formed - by a natural accumulation of sand at that point in Dublin Bay. The island wasn't a big one - about 365 metres long, 36 metres wide and 5 metres high, but it was an attractive romantic place. It was the forerunner of the present extensive Bull Island in providing a favourite recreation ground for Dubliners with free and easy access. The island was a ribbon-shaped piece of land, with one end facing the East Wall Road. It always had a residence known as the 'Island House'. But its main feature was a bathing pond, (the island was also known as the bathing island), some 30 metres in length and sloping gently from a shallow end to a depth of 2 metres. The pool - enclosed by wooden stakes and tree stumps with a shed as a changing room - was safer for swimming than the sea between the Island and the East Wall Road which had a dangerous current on the ebb tide. At low tide it was possible to wade across but when the tide was in, the 'Bathing Island Ferry Barge' operated between the Island and the wharf and a wooden causeway led from the Ferry's landing place to the Island House. Also, in the same way as today's Bull Island, ornithologists frequented the Island in pursuit of their favourite hobby. The Island flourished as a recreational haven mainly in the last years of the 18th century and in the first few decades of the 19th century. One could say that today's Bull Island merely perpetuates a tradition of Clontarf always providing Dublin citizens with a recreational Island.

Isolation

Clontarf Island had other uses too. Dublin, like all medieval cities, suffered many times from plague. Between 1204 and 1604 there were eighteen deadly plagues in the city - epidemics of cholera, bubonic plague, smallpox and fever. 'Black-Death' was the name given at the time for many pestilences. This may or may not have been the correct term for all the ailments to which it was applied. Clontarf Island was at times used by people fleeing from the scourge of the 'Black-Death'. But it was more often used as a place of isolation or quarantine for people suffering from plague or fever. Dublin Corporation especially used the Island for this purpose during one of the worst outbreaks of plague ever to afflict the city in 1650.

Like Bull Island in later years we know that Clontarf Island was used for duelling. A famous incident concerning duelling and the Island is recorded in the 'Book of Howth'. The story goes that Nicholas St. Lawrence, Lord of Howth, entertained Sir James Butler to a meal at his mother's residence in Killester about the year 1492. This was the period when the Geraldines and the Butlers (the top two Anglo-Irish Ascendancy dynasties at the time) had been at considerable variance. (They actually had managed a 'reconciliation' to the extent that their two leaders, Sir James Butler and the Earl of Kildare shook hands through an opening in a closed door of St. Patrick's Cathedral!) Feelings still ran very high and Lord Howth resented some attacking remarks which Butler made on the Earl of Kildare during the meal. Lord Howth angrily replied "I swear by our Lady of the North Church of Howth that Butler nor wine-drawer, not tapster is not in Ireland but I daren't stand to defend this quarrel, and if your Lordship is so stomached, and would ease your heart, let us both take a boat and go to yonder Island of Clontarf, there to easy your stomach or mine, for our companies here are not indifferent." Butler, however, did not accept the challenge and stormed out of the house in a fury stating that Lord Howth's 'stout and bullish nature' would bring about his early death.

We have reason to believe that the Danes used the Island as a focal point for their ships and most likely found it convenient for organising their sea forces before the Battle of Clontarf. Indeed the Island would have been a fine vantage point from which to view the thick of the battle at the mouth of the Tolka. Clontarf Island was a place of work also. Fishing nets were repaired there and various kinds of sea craft 'wintered', out of the tides reach. Towards the end of the Island's life a Dublin City publican of Beaver Street named Christopher Cromwell who was fond of fishing, spent much of his spare time on the Island as a tenant of the Vernon Family. (The ownership of the Island remained in the same name as the entire Clontarf estate and castle.) Some accounts, which suggest that the Island was at some stage granted to a Captain Cromwell a kinsman of Oliver the 'Lord Protector' and that this Christopher Cromwell was a descendant, bear no real weight. That this last occupant of Clontarf Island was named Cromwell is nothing more than coincidence. Cromwell built a wooden 'summer residence type of hut' on the Island for £45 where he often spent a week at a time. This habit was to cost him his life.

Storm
On the night of October 9th, 1844 probably the greatest storm ever recorded in this country, lashed the east coast of Ireland, raging particularly furiously in the port of Dublin. The south easterly storm that night literally washed Clontarf Island into the sea. A police constable on duty and watching from the nearest safe point saw the light go out in Cromwell's Island house at 10 p.m. Next day when the storm subsided the bodies of Cromwell and his ten year old son William were found on the Island shore - the heavy fishing boots they wore prevented them from being swept out to sea. Their boat and other boats had been carried by massive waves up to Annesley Bridge. Their wooden hut had been shattered and swept off the Island to be dashed against the embankment of the Great Northern Railway, where it crossed the sea. The embankment had only been built the previous year, 1843. It thus endured its most severe test while still a 'baby'. The railway line crossed the open sea then as Fairview Park had not yet been reclaimed.

In reality the storm only finished off the destruction of the Island as it was being gradually eroded by locals constantly carting away its sand. Indeed much of the Island that featured in the 17th and 18th century maps had vanished when Captain Bligh drew his map of Dublin Bay in 1800. Part of the sand, with a mixture of mud, was used as fertiliser. The Island had a gravel base and as the use of concrete grew, the Island began to diminish. Slowly, horses pulled cartload after cartload of gravel away. At low tide they made the journey to and from the mainland at Clontarf. At high tide iron and wooden barges came from the Liffey to be filled. The Island also provided gravel for the pioneering use of concrete by Bindon Blood Stoney in the construction of the Alexandra basin in the middle of 19th century. The construction of the Bull Wall also helped the demise of the Island in that it prevented fresh sands form drifting towards Fairview. For a considerable time after the great storm of 1844 the outline of the Island could still be distinguished, especially at low tide, by its stoney surface, its slightly higher elevation than its surroundings and by the remains of some wooden structures in the form of a few posts or stakes on its western extremity, the site of Cromwell's wooden hut. The entire site of the Island has, long since, been swallowed up by reclamation in the docks of Dublin.

Needless to say we look back with a mixture of horror and anger at the generation who allowed such a unique and historic little Island to be literally carted away. A feeble effort was made as late as 1883 to preserve, the by then, little remains of the Island. The Port and Docks Board erected notices at several points along the Clontarf Road prohibiting, under penalties, the removal of sand from the Island. It was the classic case of closing the door after the horse had bolted. In any case the prohibition appears to have been enforced only against those who neglected to pay for sand they removed. It was certainly wanton destruction and unlike today there were no organised groups around to clamour for its protection. In this respect, at least, the North Bull Island has friends who have managed to secure legislation - however inadequate - to ensure its protection. Clontarf Island was but a small part of Dublin Bay.The site of which lies beneath the area today occupied by the East Point Business Park and surrounds.

However it is alarming to notice the gradual devouring of the natural amenity that is Dublin Bay by the spread of the Dock's area, which has changed and will further change the entire sea scape around Clontarf.

The North Bull Island

Clontarf appears to have always liked the presence of a companion in the form of an offshore Island - like an offspring! When the old Clontarf Island disappeared into the bosom of the sea in the great storm of October 1844. Clontarf had a ready made replacement in the fast accumulating sandbank we have come to know as the North Bull Island. In its early years the Island was often referred to by locals as "Oileán na gCorr" (Herring Island) because of the profileration of the Herring bird there. To this day there remains a colony of Herrings on the Island. Part of the northern end of the Bull Island is not Clontarf "territory" as its postal address is Raheny. The history of this unique Island is not a long one - the Island is a little over 200 years old. Strictly speaking it is no longer an Island since it is joined to the mainland by means of two access routes - the old wooden bridge and the more recent Causeway Road. As the Island is, perhaps, Clontarf's most documented and written about topic, it is not my purpose to try to ascertain much that is new but rather to record the main existing data regarding the Island. To date over one hundred works have been published on aspects of the Island's fauna and flora. It is the most written up Island of all around our coast. Scientific papers, books, articles and theses have been written about the Island on subjects such as "The fleas of the North Bull Island". and "Nitrogen Fixation and Water Relations in a Dune Lichen". Most is material compiled by scientific specialists generally dwelling on just one aspect of the Island's natural history. The Island is often described as "a gift from the sea".

Situation and Size

The North Bull Island, a low lying sandspit, is situated very close to the Clontarf mainland in the northern half of Dublin Bay and runs parallel to the shore. Including lagoon, mudflats saltmarsh, dunes, foreshore and offshore areas it covers some 1500 hectares of the bay and is constantly growing by accretion. It is 4.85 kilometres long running along the coast in a north easterly direction between Clontarf and Sutton. Its maximum width is 1000 metres. On the south side it is bounded by the North Bull Wall. On the north, Sutton Creek separates it from the Howth Peninsula. The Clontarf, Raheny, Kilbarrack, Bayside and Sutton shore line form its western boundary while to the east is the extensive Dollymount Strand and open sea. The shape of the Island tapers from south to north. It is the largest public park in Dublin run by the City Council's Parks Department.

History of the Growth of the North Bull Island

(a) The Background

The development of the North Bull Island represents by far the most spectacular growth in land around our coast in relatively recent history. To trace the reasons for the phenomenal growth of this low-lying, dune-covered sandspit we must look at the development of Dublin port itself.
Old Dublin Harbour was divided into two strands - the North Bull Strand and the South Bull Strand. These were extensive sand flats at low tide and the North and South Bulls were separated by the combined estuaries of Dublin's drainage rivers - the Tolka, the Liffey and the Dodder. One thousand or so years ago the port of Dublin was just a muddy estuary where these rivers contended in vain with the tide. The interaction of these rivers with the sea and the sand it brought in caused the two great sandbanks to be formed one to the north and one to the

south. Two maps of the Port of Dublin one by Thomas Phillips in 1685 and another by Captain Greenval Collins in 1686, show a huge expanse of sand across Dublin Bay from Sutton to Dun Laoghaire. Both cartographers marked the North and South sides of this expanse as the North Bull and the South Bull respectively. These are certainly some of the earliest records of the use of the name 'bull' and we are told that the name most likely came from the fact that the sandbanks were so called because of the roaring of the surf on the exposed sands especially in stormy weather - resembling the bellowing of a bull. Bull, also, may possibly by a derivation of the term 'ball' meaning an offshore sand bank.

In 1590 the depth of the Liffey river opposite the two quays then in use varied from one to two metres. Whereas Viking boats were content with a little depth of water, as centuries passed, boats became narrow in the beam and deep in the water and thus the Liffey estuary presented great difficulty for navigation. In 1649, for example, vessels drawing one and a half metres could not get farther up the river than Ringsend. The river channel through or between the two 'bulls' was constantly silting up and thus the harbour bar was most dangerous. The birth and growth of the Bull Island was a direct result of efforts made in the 18th and 19th centuries to improve the port of Dublin and to create a worthy port for the city. For example by the 17th century it was necessary to have proper navigational facilities for the importation of coal alone, as Dublin city had by then become totally dependent on imported coal. In reality this meant (1) deepening the channel, as ships were being ruined. (2) improving the approach by removing the sandbar and (3) creating shelter for vessels.

Principal among these improvements was the construction of the two great walls, the South Bull Wall and the North Bull Wall. It is particularly from the erection of the great South Wall that the growth of the Bull Island became noticeable. Basically the construction of, first, the South Bull Wall caused an alteration in the pattern of currents in Dublin Bay and led to part of the sandbank known as the North Bull to appear above high tide as the North Bull Island. Indeed the erection of the South Wall may also have been responsible for the disappearance of certain promontories on the Clontarf Coast - such as 'Cockle point', 'The Furlong', and 'Cold Harbour'.

(b) The South Bull Wall

The original South Bull Wall - known as 'The Piles' was begun as early as 1715 and completed in 1730. It was built by driving oak piles through the sand into the gravel and boulder clay in the bay. These piles were reinforced by kishes (or baskets) filled with gravel, and by wattles. It was really a wooden jetty. It was built across the South Bull, from Ringsend in Dublin Bay for about 5 kilometres to the eastern limit of low water. Much of the gravel for its construction was taken by boat from Clontarf. The wall helped provide some shelter for ships to anchor and stopped some sand from drifting into the navigational channel. But the piles rotted (with the help of seawater worms) and storms breached the wall and once again sands encroached.

In 1761 it was decided to replace 'the Piles' with a stone pier. In that year work began at the seaward end and by 1768 Poolbeg Lighthouse was completed. The wall was constructed with great granite blocks which were quarried and cut in Blackrock and Dalkey and ferried across the bay in barges. No bonding material was used as the mass of their own weight held the rocks together. As the wall was being constructed gravel and sand were dredged from the channel at the rate of 100,000 tons per year and some of this was used to fill in the wall. Estimates indicate that thirty two million tons were removed from the harbour in an effort to deepen it. The work was completed in 1795.

The effect of building the great South Wall was to straighten the river channel somewhat and create a wash or scour of water. The great South Wall is about 18,000 feet long from Ringsend to Poolbeg. It is one of the longest such walls in Europe.

While the completion of the South Wall was hailed as an engineering feat without parallel, improvement of access to the port itself was not drastically improved. The channel was still found to be unsuitable - not being deep or wide enough for ships. It was still found that boats requiring a depth of more than one and a half metres couldn't come right into port in Dublin. Thus the inconvenient practice of using deeper outlying pools - e.g. Clontarf pool, Poolbeg and Salmon pool, - for anchorage and taking cargoes ashore on small boats continued.

(c) The Birth of the Bull Island

During and after the construction of the South Wall it came to the attention of the Ballast Board that an area of the North Bull began to increase in size, height and extent above high tide. The Board Secretary, Richard Broughton, noted this in a letter to the Directors General of Inland Navigation in Ireland in 1801[2]. But the erection of the South Bull Wall, alone, did not explain the ensuing phenomenal growth of the Bull Island.

An experiment carried out at the time by Captain Daniel Corneille an engineer for the Ballast Board, (at the request of the Directors General) recognised a local sea water movement as greatly helping the growth of the Island. He observed that in various movements of sand carried into Dublin Bay by waves and wind, the sand was first drifted towards Sutton, then in the flood tide the sand was carried northwards directly upon the North Bull and lastly in a north west direction towards Clontarf. This tidal movement is explained by the main flow northwards of the rising tide in the Irish Sea. Captain Corneille's experiment investigating the tidal currents in the northern part of Dublin Bay also explains why the Bull remained detached from the mainland. Writing in the year 1803 (approx). He stated: "A very great proportion of the tide flows into the harbour by Sutton Creek, round the northward side of the Bull along the Clontarf shore, and its influence is seen so far up in the harbour as the back of Clontarf Island. Now upon the return of the tide (or ebb) a great body of water escapes and runs out through the channel at the back or northward of the North Bull by Sutton Creek, from the time of high water until the half-ebb, after which time its passage is prevented by the height of the sand in the channel opposite or near "Cold Harbour". (Cold Harbour was a coastal spot along the seafront at present day Dollymount). This tidal current in the channel also created the slob or mudflat, which was the forerunner of the salt marsh on the north side of the Island. For many centuries the city's waste, including sweepings from the streets, was consigned to the Liffey for removal by the retreating tide. The southward flowing ebb carried the waste deposits towards Killiney where it was met by the rising tide and carried across the bay towards Howth. The incoming tide then carried it up Sutton Creek and into the north channel. By now the waste matter had become soft ooze (or loam) and was carried to the strand between Ballybough and Sutton Creek. The actual amount of ooze deposited must have been ever increasing during the 19th century as the city grew. (The city's present drainage and sewage system was only completed in 1906.) In 1868 the Corporation granted a concession to Messrs Barrington and Jeffries for the disposal of city sewage at the sand and sloblands of the North Bull to help reclaim that area. However the coastal landlords - The Vernons of Clontarf Castle, Benjamin Lee Guinness of St. Anne's and Lord Howth - objected and defeated the idea.)

The Island thus grew due to the configuration of currents in Dublin Bay and was aided and abetted by the erection of first the South Bull Wall and later the North Bull Wall. The Island formed on top of a system of ridges and runnels on the sand bank of the North Bull - which itself was basically formed over long years of sand deposits accumulating below sea level until it reached the high water level. The Island proper appeared with the emergence of the most landward of the ridges of the North Bull. Further development occurred due to the (already referred to) prevailing current which developed the North Bull into a trap where all sediment particles became trapped - cobbles, pebbles, granules, sand, silt, clay and loam. As more and more sediment accumulated in the area, much wind-blown, the first intertidal ridge built above the high tide level. Eventually grasses colonised the sand and grass- stabilised dunes formed.

Once the super tidal sand-bank had been established its growth direction was dictated by the combination of current direction, wave direction, wave energy, the amount of sediment available and water depth. The Bull Island grew parallel to the shore south-westwards an north-eastwards. South-westerly growth was halted by the construction of the North Bull Wall but growth continued towards Sutton Creek, assisted by dominant wave-fronts flowing from the south/south-east.

The actual growth of the North Bull Island is quite well tabulated. All experts agree that the first sand dune of about 1800, from which the Island has grown, unquestionably developed on the edge of the slob which had formed from the city's ooze on the highest part of the North Bull Strand. On a map of Dublin Bay made by Captain William Bligh[3] in December 1800 the Bull Island is first represented on a map as a small 'bump' of dry land just off shore from Baymount Castle (now Manresa House). This small dry oval patch on top of a huge sandbank had, by 1804, become 'a considerable stripe'. The growth was of course due to the influence of the South Bull Wall. By 1819 the "stripe" was about one kilometre long. Since then evidence from observation via ordinance survey maps and aerial photographs record the constant growth of the Island area, and its changing shape. In 1837 the Island consisted of the area now occupied by the Royal Dublin Golf Club with a small marsh. In 1837 the first O.S map of the area was drawn and the Bull Island is recorded as fifty hectares (approx) with three extra islets. The Admiralty Chart of 1838 indicated that the highest point of the Island had reached seven and a half metres above low water or about three and a half metres above high water. In 1843 the head of the Island extended north a little beyond the present causeway. By 1847 the Island had grown to about half its present length. By 1869 a new 'green isle' had been formed about 150 metres offshore of the northern tip of the Bull Island. However by 1902 the Island had reached its present length and subsequent growth has caused an increase in width rather than length. Since about 1936 a series of parallel ridges have noticeably added to its width - with rapid growth more pronounced at the southern end. Today the Island increases in size each year towards the open sea as each tide brings fresh sands, and it is obviously still very much in the developing stages.

(d) The North Bull Wall

As we have outlined, much of the growth of the North Bull Island was due to port improvements, especially the construction of the two great harbour walls which were built to increase the 'scour' of the Liffey. After being given responsibility for improving Dublin harbour in 1799 the Directors General sought expert advice from eminent marine specialists as to what improvements could be made to solve the main problems of lack of shelter, lack of depth and the problem of the sand bar blocking the mouth of the port. Among the specialists who submitted proposals to the Directors General was Captain William Bligh R.N who was commissioned to carry out a survey of the bay. Captain Bligh showed his undoubted skill with a beautiful map and detailed report which he submitted to the authorities in January 1801. He proposed the erection of the Bull Wall but his proposal was not accepted.

Bligh was not however, contrary to popular belief, the first to suggest the idea of the North Bull Wall. Such a project had, in fact, been proposed as far back as 1786 by an English engineer called William Chapman whose proposal was later supported by Captain Daniel Corneille. The idea of the wall was simply a practical method of overcoming the stubborn problem of improving the approach to Dublin Port which over the centuries had grown to become the chief importing centre for the county. Even after the completion of the South Wall the shallow approaches to the port left the quays totally inaccessible to deep-sea ships which had to anchor out in the open estuary[4]. It was a navigational hazard to cross the sand bar at the entrance to the channel, especially after the building of the South Bull Wall. The purpose, therefore, of constructing the North Bull Wall was 'for making the harbour a secure station for trade and improving the approach to it'. It was envisaged that such a wall on the northern side of the harbour would prevent the sands of the growing North Bull from encroaching onto the Clontarf foreshore and would also concentrate the outgoing tide across the bar. It was hoped that the resulting natural scour between the two walls would deepen the river and its approaches without the assistance of any other works.

Financial considerations delayed the building of the mole for some time. But in 1814 the Ballast Board sold the Pigeon House to the British Army for £100,183 to serve as a fort and were thus in a financial position to go ahead with the construction of the Bull Wall breakwater. From the start the wall was officially designated 'The Great North Wall' but became popularly termed the 'Bull Wall'. In 1818 Giles and Halpin (for the Ballast Board) prepared a plan for a groyne to extend from the Clontarf shore to the north spit of the Poolbeg. On a map, prepared by Giles in 1819 the Bull Island is represented as spear shaped and about 3 kilometres long. Giles marked it on the map 'Sand Island', but later referred to it as 'The Green or Bull Island'. Giles determined the site for the new wall on a more direct line to the spit Buoy than originally proposed by Broughton in 1801.

 Construction of the 'great dyke' actually began in 1820 and was completed in 1823 at a total cost of £95,000. We are told that much of the labour during the project was carried out by convicts who, we are informed, endured torturous hardships in bringing stone, for its construction, in barges from Dalkey. It was built on a base about 25 metres wide constructed by piling boulders on top of each other in a long strip. Some were also drawn in carts from local quarries. The wall is 2,750 metres long in all - from the shore to the lighthouse. 1,680 metres of this - from the wooden Bull Bridge to just beyond the Realt na Mara statue - is approximately 7 metres high and remains above water at all tidal stages. At high tide the water reaches about half way up its sloping side. Beyond the monument the wall stretches for another 1,070 metres but at a lower level. It is known as the 'half tide wall' and the sea covers it at high tide. The tide drops below this section of the wall midway through the ebb tide, so that for the second half of the outgoing tide the water is forced out between the two lighthouses - the North Bull and Poolbeg. Silting on the Island side of the pier has left the sand at a higher level than on the Dublin City side.

The result of the building of the Bull Wall was in effect the forcing of the tidal scour to cut a channel across the bar and thus prevent Dublin Bay from silting up. For some years dredging went on but nowadays with a depth of up to 9 metres at low water the scour itself has had no dredging effect for many years. The sand dislodged from the bar was carried further out into the bay where it was picked up by currents which then deposited it on the North Bull bank. This helped the growth of the Island together with the fine sand carried by the rising tide coming up the Irish coast from the large banks off Wicklow and Wexford. This 'south tide' previously deposited its sands on the coast from Fairview to Clontarf. But the South Bull Wall diverted the tidal current towards Howth and its sand was deposited on the highest point of the North Bull. The currents also collected the sludge from the city sewers as well as the flotsam and jetsam of the three main Dublin rivers,[5] The Bull Island had ample 'food supplies' to grow rapidly!

The North and South Bull Walls, confining Dublin harbour, have been a brilliant success. They represent a triumph for civilisation in producing an outstanding example of natural tidal scour controlled to act as an agent in removing river bars. The walls shut off and render harmless hundreds of acres of useless muddy spaces while at the same time keeping open a navigational channel 1,000 feet wide between those familiar landmarks in Dublin Bay - the North Bull and Poolbeg lighthouses. (The North Bull lighthouse is controlled from the larger Poolbeg lighthouse.) The terminal portion of the Bull Wall recedes to the shore in a north-westerly direction. It originally left a huge area of the bay as an open space on the north side. However much of this has been closed, little by little, by reclamation and by the gradual extension of the docks area.

(e) The Bull Bridge
The old wooden Bull Bridge, a familiar landmark to so many people, was for a very long time the only means of access from the Clontarf mainland to the Bull Island. Constructed first in the Autumn of 1819 to facilitate the building of the Bull Wall itself, the bridge represented a fundamental change in the original plan in that the wall could not reach the shore and interfere with the tidal flow. The bridge, first known as Crab Lake Bridge, was a timber structure from the start and was built under separate contract from the wall itself. Giles made a case to leave 185 metres of the channel open between the wall and the shore. The first bridge was only a footbridge and it decayed gradually over the years and the present structure was built in 1906/07. It consists of an open lattice work of cross beams. The bridge is presently subject to a load restriction limiting its use to vehicles of laden weight not exceeding five tons and is also subject to a special speed limit of five miles per hour. The bridge has been renovated and upgraded a few times since and is now protected by a preservation order.

Geography of the North Bull Island

Basically the Bull Island can be divided into two areas - supra tidal and inter-tidal. Within these two areas six sections can be identified. The Island's ecosystem is different from most eco systems due to the Island's unusual 'birth', its sandy base and its unique vegetation.
1) Dollymount Strand. This is the famous north city beach 4.85 kilometres long. It is a beach with sands varying between gravel and very fine. It runs the whole length of the Island and varies in width (at low water) from 880 metres at the Bull Wall to 620 metres at St. Anne's Golf Clubhouse
2) The Dune Complex. The supra tidal part of the Island is the backbone of dune ridges. The ridges run parallel to the beach line. The dunes are about 900 metres wide at the Bull Wall and taper off in the north-east to a recurved hook. The dunes comprise of a wind blown very fine sand. The average height of the dunes is 6-7 metres but they attain their maximum height of 10.21 metres at the northern end. The vegetation growing on the dunes plays a very important part in stabilising the mobile sand.
3) Landward of the Dune complex is a Salt Marsh. It is an area of fine sand and clay between the dunes and the lagoon. The areas of European shorelines near rivermouths and sheltered from wave action are covered by a very characteristic type of vegetation usually called 'saltmarsh' and with areas of mud next to it.

The Bull Island Salt Marsh is typical.

4) The Lagoonal Mud Flat is part of the northern lagoon adjacent to the Causeway Road. The mudflat has been deposited within the last fifty years and covers normal lagoon sand. It is about 5 centimetres thick. It owes its origin to the presence of the Causeway where the lack of current in the ebb-flow leaves materials taken in on the tide deposited in the lagoon. Sedimentation is taking place here continuously.

5) The Salicornia Flat gets it name from supporting dense stands of glasswort salicornia. It occupies some of the mud flat but is more elevated than the mud flat. It is an ever increasing area and will most likely become part of the adjoining salt marsh.

6) The Lagoonal Sand Flats occupy the largest part of the entire lagoon, and its sediment comprises of sand, silt and other organic matter formed from algae growing here.

The fact that Sutton Creek is a permanent channel means that Bull Island has reached its maximum length. But sand accumulating there has meant that the northern end of the Island has built up a higher sand mass than elsewhere. Also, since 1902, three recurves have occurred to accommodate extra sand. The tide cycle is twice a day - high and low water. Thus parts of the intertidal flats and the beach are flooded with sea water twice in twenty four hours and then drained. It takes the tide 6 hours and 40 minutes to flow from low to high water while the ebb tide takes 5 hours and 40 minutes.

In the northeast end of the Island the distinct feature known as The Alder Marsh can be found. This is a slack between two dune ridges. It is the lowest point on the Island and has almost acquired the character of a fresh water marsh. On it a layer of peat has evolved. This represents the highest stage of evolution so far reached on the Island. The Alder Marsh is so called because of the 200 or so Alder trees growing there. It is about 700 metres by 70 metres.

The lagoon landward of the Island is divided into two by the Causeway Road. Each lagoon is emptied through a permanent channel. In the southern lagoon the flood tide enters beneath Bull Bridge. It fills the permanent channel which also acts as an outlet for the Naniken river. As the tide falls the water is conducted back south westwards under Bull Bridge. In the northern lagoon water is channelled in and out through Sutton Creek which also receives the water of the Santry River.

Ownership of the North Bull Island

Ownership of the Island originated in the Royal Charter granted by Charles II to the Vernon estate and related to tidal flats and other sections of the sea floor on the northside of Dublin Bay. It remained part of the Vernon Estate until 1930. In 1954 the Royal Dublin Golf Club bought the whole Island but in 1955 Dublin Corporation acquired the entire Island exclusive of Royal Dublin's own links and the area owned by Dublin Port and Docks Board. Currently three owners are involved in the ownership of the Bull Island.

1) The Royal Dublin Golf Club owns its own links which cover 66.7 hectares. The club acquired this land from Colonel Edward Vernon in 1889.

2) The Dublin Port and Company own a narrow strip of land adjoining the Bull Wall which was acquired before the erection of the Bull Wall in 1820. This covers about `10.5 hectares, including the Bull Wall itself and a small area adjacent to the Royal Dublin Golf Club which is used for maintenance purposes. The bridge and the seven Island cottages are the property of the Board also. To demonstrate its ownership of the bridge the Dublin Port Company close it to traffic one day each year. This however is changing and in September 2013 the Port Company announced its intention to transfer this area to Dublin City Council so it can become a full part of the public park and amenity that is Bull Island and the whole Island can be administrated as one unit for the benefit of the local community, Dubliners in general and visitors, from environmental, tourism and social inclusion points of view.

3) Dublin City Council own the rest of the Island (down to low water mark). The then Corporation acquired the Island in 1955 and it is treated as a public park. It is in the care of the parks department and is managed by that body for the use and benefit of the community. The Island area increases annually by accretion. St. Anne's Golf Club rent their 26.1 hectares links from Dublin City Council. The club first rented their playing area from the Royal Dublin Club in 1921, an agreement formally ratified in 1929.

The presence of two golf courses on the Island irritates many people. Firstly they feel that the entire Island should be at the disposal of Dubliners as an amenity. Secondly conservationists complain that golf clubs modify much of the dune coverings to create proper fairways. This involves the use of fertilisers and continuous mowing which produces a dry 'suburban lawn' type of landscape which is not at all characteristic of the natural vegetation of the North Bul!. It is also pointed out that apart from some furze bushes both courses are somewhat flat and plain and the planted pine trees (for visual relief) do not fit in to the habitat.

BUILDINGS ON THE NORTH BULL ISLAND
Inhabitants on the Island occupy seven houses (or cottages) originally built as coastguard dwellings for harbour police (and such as tug boat operators) to guard against pirates and smugglers. (A coastguard brick house station known as 'The Crane' stood for many years opposite the Royal Dublin clubhouse from where a look out was kept on sea traffic using the famous brass telescope.) Each of the houses has six rooms and a two roomed cellar. The cellars were used for storing boating tackle. The Island inhabitants are very familiar with the often harsh south-westerly gales. Traditionally a harbour policeman is responsible for traffic crossing the wooden bridge. He is mainly preoccupied with ensuring that no very heavy traffic uses the bridge because of the danger of the wooden supports collapsing. For 'individuality of identity' some of the Islands residents consider it complimentary to be referred to as 'Islanders'. Each house once had a plot of ground where much intensive gardening was carried on. But this ground is now the Royal Dublin Golf Clubs 18th hole - not surprisingly named 'the garden hole'. The only other buildings on the Bull Island - apart from bathing shelters, lifeguard huts, public toilets, the statue monument, the North Bull lighthouse and the sea scouts pavilion - are the two golf club houses and the building housing the Interpretive Centre.

Conserving the Island

Being just over 200 years old, new plants and animals are constantly arriving to colonise the Bull. One of the facts that make the Island unique is that, as it exists only for such a short time, it has been possible to detail and graph the growth of each sand dune ridge and follow the sequence of its evolution. Fundamentally a sandspit, the Island is always changing and is always an exciting place. The first time visitor to the Island would be very foolish to dismiss the place on first impressions - as the Island gives the impression of being a desert-like, barren, insignificant, weed infested, windswept and bleak wilderness of sand....unhospitable and isolated. On the contrary the Island offers a fascinating combination of habitats rich with plant and animal life. Conservationists and general lovers of the Island want long term rigid and permanent legislation giving everlasting peace to the fauna and flora of the Island. They want legislation specifically drafted for the Island to ensure its protection as an amenity area, a nature reserve and a bird sanctuary[6]. However, annually renewed ministerial orders are the extent of government 'protection' of the Island to date. These are: The protection of birds act 1930 in which the minister of Justice (and later other ministers) has annually made ministerial orders declaring the North Bull Island, its lagoon and mudflats to be a bird sanctuary. The local government planning and development act of 1963, especially sections 42 and 43 under which Dublin Corporation has made a special Amenity Area Order in the context of Dublin Bay and including the Bull Island. Section 15 of the 1974 Wildlife Bill concerns itself with Reserves and would be relevant to the Island but it has not yet been enacted. (Since 1977 the Island is also protected under the Wildlife Act 1976, when the Island was declared a no-shooting area.)

The 1933 Foreshore Act covers the Island but is not really relevant.

The bye-laws made by Dublin Corporation and operating on North Bull Island are in accordance with the Open Spaces Act 1906. Legislative protection for the Island is thus discretionary in that an annual Ministerial Order is required to protect the bird sanctuary and maintain its status. Also a sub-section of the Special Amenity Area Order made by Dublin Corporation in respect of Dublin Bay, relating to the Bull Island requires to be renewed in each five yearly revision of the city plan. It is fair to say that such an unusual and unique place as the Bull Island surely deserves permanent protection for the sake of the generations who will come and go and experience all the Island has to offer. It is an expanse of land readily available and accessible to the city masses, and yet is so remote in its feeling. As well as being a prime amenity area for Dubliners the Island is ready made as an educational and scientific study area. This is the central importance of the Island - the unique combination of its values and its immediate proximity to a densely populated area.

Wildlife and Vegetation on the North Bull Island

(a) Birds of the Bull Island

The Bull Island can only be described as an ornithologist's paradise. Because of its favoured position the Island has become the haunt of many many birds. The bird watchers are at their busiest in winter when about 30,000 birds, of various species, winter on the mud flats after migrating from the Artic. The birds have unquestionably helped to give the Island a special character and a popular appeal. The Island gets more attention from bird-watchers than any other bird watching 'centre' in the country. Indeed to the true bird lover the real importance of the North Bull Island lies in the food and shelter it provides for a variety of birds. The Island is a bird sanctuary of international importance, especially for wader and wild fowl. This gives international responsibilities in that the Bull Island sanctuary has one of the greatest densities in Europe of over wintering waders and wild-fowl. The Bull Island has international importance for Brent Geese, Grey Plovers, Curlews, Bar-Tailed Godwits, Redshanks and Knots. It is nationally important for Wigeon, Pintail, Shoveler, Shelduck, Oyster Catchers and Dunlins. The freedom from shooting, which the Island affords them, is a very significant factor in the conservation of birds[7].

Wildfowl species occur on the North Bull in a seasonal pattern. Many of them breed in Northern Europe and Greenland and come south in the autumn as food and climate begin to deteriorate. The Bull Island is a crucial link in this north-south migration of birds as it provides a base for a wide variety of birds (some very rare) who use it as a staging ground to build up reserves for further travel. After our summer when the biggest variety of birds can be seen, the Bull Island is like an international airport for birds. The joy of the birdwatcher is to pick out the one that is different from the flock, even vagrant birds, thrown off course by weather conditions.

From late November to early February, when the tide is out, the mud feeding area is darkened by great packs of wildfowl. Geese and Dabbing Duck are the most conspicuous birds on the Island. The Brent Geese are, for many observers, the 'darlings' of the Bull. Everyone seems to herald their arrival as a milestone in the year. Familiar by their V-shaped flying column the Brent Geese breed in summer in Artic Canada and Greenland and about 1,000 of them come to Bull Island for our winter, a distance of 3,000 miles. They stay in families of adults and young until the following Spring. Dublin is about the only place in the world, where one can observe these birds from the top of a city double decker bus. The Brent Geese breed closer to the North Pole than any other species of goose and all but a few species of birds. They arrive usually in late October. The feed on the zostera plant or eel grass. They leave again about the end of April.

The ducks are there in their hundreds - Shelduck, Wigeon, Teal, Pintail, Shoveler and Mallard. Wigeon nest in Iceland, Scandanavia or Russia. Teal, Shoveler and Pintail breed across much of North West Europe. Shelduck nest in Ireland - but leave in huge flocks temporarily to moult in Heligoland. The Teal and Shoveler are first to come to the Bull Island each season - in August. Wigeon and Pintail arrive from early September. From then on all species arrive on their turn - the Shelduck in late October, just before the Brent Geese. The dedicated bird watcher may be rewarded by spotting a rare bird among the arriving masses - a White Fronted or a Pink Footed Goose or maybe a few Gadwall Ducks.

The wader birds are the most numerous group of the Island's avifauna, numbering about 24,000. Most of these are carnivores and feed on the abundant animal life in the mud. They include Knots, Dunlins, Plovers, Sanderlings, Curlews and Redshanks. They must have good food in order to grow a proper set of flight feathers after moulting each year. The Bull Island also has its share of seabirds. Shags and Cormorants are common off the strand. Razorbills,

Guillemots, Fulmars and Terns are also regulars. Great Black-Backed, Black-Headed, Common and Herring Gulls are there all the year round. Lesser Black-Backed Gulls are regular in summer but migrate south in winter. Two common species of diver birds are to be found in the open sea, off the strand - the Great Northern and the Red-Throated. The shore birds use the two habitats- the mudflats and the saltmarsh. They feed on the mudflats, when the tide is out, so that twice a day, at high tide, they must find dry land to rest. They cannot waste energy in extra unnecessary flying. The saltmarsh with its all round visibility is good for resting. Indeed the Island provides a very safe roosting and digesting area for the entire shorebird population which feeds in Dublin bay - while the mudflats are a feeding area for a large part of that population.

The great flocks of birds remain on the Bull Island well into February. Each week sees a change in the number of each species present. The rich and varied feeding base provided by the mudflats supports these thousands of birds each day. And all the birds of various breeds have different types of bills and different ways of feeding so they don't get in each others way. As the tide comes in and out twice each day and covers the feeding grounds, they eat whenever the tide is low - even at night. Then they roost on the saltmarsh. The Island is more important as a wader haunt than as a duck haunt but the waders do not nest on the Island - it is primarily a feeding, roosting and preening ground. In fact it is only when the enormous dense flocks - of all different species - settle together to roost that the observer can really appreciate the great numbers involved. In February the flocks begin to decrease in size and coast towards their breeding grounds in the Artic. Some travel as far as Siberia, others to Canada, with the majority finding nesting places in between. Many land birds may also be viewed on the Island, - including birds of prey such as Owls, Kestrels, Sparrowhawks, Peregrines and Raptors. Numerous Woodpigeons, Skyhawks, Magpies, Crows and Linnets can also be seen.

It is the fact that the Island is a bird sanctuary that makes it so important - and it is a sanctuary only because of its wealth of wildfowl and waders. It was established as a sanctuary in 1931 and as such the birds enjoy close time conditions all the year round. It means that all bird catching, shooting and taking of eggs are forbidden. One could argue that the lack of shooting has led to the birds becoming quite tame. The early departure of so many wildfowl at the beginning of February coincides with the end of the shooting season - suggesting that security from shooting is one of the factors which attracts ducks to the Bull in such numbers. Certainly the continued status of the Island as a sanctuary seems certain to lead to the present trend of a very high density of wildfowl population wintering there. Also the general lack of disturbance for roosting, preening, sleeping and resting afforded by the Island is very attractive, especially to the waders. And the feeding habitat is excellent - on a short visit to the Island any day one can observe the birds feeding assiduously. Perhaps we need to protect the Bull Island as one of North West Europe's most suitable estuaries for bird support. This means preventing industrialisation and reclamation from ruining the Islands feeding grounds. Their aesthetic presence, alone, enhances the whole city, with their proximity. For now the yearly establishment of the sanctuary means adequate protection, adequate food, and a resting and nesting place for all the Island's birds. It affords the genuine ornithologist a chance of studying the habits and migrations of birds. It provides an opportunity to save threatened species from extermination.

(b) Mammals on the Bull
Birds are very mobile and can colonise a new habitat very quickly. Most other animals are sedentary and move only when forced or by chance passage. This was what happened in the famous case of the 'Bull Island Mouse' which gave the Island world wide scientific fame. A Mr. Lyster Jameson, near the end of the last century, discovered a species of mouse on the Island which was pale and sandy coloured and quite unlike the normal house mouse which is greyish brown. It was immediately assumed that a new sandy coloured mouse species had evolved to give it more protection from the predators by being of similar colour to the Island's sand. However this 'new mouse' soon proved to be a 'pretender' and not a valid species. It was merely the result of inbreeding which caused the colour to change - probably only a very small number of mice arrived on the Island originally. The mouse was, nevertheless, nicknamed, "Mus Jamesonii"

As well as House Mice, Field Mice are abundant on the North Bull Island and these are no different from those on the mainland. The number of Irish Hare on the Island is high - but fluctuate. Hares are quiet animals but are often chased by dogs on the Bull. When the numbers of Hare on the Island were at their highest, suggestions were jokingly made, that the name of the Island should be changed from Bull Island to Hare Island.

Rabbits have colonised the Island since 1970. They are not too welcome as their burrowing can cause sand erosion. Rats, Foxes, Stoats, Badgers and Pigmy Shrews are other mammals that can be spotted on the North Bull Island.

(c) Shells
Common shells on the Bull Island are:
Bivales - the hinged double shells such as the Cockle.
Crustacea - from arthropods with hard shells, like the Crab and Lobster.

Polychaeta - from Annelid worms.
Mollusca - from soft bodied creatures with hard shells such as Limpets, Snails, Oysters and Mussels.

(d) Fauna of the Saltmarsh and Dune Complex
A collection of the fauna on the saltmarsh will include Mud Snails, Rough Winkes, Amphipods, Shorecrabs and Common Shrimps. Of the winged variety one will find the yellow and black Soldier Fly, the Rush Moth, the Midge, and the Cranefly (or Daddy Long Legs). Other species present include the Water Beetle, The Ground Spider, the Wolf Spider, the Jumping Bug, Beetles and Worms. On the dunes the 'regulars' one tends to find are the Large Black Slug, the Cuckoo Spit Bug, the Hoover Fly, the Ground Beetle, the Bee Fly and the Robber Fly. Regular visitors to the dunes will be familiar with the distinctive red and black Burnet Moth.

(e) Vegetation
The vegetation of the intertidal flats area of the Bull Island consists mainly of Glassworth, Gras-Wrack, Ruppia and Green and Brown Algae. The main Salt Marsh plants are Common Saltmarsh Grass, Sea Spurry, Sea Blite, Sea-Milkwort, Red Fescue, Sea Aster and Sea Arrow Grass. On the Dune Complex one cannot expect to find the same flora as in a normal field or garden - due to the porous, sandy nature of the soil which does not retain enough fresh water to support a 'mainland type' vegetation. Lack of adequate nitrogen also considerably limits the variety and growth of plants. A list of plants of the dunes include Sand Couchgrass, Marram Grass, Lyme Grass, Ragward, Calsear, Sea Spurge Field Speedwell, Whitlow Grass, Sand Dune Violets, Yellow Kidney Vetch, Pink Rest Harrow, Meadow Grass, Quacking Grass, Clover and Orchids. The Alder Marsh had its own distinctive Alder tree vegetation.

The North Bull Island as a Biosphere Reserve
In 1971 Unesco (United Nations Educational Scientific and Cultural Organisation) launched an ecological programme called 'man and biosphere'. It was aimed at conserving the earth's resources by improving man's relationship with his environment. As the premier international body responsible for education, science and culture, Unesco organised an international network of what are called biosphere reserves. These are areas which are internationally unique and have 'unusual' natural features. The reserves function as watchtowers for monitoring environmental changes. Each one is an important conservation area which contributes to education and research.

In November 1981 Unesco considered the North Bull Island of such importance (due to its great diversity of flora and fauna and its general ecological richness) that it named the Bull, as Ireland's first biosphere reserve, which ranks it in the same status as renowned reserves such as Yellowstone National Park in America and the Camargue National Reserve in France. It is one of only about 250 such reserves in the world in countries as diverse as Australia, Kenya, Chile and Thailand. Unesco declared the Bull a biosphere reserve in honour of its international importance to science, scientific research, and because of its educational and amenity value to Dublin. It is different from the other biosphere chain of reserves worldwide, in that it is the smallest and is so near the centre of a large city. It is also unique because it hasn't got the long term legal protection from its national parliament, normally a strict requirement for a biosphere reserve.

The North Bull Island Interpretive Centre

Just to the right of the Island end of the Causeway Road is an interpretive and visitor centre. It is an exhibition centre providing those interested, with adequate facilities to study the birds, flora, fauna and general history of the Bull Island. The centre acts as a watch tower for the bird watchers and has staff from Dublin City Council's Parks department. The centre is a kind of information bureau which provides information leaflets, videos and exhibitions. Experts lecture and tours are conducted. Members of the wildlife and conservation bodies help man the centre. It is a meeting place for various groups and in general provides environmentalists, students and the general public with a base from which to study the Island. The amenity, built by Dublin Corporation, was officially opened to the public on Sunday March 9th 1986 by Alderman Jim Tunney T.D. Lord Mayor of Dublin. £60,000 of the €200,000 overall cost of the project came as a grant from E.E.C. funds.

The Causeway Road

This connecting road between the mainland and Dollymount Strand was completed in 1964. The four lane 2.4 kilometre road sweeps from Watermill Road across the lagoon to a roundabout just short of the beach. The base of the road was constructed from dumped refuse.

The road was part of the Corporation's scheme to open up the "Sutton end" of Dollymount Strand to the public. In a decision taken by the Corporation in 1961, it was agreed to build this new road rather than adapt a proposed scheme to demolish the old wooden Bull Bridge and erect a new wider one. Up to then the only access to the beach was via the 'woodener' which the Corporation didn't own or control. But even in the 1950's, traffic had become so heavy on a fine

Sunday that the new wooden bridge couldn't cope and was almost impassable. Building the new road the Corporation hoped to attract the ever increasing volume of traffic streaming to the Island to it, and hoped the old route would be left to cyclists and pedestrians. The new road was a tremendous success in creating access to the entire Island - especially as its allows double decker buses to ferry people practically on to the strand, and home again. But for years before the Causeway road was built, arguments raged as to whether or not such a project would affect the level of water in the lagoon and cause silting. It was thought that a bridge would have been the proper answer, so to allow the tide to circulate, but on analysis it was realised that the tide filled the lagoon from both sides. At the meeting point of the tides the road was constructed.

An Foras Forbartha began a five year survey in 1979 to study the effects of the Causeway, if any, on the lagoon. The details of their survey released in April 1985 proved that although rapid silting did occur (after the causeway was built) to the north eastern side of the Island it slowed up after 1970 and became hardly noticeable. The Foras Forbartha investigation into the ecological effects of sediment at the Causeway Road, Bull Island, concluded that although the channel would narrow slightly there was absolutely no fear of it closing completely. It also concluded that no practical benefit would be gained by rejoining the two parts of the lagoon via a channel under the Causeway. However, a far more interesting find by the survey was that the explosive spread of spartina grass in the area will most likely greatly effect bird life on the Bull as it destroys their feeding grounds. The spread of spartina grass began in 1958, and was not a result of the construction of the Causeway. But the spread of the grass was aided by the structure and by the sandbanks the new road created. The real danger is that if the mud flats are destroyed by spartina grass the visiting birds will eventually give up using the Island as a winter ground and move further south.

Uses of the Bull Island
"Across the wooden bridge,
Above the flotillas of seabird and duck,
Under the swooping squadrons,
I go to you to say goodbye.
How many years have you given me sanctuary?
How often have I stumbled across to you,
Holding my mind like an aching limb;
And lain among your grasses and walked your sands,
Until the thunder of the surf vanquished despair
And my heart was hopeful with the song of birds?

Have you no other lovers
That men should heap excrement on you
Banish your birds and bury you
In a vault of stone and iron." **Kevin Faller**

The uses of the Bull Island, mainly recreational, are almost endless. Its proximity to over one million city dwellers (it just 7 kilometres from Dublin city centre) makes its extensive beach situated on the eastern side of the Island, a favourite haunt for Dubliners. With two access roads and 4.85 kilometres of a strand even the litter problems often experienced there cannot diminish Dollymount as a really attractive beach[8]. While on the beach, especially in summertime, the activities engaged in are many and varied. As many as 10,000 people can be on the Island on some fine summer days. This includes those using the facility as a public park, as a beach and the golfers.

One can simply appreciate the scenic seaside area for its own natural beauty and enjoy a day on the beach. One can enjoy a panoramic view of Howth and the Dublin Mountains, the spires, towers and chimneys of the city, Dublin harbour and its shipping and the mainland of Clontarf, Raheny, Kilbarrack, Bayside and Sutton. The water can be used for swimming, bathing, fishing or sailing. The beach itself is ideal for sunbathing in the summertime, for picnics and barbeque parties, for walking, jogging and running. Children can play, paddle and build sandcastles[9]. The Island is patrolled by wardens and Dublin City Council provide facilities or special zones for the various activities engaged in on the Island, and for special events. The dune complex is a public park with a difference - its natural character is quite distinct from the conforming landscaped environment of the regular urban park. And when weather conditions are unfavourable on the Bull Island people tend to make use of Clontarf's nearby more sheltered St. Anne's Park. In this way the Island and St. Anne's complement each other.

The importance of the Bull Island as an educational centre cannot be over stated. It is a natural environment set in the middle of a built up area - it is accessible, large and safe. The whole Island can rightly be described as an outdoor, living, ecological laboratory. The Island provides habitats of great ecological importance. Its sedimentology and geomorphology can be studied in detail. The beach area supplies ample scope for the study of living organisms being transformed into fossils..........even a variety of ripple marks can be examined. The whole Island is a major national scientific resource actively in use. It provides an exploration area for botanists, ecologists, marine biologists, insect hunters and natural historians. The very fact of its permanently changing physical form - its continuing growth, changes in soil type and plant cover, give scientists an exceptional interest in the Island and its purposes. Estimates suggest that 10,000 students a year study the development of the Bull Island.

As a scientific and educational workshop, then, the Bull Island is available to everyone to study. Surveys show that its greatest users are post-primary and third level students of Dublin City and county for areas of their Biology, Geography, Geology and Natural History curricula. In fact about 1,000 University students in Dublin each year have their degree courses in Biology and Earth Sciences associated with the Island. These range from excursions, to long term research. Teachers in the primary school system also, quite regularly, bring their classes for a day on the beach, or for some practical work on a field trip. Other amateur organised groups such as the Dublin Naturalists Field Club, the Irish Wildbird Conservancy and the Geographical Society of Ireland, use the facilities of the Bull Island for various projects. And conservationists and individual wildlife admirers simply like to visit the Island, walk around and appreciate all it has to offer. For ordinary everyday study - maybe just reading notes, or a book, - many like to find a little corner - 'a haven of tranquillity' - among the sand dunes of the Bull and study in the peaceful atmosphere provided, weather permitting of course! In the same way many writers, artists and poets use the Island. They find it the ideal retreat where the permeating peace, the sea breeze and the lapping waves remove them from regular everyday life and bring inspiration to the pen or brush. Many nature lovers like to simply retreat to the solitude the Island provides.

The hobbies practiced on the Bull Island are many, but ornithology must be the most popular. There is no better scope offered anywhere in the country for bird watching than the Bull with its thousands of birds. Bird watchers operate alone or in organised groups. Various individuals use the Island and the beach for activities as diverse as exercising the dog, learning to drive, shell collecting and kite flying. Basic orienteering is practiced. Sand yachts and small hovercraft can also be seen in use. Sailing Clubs such as Kilbarrack Sailing Club and Clontarf Yacht and Boat Club, use the Bull Island waters. Canoeing and water-skiing are also practiced, by among others, sea scout troops. Many sports are practiced on the beach including all kinds of football as well as tennis. And many dedicated sports people do much of their training on Dollymount Strand. The Bull Wall itself is ideal for a good healthy stroll and passing over the Bull Bridge, one normally encounters the leaning figures of rod fishers from the bridge trying to catch mackerel, trout, bass or whiting. Many courting couples use the Bull Island regularly. On fine summer nights when the shutters come down in the local hostelries lovers often head for the curves and hollows of the sand dunes. Many a courting couple have had the embarrassing experience of gazing too long into one another's eyes and allowed the tide to encircle their parked car! It is a rather face reddening experience to knock up some friends for help at an ungodly hour of the morning and explain just how a vehicle came to be stuck in several feet of water on Dollymount Beach!Historically the Bull Island has seen its share of smuggling. And when 'gentlemen' settled their differences, at dawn, with pistols, the Bull Island was a favourite choice of venue.

On the outbreak of World War 1, in September 1914, the British army commandeered the Bull Island, closed it to the public, festooned it with barbed wire and practiced trench warfare in the sand hills. It was used by the Hythe school, under the Hythe command, as a school of musketry for Ireland. Dubliners in general and locals especially sorely resented this usurpation of their heritage, The Easter Rising of 1916 led to the departure of most of these troops. Older Clontarfites recollect stories of a garrison of Volunteers on the Embankment 'Skew' bridge near Fairview ambushing troop reinforcements heading from the Bull Island to the city centre during the Rising. At the end of World War 1 the military vacated the Island. The broad outlines of some of their trenches can still be identified on the Island and bullets can still be unearthed in the saltmarsh.

Dollymount has witnessed its share of tragedies. There have been drowning's while swimming. Sea tragedies have occurred from yacht and boat accidents as well as fishing mishaps. Dollymount has experienced shipwrecks especially in the 18th and 19th centuries. More recently many Clontarfites will remember the plight of the Wexford built schooner 'Antelope' which was driven ashore on the North Bull in December, 1950 and destroyed. Suicides - jumping off the Bull Wall - have occurred. Bodies have been found dumped on the beach. In the past a notable death on Dollymount Strand was that of the eminent physician of the late eighteenth and early to middle nineteenth century Dublin, Doctor Richard Carmichael who had the distinction of having the Carmichael School of Medicine named after him. He died while crossing the strand on horseback in June 1849.

Curley's Hole

Curley's yard or fort is situated on the Royal Dublin Golf Course between the present 3rd and 13th fairways. A family named Curley once resided on the Island. In the Clontarf Boys N.S roll book for the year 1881 a John Curley of 'North Bull' is listed as a pupil with his parents occupation stated as 'herd'. The name 'Curleys Hole' was given to a killer hole in the nearby sea. This hole must have claimed the lives of many bathers over the years. The hole was formed by

the meeting of currents on both flood and ebb tides which caused a fatal whirlpool to be formed, which was not obvious from the shore. To make it an even more deadly trap its location changed almost weekly. The hole was so named after a Curley family member was drowned there with his horse. The writer James Joyce mentions it in his satirical poem "Gas from a Burner"
- *"Its a wonder to me upon my soul*
he forgot to mention Curley's Hole"

The Island is the property of the plain people and serves as a brilliant recreational facility - which, it can be justifiably argued, should be its prime purpose. Its rugged features offer the visitor free space to stroll, and its ecological complexities helps educate our youth. It has become part of Dublin and since its growth from 1800 it has changed the image of Clontarf in the 19th century by opening up the area as a seaside resort.

Statue of Our Lady of the Port of Dublin

The dominating monument at the seaward end of the supra-tidal part of the North Bull Wall with our Blessed Lady's (mother of Jesus Christ) statue on top is visible from all points of the port and indeed from the whole of Dublin bay. The idea of such a monument honouring Our Lady by giving her a commanding view of the entire port of Dublin, thereby imploring her to look after all who have dealings there, was first mooted by a cross section of port workers on a one day retreat at Roebuck (south Dublin) in 1950. After much fund raising, especially by a docker called Billy Nelson, the project took firm root. Dock workers contributed sixpences and shillings weekly to earn the 'guinea certificate' which to this day hangs honourably framed in thousands of Dublin homes. Checkers, carters, storemen and clerical workers in the port all contributed. Support also came from, among others, Guinness workers, the Gas Company, C.I.E and Dublin Port and Docks Board. The search for a proper site went on for some time around the bay, until finally agreement was reached on the present location. The monument consists of a tall concrete tripod - three solid concrete columns meeting at the top to form a resting place for the statue which is protectively facing in over the docks area. The foundation stone for the project was blessed by the papal personal legate (in Patrician year) Cardinal Gregory Agagonian on June 19th, 1961. The statue is called Our Lady of the Port of Dublin or Réalt na Mara. On Sunday September 24th 1972, the Feast of Our Lady of Mercy, his Grace the Archbishop of Dublin Most Reverend Dermot Ryan performed the solemn unveiling and blessing of the statue. At night the monument is floodlit and dominates the port skyline. It can be seen from many parts of the city as well as from far out to sea. It is a radiant beacon and a fitting reminder to all entering and leaving the port that Our Lady is watching over them.

Bull Island
"The shrill snipe, sniping up with plaintive cry,
a bullet from a rifle gun
left and right and left again
straight into the moon's astonished jaws
now a fading yellow hook balanced on chalk-purple mist,
the mist, a faded curtain from deserted playhouse rail.

The snipe has circled in a ring
wheeling back again to see
who the intruder might have been.

Howth Head -
a giant's hand that's closed into a knuckle-fist
a rosary beads of orange lights like coloured stones
about the joints.

Coast Road
curved circle
studded match-stick tops, golden horse-shoe nails
brazed into the resin dark
along the verge
where night hangs out black cloaks to dry
on witches' brooms.

The posts along the curve get small and small
and smaller still -
till they are tiny pencils stuck into the ground -
little blobs of yellowness.

An echo curlew wail
old woman's keen of desperation
rising, falling
the hooded gull on the coming tide into the wind.

A timber ship

Norwegian flat
Its megaphone a laryngitised ghost -
Farewell -
out into the open deep
then North to Baltic seas with iced-up fjiords.

Ringsend chimneys -
giant phalii, scarlet, white and slate-stained grey
orgasming bellyfuls of smoke that sperms
like a wounded Conger eel
ejaculating out to sea, a pinnioned python thing
till it thins out into a wormy line
flamingo-pink and blue and sun-stormed red.
Child scribble on the concrete paths above
way out beyond The Porcupine."
Uínsín O Donovan

Footnotes
(1) In 1712 the Corporation decided to reclaim land "east of the North Strand clear to the Clontarf Strand". The area was divided into sections which were raffled among the citizens. Because of this 'lottery' system the scheme was called the 'North Lotts'.
(2) The Old Ballast Board, the first port authority for Dublin, was originally established in 1707 to ensure that any ballast taken from the channel would be removed from the channel bed at lower water and not from the sides. This helped somewhat to create a deeper and more sheltered anchorage. It was essential to stop the practice of sailing ships taking their ballast (which they required when sailing without cargo) from the channel banks as the banks tended to eventually collapse causing serious silting. The old board had much of the South Wall completed when it was replaced by the new Ballast Board. This body was established by the Irish Parliament in 1786 and was to function until 1867. Its official title was "The Corporation for Preserving and Improving the Port of Dublin." In 1799 the Directors General of Inland Navigation in Ireland were given responsibility for the improvement of Dublin harbour.
(3) This was the same Captain Bligh who was earlier in charge of the "Bounty" when Fletcher Christian and the crew mutinied. Bligh and Christian were firm friends when the Bounty began that doomed voyage in search of breadfruit, to feed slaves, in 1789. Bligh was 32, Christian 22. Bligh has carried the reputation of being a sadist for over 200 years. He certainly ran a tight ship but perhaps it wouldn't be too generous to remember him as a hard but fair man. When he carried out the Dublin survey he was 46 years old and earned a fee of £682. Prior to the 'Bounty' affair he had much experience as a cartographer

on Captain Cooke's ship "Resolution" in the south seas. It was on his map of Dublin Bay (made in December 1800 and later published in London in 1803) that the existence of the Bull Island was first noted and recorded in accurate detail. Bligh was a strict disciplinarian and somewhat puritanically inclined. He had come from artisan stock and he never forgot that.

(4) Cargoes were taken ashore via sailing barges (gabbards) and other smaller boats. As the port got busier many had to unload at low tide and merchandise had to be carried ashore on hand-borne litters which was time-consuming and expensive. Many ships were lost or damaged while at anchor - pounding against the hard bottom in storms at low tide. As far back a 1707 the Dublin merchants petitioned the Irish parliament and secured legislation giving Dublin Corporation authority to deepen and straighten the 'approach by water to the city'. This authority was transferred to the Ballast Board in 1786.

(5) These materials, carried to the sea by the rivers, are now carried by the scour beyond their natural dropping point (the bar) and caught in the currents which carry them to the Island. The two walls altered the sea currents in Dublin Bay and increased the accumulation of sediment in the area. They cause the natural current to clear the harbour by compelling the Liffey current to run with greater force.

(6) Precedents in this area were special acts passed for St. Stephens Green in 1877 and the Phoenix Park in 1925. Many people argue that the Island is most valuable as a nature reserve and as a scientific 'working area'. To give the Island 'nature reserve status' would mean regulation of access and activity within the Island so that nature conservation, scientific research and education are facilitated.

(7) Father P.G. Kennedy S.J. is very closely associated with identifying and establishing the Island as a bird sanctuary. To this end he devoted much of his leisure time. He wanted to preserve the Island from encroachment and to publicise the birds - on which subject he published a book in 1953, called "An Irish Sanctuary - Birds of the North Bull Island."

(8) As well as regular beach litter left behind by day trippers Dollymount Strand receives much litter and debris from the sea because of the direction in which the Dublin Bay currents move.

(9) An older colleague once related a little story to me which concerns the Bull Island and identifying children - his own! The man in question had five sons who annually spent almost the entire school summer holidays paddling, running, swimming, ect. on Dollymount Strand with the result that the effect of the Dollymount breeze left them with rather bronzed bodies - brown legs in particular. Now invariably the country cousins or other friends would call on some of those Summer Sundays, bringing three or four more children of their own - add in a few neighbours kids and you had a right gang! Inevitably a disagreement would arise between the children - what's new? - and of course a free for

all fight would ensue in a room or in the garden. When the screams and banging became too much my colleague would go to sort out matters only to be confronted with anything up to a dozen boys punching and kicking in a heap on top of each other. "Lucky enough," he said " I could always identify my own by their tanned brown legs sticking out of the 'pack' and thus could begin sorting the matter out by first ejecting them from the melee."

Shooting Competition on Bull Island

In 1874 at Creedmoor, Long Island, New York the Irish Rifle target shooting team lost narrowly (with a little controversy) against their American equivalents for the World Title. A rematch was granted and took place on the Bull Island on the 29th June 1875. In an event that gripped Dublin's imagination reports stated that some 60,000 people made their way to Clontarf. However the Americans were the winners.

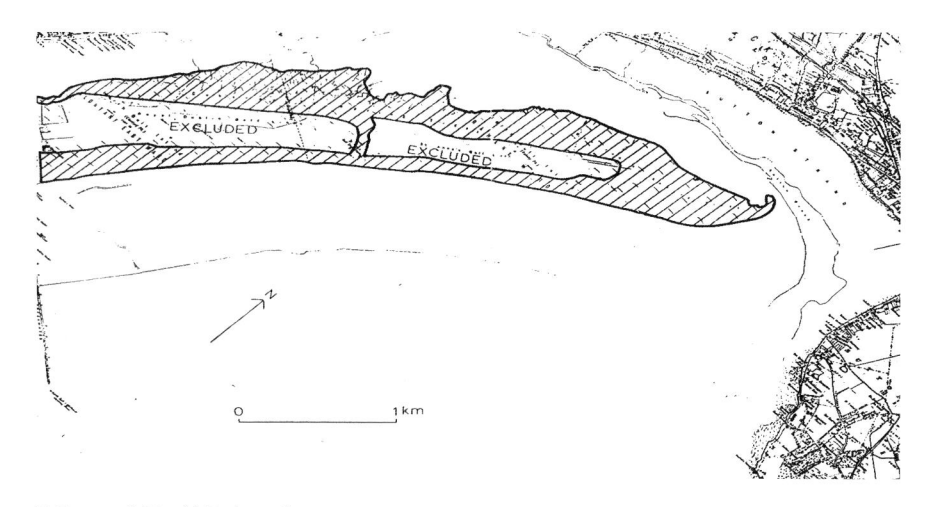

Map of Bull Island

Bull Wall and Statue

Bull Bridge

Bull Island Cottages

Bull Island Interpretive Centre

Brent Geese

A Curlew

CHAPTER SEVEN

St. Anne's Park
Dublin City Council has more than 3,000 acres of public open space under its administration, including about 80 parks. But St. Anne's is, in many ways, the park's, department showpiece with an appeal all of its own. Technically most of it lies in the Raheny Dublin 5 area, but it is historically, almost always, recorded and regarded as 'St. Anne's, Clontarf', and is a central ingredient to the character of the Clontarf area[1]. The park enhances the district with its serene, placid presence, and supplements in its own special way Clontarf's two other great natural amenities - Bull Island and the sea itself. Originally, St. Anne's was developed, as a beautiful nineteenth century estate complete with luxury mansion. The money for the development came from that accumulated by the Guinness family and their famous St. James' Gate brewery. In any study of the estate itself it is necessary to spend a little time tracing the Guinness family's connections with the demesne.

The Guinness Family
The whole Guinness dynasty are direct descendants of Richard Guinness of Celbridge, County Kildare, an Anglo-Irish rent collector born about 1690. His son, Arthur Guinness (the first), born in 1725, had a small brewery in Leixlip. In 1759 he bought another at St. James' Gate, Dublin. It was in a somewhat dilapidated condition but considered a practical and sound investment due to its position beside the river Liffey, the city's water supply. It was from this base that Arthur, and his successors, developed the world famous drink and the Guinness empire that came into being[2]. Arthur was a man of high principles with a good sense of community service. In 1764 he came to live in a fine house and estate which he had bought at Beaumont, (now Beaumont Hospital) on the northside of Dublin. He served as governor of the Meath hospital and did some campaigning for the upgrading of prisoner's conditions in Irish jails. Though a staunch supporter of his own church - the established Protestant Church of Ireland - he disliked any kind of religious discrimination. He opened the first Sunday School in Ireland in 1786. Arthur died in 1803.
Of his large family of ten children only Arthur Guinness (the second) followed his father's trail. In 1820 he became Governor of the Bank of Ireland and developed into a public figure with wide interests. A deeply religious man, he kept close contact with the bible. He advocated Catholic Emancipation and reform of Parliament. Arthur married a Dublin girl Ann Lee and eleven years later his brother Benjamin married Anne's younger sister Rebecca Lee - thus 'Lee'

became entwined in the Guinness name. Two of Arthur's sons, Benjamin Lee Guinness and Arthur Guinness (the third) moved to a house with some land called Thornhill at Blackbush, Heronstown, Raheny in 1835 which they bought from John Vernon of Clontarf Castle. This move established the first Guinness connection with the Clontarf district which was to last until 1939. (In 1814 Thornhill House was listed as owned by Sergeant John Ball who first built it). Two years later Arthur withdrew from the family firm. Benjamin Lee married his cousin Elizabeth Guinness in 1837 and also acquired his brother's interest in the new Clontarf property. At this stage Benjamin Lee was already a very wealthy man. On the death of his father (1855) he assumed full control of the brewery business. Benjamin Lee's 'reign' was an era of tremendous prosperity for the Guinness 'empire'. And Benjamin Lee achieved much personal distinction himself. He was made Lord Mayor of Dublin in 1851. In 1865 he entered Parliament. In 1867 he was created Sir Benjamin Lee Guinness, the family's first Baronet, in recognition of his service to the community. While a member of Parliament, he represented Dublin city as a Conservative and a Unionist. He was in fact the first of the brewery chiefs to take a public stand alongside the political establishment. He was totally against the emerging Home Rule movement which was aimed at total independence for Ireland. The Baronetcy was his reward for his loyalty[3].

The Thornhill house estate contained 52 acres, and the original entrance was from what is now Mount Prospect Avenue. It had previously been occupied by Hugh O'Reilly and was originally a portion of the lands in the area owned by successive owners of Howth Castle and Clontarf Castle. Sir Benjamin Lee is reputed to have demolished the house, which was a large Georgian one, and built anew. However it seems more likely that he renovated the old house and added to it, the new building having an Italian architectural flavour. He renamed it St. Anne's (in 1877) from the nearby ancient holy well known as St. Anne's Well[4]. The renovating of this to become a new finer house, the addition of the out buildings and the improvement of the general layout of the ground, in a tone reflecting his ever increasing wealth, took some years. To add to his prestige he bought a Palladian town mansion on the south side of St. Stephens Green for £2,500, and later the adjoining house. He merged the two into what later came to be known as Iveagh House (today's department of Foreign Affairs). Sir Benjamin Lee also bought the magnificent Ashford Estate in Cong, County Mayo, on the shores of Lough Corrib.

After 1850 Sir Benjamin Lee began the process of enlarging St.Anne's estate by availing of opportunities offered in purchasing adjoining farms and absorbing them into St. Anne's. Just how the locals of the time viewed this usurpation of land, we cannot say, but at least the Guinness family weren't guilty of open grabbing via dispossession by eviction which was an all to common process in nineteenth century Ireland. Guinness land was acquired, not by eviction, but by purchase[5]. It is difficult to establish the exact chronological sequence of the series of purchases made by the Guinness's in Raheny. The following list and order can only be accepted as approximate. Many of the purchases were actually made by Benjamin Lee's son the later Lord Ardilaun. His house and estate were the envy of dynasties and Royal families around the world. A statue of him was erected in the grounds of St. Patrick's Cathedral.

Two early acquisitions were Miss Sarah Wade's 40 acres and Mr. Joseph Robinson's 33 acres in the townlands of Bettyville and Charleville. At the same time Patrick O'Rourke's 13 acres were purchased to complete the absorption of Charleville townland. Then followed the purchase of Fottrell's fields (which are now used as football playing grounds) and Thomas Huston's 24 acres as well as a number of other quite small holdings, and Bedford Lodge.

Sir Benjamin Lee Guinness died in 1868, and by then his wealth was colossal. Even though he had set up various family trusts, he nevertheless died, reputedly, the first Irish millionaire, leaving £1,000,000 in his will. In today's terms that would be closer to £50,000,000. Of the character of the household of Sir Benjamin Lee, one account states; "Whether they were at St. Anne's, their quite house on Dublin Bay, in the handsome town house on St. Stephen's Green or in the wild magnificence of Ashford, the atmosphere in which they lived was distinctively pious, serious, yet far from solemn. Frivolity was as far from Sir Benjamin Lee as it had been from his father. Their guiding impulse was high-minded and their comfortable lives demanded constant recognition of God's grace and thanks for his bounty. Their surroundings were opulent but their lives were sober, in some ways austere, and the day began and ended with family prayers.

Sir Benjamin Lee had a daughter and three sons. His daughter was later to be Lady Plunkett wife of the Protestant Archbishop of Dublin, the Honorary and Reverend William Conyngham 4th Baron Plunkett. His three sons were Arthur (the fourth), Benjamin Lee and Edward Cecil. Benjamin Lee opted for a career in the army with the Royal Horse Guards. The St. Anne's and Ashford Castle estates fell to Arthur and the St. Stephen's Green house to Edward Cecil. These two latter sons became co-partners in the brewery. The will was so designed that if either should wish to withdraw from the business the expansion of the brewery would not suffer.

Arthur, now 27, as the oldest son inherited his father's Baronetcy. He had been educated at the famous English school of Eton - the first in a long series of

Guinness Etonians. Edward Cecil who served an apprenticeship to the brewery from the age of 15, was the more active partner in the firm and a far more shrewd businessman that Sir Arthur, whose experience with the brewery was limited. Besides, Sir Arthur was much more interested in politics and philanthropy, being governed by something of an artistic nature. On inheriting St. Anne's Sir Arthur continued his father's policy of extending his estate as much as possible, especially in the years 1874-78. He first purchased the property of John Harden (a barrister and official of the Public Records Office) at Brighton Lodge to the west of St. Anne's bringing his domain up to the southern boundary of Maryville. (In 1873 St. Anne's is listed in a parliamentary return as 156 acres). Between 1870 and 1876 properties along Watermill Road (then Watermill Lane) were added. These ran from the coast road at the seafront to the Howth Road at Raheny. They belonged to Patrick Boland at Watermill House, Major Williams at Bettyville and Anthony O'Toole - whose land was the most northerly, touching the Howth Road. The last and biggest addition to the estate was made about 1878 when the Sybil Hill lands were bought by Sir Arthur. Mr John Barlow had owned Sybil Hill and held Maryville under lease from Lord Howth. It was Mr. Barlow's sons who sold their entire interests to Lord Ardilaun.

Thus, as outlined, various townlands and estates in the Clontarf - Raheny area went to make up the present St. Anne's Park. Bettyville, Charleville, and Maryville were little townlands made up of patches of land. The original Thornhill House on Blackbush with Bedford Lodge and Sybil Hill were demesnes in themselves. The total acreage of St. Anne's was now just 4 short of the magic 500 acres.

In 1871 Sir Arthur married into 'quality' when 19 year old Lady Olivia White, oldest daughter of William White the 3rd Earl of Bantry became his wife. From the beginning Olivia (or Olive) was hostile to her husband's involvement in the brewery trade. With her background any business affair with the odour of Guinness just wasn't right for delicate nostrils. Sir Arthur was never really suited to the trade in any case. Indeed his spasmodic intrusions into the dealings of the brewery were both an irritant and an embarrassment to his most efficient younger brother-partner Edward Cecil. So, gradually after his marriage, Arthur began to concede his partnership in the business to his brother. In 1876, after eight years involvement he withdrew completely from the firm. But what a golden handshake he received! First of all he had, as compensation, his share in the eight year profit - the first year alone yielded £42,000 and in all accumulated to £530,000. For his half share in the actual firm itself he received a generous 'good-bye old chap' inducement of £686,000 from Edward Cecil. He had also various smaller legacies from his father. Thus he was left, in his mid-thirties, with enormous wealth in his purse - not forgetting his two estates, St. Anne's and Ashford in Cong - and plenty of time on his hands.

The Making of Lord Ardilaun

Aided and abetted by his very class conscious wife Sir Arthur decided to use his time and money to work wholeheartedly towards the acquisition of a peerage. They settled in St. Anne's estate and it is with this couple that St. Anne's will always be mainly associated.

In 1868 Sir Arthur had contested, and with the help of his bulging Guinness bank account, won the by-election for his father's parliamentary seat. Later that same year he held the seat in a general election. However his election agents were later accused of bribing the electorate and his election was declared void. He was out of parliament - though not out of politics - for five years until he won back his Dublin seat (in 1874) and held it until 1880.

He helped finance the famous Dublin exhibition of 1872. He completed the reconstruction of Archbishop Marsh's Library in Dublin, re-built the Coombe Lying-in Hospital and saved the Muckross Estate in Killarney from speculative builders by buying it for £60,000[6]. He served for sixteen years as president of the Royal Dublin society. But probably his greatest benefaction was his acquisition of the 30 acres St. Stephen's Green from the house-holders by whom it had been fenced off as a private park. Sir Arthur beautified the park with little walks, flower beds and an artificial lake and handed it over to the public. The reward for his generosity came in 1880 when he was raised from Sir Arthur Edward 2nd Guinness Baronet to Lord Ardilaun of Ashford with the 'complimentary' seat in the British House of Lords. In 1892 a statue of his lordship was unveiled in St Stephen's Green.

The name Ardilaun (meaning "High Island") was adopted from that of an Island in lake Corrib on his Ashford estate. This was the first peerage granted to the Guinness family. He was however the 'first and last' Lord Ardilaun for he died without issue in 1915. He achieved his ambition of a peerage by playing the game strictly according to the 'rules'. He married an Earl's daughter, got out of 'trade' (the brewery) and kept the Conservative Party's treasurer busy accepting 'donations'. On his death the peerage became extinct, but the Baronetcy Arthur had inherited from his father Sir Benjamin Lee passed on to his nephew Algernon Arthur Guinness, eldest son of Lord Ardilaun's brother, Benjamin Lee (who died in 1900).

A reserved and taciturn member of the house, as one of Ireland's biggest landlords - with estates, (in addition to those at Clontarf), in Cong, Killarney, Ballykyn, Strandhill, and Lisloughoey - he took part in House of Lords debates at every possible opportunity, to defend Irish Landlords against what he saw as the injustices of the various Land Acts after 1880 and especially the Land Act of 1896. This latter Act he saw as having an overwhelming bias towards the rent-paying peasantry. His politics also embraced a totally Unionist anti- Home Rule stance.

To ensure a good Dublin airing for his views he bought control of no less than four newspapers - the Dublin Daily Express, Morning Mail, Evening Mail and Weekly Warder.

After Sir Arthur became Lord Ardilaun, (in 1880) he obviously felt that the fine house of St. Anne's built by his father (Sir Benjamin Lee) no longer measured up to what was expected of a man with his wealth and social eminence. Indeed from about 1873 on, he infused large sums of money into re-building and revamping St. Anne's from the Georgian style villa of his father to become an Italianante Palazzo of the later Italian renaissance style, with accompanying improvements to the grounds. St. Anne's Mansion has long since disappeared, but no account of the estate would be complete without a description of the magnificent villa so fondly recalled by many older Clontarfites. Indeed many of the latter feel that the house would have been as good and as fitting a presidential residence as the present Árus and Uachtarán in the Phoenix Park.

The first documented improvement to the estate had been carried out by Sir Benjamin Lee in 1839 to commemorate the birth of his first child Anne Lee. He erected a sham ruin in the form of an ornamental bridge and tower over the old entrance drive. Other follies built by Sir Benjamin in the pleasure grounds included the clock tower, sporting a large bell with the family motto engraved on it - "Spes mea in Deo" (My hope is in God) - which is a nice example of the architecture of the period, and a replica of a Herculanean water house or temple, (pseudo Greek) with Doric Pillars linked to a metal footbridge over the river Naniken, which flows through the park on its way to the sea. The river was dammed just short of the seafront edge of the estate to form an artificial lake. The lake is allegedly, fed by the spring that originally gave rise to St. Anne's Well. At the edge of the lake he erected an Italian style boater tea-house temple based on a Pompeian model. The lake was stocked with fish and two Islands built in the centre - which nowadays provide shelter and nesting space for mallard duck and water-hen. Near the mansion itself was a walled garden which incorporated a yew walk complete with classically sculptured statues brought back from Italy. Sir Benjamin carried out further improvements to the house proper in the early 1860's. He also had a Richard Turner conservatory built, leading off the dining-room.

Lord Ardilaun, and his architect, the somewhat eccentric Kerryman, James

Franklin Fuller[7] effectively rebuilt St. Anne's between 1873 and 1881 and doubled the house in size. Fuller engulfed the earlier house and removed the observatory (a Roman Tower) from the roof to a mound beside the lake. His final building was splendid from the outside but somewhat cold and uncomfortable inside with spacious rooms. A new entrance wing was added as was a monumental marble and Portland staircase. A drawing-room complete with organ was added. Perhaps the main attraction was the new central hall and ballroom which was of double-storey height with a gallery supported on Iconic Columns, the shafts being of different kinds of Irish marble. The coat of arms of Lord Ardilaun - flanked by unicorns - was carved into the tympanum of the pediment of the new entrance. The house had eight reception rooms, thirty one bedrooms, six bathrooms and extensive stables and garages.

In her book "Bricks and Flowers" Katherine Everett did not find the splendour and grandeur of St. Anne's a real success. "It was a vast building in pseudo-Palladian style, the huge portice being flanked on either side by seven high plate-glass sash windows, and surmounted by fourteen others. Externally, its great size and fair proportion gave it a certain dignity, but nothing can be said in favour of the interior...The dark enormous hall was intersected midway by a wide, cold, white marble staircase, and on the landing, where the steps divided, to ascend in two flights, sat a female figure, also in cold white, marble, hampered in her clearly expressed desire to appear modest by the lack of any rag of clothing...A London firm had furnished this mansion throughout and the effect achieved was of an out-of-date luxury hotel...Olive (Lady Ardilaun) hated the place in winter." Until it disappeared, however, the house remained a solid impressive, enchanting character-filled mansion. Lord Ardilaun had his gardeners prune certain branches on certain trees near the house in order to afford him a splendid view of the Bull Island and Dublin Bay through the leaves. 'Modern' elements such as electric light, a telephone, central heating and a passenger lift were installed in time. To find the exact location of St. Anne's house, one follows the main avenue through the park from Sybil Hill Road, for its duration, to a mound which was the site of the house. When operating at its peak, one man had the sole duty of bringing fresh fruit, vegetables and flowers to the house each morning from the gardens.

In developing the grounds the Ardilaun's followed along Raptonian lines[8]. Both Lord and Lady Ardilaun loved trees so they planted great belts of evergreen Holm Oak and Pine (which are now a distinctive feature of the Clontarf precinct) to provide shelter and as a dark green background against which to view the lighter colours of ash, beech, elm, chestnut, lime and sycamore. To add to the character of the woodland patches they also planted yew, maple and many flowering trees.

All the planting was carried out in the years around 1880. The trees gave shelter throughout the estate from the cold easterly winds which blow across from the sea. These elegant trees, which have by now well matured, have a somewhat stately presence - serene, grand and proud, and their scent alone gives the park a distinct and unique atmosphere and an aura of sylvan deity, no matter what season prevails. Indeed the park would, today, be a bleak and cold place without the warmth generated by the trees which create shelter for young and old who stroll through the grounds. The trees surprise foreign aboriculturists who wonder at how they withstand all the salt blown on them by the Irish Sea winds even allowing for the fact that Holm Oak is quite resistant to salt-laden gales. Incidentally, all the evergreen oaks were supposedly raised by Lord Ardilaun from cuttings of one specimen tree which he reputedly got from Lord Powerscourt. The original tree, 'the father', can still be seen proudly standing to the east of the site of the house.

Lord Ardilaun carried out much work on the demesne. He created grand alleys radiating from the house, flanked by trees. He built a new driveway from Sybil Hill to the house as an absolutely straight road for about one and a half kilometres, flanked on each side by alternative plantings of Holm Oak and Austrian Pine. He intended it to be a longer one but could not persuade the owner of Furry Park (Killester) to part with some of his land[9]. Instead, the driveway had to kink to join the Howth Road (opposite Brookwood Avenue.). One notable alley through the park began beside the present rose garden at Mount Prospect Avenue and terminated with the spire of All Saint's Church Raheny. It was in fact a pathway for Ardilaun's hamlet of workers who lived at Dollymount to make their way to Church services. The path crossed under the main avenue to the 'Manor house' on the Vernon Avenue side of the Clock Tower, by means of a tunnel. The tunnel was created to keep those crossing the estate from becoming too 'familiar' with activities around the house and to preserve an existing public right of way. This was totally in keeping with the Ardilaun's style in which they jealously guarded their privacy. One observer at the time remarked that "not even a crow was allowed fly around the house." However a burglar once managed to breach the security net and robbed the house. Before he left he took a hot bath. No wonder he got clean away! The tunnel has been misrepresented in some accounts as an 'underground passage' for Catholics passing by. It has also been wrongly stated that it was originally opened as a cattle crossing. Also its use by 'bands of Sinn Feiners who haunted the park' in the period after 1916 has been quite overstated, especially in relation to their 'contacts' with Lady Ardilaun and Katherine Everett. In general the grounds were adorned with sun houses and shelters. The grounds even had a dogs' graveyard, complete with tombstones - surely a relic of Ascendancy days! (Lord Ardilaun's provision of All Saint's Church of Ireland in Raheny is dealt with above, in chapter two.)

Lady Ardilaun

Lord Ardilaun one time brewer, parliamentarian and philanthropist died in 1915, without any offspring. His strong willed and purposive wife, Lady Olive Charlotte White Guinness, outlived her husband by ten years, (Dublin wits alleged that she wished to give him ample time to make the proper acquaintances in 'the eternal state'! Born in 1850 she was chronologically, in any case, ten years his 'junior'!) In his will, laid out in 1902, he allocated his estates to his only surviving brother Edward Cecil in case "that the care of my estates would impose too much upon my wife." His personal estate, however, valued, after death duties at £495,638, he bestowed on her together with his London house at 11 Carlton House Terrace, his Dublin house at Leeson Street and of course the entire house and estate of St. Anne's Clontarf. After the Lord's death, and no longer requiring it, Lady Ardilaun sold the London house (which had been his base for commuting with the Houses of Parliament) and settled in Ireland. She divided her time between Dublin and her castle at Macroom (which she inherited from her father), 20 miles from Bantry in County Cork.

For ever an even more intense Conservative and Unionist then her husband had been, Lady Ardilaun reviled the Westminster government for any concessions to the Irish nationalists and their Home Rule movement, and later the militant Republicans of Sinn Fein. Her Macroom Castle was burned down by local Republicans whose action, in her will, she blamed on Erskine Childers. (This was the Erskine Childers, father of the later 4th President of the Republic who was involved with "the Asgard" and the Howth gun-running of 1914). But with no real logic she also blamed the Government's notorious 'Black and Tans', whose presence in the castle incited the Republican action.

St. Anne's had many times been the scene of dazzling high-society functions and garden parties. In April 1900 Queen Victoria visited St. Anne's as part of her Irish tour... she entered the estate by way of an elaborate ornate gate which stood a little east of the seafront end of Mount Prospect Avenue where today there is a former gate lodge called "Sea Lawn House". For the record she left via the main avenue and took the Howth Road back into Dublin City! Lady Ardilaun continued this trend and in Dublin she was much appreciated by the local intelligentsia for her elaborate entertainment of them. The aromatic scents from the herb garden were a fitting ambrosial aroma for one party thrown by Olivia for the doctors of Dublin - it was a hot summer's evening and amid fluttering butterflies and humming bees the doctors sat long into the evening discussing the origins of their drugs, 'the old pharmacopeia' used by herbalists of medieval days. As she had no children, Lady Olivia was a forlorn figure. Lady Gregory (Irish Writer) wrote of her living in St. Anne's in the 1920's as "a lonely figure in her wealth, childless and feeling the old life shattered around her." Her cousin and godchild, Katherine Everett, described her as "tall, dark, very uptight and good-looking, with charming expressive grey eyes and dignified in a manner that was slightly alarming." In 1916 Katherine excepted Lady Ardilaun's offer of a home at Sybil Hill[10] in return for her companionship at St. Anne's. Katherine lived at St. Anne's for eight years and also acted as Lady Ardilaun's secretary. In contrast to Olivia, who had led a sheltered life attended by servants, Katherine was independent and courageous. The two ladies became familiar figures during those eight turbulent years in Dublin. (1916 -1924 embraced the 1916 Rising, the rise of Sinn Fein, the setting up of Dáil Éireann, the 1919-1921 War of Independence, the Anglo Irish Treaty the Civil War and the setting up of the Irish Free State). They spent the winters in the town house as St. Anne's house was showing signs of 'wear and tear' being cold and draughty with leaking conservatory and flooded cellars.

But it was during the summers, spent in the gardens and woodlands of St. Anne's that they had their happiest times. They continued the Ardilaun trend of developing and beautifying the estate. No matter how disturbed the country around them was, they found peace of mind and an outlay for their creativity - which was considerable when Olivia's vast financial resources and large labour force were coupled with Katherine's skill in craftsmanship, her love of architecture and her training in proportion and design. Both ladies had absorbed in childhood a common affection for the magnificent scenery to be viewed from the great houses with which they were familiar in West Cork and Kerry. This produced some wonderful results in St. Anne's. Olivia took over the walled vegetable garden, turned it into a setting for flowers, and assisted by Katherine in the layout of the borders, it became a show piece. It contained a fine twisted Italian pillar, topped by a stone basket of carved flowers. This was a focal point, and can still be viewed. It also served as a memorial to the old head gardener, Andrew Campbell, a devoted family friend. To Campbell, who died in 1917, is attributed much of the overall development of the park. Much of his patient planning is retained in today's St. Anne's. They also created the famous herb garden (which was to be regularly visited by many eminent physicians), with a background of clipped grey-green llex trees in the formal Elizabethan knot style - oval beds in a large circle graduating to tiny ones in the centre. The garden had narrow paths of crushed shell twisting in and out with four lead figures of the seasons at its centre. The beds contained endless varieties of herbs - rosemary, borage, fennel, worm wood, penny royal, balm, poppies, horehound, hyssop and basil.

Lady Ardilaun died at her Lesson Street town home in December 1925. She left an estate valued at more than £900,000. After various charitable and personal allocations had been executed[11] the residue of her estate, including St. Anne's, was inherited by Lord Ardilaun's nephew Most Rev. and Honourable Benjamin John Plunkett, Protestant Bishop of Meath. In her will she advised him to dismantle the house and reduce it to its pre-Ardilaun dimensions stating "St. Anne's is far too large and expensive for anyone to live in, in the future. The enormous taxation and increase of wages and cost of everything will make it impossible." The Bishop moved in to the house in 1926 and erected a plaque to his mother (Lord Ardilaun's sister Anne) on the rustic arch put up by Sir Benjamin on her birth in 1838. However he found the estate expensive to maintain and in 1932 he made attempts to dispose of St. Anne's and its 496 acres. Only two parties were interested and eventually in 1938 one of them, Dublin Corporation, compulsorily acquired almost the entire property for £80,000 - most of which went to buy out the freehold and subsidiary interests. Now retired, Bishop Plunkett moved into Sybil Hill house with his family, retaining 30 acres of the vast estate as private grounds. On the bishops death in 1947, his son, (also called Benjamin) sold Sybil Hill House and grounds to the Vincentine Fathers, who founded St. Paul's College there in 1950. A sale of contents of St. Anne's house planned for October 1939 was advanced on the outbreak of the Second World War in September. During the war the house was used as a headquarters by the local defence force and A.R.P. (breathing) equipment for the city was stored there. In December (Christmas Eve), 1943 the building was gutted by a fire which started in the east wing and destroyed the entire building. The fire was caused, it is thought, maliciously. The outer walls remained intact but were vandalised. The remaining shell of ruins was eventually demolished and removed in 1968. When burned, the house was insured for £100,000, so the Corporation got more than its original investment of £80,000 back. The residue was invested in the development of the park.

While the era of the Ardilaun's has long vanished there exists in Clontarf a genuine fondness and affection for the house and grounds of the 'Lord and Lady'. Their 'own' local Lord was a symbol of status and thus much esteemed. The only remains of St. Anne's house which still stand are the Victorian courtyard style 'Red Stables' which were formerly used as horse stables with livery men and general workers living above the stables. They were used later by the Corporation as a store and a works department for park maintenance and as a canteen and are preserved as the magnificent example of Victorian architecture they are. At the time of its sale, besides the palatal residence, the other buildings, on St. Anne's included eight houses let to 'substantial' tenants, four gate lodges and six other cottages. Its stated size was 484 acres, 0 roods and 10 perches. The land of the estate helped greatly during the 'emergency' war years of the Second World War. Food crops of wheat and oats were extensively grown to supply food for the city of Dublin. Indeed 'allotments' were common in St. Anne's for many years after the war. And older locals well remember the familiar sight of stacks of turf lining the avenues.

After the war the 'great debate' began in the Corporation as to how best to utilise this great municipal acquisition. Various proposals were discussed. Eventually, under the guidance of the city manager of the time (Mr.P.J. Hernon), the city engineer, the city housing architect and the city planning officer worked out a plan which was to be the blueprint of the St. Anne's we know today. Their proposals were heralded as revolutionary as they contained the biggest development scheme up to then (1945/1946) ever attempted by Dublin Corporation.

The 496 acre St. Anne's Estate was to be split up. 200 acres, including "all the main avenue, pleasure grounds and gardens, the land to the seafront and all the tree-planted portion of the estate" was to be laid out as a national memorial public park dedicated to the people forever. Two sections of 60 acres - one on the Clontarf/City side, the other on the Watermill Road/ Raheny side were to be utilised for public and private playing fields. Portion of the side adjoining Vernon Avenue/Sybil Hill was to be allocated for secondary and primary schools. The rest of the land - about 103 acres - was to be reserved for housing development. This is the tranquil little housing estate of St. Anne's, "Raheny Corner" bounded in the triangle formed by the Howth, Watermill and All Saints Roads. The housing committee directed that 74 acres of the building land should be reserved for an 'an improved type of working-class house.' A private builder would have a free hand in the remaining 30 acres or so. Today it has become a compact little community. As well as the comfortable houses, the estate also contains the All Saints Protestant Church with the accompanying Parish Hall and rector's house. It contains Raheny National Schools, Raheny Gaelic football clubhouse, Raheny Garda barracks, the meeting rooms of St. Anne's Community and Residents Association, the premises of Raheny United Soccer Club, a little shopping centre, Cara Hall on All Saints Drive and a sizeable block of comfortable residential flats for senior citizens, called St. Anne's Court. Tied up with this plan for St. Anne's the city planners also earmarked an area of about 650 acres north and north-east of St. Anne's for further housing development - giving Dublin in all about 7,000 new houses. The development of the Bull Island at Dollymount as a recreation centre was involved in the total plan and this included an embankment road connecting the Howth Road, where it meets the Coast Road with the Island. Also the plan envisaged going ahead with the then proposals for the Marine Lake at Dollymount known as the 'Blue Lagoon' scheme.

Today St. Anne's estate is about five and a half miles in circumference, as it was in 1880. It is bounded by the Howth Road, Watermill Road, James Larkin Road, Mount Prospect Avenue and Sybil Hill Road. Between the Mount Prospect Avenue/Mount Prospect Drive junction and Sybil Hill Road, St. Anne's does not run neatly along a road as such. It adjoins the houses of Mount Prospect Drive, Mount Prospect Park and Vernon Avenue. The environment created by St. Anne's public park of landscaped grounds is much appreciated and admired by residents of the Clontarf area, and indeed by visitors from all over Dublin city and elsewhere. It provides an ideal escape from the busy city and from the rigours of everyday life. Its beautiful leafy glades and avenues provide lovely grounds for adults to stroll, lovers to wander, teenagers to gaggle and children to play.

There is no more fitting a scene to admire the splendour of nature and the seasons than in St. Anne's park. Despite the work of vandals, many of the follies created by the Ardilaun's can still be viewed (indeed have been refurbished), together with the rose garden, the rockeries, the woodlands, the bridges, the beckoning paths and the ornamental lawns. An abundance of wildlife species - squirrels, rabbits, foxes and hedgehogs - roam the park. The birds are there in their numbers - owls, magpies, blackbirds, thrushes and all the other familiar everyday countryside birds. Many birds more associated with the seashore and the Bull Island often feed in St. Anne's - curlews, oyster catchers, gulls and brent geese. And the Naniken River flows gently by through semi-woodland, helping to create an atmosphere of relaxation and tranquillity for passive recreation. For schools, the park is ideal for nature trails, field trips and nature walks.

The park is famous for its gardens, many already referred to. In 1875 the development proper of these gardens was begun by Lord Ardilaun and early in the 20th century the estate included an Italian garden, a flower garden, a fruit garden and a herb garden. Nowadays these gardens are used as nurseries by Dublin City Council's Parks Department, which is constantly building new model gardens. From these nurseries come the flowers, shrubs and foliage for all of Dublin's open spaces, as well as the floral decorations for city centre streets.

St. Anne's is an intensively used open recreation centre. It incorporates over forty playing pitches for all forms of football used by a plethora of clubs and groups. As well as Gaelic football the G.A.A. clubs also play hurling and camogie. The parks contains eighteen hard tennis courts, a pitch and putt course, a one-time band stand for the odd 'lark in the park' , a dogs playground and a miniature racing car track.

St. Anne's Rose Garden

"The cowslip is a country wench.
The violet is a nun,
But I will woo the dainty rose,
The queen of everyone."

The first attempt to establish a rose garden in Dublin was made by the rose group of the Royal Horticultural Society of Ireland in 1963. They had a site in St. Anne's Park - in front of the villa itself. The project was, however, stillborn. After this, the Clontarf Horticultural Society for many years advocated the provision of a major rose garden in the district which has a very suitable climate for the purpose of the cultivating roses. Committee members (of the horticultural society) realised, having visited major shows abroad, that Dublin had nothing comparable to the formal rose gardens of major cities in other countries. Finally, in 1970 the Clontarf group took their idea to the parks department of Dublin Corporation, and the 'rose garden project' began. Today St. Anne's rose garden is the national rose garden and its roses are used to decorate Dublin City streets on festive occasions. The Parks Department agreed to provide and maintain the site. The Clontarf horticultural society undertook to use its influence, and contacts, with commercial rose growers to obtain an initial stock of rose trees. From the beginning the society also provided the stimulus of public support generated by its membership and contributed much by way of technical expertise. When the garden plan was first being laid out 10,000 cubic yards of soil was excavated from the central area of the garden and placed around the perimeter of the site to give a 'sunken garden' effect with sloping banks. This also helped create intricacy, variety, space division and unity. 2,000 young beech plants were set on top of these banks around the garden to form hedges, to provide shelter and to form a nice pleasant background against which visitors can view the roses. To help cater for visitors - as the rose garden is a public one - 4,500 square yards of paths have been laid. And the whole garden is set within a frame of oak, pine and lime trees. The main (oval) Rose Garden has some 25,000 various roses.
Today's St. Anne's rose garden is one of the leading rose gardens in the world and is included in the international rose garden trials. The City of Dublin International Rose Trials are the joint effort of Clontarf Horticultural Society and Dublin City Councils Parks Department in conjunction with the British Association of Rose Breeders. St. Anne's rose garden has won many awards,

both nationally and internationally. The garden is a living factory of colour and fragrance. Rosarians from all over the world visit the garden, and it is now an established fact that the best roses in Dublin are grown in Clontarf, where the soil and the influence of the sea air contribute their beneficial effects. The varieties of roses in the garden represent what experts consider the best in cultivation today - and are being constantly expanded. There are roses for sunlight and roses for moonlight, roses for youth and roses for age. There are tall roses and small roses, giant roses and dwarf roses, old roses and new roses, climbing roses and rambling roses....Shot Silk, Yesterday, Peer Gyant, Kiskadee, National Trust, Brasila, Picasso.... the list is endless. The garden has a wide selection of Hybrid and Floribundas which are so popular.

"No one knows
Through what wild centuries
Roves back the rose."

The tradition of rose cultivation in St. Anne's dates mainly from Mr. Andrew Campbell, already referred to in this chapter. He developed a Malmaison Hybrid rose or the "souvenir de St. Anne's" which is the 'queen mother' of the garden. This rose is a fitting tribute to the memory of his skill and will always hold an exalted place in the garden.In St. Anne's Park, with its many attractions including romantic tree shaded paths and some enchanting and mysterious by-ways, the beautiful rose garden is a charming extra amenity. Indeed, needless to say, the garden is never without admirers in the summer season. Today the nurturing planning and arranging of the rose garden is carried on in its best traditions by Dublin City Council's Parks Department team of trained experts.
Clontarf Horticultural Society, founded in 1954, as well as initiating the project that gave rise to the rose garden, generally promotes interest in horticulture in all its aspects and organises many horticultural shows with the support of the community and the Environmental Department. From its earliest days the society has been involved in the growing of roses and constantly advocates the planting and cultivation of roses. The society takes an active part in the City of Dublin Rose Trials.

Footnotes

(1) One of the finest natural parks in Europe, the Phoenix Park consisting of 1,752 acres is Dublin's largest public park. St. Anne's never quite reached the 500 acre mark.

(2) Not really relevant to our story...but...many colourful myths have, over the years, grown to explain the 'secret' of Arthur's unrivalled success in developing the famous dark

ale we know today. They are interesting and worth recording. One such story says that Arthur's father Richard accidentally burned the malting barley while brewing beer for his boss, the Archbishop of Cashel. This gave a dark, somewhat bitter but quite pleasing drink and its secret passed on to Arthur. A second legend tells us that Arthur stole the recipe for his guinness from monks who had discovered a method of "giving body" to their home made beer. Another theory declares that the secret of the famous stout lies in the individual quality of the water in the River Liffey. However the truth is that porter (which is really only a stronger and darker version of ale, made by supplementing hops to malted barley, boiling and straining the compound and fermenting it with yeast) was brewed and drank in England at least a hundred years before Arthur Guinness entered the trade. But nobody can deny that the stout developed by Arthur, and to which he gives his surname has a uniqueness all of its own (Stout is really porter with knobs on, stronger than normal with 8% or more abv). Up to 1825 the market for Guinness was confined to Dublin and its surroundings. In 1825 the firm began to export and as this market broadened the family wealth began to accumulate. A stamp was issued by the government in 1959 to commemorate the bicentenary of the founding of the Guinness firm in 1759.

(3) Much of this service was demonstrated in practical terms, for instance his donation of £150,000 for the repair of the neglected and decaying St. Patrick's Cathedral. In its restoration, he himself was the architect. This proved his allegiance to the established Church which at the time was seriously threatened with disestablishment by the Liberal, Gladstone.

(4) The bed of St. Anne's well is situated on the eastern side of the park near the James Larkin Road, and beside the artificial lake. The well has been dry for at least 70 years. Corporation staff have tried in vain many times to find the original source or spring for the well. St. Anne's well was a place of pilgrimage for Dubliners up the close of the 19th century and a "pattern" was held there annually.

(5) Among the many questions asked by a Government enquiry in 1835 into the state of the poor in Ireland in each parish was "to what extent has the system of throwing small farms into larger ones taken place in your parish and what has become of the dispossessed tenants?" The usual answer to the latter part of the question was" they have settled themselves on bog edges in the neighbouring parishes"

(6) Marsh's Library is the oldest public Library in Ireland. It was founded by Archbishop Narcissus Marsh in 1703. Sir Arthur's interest in Muckcross house arose from the fact that his mother in law was a Herbert originally from Muckcross House. The house is now a folk museum.

(7) Fuller was the official architect to the Representative Church Body. Lord Ardilaun later replaced him as architect by George C. Aslin a Catholic who revamped some of the interior of St. Anne's and designed the still existing 'red stables' as well as All Saints

Church. St. Anne's was not the sole recipient of Lord Ardilaun's attention. Vast improvements were made to his town house at 18 Lesson Street. He also transformed Ashford Castle, Cong, into a quite magnificent country 'palace' to satisfy his vanity and also carried out substantial forestation schemes on the estate. The architectural work on this was also done by Fuller. It will not be forgotten that this same Ashford Castle - later a hostelry of the most elite order - was chosen by United States President Ronald Reagan as his West of Ireland 'base' during his presidential sojourn in Ireland in June 1984.

(8) Humphrey Rapton was an eighteenth century English landscape designer whose basic idea was to flood the hollows and plant the hills. He and his successor Capability Brown were completely opposed to the rigid formal style of designers such as Lenotre who designed Versailles.

(9) The then owner of Furry Park was Sir Ralph Smith Cusack J.P. Chairman of the Midland Great Western Railway. A story goes that when Lord Ardilaun approached Sir Ralph about purchasing the land necessary to complete the avenue as far as the Howth Road (close to the top of Castle Avenue) Sir Ralph informed Ardilaun that the latter's 'beer money' was not acceptable! (This was a reference to Ardilaun's connections with the Guinness brewery).

(10) Sybil Hill is the house now occupied by the Vincentian Fathers on St. Paul's College campus. Katherine Everett, in a book called "Bricks and Flowers" tells her own story. Born into the Cahirnane branch of the Herbert family she left home while quite young to study in London at the Slade School of Art, thus escaping a neurotic mother. When her own marriage ended she supported her two sons by using her considerable artistic gifts moving between wealthy relations advising them on the upkeep of their homes and gardens.

(11) A £20,000 trust was set up for the education of Protestant sons of Irish gentry "in reduced circumstances owing to loss of income from their Irish landed estates," and for assistance in the education of protestant clergyman's sons. The trust was called, "the Lady Ardilaun Educational Endowment" and the recipients were to be known as the "The Lady Ardilaun Scholars." A trust fund of £500 was also set up, the income from which patients, and workers at Mercer's Hospital, Dublin, were to be provided each year with a special Christmas Dinner called the 'Lady Ardilaun Dinner'.

Lady Ardilaun

Clock tower

Pond and Tea House

St Annes Well

Red Stables

Rose garden

Follies at St Annes

Benjamin Lee Guinness

Lord Ardilaun

St Annes Mansion

CHAPTER EIGHT

Lord Charlemont and Marino

In the middle of the 18th century Thomas Adderley built a big mansion (later known as Marino House) on the south-eastern end of Donnycarney estate. Some accounts allege that the house incorporated portion of an earlier house built by Basil, Cromwell's Attorney - General in Ireland. The house made all others in the area look rather insignificant and it had a splendid view of Dublin Bay - not being far from the Fairview end of the present Malahide Road. Adderley came from Inishannon near Bandon in County Cork. He married a girl of the Bernard family, the Lords of Bandon, but she died a few years later. He built a thriving linen industry and devoted his life and fortune to the education of his step-son, James Caulfield. Indeed Marino House was built as a present for James.

The Caulfield's owned vast estates in the North of Ireland which together with their titles originated in the plantation of Ulster. The name Charlemont was adapted from a fort built in 1600 by the Lord Deputy Charles Mountjoy at the height of the nine years war against Hugh O'Neill. The first Caulfield came to Ireland with the Earl of Essex in 1599. James Caulfield 4th Viscount, 1st Earl of Charlemont and later Lord Charlemont was born on August 18th, 1728 in the family town house at Jervis Street - now the site of Jervis Shopping Centre. Being of delicate health James was unable to attend regular school or college but was well educated at home with the aid of various tutors. He was then sent on an extensive tour of continental Europe which lasted nine years mainly to resolve his tendency to gamble and live its (often) associated lifestyle of such as irresponsibility. He spent the last three years, or so, of the tour in Italy where he acquired a deep interest in Arts and Classics that was to last throughout his life.

Grandeur and Eloquence

When he returned home, at 26 years of age, he was presented by his stepfather with the big house and its 200 acre estate, which because of its proximity to the sea, he named Marino (which means "a small sea") and set up home there. Marino House itself was a squat, square mansion of Portland stone standing close to the old Malahide Road at the junction of today's Brian Road and Brian Avenue. He proceeded to spend a fortune making his estate one of grandeur and eloquence in the manner of his aristocratic contemporaries. He used his privileged position in the Protestant ascendancy class to sway the city council to divert the Malahide Road away from his house, in order to give more parkland 'setting' to the building. He erected a high wall around his entire estate - many locals well remember part of the demesne wall in Marino Mart as well as the beautiful ornamental gateway he had erected at the entrance to his estate, which is today Marino Park Avenue. The actual gates themselves now stand at the entrance to St. Mary's, the Christian Brothers' house, on nearby Griffith Avenue. The gateway displayed the family arms and chivalrous motto - 'Deo Duce Ferro Commintante' (With God as my guide, my sword by my side.) He filled the lofty rooms of the house with works of ancient and modern art and treasures he had amassed during his continental travels. The art gallery in Marino House was sixty feet long. Writing of his decision to settle here, Lord Charlemont wrote "I was sensible that it was my indispensable duty to live in Ireland, and I determined by some means or other, to attach myself to my native land and principally with this view, I began those improvements at Marino, as without some attractive employment I doubted whether I should have resolution to become a resident."

Distinguished Irishmen
Having mixed in 'polished' circles in the most splendid courts during his European sojourn, Lord Charlemont developed a taste for interesting and witty conversation with the elite of society. Indeed all the distinguished Irishmen of his age came to wine, dine and converse at his residence in Marino - politicians Henry Grattan (who owed his parliamentary seat to Charlemont), and Henry Flood, nationalist John P. Curran, patriot Charles Lucas, pickpocket and author George Barrington, writer Jonathon Swift, political writer and orator Edward Burke, united Irishman Lord Edward Fitzgerald and a host of others. The nobleman 'above middle size with a dark beard and very high thin eyebrows' has often been described as the most accomplished and polished man of his day and the most agreeable....fond of humour and full of spirit, integrity and public virtue. He was also fond of fame and very ambitious. In London he was greatly admired by literary friends such as writers Johnson, Goldsmith and Boswell. As he was one of Dublin's most eligible bachelors countless 'fair daughters' were paraded in his sight with a view to matrimony. But he confounded everyone by marrying a fisherman's daughter - Mary Hickman, a native of County Clare. Considering his liberal tastes and his all round benevolent manner it seems strange that Charlemont strongly opposed Catholic relief and emancipation all his life. Yet he remained a staunch supporter of the Irish Parliament and the Volunteers. He became nicknamed the 'Volunteer Earl' because he had helped achieve some measures of independence for Grattan's Irish Parliament as Commander-in-Chief (from 1780) of the Irish Volunteers.

The uninterrupted sea view from Marino House was something Charlemont soon had to learn to live without. A builder with whom the affable Lord had a somewhat uncharacteristic disagreement built the waxing moon shaped row of houses known as "The Crescent" to deliberately destroy the cherished view of Dublin Bay enjoyed from Marino House. (See chapter nine below.)

Aesthete
Many people will remember Lord Charlemont most of all for his patronage of the Arts. As the leading aesthete of his day he was the founder of the Royal Irish Academy. He had his town house - Charlemont House - on Parnell Square North (then Palace Row on Rutland Square). This Georgian house, also designed by Sir William Chambers, nowadays houses the Hugh Lane Municipal Gallery of Modern Art. The house was built in 1765 and remained in the Charlemont family until it was sold to the Government as offices of the Register General for Ireland in 1876. In 1929 it was leased to Dublin Corporation for the purpose of housing a modern art gallery which opened in 1933. In the latter decades of the 18th century Lord Charlemont presided over many gatherings of the artists and literati of the time, in his town house. His gatherings of intelligentsia were referred to at the time as the 'society of Granby Row'. Charlemont was a member of the House of Lords, first taking his seat in 1755.

Towards the end of his life Lord Charlemont's health became quite delicate and he moved for a time to a warmer continental climate. He died at his town house in 1799 aged 71 years. He was buried in the family vault in the Cathedral of Armagh. His successors remained at Marino until 1876 when the last of the Caulfield's left the district. In his papers the 'Volunteer Earl' left his own epitaph which read; "Here lies the body of James, Earl of Charlemont a sincere, zealous, and active friend to his country. Let his posterity imitate him in that alone and forget his manifold errors."

City Slums
The modern area known as Marino adopted its name from Caulfield's mansion - which itself has long since vanished, being demolished to make way for Dublin Corporation's house building plans. In 1876 Marino Estate was purchased by the Christian Brothers from Lord Charlemont's grandson. In the early 1920's the southern part of the estate was acquired by Dublin Corporation, which carried out the first house building programme of an Irish Government on it. This Marino project turned out to be an immense scheme which had been planned years before it actually occurred in 1925. Hundreds of new houses were built in Dublin Corporation's first effort to solve the problem of the city slums. It was a pilot scheme by the fledgling Free State to relieve overcrowding and provide adequate living accommodation for workers. Needless to say the Marino housing scheme changed the whole face of this part of Clontarf and Fairview.

The rural aspect of the area was totally transformed as rows of houses with new service roads and avenues replaced the green fields.

The Casino

Probably Ireland's most perfect building and perhaps the best surviving example of 18th century Sicilian Doric architecture in the world is the enchanting structure known as the Casino sometimes called "the Temple". Situated on the left, past the end of Griffith Avenue, (actually on Cherrymount Crescent)as one travels from Dublin city up the Malahide Road, the Casino is in Marino but has traditionally been associated with Clontarf. The Casino is the only remaining memorial in the area to Lord Charlemont. Now renovated and restored it is open to the public for visiting as a heritage house since 1984. It is essentially a Palladian pavilion in classical architecture, which was completed in 1773 at a total cost of £60,000. To many people the very name Casino projects images of a gambling den or even a brothel but it was designed and built in the grounds of Lord Charlemont's Mansion, Marino House, as a companion to the parent house. It was intended to be the 18th century architectural gem it is and perhaps surpassed the owners expectations in evolving as such a breathtakingly beautiful building. It is now one of Dublin's major tourist attractions.

The exquisite, unique and ornate building was built first of all as a wealthy Lord's showpiece in his search for excellence. But Lord Charlemont also had in mind the lavish entertainment of his high society associates 'in seclusion away from the main building in a natural parkland setting (and there were parties on the "4th floor" i.e. the rooftop!) Care was also taken in positioning the Casino to best benefit from the views available of Dublin Bay and the Dublin and Wicklow mountains. Charlemont also used the Casino as 'a pleasure house for the pastoral life' - a summer house and a rural retreat into solitude and retirement. In keeping with his reputation as a patron of the arts, he had much of his comprehensive private library collection stored there, where he often retreated to study as well as to view and admire his valuable and extensive art collection.

The Casino, which had an Irish postal stamp depicting the building issued in 1973 to mark its bicentenary, was designed by an Englishman, Sir William Chambers. Chambers designed many other notable buildings in England, Ireland and elsewhere, but the Casino was his masterpiece. Chambers (who never actually came to Ireland) sent on his design to Lord Charlemont in 1758 and kept up protracted correspondence with Charlemont on all aspects of the building - design, construction and decoration - until it was finally completed in 1773. Local streets Casino Park and Casino Road are called after it. The man who actually built it was an Italian sculptor called Simon Vierpyle whom Charlemont had brought to Ireland in 1750. Regarding the cost of the erection of the Casino a traditional story survives in the Marino area that workmen engaged in the building constantly reminded each other to be careful handling the specially carved stones for the cornices...so great was the cost of cutting them that each one harmed would mean "another townland gone!" This was a reference to the fact that Charlemont had sold some of his estates in the north to meet the bill for the construction of the Casino. Indeed he admitted that the cost of the Casino would be a burden on his estate forever.

The Casino then, constructed during the Penal days in Ireland, is a relic of the English dominated past and typically depicts life in the Georgian era with the domestic and servants' area in the basement contrasting sharply with the upstairs grandeur. The word 'Casino' (which may have been taken from the Italian town Cassino) means 'little house' and from a distance it looks quite small. However on closer examination subtly designed it is deceptively large, being of three storeys even though externally it appears to be only one, and containing sixteen rooms. It also had underground passages. One tunnel - large enough to accommodate a donkey and cart driving through - led directly to Charlemont's main residence at Marino House (see above). This passageway is now blocked off by the foundations of the distinctive red bricked building that houses Dublin Fire Brigade and formerly known as O'Brien's institute. After the 1914 Howth gun running some arms were hidden there and the tunnel was searched by the authorities.

Its basic structure is the design of a Greek cross and the inside disposition is that a small scale dwelling house - although it is as large as any town house of its era. It was constructed of dazzling white Portland stone and it measures seventy square feet in area and is fifty feet high. There are eight rooms in the basement, four on the ground floor and four on the first floor. The rooms included a wine store, a vestibule, a saloon, a dining room, a boudoir, a library or book closet and four bedchambers. Because of its structure and history it is simply an outstanding building.

All the fine sculpture work on the ornaments within and outside the building is the carving of Joseph Wilton and the interior decorations were executed by Cypriani. The building has twelve Tuscan columns four at the corners and eight in the four porticoes, outlining the basic plan. The rooms are very finely proportioned and timbers for the original intricate parquet floors were brought from all over the world. The plaster work on the walls was of such excellence as to be unrivalled in Europe. Highlights of the sculpture and decorations include the four statues on the roof - Bacchus, Venus, Ceres and Apollo - together with the graceful ornate urns. At ground level the four corners of the balustrades have four stone lions as 'sentries'. The main drawing room had a splendid golden sun in the ceiling and Charlemont's master bedroom was dominated by a large golden leaf decoration. All round the building the pediments, festooned panels and the mantelpiece are quite beautiful. In his renowned book on World Architecture Norbert Lynton refers to the Casino as one of the most perfect of the Renaissance buildings. Indeed, architects today are rediscovering some of its quite outstanding and 'modern' features. For example there are no noticeable drainpipes to in any way detract from the all round splendour of the building. Instead the columns were hallowed to cater for the rain water. The ornate urns on the roof act as chimneys. Also the Casino had an arrangement whereby hot air from the basement kitchen ovens was conducted through the cavity walls to keep the entire building warm - showing that there was central heating in the 18th century!

The Casino was left derelict and allowed fall into ruin and decay at the end of the 19th century as the fortunes of the Charlemont family declined. Now Dublin City Council own the Casino and the land immediately around it. In 1930 the Irish Government designated the building a national monument to be preserved under the care of the Office of Public Works who in 1975 (European Architectural Heritage Year), began to meticulously and painstakingly restore the building to its original splendour. In this they have been superbly successful and the building once again can be referred to as 'one of the most beautiful pieces of architecture ever created.'

Furry Park House

(This is the original piece that appeared in "The Meadow of the Bull" in 1987.)
Furry Park House, the eighteenth century building which stands on the right on the Howth Road just past Killester village, as you travel towards Raheny, is believed to be Dublin's oldest continuously inhabited house. Today, it stands in a lazy farmyard style setting, somewhat landlocked, yet it has a very busy city highway beside it. It has the "land that time forgot" type of appearance and demeanour. It was built in 1730, by a Dublin banker named Joseph Fade, as a country villa to act as a weekend retreat. Since then the house has attained an illustrious history and is of national importance being the home of many eminent persons, who were closely associated with the political and cultural life of the country and being of much architectural splendour in its own right. The house, of the early Georgian style, is thus of considerable historical and architectural significance. However, the building had no legal protection and has been saved 'from the gallows' (or the bulldozer) in recent years only by the vigilance of the local community. All those concerned with the preservation of Furry Park House

expect it to be listed for preservation in Dublin Corporation's next city development plan. An old spelling 'Furrs-parke' or 'Furrsparke' suggests that the name was adapted from Furze Park. Furry Park Road is today translated into Irish as Bothar and Aitinn (Furze Road). One of the last houses of its type on Dublin's northside Furry Park House has been at the centre of a planning controversy since F.P.H. Properties U.S.A. (a Swiss firm) were given permission to demolish it in 1977. Since then Killester residents (especially Furry Park Action Group), an Taisce, an Foras Forbartha and conservationists in general, have successfully fought the demolition permission. In the last development of the case An Bord Pleanála granted F.P.H Properties permission to build over eighty apartments on the remaining two an a half acres of grounds around the property, but it refused to allow the house itself to be replaced by a commercial car park. In fact the Bord ordered the developers to retain and restore the 18th century building - an order which is a first and may well set a precedent for other historic buildings throughout the country.

After its first owner Mr. Fade the house was occupied by Peter Paumier who owned a sugar refinery at Mullinahack. He later sold it to Charles O'Neill of County Antrim who in turn disposed of it to Edward Howard in 1765 for £300. In 1780 Howard sold the house and estate to Richard Boyle, Earl of Shannon for £1,300 'plus £100 per annum'. Boyle was a Member of Parliament and in 1800 he voted in favour of the Act of Union. After Boyle, Thomas Disney occupied Furry Park House and then the Honorary T. Burton Vandaleur, Privy Councillor and King's Bench Judge resided there. In 1835 Thomas Bushe acquired the Furry Park Estate. He was secretary of the Ecclesiastical Commissioners who had responsibility for the tithe. His Father Charles Kendal Bushe a distinguished parliamentarian who advocated Catholic emancipation and was Lord Chief Justice from 1822 to 1841, spent his declining years in Furry Park House where he died in 1843. Charles' nickname was 'The Incorruptible' a title he earned when - unlike so many of his colleagues - in vehemently opposing the Act of Union he steadfastly refused to be bribed by British politician Cornwallis to change his mind. Sir Ralph Smith Cusack J.P., chairman of the Midland Great Western Railway, bought Furry Park in 1874 and he was succeeded as owner by Major M. Fetherston Whitney who in turn sold the estate to Crompton and Moya Llwelyn Davies in 1920. Since the mid 1930's, Furry Park House was occupied by the MacAnulla family.

Architecture

Furry Park House - most of its estate has been built upon for many years now - is among the most intact of the remaining medium sized early 18th century houses in the country. It is a three storey edifice in very good and sound condition with a basement and outhouses. On the wall of one of the outhouses - a granary - is a sundial or clock with the original builders name and date, 1730. Much of the original plaster work of the house is still intact. The entrance doorway is formed by a heavy stone architrave moulding. The original panelled entrance door still survives. Inside, the main staircase is also the original, and is completely unimpaired with robust handrail and balusters and original panelling running to full ceiling height. In fact it is the survival of this staircase and panelling coupled with the unaltered state of the front entrance which makes Furry Park House a building of such architectural importance nationally. Many alterations, repairs and extensions were carried out on the building in the late 18th century and from time to time during the 19th century. But the restoration work ordered by An Bord Pleanála (referred to earlier) includes preserving, or replacing with facsimile items, the wood panelled hall, the fire place and ceiling cornices. In general all interior features and fittings of the mansion must be retained and restored. The interesting and attractive 18th century sundial is to be set in the facade of one of the proposed apartment buildings.

While they resided in Furry Park Crompton and Moya Llewwlyn Davies, leading lights in Dublin's political and social scene at the time, entertained many of the country's leading personalities of the day including academics and politicians. Crompton was a member of the British Liberal Party. He was appointed Solicitor General to the British Post Office, a position he lost in 1921 (despite his close associations with Lloyd-George) on account of his support for his wife's Irish nationalist activities. He supplied Michael Collins with pen pictures of the British negotiating team prior to the 1921 Anglo Irish Treaty. Some historians argue that it was Crompton Davies who actually drafted the treaty document and also the famous Oath which was to cause such dissention. However other historical commentators are far from convinced that there is ample evidence to prove that Davies was really fully committed to the good of the Irish cause. In Furry Park House, it was his wife Moya who became the much renowned and celebrated 'character' of the villa. She was a daughter of James O'Connor, Fenian journalist and M.P for West Wicklow. He had been imprisoned in 1866 with the entire staff of the 'Irish People'. He later aligned himself with the anti-Parnellities. The O'Connor family lived in Blackrock and in 1890 tragedy struck when the mother and four daughters died after eating contaminated shellfish, which they cultivated in their own large private pond. James was absent on that occasion and Moya was the only family member to survive. She had good French and German and spoke Irish fluently, having spent several holidays in the Aran Islands. She also did some writing mainly on economic and medical topics under the pen name

'Delta'. The Davies had two children - Richard and Katherine. Guests entertained in Furry Park House from time to time included General Michael Collins and many of his friends in the Irish Nationalist Movement. Indeed the Davies hosted a 'Friend of Ireland' reception for the Irish delegation which went to London in 1918 to seek a meeting with President Wilson of the United States hoping that Ireland would be included at the Paris Peace Conference. Collins was a member of this delegation and John Charters was also at the reception - he was later to appear as one of the four secretaries of the Irish team for the 1921 Treaty negotiations. (See chapter ten below)

Attempted Assassination

Perhaps the most popular tale people like to recall about Furry Park House is the attempted assassination there of Michael Collins on the night of August 19th, 1922, at the height of the Civil War. On that night a group of distinguished guests were being entertained in the house by Crompton and Moya Llewelyn Davies. The guests included the inimitable Dublin writer George Bernard Shaw, the artist Sir John Lavery and his wife Hazel; Horace Plunkett, pioneer of the co-operative movement in Ireland, Desmond Fitzgerald then a minister in the Free State Government (and father of later Taoiseach Garret Fitzgerald) and his wife who had been private secretary to George Bernard Shaw. Also there was the 'magnetic' Collins himself with close associate Piaras Béaslaí - a journalist who became editor of the revived Volunteer's journal "an t-Óglach" in 1918. During the course of the evening a fifteen year old courier called Bill McKenna arrived to the house with a warning message that 'information received' indicated that an attempt would be made on the life of Collins that very night. This was a particularly dangerous time for Collins. Only a week earlier (August 12th) Arthur Griffith had died and just the day before, an attempt had been made to assassinate Collins in Stillorgan. When this message came through from McKenna, Collins, who was sitting with his back to the window 'eating a cream bun and discussing the Palestinian question with Moya Davies', refused to move while the Furry Park Grounds were being searched. Sure enough an armed ex-Connaught ranger called Dixon was discovered in a tree in the garden preparing to shoot Collins through the window. Dixon was escorted down the Howth Road to the sloblands at Fairview (now Fairview Park) and executed. The following morning Collins accompanied by the young McKenna left Portobello barracks at six a.m. on the doomed trip to his native Cork. No other commander-in-chief would have undertaken the reckless expedition that led to his death in the famous ambush at Béal na nBláth on Tuesday 22nd, August, 1922. This was characteristic of Collins who probably had accepted that his end was going to be violent one.

Among the other regular visitors to Furry Park was the poet William Butler Yeats. Professor George Thompson, the distinguished student of Greek culture, Muiris O Súilleabhán the Blasket Islands author of "Fiche Bliain ag Fás " and Bertrand Russell the noted British philosopher. Thompson - who had a deep interest in Ireland and the Irish language - together with Moya Davies translated "Fiche Blian ag Fás" into English. Muiris O Súilleabhan described Furry Park as "a castle. . . covered in ivy. . where there is comfort and delight". Yet another distinguished and frequent visitor to Furry Park House was the English born composer of the Peter Pan story - J.M. Barrie. He became a close friend of Michael Collins and many people suggest that Collins' boyish, flamboyant and 'eternal youth' attitude sowed the seed of 'Peter Pan' in Barrie's mind.

William B. Yeats rehearsed some of his famous 1930's B.B.C broadcasts in Furry Park House. The poet is alleged to have rather 'excelled' himself on one visit. Announcing that he could fill a room with the scent of roses by merely rubbing his hands together, his audience sat in considerable discomfort while he tried in vain to practically illustrate this 'gift' - all to no avail! On another occasion both Yeats and Moya were highly amused by Percy French's skit on Queen Victoria's address to her Irish Lord Deputy in Dublin Castle, which he parodied thus:

"I think there's a slate, says she,
Off Wille Yeats, says she,
He ought to be home, says she,
French-polishing a poem, says she,
Instead of writing letters, says she,
About his betters, says she."

Crompton Davies died in 1936. Shortly afterwards, as the original large Furry Park Estate was being extensively built upon, the remarkable Moya Davies went to live in Coolock and later in Newtownmountkennedy in County Wicklow where she died in 1944.

. . . .

Threatened with demolition in the 1980's, Furry Park House has been saved in that the building has been incorporated into the Furry Park Court Residential Scheme.

Lord Charlemont

Marino House

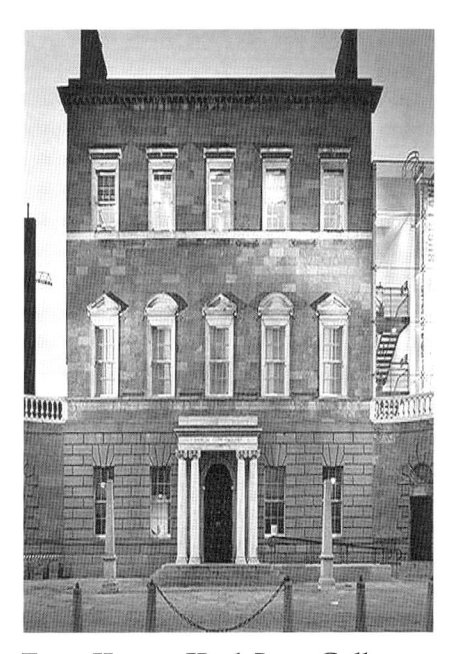

Town House - Hugh Lane Gallery

The Casino

Furry Park House

Old Sundial Clock

Moya Llwellyn Davies

CHAPTER NINE

Origin of Place Names in Clontarf

One need not be a Sherlock Holmes to compile a potted history on the origins of the street names in the Clontarf area. Many are derived from the cornucopia of historical characters and events that dapple Clontarf's heritage. Others are adapted from the 'handsome seats and pleasant villas that once adorned the richly wooded and finely cultivated Clontarf area.' A third source of origin for many names is the sea itself. But it is amazing to see quite a number of building schemes being labelled with names with no connections, significance or meaning to the traditions of this most historic of regions. Many of these are maverick names that sound enticing - or even trendy - which are haphazardly chosen by builders. Surely residents should have some voice in naming new residential areas in order that names with some background and relevance to Clontarf would be chosen - especially as historically steeped and traditional Clontarf names such as Crab Lake, Cockle Point, The Furlong, ect. are now redundant? And while a host of such names stand idly by its quite baffling to perceive identical names adopted for more than one residential scheme.

Clontarf - Street by Street, Road by Road

Alfie Byrne Road,	Bóthar Ailf Uí Bhroin.
Baymount Park,	Páirc Árd an Chuain
Bayview Court	Cúirt Ard an Chuain
Belgrove Road,	Bóthar Sárchoille
Blackheath Avenue,	Ascaill an Dubh-Fhraoigh
Blackheath Court,	Cúirt an Dubh-Fhraoigh
Blackheath Drive,	Céide an Dubh-Fhraoigh
Blackheath Gardens,	Gairdiní an Dubh-Fhraoigh
Blackheath Grove,	Garrán an Dubh-Fhraoigh
Blackheath Park,	Páirc an Dubh-Fhraoigh
Brian Boru Avenue,	Ascaill Brian Bóirmhe.
Brian Boru Street,	Sráid Brian Bóirmhe.
Brighton Avenue,	Ascaill Brighton
Bull Bridge Road & Cottages	Droichead Bóthar agus Teachini an Bhulla
Byrne's Lane,	Lána Uí Bhroin

The Alfie Byrne Road was first opened in 1984 and known as the East Link Road until it was formally named the Alfie Byrne Road after the 10 times elected Lord Mayor of Dublin. Essentially a Fairview/City Centre by-pass it gives the motorist easy access to the south-side of Dublin City via the EastLink Toll Bridge. The bridge that takes the road across the Tolka river was called the John Mc Cormack Bridge in honour of the famous singer in the centenary year of his birth (1984).

Baymount Park takes its names from the local Baymount Castle (now Manresa House). The name Belgrove comes from Belgrove house and Belgrove Park stands on the grounds of what used to be Belgrove Football Club. The last addition to the Blackheaths is the little nest of townhouses called Blackheath Court on the site of the old St. Michaels House on the junction of Blackheath Avenue and Blackheath Park. Blackheath estate, now the Orthopedic Hospital, was the home of the well known Gibson Black family and Blackheath Grove - still no more than a laneway - was their private entrance. Brian Boru Avenue and Street with its little park commemorate the famous High King of Ireland. (Its worth noting that the only 'street' in Clontarf is Brian Boru Street!) Brighton Avenue is called after the Brighton Lodge part of St. Anne's Estate. Byrne's Lane is a laneway connecting Dollymount Park and Avenue. The Bull Bridge, Road and Cottages are dealt with in chapter six above.

Castilla Park,	Páirc Chastilla.
Castle Avenue,	Ascaill an Chaisleáin.
Castle Court,	Cúirt an Chaisleáin.
Castle Grove,	Garrán an Chaisleáin.
Castle Road,	Bóthar an Chaisleáin.
Castle View,	Radharc an Chaisleáin.
Causeway Road,	Bóthar an Chabhsa.
Cecil Avenue,	Ascaill Cecil.
Charlemont Road,	Bóthar Achadh.
Chelsea Court,	Cúirt Shealsai.
Chelsea Gardens,	Gáirdíní Shealsai
Churchgate Avenue,	Ascaill Gheata an Teampaill
Clontarf Bay,	Bá Chluain Tarbh
Clontarf Court,	Cúirt Chluain Tarbh
Clontarf Mews,	Stáblaí Chluain Tarbh
Clontarf Park,	Páirc Chluain Tarbh
Clontarf Road,	Bóthar Chluain Tarbh
Conquer Hill Avenue,	Ascaill an Choingéir

Conquer Hill Road,	Bóthair an Choinigéir
Copeland Avenue,	Ascaill Cóplainn
Copeland Grove,	Garrán Cóplainn
Crescent Place,	Plás an Corráin

The Spanish sounding Castilla Park commemorates an old house of that name which once stood on the site. The house was for many years the residence of the Bradstreet family. The name "Castle" is adopted from the twelfth century Clontarf Castle. Castle Avenue is the oldest road in the vicinity and was part of an old road connecting Artane and Killester to Clontarf and the sea, while also serving as an avenue to the castle itself. Cutting Clontarf in two it is one of Clontarf's five "highways" - the others being the Malahide, Howth and Clontarf Roads and Vernon Avenue. There were two Castle Courts in Clontarf - one the neat little hamlet of houses almost directly opposite Lawrence Grove on the Howth Road. The other is the pocket of town houses to the left after Victoria Road as one ascends Castle Avenue, but this one is now called Clontarf Mews.

The building development known as "Auburn" shares the same entrance as Castle Court off the Howth Road. On its junction with Clontarf Road Castle Avenue has, on the city side the complex of apartments known as Alverno called after and built on the site of Alverno House - which was once named Tivoli House. Further up is Rathmore House and just past Victoria Road is the dwelling known as Balmoral Lodge. On the other side of Castle Avenue, again ascending from the sea, the seafront corner site, originally occupied by Danesfort House which had Baymount House just to its east, now has the sites of both houses occupied by the Danesfort estate of town houses and apartments. Further along are the twin houses called St. Elma and St. Andrew. Then we have the residence known as Hughenden called after original residents connections with Hughenden in Buckinghamshire in England. Further along are St. David's Court Apartments, Moyville residence, Sandon Court Apartments, Lissadell House and the modernised Lucerne with some town houses. On the junction of Castle Avenue with Castle Road is the familiar and sizeable rectangular Post Office building with its distinctive "elongated" windows. It was a telephone exchange of the older 'step by step' type. The row of eight houses opposite Clontarf Castle (or St. John's Wood to be precise), between Kincora Road and Seafield Road West, were built by Dominic Dolan of Belgrove House. They are named St. Dominic's, Courtview, Clifton, Mount Olive, Cataloga, Glenburn and St. Michael's. Courtview comprises of two houses and has long since been converted into apartments.

The Causeway Road is dealt with in chapter six. Cecil Avenue is so called in memory of Edward Cecil Guinness, the first Earl of Iveagh. Charlemont Road recalls Lord Charlemont. Chelsea Gardens is built on the site of the old Brian Boru G.A.A. grounds. Churchgate Avenue (formerly Chapel Lane and also once named Ruthland Lane) obviously is 'dedicated' to the nearby St. John The Baptist Church. Its tiny little houses are the last of the old fishermen's cottages in the area. Clontarf Bay is the little commercial development at the junction of Dollymount Park with the Clontarf Road. Clontarf Park encloses a nice little green for its residents. This was once the playing fields for two football clubs - Corinthians and Queens Park. The entrance to Clontarf Park from Vernon Avenue was known as Ruthland Place.

Clontarf Road itself, sweeping along the seafront from the Fairview end of the Howth Road to the seafront end of Mount Prospect Avenue is Clontarf's longest roadway. This swirling road, starting property at the 'Skew Bridge', is the one that escorts the visitor into the heartland of Clontarf. The road marks the route of the old tramline from the city centre and many younger readers will, perhaps, be surprised to learn that it is in fact one of Clontarf's newer highways. Affectionately known as the 'coast' 'seafront', 'front', or even the 'tram' road it is flanked by a wide grassy promenade with a concrete walk and wall along the edge of the sea. This neat 'skirt' along the seafront is a far cry from the slob of messy, wet and muddy foreshore ooze which older residents will recall, with only a three foot high wall attempting to discourage the advances of the sea. In 1925 moves were begun by Dublin Corporation to complete a promenade between 'the railway viaduct at Clontarf Road Fairview and the Bull Wall Dollymount'. In 1930 the Corporation voted a sum of £70,000 towards the project. For a time it was envisaged that the Clontarf coastal boulevard (as it is often called) would be part of a scenic seaside drive unbroken to Malahide. As far as old St. Anthony's Church the boulevard was filled in with city rubbish. From St. Anthony's to the Bull Wall it was filled in with sand. The Clontarf promenade was eventually completed in 1965, much of the work being done by Dutch dredgers who pumped sand from outside the boundary wall of the promenade into the space between the wall and the road. This was then covered with top soil and seeded to bear a healthy crop of grass - and the quite stifling odours which accompanied the work will long be remembered by the residents who had to endure them. However it would be hard to imagine Clontarf today without the promenade which also has many decorative palm trees, shrubs and flowers as well as frequent shelters and a footpath and now a bicycle lane. The promenade is often (illegally) used for training by football teams and became the 'unofficial jogging capital of Ireland'. (see appendix 9 below)

Along the Clontarf Road, at a spot approximately half way between Seaview Avenue North and Haddon Road lie numbers 84-90 Clontarf Road - a block of terraced houses. The spot is colloquially known as Warrenpoint. The entrance is guarded by two spinx. This location once had a quarry for calp stone and is marked on Taylor's map of 1828 as Cockle Point and a house known as Cockle Hall once stood there. The name "Warrenpoint" was given to the place by its builder who had intended to build a full terrace of houses, but found funds in short supply. Keen observers will notice some old name plates at various points along the Clontarf Road such as "Whitehall Terrace" and "Cabra Villas". These were merely names for the various terraces of houses built along the road at different times and in use until the umbrella name "Clontarf Road" was adopted in 1929. Indeed the road was originally known as Strand Road or Strand Street. Just landward of its junction with Strandville Avenue on the Clontarf Road is Clontarf Garda Station, with the Seapoint office block beside it. Number 162 Clontarf Road, between Oulton Road and Summerville Estate is the entrance to the office complex of Tara (mines) Exploration and Development Company Ltd. The Summerville housing development covers the site and sourounds of the house once known as The White House and previously as Summerville House and Strand House. At the junction with Conquer Hill Road is the Clontarf Dublin Bus depot. At the Dollymount end of Clontarf Road Danesfield House stood where a Danish sword was dug up in 1830. Danescourt flats now occupy the site. A little further on are three houses, Mount Vernon (which is effectively two semi-detached houses) and behind it Iverna House, formerly Eagle Lodge. Situated between the old (and now non existent) Albert Terrace and Byrne's Lane (at the seafront end of Dollymount Avenue) once stood the Dollymount Inn - at times hotel, restaurant and public house. It was once owned by the Connolly family – more associated with the Sheds, public house. In time the Dollymount Inn was transformed into the flourishing Dollymount House by the Fitzgerald family. It was demolished in 2013 and today a block of apartments called Seascape stand on its site.

Many Clontarfites proclaim Conquer Hill to be the true heart of Clontarf. It houses a traditionally close-knit loyal and proud community of people. Much confusion surrounds the origin of the name itself. Many maintain that the spot marked the final vanquishing of the Danes at the end of the 1014 battle. However this is rather unlikely. It was to have been the site for Daniel O'Connell's Monster Meeting of 1843. The Irish translation of the name being quite close to 'coinicear' suggests it may have connections with a rabbit warren. Another source alleges it to be the English adopted translation of the 'ceann-cor' the herring's head. The area originated as the site of an old village - perhaps remnant fishermen from the

Old Sheds village who were pushed further north and slightly inland as Clontarf developed as a seaside resort. The village (and the remnants of the original village survived into the 1950's) comprised of cabins erected with somewhat carefree orientation ending with a haphazard maze of meandering rows which were locally nicknamed 'The Puzzle' and 'The Keyhole' and covering an area once known as Danespark. The present Conquer Hill Avenue was originally 'Tram Terrace' - which sports delightful period tramwork cottages, built by the tramway company for its workers. Originally council houses, the Conquer Hill houses are now privately owned. The name Copeland is taken from the Copeland Islands which are situated north of Donaghadee on the entrance to Belfast Lough. Crescent Place derives its name from the nearby Crescent.

Dollymount Avenue	Ascaill Chnocán Doirinne.
Dollymount Grove,	Garrán Chnocán Doirinne.
Dollymount Park,	Páirc Chnocán Doirinne.
Dollymount Rise,	Ard Chnocán Doirinne.
Doyles Lane,	Lána an Dúill.
Dunluce Road,	Bóthar Dhún Libhse.
Dunseverick Road,	Bóthar Dhún Sobhairse.
Fortview Avenue,	Ascaill Redharc an Dúna.
Fortview Quay,	Cé Radharc an Dúna.
Furry Park Court,	Cúirt Páirc an Aitinn.
Furry Park House,	Teach Páirc an Aitinn.
Furry Park Road,	Bóthar Páirc an Aitinn.
Grosvenor Court,	Cúirt Grosvenor.

It is often claimed that Dollymount (which essentially lies between Seafield Road East and Mount Prospect Avenue) acquired its name in memory of Dorothy (Dolly) Vernon, the daughter of Sir George Vernon of Haddon in Derbyshire, England. However this is unlikely. Rather it appears that a tiny village grew up in front of a house (later known as Kincora or Kinkora House) 'between Seafield Avenue (now Seafield Road) and Blackbush Lane (now Mount Prospect Avenue'). Dollymount Rise is built directly on the site of Kincora House. Captain William Bligh on his map of 1800 marks the nearest sea point as 'Cold Harbour'. Another house stood on or beside the site known as 'Seapark' (shown on Duncan's map of 1820) on Mount Prospect Avenue. The name Dollymount was first applied to this house and Dollymount house appears in the Dublin directories up to 1836, after which it disappeared - being perhaps renamed. The name first appears in 1838 as the name of a district. Until well into the 19th century Dollymount was a country seat quite removed from, and not even connected with, Dublin. Then the villa-building era resulted in its absorption first into the Clontarf township and later into the Dublin metropolis. Some of the older cabins and houses - dating back to the original village were inhabited until close on 1950. The growth of the Bull Island gave Dollymount its extensive beach of smooth sands. The older nameplates on the present Clontarf "Dollymounts" translate it as the more original 'Baile na gCorr' but that name refers to the old area from the seafront inland once known as 'Heronstown, Raheny' and also as 'Blackbush'. Dollymount Park has the Clontarf Bay development at its seafront end. The names 'Dunluce' and 'Dunseverick' are effectively adopted from two old castles near Bushmills in County Antrim. Fortview Avenue and Quay assume their name from the panoramic view afforded to them of the Old Pigeon House Military Fort on the southside of Dublin Bay. The name Furry Park alludes to the local historical Furry Park House. Grosvenor Court houses are built on what was once part of the ground of Verville (Retreat) House and lands.

Haddon Court,	Cúirt O'hAidín.
Haddon Park,	Páirc O'hAidín.
Haddon Road,	Bóthar O'hAidín.
Hampton Court,	Cúirt de Hamptún.
Hazel Lane,	Lána an Chuill.
Hollybrook Court Drive,	Céide Chúirt Chuileannsruth.
Hollybrook Grove,	Garrán Chuileannsruth.
Hollybrook Park,	Páirc Chuileannsruth.
Hollybrook Road,	Bóthar Chuileannsruth.
Howth Road,	Bóthar Bhinn Éadair.
Hunter's Row,	Rae an tSealgairí.

The name Haddon recalls the family and property connections the Vernon family of Clontarf Castle had with Haddon in Derbyshire, England. The famous 'dip' in Haddon Road was caused when old tree stumps - used to fill in a closed down quarry over which the road runs - rotted causing subsidence. On the corner of Haddon Road and the Clontarf Road (Howth side) are Haddon Court apartments. This was formerly the site of the manse (which has been subsumed into the apartments) wherein resided the various ministers of the Clontarf Presbyterian Church. Directly across Haddon Road stand those very conspicuous large and serene twin houses known as St. Raphael's and Padova. The seafront end of Haddon Road had for many years a row of Bathing Boxes at the spot known as 'The Shingle'. Bathing boxes were fashionable in the early years of this century and the Haddon Road boxes were operated by Mrs. Coyne. Haddon Park leads into the Paddocks. The name Hollybrook is derived from the local Hollybrook River. Hollybrook began as a small cluster of houses on the Howth Road. Hollybrook Road was opened about 1900. Hollybrook Court Drive has Hollybrook Court Flats at its seafront end. On Hollybrook Park stands Tullyallen House which is a 'twin' of the house named St. Dympnas. Beside these is the assemblage of apartments named St. James' after the house of that name. Also on Hollybrook Park are two serene "Queen Anne" houses allegedly the oldest buildings in Clontarf. (See Verville retreat chapter twelve). They were built back in the 1740's. The one nearest the Howth Road still has its coach house gate. Glaslyn apartments occupy the Junction of Hollybrook Park with the Howth Road.

The Clontarf section of the Howth Road stretches from Fairview to Sybill Hill Road - thence it proceeds through Raheny Village to join the James Larkin Road (as it becomes the Dublin Road) at a spot known as the Whip O' Water. The Howth Road is the original highway to Howth, but it was not always known as the Howth Road. In old directories the road approaching Killester from the city is termed 'Killester Road' and in John Rocque's 1752 map of Dublin the section from Raheny North to Blackbanks (then part of Black Bush) is marked 'Fox Lane'. Indeed the original Clontarf seafront end of the road extended only as far as a place known as the Black Quarry. Once a regular quarry this became a romantic little place and was situated between the present Dublin-Belfast Railway line and Mount Temple Comprehensive School. From the Black Quarry the road petered out into country laneways. In 1805 the British Government decided to direct all Irish mail through Holyhead rather than Liverpool. Fierce and vigorous controversy arose on this side of the Irish Sea as to whether the departure/arrival point should be Howth or Dun Laoghaire (which was renamed Kingstown after the visit of King George V in 1821). Up to then the Pidgeon House had been used as the Irish 'Station'. One pamphleteer viewed the possible choice of Howth with a dismaying terror. He wrote " what would become of the passengers if a coach wheel broke on such a road as that leading from Raheny down to the whiskey forge at the foot of the hill", And what about the following words from an antagonist of Howth being chosen: "Let any man of common sense travel along the road from Dublin to Howth. Let him see what security he can find for his person and property on a dark night. He should have a troop of horses to guard him against land robbers. And at high water, which at times it must be when the mail boat goes that way, he ought to have a gunboat sailing along the strand inside the North Bull to prevent the sea pirates attacking him and plundering him on the coast." It must be stated that such hazards didn't seem to worry the ordinary Dubliner of the day as a jaunting car trip to Howth was one of his favourite treats!

In any event Howth was chosen as the plum centre to act as mail pack station. Great activity ensued on the northside and preparation of the harbour began in 1807. In order to accommodate the mail-coach and other traffic a big reconstruction scheme began, the legacy of which is the Howth Road as we know it today. The work undertaken by Telfords (then a giant British engineering company) began in 1808. It was known as the Dublin-London Road as it was regarded as a continuation of the route from London to Holyhead - a road which was in fact built under the same contract. The road turned out to be one to compare with the best of its time, complete with granite milestones (many of which still stand along the road). A rather fittingly named mail-boat 'The Escape' (there were six in all) inaugurated the Howth-Holyhead service in 1814. Each night the Royal Mail Coach left Falconers Hotel in the city centre at 9.45pm and took one hour to reach Howth. But alas, and unfortunately for Howth, it soon became clear that the new Harbour was not suitable. Almost immediately it began to silt up and arrangements were made to switch the mail packet station over to Dún Laoghaire. This became permanent in 1836 and Howth relapsed into an ordinary fishing village. And perhaps the great memory of Howth as a harbour is the fact that King George IV landed there on August 12th, 1821.

The house names on both sides of the section of the Howth Road between Hollybrook Park and Killester Village have various origins - some recall different traditions and represent family prides and memories. Others are place names transported or events commemorated, or to quote the poet William Wordsworth *"old forgotten far off things and battles long ago."* On the right hand side coming from the city at the junction of Hollybrook Park and the Howth Road stands Glaslynn, one of the oldest houses in the district - the name being an adaptation of the Irish form of 'Green Brook' from the local Hollybrook stream. Further on are Abbeyfield, Norabrook, Loyola, Redpark, Ferndale, Kentucky, Hibernia and Lissue as well as the De La Salle Provincialate house. On the left hand side stand many stately houses (set in their own extensive grounds) that recall the era of the big houses. They include Auburn, Greenmount, Kelburne, Iona, Belvidere, Killronan, Lyndale, Hazeldene, Tuly Herron, Beverly Hall and Rivendall. Hunter's Row is part of Seapark Road.

James Larkin Road,	Bóthar Séamus O Lorcáin
Kincora Avenue,	Ascaill Cheann Córa.
Kincora Court,	Cúirt Cheann Córa.

Kincora Drive,	Céide Cheann Córa.
Kincora Grove,	Garrán Cheann Córa.
Kincora Park,	Páirc Cheann Córa.
Kincora Road,	Bóthar Cheann Córa.
Kincora Walk,	Siúlan Cheann Córa.
Knights Bridge,	Droichead na Ridirí.
Lambourne Village,	Sráidbhaile Lambourne.
Lawrence Grove,	Garrán Lamhrás.

The James Larkin Road recalls the great Dublin trade unionist and joins the Clontarf Road from Mount Prospect Avenue to the Howth Road at Blackbanks. It was opened in 1949. Prior to that the only route along this part of the seafront was the Old Tramway. The name Kincora is another reminder of that irrepressible monarch Brian Boru. Kincora was his birth place and the ancient fortress of the Dalcais tribe in County Clare where Killaloe stands today. Kincora Avenue, Drive and Grove were part of the Clontarf Castle estate which was sold in the 1930's and acquired for building purposes. The houses were finished in 1958. Kincora Court is an extension of Kincora Road and its continuation is Parkview. It consists of a cluster of bungalows and townhouses on a site traditionally known as Crab Lake. Off Kincora Grove on another section of the Castle grounds are Lambourne Village townhouses. Knightsbridge recalls the fact that both the Knights Templars and the Knights Hospitallers (or the Knights of St. John of Jerusalem) occupied the Castle at different times. Off the Howth Road, on the city side of St. Lawrence Road is Lawrence Grove, a neat modern nest of houses.

Malahide Road,	Bóthar Malahíde.
Marino Avenue,	Ascaill Mhuiríne.
Mount Prospect Avenue,	Ascaill Árd na Teamhrach.
Mount Prospect Drive,	Céide Árd na Teamhrach.
Mount Prospect Grove,	Garrán Árd na Teamhrach.
Mount Prospect Lawns,	Faiche Árd na Teamhrach.
Mount Prospect Park,	Páirc Árd na Teamhrach.

The Malahide Road adopts its title from the seaside town to which it leads. The name Marino is the legacy from the name Lord Charlemont gave to his residence and estate (see chapter eight above). Mount Prospect acquires its name from an old house of that title which stood on the site now occupied by Immaculate Conception House, the home of the Sisters of Charity of St. Vincent's de Paul (see chapter two above). The seafront section of Mount Prospect Avenue (once named Blackbush Lane) is one of the most desirable residential spots of a very desirable (Clontarf) residential area, incorporating as it does the best of all worlds - a country setting in the city (Clontarf's "Rus in Urbe") with the sea and Bull Island thrown in as extras! The headquarters of Dublin Corporation Parks Department (from the 1978 until 1995) was Bedford Lodge House in St. Anne's Park on Mount Prospect Avenue. It is now a private residence. Nearby are the famous Red Stables, in a magnificent Victorian courtyard setting (see chapter seven above). Further "Inland" opposite its junction with Seapark Road, Mount Prospect Avenue has the complex of flats known as "Seapark", once the site of Dollymount House later known as Seapark House. Mount Prospect Grove has the facility of a very neat little green in its centre while Mount Prospect Park has some town houses named Woodside on its "extension" close to St. Anne's Park.

Oakley Park,	Páirc Oakley
Oulton Road,	Bóthar Oulton.
Parklawn,	Páirc an Faiche.
Parkview,	Radharc an Pháirc.
Redcourt Oaks,	Doire an Cúirt Dearg.
Seacourt,	Cúirt na Mara.
Seafield Avenue,	Ascaill Ghort na Mara.
Seafield Close,	Clós Ghort na Mara.
Seafield Downs,	Isle Ghort na Mara.
Seafield Grove,	Garrán Ghort na Mara.
Seafield Road (West and East),	Bóthar Ghort na Mara (Thiar agus Thoir).
Seapark Drive,	Céide Páirc na Mara.
Seaview Avenue North,	Ascaill Radharc na Mara Thuaidh.
Seaview Court,	Cúirt Radharc na Mara.
St. Gabriels Court,	Cúirt Naomh Gailbriél.
St. Gabriels Road,	Bóthar Naomh Gaibriél.
St. John's Wood,	Coill Naomh Eoin.
St. Joseph's Square,	Cearnóg Shan Seosaimh.
St. Lawrence Road,	Bóthar Shan Lamhrás.
Strandvill Avenue East,	Ascaill Bhailtín Trá Thoir.
Summerville,	Cnoc an tSamhraidh.

Oakley Park is named after Oakley House which stood nearby. The name Oulton comes from the last owners of Clontarf Castle. When the male Vernon line finished a female Vernon married into the Oulton family. Beechfield House and Tudor House are the two 'big house' names associated with the Howth side (seafront end) of Oulton Road. Originally a laneway called Beechfield with a turnstyle, it led to Seafield Road West. Today's Oulton Road joins Kincora Road but the old laneway still leads to Seafield Road - joining it beside Clontarf Protestant Church. The entire lane was also known as 'Tudor Lane' and 'Church Lane' and today's existing stretch has been nicknamed 'Ministers Walk'. Close to its junction with Dollymount Avenue on Mount Prospect Avenue is the compact little housing estate called Parklawn, built on a plot that was once part of Baymount Castle, now Manresa House (see chapter two above). Parkview is reached from Kincora Court. Redcourt Oaks is built on the grounds of Redcourt House, off Seafield Road East. The house was long associated with the Hardy Family and its ruins sit emptily there. It is not surprising to find the word "sea" in so many Clontarf placenames considering the regions' proximity to the sea. The name "Seafield" commemorates the old Seafield House which stood slightly inland of the seafront end (city side) of Seafield Road (East) a spot now occupied by Seafield Downs, a little group of houses built almost directly across the Clontarf Road from Bull Bridge. Beside the junction of Seafield Road (East) and Vernon Avenue, on the seaside, stood two big houses called Merchamp (meaning Seafield in French) and Koska (once called Rosetta House). Koska was used as a college for a time, but the site and grounds of both houses are now occupied by the spread of apartments called Merchamp. Where Seafield Road (West) meets Castle Avenue a block of apartments called Seafield Court stand. This block is on part of the grounds of the villa and estate once known as Yew Park, and previously called Yew View and Elm Park, the gatehouse of which still stands. Part of a route to Howth once passed along a section of Seafield Road then known as Green Lane. However it became nicknamed "Robbers Row" as a result of the activities of highwaymen active in the area. Seaview Avenue (North), its houses dating from the 1920's shares its name with another Seaview Avenue (East) on the North Strand. Seaview Court consists of a few townhouses on the Clontarf Road close to the Bull Bridge. The Saint Gabriel's name is derived from the local church of that name and St. Gabriel's Court features residences for senior citizens.

St. John's Wood on Castle Avenue and once part of Clontarf Castle grounds is named after Clontarf's patron saint, John The Baptist. The tranquil and nesting St. Joseph's Square is surely one of Clontarf's treasures. Directly inland of the Holy Faith Convent it is perhaps Clontarf's oldest existing hamlet of houses. There are some 30 dwellings on the little jewel of a square and all the houses are of the type once known as 'up and down' houses. One residence is traditionally known as 'the bachelors house' having once accommodated four bachelors! The Square was part of the area known as Snugborough or 'the Burrow' which was originally constructed to house the poor of Clontarf, from the old Sheds fishing village.

St. Lawrence Road recalls the famous Howth family of that name and was once part of Killester. The St. Lawrence's owned some land in Killester including a strip through the property of Clontarf Manor from the Howth Road to the sea. The Howth family apparently inherited an inland convent's ancient right of access to the sea. When the nuns were originally given this access they were told to mark off "a corridor to the seafront". So the entire community of nuns marched down the route of today's St. Lawrence Road abreast, with arms stretched, and commandeered all the land they could span. That is why, the story goes, St. Lawrence Road is so wide! Today the elegant road with houses dating back to 1872, is beautifully shaded with trees which were originally planted by courtesy of Lord and Lady Ardilaun of St. Anne's. The road has three apartment complexes - Kilronan Court at the Howth Road end (city side). St. Lawrence's Court on the left about half way to the seafront and Carlton Court at the Howth side of the junction with Clontarf Road. Strandville Avenue (East) has a 'twin' in Strandville Avenue North on the North Strand. However the Clontarf one is the 'senior' of the two! Number 16 on this road is a preserved house. Brooklawn and Strandville House represent multi-apartment residential development schemes on Strandville Avenue. For Summerville see Clontarf Road (above).

Stiles Court,	Cúirt na Strapaí.
The Court,	An Cúirt.
The Crescent,	An Corrán.
The Laurels,	Na Labhrais.
The Mews,	An Eachlann.
The Paddocks,	Na Banraí.
The Stiles Road,	Bóthar na Strapaí.
Vernon Avenue,	Ascaill Bhearnon.
Vernon Court,	Cúirt Bhearnon.
Vernon Drive,	Céide Bhearnon.
Vernon Gardens,	Gairdíní Bhearnon.
Vernon Grove,	Garrán Bhearnon.
Vernon Heath,	Fraoch Bhearnon.
Vernon Park,	Páirc Bhearnon.
Vernon Rise,	Árd Bhearnon.
Vernon Wood,	Coill Bhearnon.
Verville Court,	Cúirt Verville.
Victoria Road,	Bóthar Bhictoria.

Victoria Terrace,   Sraith Bhictoria.
Victoria Villas,   Bailtíní Bugidhe.

As the name suggests the Stiles was originally a spot or opening or gateway (this one complete with circular metal disks), where people could cross but cattle could not, and in this case was part of an area of grazing land known as The Stiles Paddock. The name Stiles first referred to the old broad laneway (still in existence) which connects the Howth Road with Castle Avenue. It later skirted the Castle garden wall and led to the farm of the Caprani family, passing the Stiles cottages which adjoined the Lido Tennis ground. Today the Stiles Road the oldest houses on which date from 1937, joins the Howth Road with the seafront via Seaview Avenue. In a garden approximately half way between the seafront and the Howth Road (on the left ascending from the seafront) is the site of St. Phillip's Well which once was in Clontarf Castle demesne. On the 1837 Ordinance Survey map it is marked St. Dennis's Well. The Court is the little pocket of townhouses on the Clontarf Road the city side of Warrenpoint. Probably the most famous street in Clontarf is The Crescent (sometimes called Marino Crescent). The quaint little semi-circular street of Georgian houses connects the Howth and Malahide Roads close to the city end of the Clontarf Road. Concave in design it was once nicknamed "Spite-Row". The story goes that in 1792 a painter-builder named (Wild) John Folliott of Aungier Street (south Dublin City) obtained land on the site of The Crescent. At the time he had a card gambling bet with the local Lord Charlemont (see chapter eight above) who owned a huge mansion and estate (present day Marino) in and around The Crescent site. Charlemont accused Folliott of being financially unable to secure the bet. Regarding this as a slur on his character, Folliott vowed revenge. So he arrived at the site and announced his intention of building houses there. However, Charlemont not wishing to have any buildings between his mansion and the sea discouraged Folliott by charging exorbitant dues on building materials the builder was obliged to take through the only roadway to the site - a toll gate of which Charlemont was a director and trustee. Folliott's answer was to transport his materials across the bay by barge and he then proceeded to exact sweet revenge by deliberately building The Crescent houses in that style and arrangement to entirely extinguish Charlemont's view of Dublin Bay. "Spite-Row" was thus, perhaps, the most expensive hate fence in the country!
Number 15 The Crescent, as well as being the home of Bram Stoker author of "Dracula", once housed the Russian Crown Jewels. Transactions concerning the jewels involved Eamon De Valera, Gerry Boland and a Bolshevik named Alexander Martens. The Russians eventually redeemed the jewels in 1949.

Residents of the Crescent had the amenity of a sizeable private park at their disposal. The park is enclosed by a high boundary wall and railings. Directly in front of their homes it allowed all the residents to use the facility. However the park later had a somewhat turbulent history for many years. Problems arose as to who was responsible for its upkeep. It has passed through phases of being a rubbish dump with heavy undergrowth to being a haven for 'Knights of the road' who used it as an open air dormitory. Many of its stately old trees have been cut down. But some years ago the then Dublin Corporation took over the park, cleaned it up and officially named it "Bram Stoker Park". Nowadays it is extremely well kept but in view of its many associations and general chequered history the tourist potential has never been realised. The Howth Road end of the Crescent has a very fitting apartment block called Crescent House (see also chapter ten below).The Laurels houses share the same site as the Seapark Apartments on Mount Prospect Avenue. The Mews development is off Dollymount Avenue and The Paddocks, a continuation of Haddon Park, recalls a local field cum corral for holding cattle.

The name Vernon alludes to the famous family who owned Clontarf Castle and lands - and effectively "ruled" Clontarf for so long. Ascending from the seafront Vernon Avenue turns sharply left at St. Anne's Park to meet Castle Avenue. This was the old throughfare from the "Sheds" fishing village and Sybil Hill Road - leading to the Howth Road - is a much later development. Near Clontarf Park, Moate Lane, formerly called "The Moat" connects Vernon Avenue with Conquer Hill, and where the shops now stand at the seafront end of the Avenue was once known as Dagmar Villas. At the (seaward side) junction of Vernon Avenue with Mount Prospect Avenue there stands Duncan Court Flats, once the site of a Dominican Convent originally called Convent House and which collapsed in the 1960's (see chapter two, above). On the other side of the junction is the stately mansion known as Calderwood House. Directly across Vernon Avenue in a little driveway, was Oakley House now replaced by Beverly Court Apartments.

Beside the Health Service Clinic on Vernon Avenue is Vernon Heath built on McMullan's farm - Clontarf's last farm. The site once belonged to a larger estate with a large villa known as Woodpark - better remembered as Wood Park Dairies. There are two Vernon Courts in Clontarf. One is the assemblage of apartments close to Fortview Avenue, the other is the little maze of town houses on Seafield Road West between Vernon Avenue and Belgrove Boys School. Verville Court is a nest of apartments built on part of the grounds of the old Verville Retreat House, beside Hampton Court. The name Victoria recalls Britain's longest reigning monarch (to date).

Other housing developments that have been built in Clontarf since our original publication, but not mentioned above include Bruach na Mara (Seafield Road), Rinn na Mara (off Clontarf Road at Doyle's Lane), Thornhill Lane - Cnoc Sceach Lána - (Mount Prospect Avenue), Yew Lane - Lána an Iúr - (Seafield Road) and Walpole Mews - Stablaí Walpole - (Kincora Avenue).

Periphery Roads and St. Anne's Housing Estate Roads.

All Saints Close,	Clós na Naomh.
All Saints Drive,	Roan na Naomh.
All Saints Park,	Páirc na Naomh.
All Saints Road,	Bóthar na Naomh.
Ballyhoy Avenue,	Ascaill Bhaile Thuaidh
Bettystown Avenue,	Ascaill Bhaile Bheite.
Maryville Road,	Bóthar Bháile Muire.
Naniken Avenue,	Ascaill Nainicín.
St. Anne's Avenue,	Ascaill Naomh Áine.
St. Anne's Court,	Cúirt Naomh Áine.
St. Anne's Drive,	Raon Naomh Áine.
St. Anne's Terrace,	Ardán Naomh Áine.
Sybil Hil Avenue,	Ascaill Chnoc Sibíle.
Sybil Hill Road,	Bóthar Chnoc Sibíle.
The Meadows,	Na Cluainte.
Wades Avenue,	Ascaill Mc Uaid.
Waterfall Road,	Bóthar an Easa.
Watermill Avenue,	Ascaill an Mhuilinn.
Watermill Court,	Cúirt an Mhuilinn.
Watermill Drive,	Raon an Mhuilinn.
Watermill Park,	Páirc an Mhuilinn.
Watermill Road.	Bóthar an Mhuilinn.

A unique fact about this particular list of streets is that each and every name is "local". The 'All Saints' is assumed from All Saints Church of Ireland in St. Anne's Park. Ballyhoy Avenue was 'christened' from Ballyhoy Bridge - where the Naniken River crosses under the Howth Road, the city side of All Saints Road. Bettystown Avenue assumed its name from the one time townland, Bettyville, long since part of St. Anne's. Likewise Maryville Road comes from the townland Maryville also long ago absorbed into St. Anne's. Naniken Avenue derives its name from the local river while St. Anne's Avenue, Drive and Terrace have the name of the park itself. Sybil Hill Avenue and Road recall the name of the lands and house once known as Sybil Hill. One cannot attach much credibility to the story which tells that the names Sybil Hill, St. Anne's and Maryville were adopted from the names of the three daughters of one time owner of Sybil Hill. He was John Barlow and his daughters were Sybil, Anne and Mary. The Meadows, named after the broad meadows of St. Anne's Park is a neat enclosure of houses bounded by St. Anne's Park, the Howth Road, Sybil Hill Road and St. Paul's College. Wades Avenue commemorates Sarah Wade whose forty acres were 'swallowed' by St. Anne's. The 'Water' roads come from the local Naniken and Santry "waterways" with the 'mill' being adapted from an old mill which once operated on the Santry River close to today's Watermill Bridge. Watermill Road itself was originally named Watermill Lane.

Clontarf Road Names

Vernon Avenue

Castle Avenue

Brian Boru Street

Conquer Hill Road

Cottages at Churchgate Avenue

The White House Clontarf Road

The Crescent

Sphinx at Warrenpoint

British Army at Skew Bridge 1916

Milestone at Howth Road

CHAPTER TEN

Famous Clontarfites - Past and Present

Over the years many famous names from all walks of life have lived in Clontarf. Some are native Clontarfites while others came to live in the area as their adopted home. Indeed the list is almost endless. Clontarf always was, and is, a very attractive area in which to reside - its comfortable relaxed position by the sea and its proximity to the city centre being two of its greatest attractions. Particularly in the fields of writing and politics we find many of our most outstanding national figures with Clontarf connections. Today's Clontarf has, as residents, a good cross-section of society in general with perhaps a majority of professional clerical and business people. Many 'high-profile' names appear on close examination of the Clontarf 'register'.

Politicians

The well known republican-Fianna Fáil Boland family have long associations with Clontarf. Mrs. Boland senior Kevin Boland's (the Fianna Fáil government minister of the 1960's) grandmother came to live at number 15 Marino Crescent with her four children Gerald, Harry, Kathleen and Ned, some years before 1916, after her husband's death. This was the house in which Bram Stoker had lived at an earlier period. They were there at the time of the Howth gun-running. Kathleen continued to live there after she married Sean O'Donovan. Kathleen and Sean later moved to a house called St. Michael's, almost opposite the Bull Wall, on the Clontarf Road, Dollymount. Sean O'Donovan, who was later a senator for some time, played centre field on the Dublin hurling team that beat Cork in the 1920 All Ireland hurling final, and is probably the only All Ireland winning Dublin hurler to have lived in Clontarf. Kevin Boland's grandfather Jim Boland (who was dead before the family moved to Clontarf) was the first Chairman of the Dublin G.A.A. County Board. Kevin's uncle Harry Boland, who won an All Ireland hurling medal as a sub when Dublin beat Tipperary in the 1917 All Ireland hurling final, was, while living in Clontarf, chairman of the Country Board for a number of years. He was killed during the Civil War in July 1922.

The Boland family moved from Marino Crescent to Lord Charlemont's old house in Marino (which was later demolished to make way for the housing estate.) They then lived for a time on Richmond Avenue, Fairview in a house where Mrs. Kathleen Clarke, wife of 1916 leader Tom Clarke, had once lived. Kathleen Clarke was a councillor, a Fianna Fáil T.D., a senator and served two terms (1939-

41) as Lord Mayor of Dublin. She later lived in Baymount House at the seafront end of Castle Avenue. Then when Kevin's father, Gerald Boland, was released from jail after the Civil War - he was one of the last batch of prisoners released in July 1924 - the family lived at number 5 Brian Road, Marino. Gerald Boland in 1933 bought 102 Howth Road, Clontarf and lived there until his death. He bought it from Denis Guiney owner of the famous Clerys city centre store, who bought and lived in the house called 'Auburn' a little further along the road. With (later Taoiseach) Sean Lemass, Gerald was principal architect of Fianna Fáil's brilliant constituency organisation in winning the 1932 General Election - organisation generally accepted as totally superior to Fianna Fáil's rivals. He was for many years a solid Fianna Fáil T.D. and minister. Kevin Boland lived at 102 Howth Road until his marriage in January, 1951. He was for a number of years minister before he resigned (as minister for Local Government) from the Lynch cabinet in May 1970,as a direct result of the deteriorating troubles in Northern Ireland. The following year, 1971, he formed the short lived Aontacht Éireann party. Kevin later lived in Rathcoole (in south County Dublin), but the 'Boland dynasty' still has members living in Clontarf.

Arthur Griffith, founder of the Sinn Féin party in 1905, lived from 1911 until his death in 1922, at 138 St. Lawrence Road. Born in Dublin in 1872 and educated at the Christian Brothers School, Great Strand Street, he became a very scholarly man. He was a gallant agitator of the Irish National cause and the Sinn Féin Party's main propagandist. He had earlier supported Parnell. He took part in the Anglo-Irish treaty negotiations of 1921and afterwards became a pillar of the pro-treaty side at home. He became first President of the Irish Free State and died in office on August 12th 1922, barely 50 years old. A self-confident and incorruptible man, loyal but not a real leader, he died as a result of exhaustion from the strain of work in those turbulent years of the early 1920's. The local broad tree lined crossover road (Griffith Avenue) linking the north city suburbs of Clontarf and Marino with Whitehall and Glasnevin, commemorates him and his zeal for Ireland. His two main written works were "Thomas Davis - Thinker and Teacher" and "The Resurrection of Hungary - a Parallel for Ireland".

Thomas Ryder Johnson was the first leader of the Labour Party in Dáil Éireann, and together with James Connolly and Jim Larkin is regarded as a founding father of the Labour Party in Ireland. In his time he was certainly Labour's major theorist and his presidential address at the 1916 Irish Trade Union Congress is regarded as the charter of the Irish Labour Movement. Johnson represented County Dublin in Dáil Éireann from 1922 to 1927. His long and distinguished career in the Irish Trade Union Movement began when he came to Belfast in 1903 from his birthplace, Liverpool. Late in 1929 Thomas Johnson and his wife

Marie came to live at 49 Mount Prospect Avenue, a house they named 'Ralahine'. They were both to have a long and happy life in Clontarf. Johnson died in 1963 exactly four months short of his 91st birthday. He was interred in the Old Clontarf graveyard on Castle Avenue after an oration by the then Labour Party Leader Mr. Brendan Corish. His remarkable wife Marie lived on until June 1974, a little over six months away from her 100th birthday. Up to 1927, in a Dáil without the abstentionist Fianna Fáil members, Johnson ensured the survival of constitutional democracy in the Young Free State by his constructive conduct as leader of the opposition. His most dramatic moment came in August 1927 (after the infamous affair involving the Sligo Alderman, John Jinks T.D.) when he came within one vote of being elected president of the Executive Council of the Free State (Taoiseach in fact). In September of that year (1927) he lost his Dáil seat in the general Election but remained a significant figure in Irish politics for thirty more years. He was a Labour Senator from 1928 to 1936 and played a major part in the Labour-Fianna Fáil alliance in the 1930's.

Another Fianna Fáil and Republican family with long Clontarf connections are the Colleys. Harry Colley set up home on Mount Prospect Avenue having originally lived in Marino. He was 'out' in 1916 and was 'left for dead' with bad wounds. He survived and served for many years as a Fianna Fáil T.D. and Minister. His son George Colley was to have a long career as a Fianna Fáil T.D. Minister and Tánaiste. Twice he contested elections for the party leadership but failed each time. He died suddenly in September 1983. The Colleys are still represented in Clontarf.

A man who, as a result of his frequent visits there, became very familiar with the Clontarf region, was General Michael Collins, first commander in-chief of the Irish army. Collins, that leader of genius with great resourcefulness and organising power, was for a long time - from the setting up of the 'illegal' Dáil Éireann in January 1919 to the 1921 Treaty negotiations - the head of the 'provisional government' and responsible for implementing policy, as practically all the other Sinn Féin leaders were in jail. He had his now legendary network of spies operating in Dublin Castle. Many historians agree that this is where the 'Laughing Boy's' real genius lay - he beat the British at their familiar game of intelligence and dirty tricks. Perhaps it was his understanding of the murky waters between politics and intelligence work that made him such an outstanding figure. The home of the Gay family on Haddon Road in Clontarf played a central role in his espionage web. Thomas Gay was the librarian in the public library in Capel Street at the time. He acted as receiver of messages for Collins from his spies in Dublin Castle chief of whom were James MacNamara, David Neligan, Joe Kavanagh and Edward Broy. Indeed Collins held a weekly conference with one of more of them at Gay's house. In his book "The Big Fellow" Frank O'Connor relates a close shave for Collins in an incident where the law officers failed to recognise him . . ."He (Collins) was returning to town after a consultation with Neligan, Broy and MacNamara at Gay's house in Clontarf. At Newcomen Bridge on Dublin's North Strand they were halted by a patrol of soldiers. It was fortunate for Collins that the detectives were with him. When they showed their passes the military informed them that an ambush had just taken place near the bridge. The officer advised them not to drive forward because some Sinn Féiner's were still there. They thanked him for the information, Broy called to Collins, who had jumped out ready for a fight, "Step in Sergeant!" and they drove off in safety." In his little book 'Old Clontarf' Canon F.W.R. Knowles refers to Collins thus "Near us (on Haddon Road) lived the Twohig family, cousins of General Michael Collins . . . of which one was commander Alphonso Twohig, Harbour Master of Dublin. In another house lived Mr and Mrs. Gay . . . One evening Mrs. Gay said she'd like to show me some of her visitors, and brought me into the kitchen, where Mr. Gay was sitting with three gentlemen. I never forgot the faces and in later years I recognised them from photographs in the daily papers. They were Arthur Griffith, Michael Collins and the third was, I believe, Eamon De Valera. Later Mr. Gay was Colonel Gay, Director of Civil Defence."

Another house in the Clontarf area to which Collins was a frequent caller was Furry Park House, Killester, (already referred to in Chapter eight), when it was occupied by Mrs. Moya Llewellyn Davies. Married to a Welshman, (Llwellyn Davies) who was a bar counsel and had encouraged and abetted David Lloyd-George early in his career which was ironic considering the parts Collins and Lloyd-George were to play in the forthcoming treaty. Mrs. Davis was a woman of wit and practical patriotism. Her own father had been 'out' in 1867, and now she entertained the hunted Michael Collins during the height of the War of Independence. Once a large-scale search for Collins of Furry Park House by the British Army took place, with troops approaching the house from Dollymount, Watermill Road and Howth Road. Collins was not there, as it was alleged he knew of the raid before the officer in charge did. Mrs. Davies was closely questioned and the following conversation took place:

First Officer	"We are looking for a man, Collins - Michael Collins."
Mrs. Davies	"But why all this horse, foot and artillery looking for one man?"
First Officer	"You appear to be educated."
Mrs. Davies	"I can read and write"
Second Officer	

(A Scotsman):	"Don't you think it foolish keeping up this opposition? We (the Scots) gave it up a long time ago."
Mrs. Davies	Don't you think we (the Irish) have more spirit?"

Collins and Mrs. Davies took occasional strolls from Furry Park across St. Anne's estate as far as the pond on the Naniken river. Another feature connecting Collins with Clontarf is the story that he regularly used the basement of the Casino (on the Malahide Road), and its underground tunnels, for rifle and machine gun practice during the War of Independence. A Clontarf resident who was a close associate of Collins, was Pat MacCrea. A tram driver, originally from Wicklow, who lived on the seafront at Dollymount, MacCrea was the driver of the car involved in Collins' extraordinary daring plan to rescue General Sean MacEoin from jail during the War of Independence.

Two nieces of Collins married and lived in Clontarf. One, Joan, was the wife of well known Colonel R.W. (Dick) Bunworth who was Battalion Commander of the United Nations 33rd (Irish) Infantry peace keeping Battalion during the Civil War in the Congo in the 1960-61 period, where in a notorious incident nine men from his Battalion were murdered by Baluba tribesmen. Colonel Bunworth is best known for his years as chairman of the Clontarf Residents Association. The other, Kathleen (Kitty) O'Mahony, is the mother of the two well-known Dublin area Fine Gael 'political ladies' - Mary Banotti and Nora Owen. Both these ladies are Clontarfites and are of course grand-nieces of 'The Big Fellow'. Other politicians who represented the Clontarf area or lived in the locality (or both) included, General Richard Mulcahy T.D. and Minister (who became leader of the Fine Gael Party), Oscar Traynor (Fianna Fáil) T.D. and Minister (also for many years President of the Football Association of Ireland), Séan Flanagan (Fianna Fáil) T.D., Minister and M.E.P, Charles Haughey (Fianna Fáil) T.D., Minister and Taoiseach, Eugene Timmins (Fianna Fáil) T.D. who also served a term as Dublin Lord Mayor. Celia Lynch was a Fianna Fáil Clontarf T.D. as was Luke Belton for Fine Gael. Vincent Brady, Séan Haughey (who served as Lord Mayor of Dublin for a term) Ivor Callely (all Fianna Fáil), and George Birmingham of Fine Gael (later a court judge) all served as T.D's.

A celebrated and colourful figure on the political scene in Clontarf was Séan Dublin Bay Loftus. A Dublin Corporation councillor for many years and Lord Mayor for a term - also a T.D. for a short period - he is remembered for his fight against pollution, his campaigning for proper planning for Dublin and especially for leading the fight to prevent an oil refinery in Dublin Bay. Other Clontarf residents who served terms as Dublin Lord Mayor were councillor Evelyn Byrne of Fianna Fáil, and councillors Gerry Breen and Naoise Murray of Fine Gael.

John Rogers, a Clontarfite, was Attorney General when his Colleague Dick Spring was Tanáiste. Another resident P.J Mara was government Press Secretary during the years Charles Haughey was Taoiseach. Much associated with Clontarf was the "elegant bicycle" Lord Mayor of Dublin, Alfie Byrne who held that office from 1930-1939 the longest ever holder of the 'Mayorship'. As well as being Lord Mayor his extraordinary career saw him elected a Westminster M.P. in 1914 and later a T.D. He was also a long standing councillor and served as a senator for a term!

Four Labour T.D's at various times had Clontarf as part of their 'territories' - James Larkin and later his son Denis Larken, Conor Cruise O'Brien (a one time government minister) and Pat McCarton later a circuit court judge. Strictly speaking not a politician but involved in the development of our nation since the beginning, Lieutenant General Michael J. Costello, who died in October 1986, had his residence on Victoria Road, Clontarf. A freedom fighter who joined the I.R.A. at sixteen, he switched to the regular army on its formation in 1922. In 1945 he became general manager of the Irish Sugar Company and was the dynamic force behind the Sugar Company's success in its early years. He also played a major role in developing Erin Foods. General Costello, who is rightly regarded as a founding father of our state, was a big man with a big mind. He fervently believed our country to be a rich one had we only the self confidence as a people to properly develop our natural resources. A man of great courage himself, General Costello believed that such development could bring us close to self-sufficiency, thus greatly boosting national morale and independence as well as creating much employment. His ideas never seemed to reach the right ears, or his contributions to our National development could surely have been greater. He resigned from the Irish Sugar Company in 1966.

Literary Figures

Perhaps the best known of all Clontarf's writers is Abraham or 'Bram' Stoker. He was born at number 15 The Crescent on November 8th, 1847. Because of the impact his novel 'Dracula' has had, he is probably Clontarf's most famous son. Stoker was ill and sickly for the first seven years of his life, but when he gained his health he went to Trinity College where he had an exceptional academic career, and became quite a competent athlete. He followed his father into the Civil Service, becoming a Dublin Castle Clerk. He loved the theatre and became an unpaid drama critic for the 'Dublin Evening Mail' newspaper, through which he promoted the appreciation of drama. It was through this channel that he met the famous English actor Henry Irving. Stoker gave Irving a very favourable review as "Captain Absolute" in "The Rivals" and afterwards the two met in a private room in the Shelbourne Hotel. Later Stoker became Irving's personal manager, staying with him until Irving's death almost thirty years later. In 1905, Irving became the first actor to be honoured with a knighthood - much due to the positive influence of Stoker on his career.

Bram Stoker resigned from the Civil Service in 1878 and moved to London to manage the Lyceum Theatre, which Irving had bought. In the same year he married Florence Balcombe of number one The Crescent. Florence had been a former girlfriend of the poet and playwright Oscar Wilde, who was a frequent visitor to the Crescent in those days. Bram and Florence had one child, Noel, born in 1879. In all, Bram Stoker wrote eighteen novels, the eighth being his masterpiece the spine-chilling horror story "Dracula" While the many facets of Dracula today - films, books, souvenirs, ect. - is nothing short of an 'industry' Stoker himself never really benefited commercially from 'Drac' (as he termed it) and he never enjoyed, while alive, the fruits of national fame and fortune. Towards the end of his life Stoker suffered a stroke. He died on April 20th, 1912 in London and was cremated at Golders Green, cemetery in North London. He was sixty four years old. The cause of death was given as 'exhaustion'. The Greater London Council have honoured his memory with a commemorative blue plaque marking his London home.

Nowadays honoured as a great writer, Stoker had two sides to his personality. Outwardly he was strong and stalwart, if somewhat impulsive and a hero worshipper, but inwardly he could be unsure of himself and had a particular obsession with the strange and supernatural.

Why did Stoker write Dracula? It certainly is the most enduring of horror stories. Indeed most critics agree that he is eclipsed by his own creation. And he certainly never realised that this gothic vampire character would achieve such fame. Perhaps he simply had a good story and wanted to tell it. A very popular theory is that the story came to him in a dream. It is believed that Stoker dined too well on dressed crab and had a nightmare!

Other experts think that he recalled childhood stories told by his mother about the cholera epidemic that swept Ireland in 1832. These concerned victims who were hastily and prematurely buried to prevent the spread of the disease. These stories would be supplemented by accounts of the 'suicide' plot beside Ballybough Bridge, where as late as Stoker's own lifetime, the bodies of suicides were interred in the time honoured fashion transfixed with stakes through their bodies which supposedly prevented their unhappy spirits from wandering around! The Dracula story might well have been set in the Clontarf area, as the superstition of the vampire was common in Ireland.

A certain number of experts argue that Dracula was analogy - the vampire representing the oppressive British Empire (and their protégé in Ireland the hated landlord class) under which Stoker and his fellow Irishmen had to live. Stoker strongly favoured Home Rule for Ireland. Bram was 31 years old before he left Dublin and we now know that the social political and religious situation in 19th century Dublin and Ireland were the real genesis of Dracula.

With Dracula, Stoker proved himself a master of fantasy and the story can only be accepted as an outstanding contribution to the literature of the uncanny. But perhaps his real achievement with Dracula was in changing our whole understanding of life after 'death'. The common theme of the regular ghost story is the ghost of a victim deprived of life returning to seek revenge. However a ghost is the spirit of a dead person. Stoker's villain is not dead but undead - a brand new concept in English literature. Sadly such a talented author as Stoker is neglectfully forgotten in his own city. Only the tireless work of the Clontarf based Stoker Dracula Gothic Organisation keeps his memory alive. Many tend to forget that we are celebrating the author of the world's biggest selling novel and the creator of the world's greatest fictional character – Dracula. People who are not "vampire freaks" should remember that Stoker was a versatile man who made a notable contribution in other areas - for example the appreciation of drama in Ireland, and laid the groundwork for the founding of our national Abbey Theatre (1904).

Brian O'Higgins, once a well known Clontarf figure, lived at 68 Hollybrook Road. He wrote the book of songs named "Songs of Glen na Mara" of which "The little ones" is probably the best known. He published an annual called "The Wolfe Tone Annual". A very religious man he also produced 'scroll type' Christmas cards.

William Carleton born in the 1790's near Clogher, Co. Tyrone, the "poor scholar" and renowned Ulster novelist of the 19th century, is said to have lived at number 23 The Crescent (but that is more likely Crescent Place) during the 1850's. He died in 1869 at number 2 Woodville, beside Milltown Park. W.B. Yeats wrote of him: "He is the greatest novelist of Ireland by right of the most Celtic eyes that ever gazed from under the brows of a story teller." He is commemorated in Marino by Carleton Road and Carleton Hall. He left the manuscript of an unpublished novel entitled "Anne Cosgrave". His best known work is "Fardorougha The Miser". Another of his respected works is "Traits and Stories of the Irish Peasantry" (1830).

Martin Haverty the author of a very respected History of Ireland called "The History of Ireland, Ancient and Modern" lived for many years at number 21 Marino Crescent. His very accurate and popular history published in 1867 was based on close scrutiny of original documents. He died in 1887 at number 40 St.

Alphonsus Road, Drumcondra. Haverty Road in Marino is so called in his honour.

The writer Charles Lever born at number 35 Amiens Street in 1806, grew up in Moatfield house, Coolock, which was built by his father James, an English architect. (It is now the site of Cadbury's factory). Charles is also supposed to have lived for a time on Philipsburgh Avenue, Fairview. Charles was to introduce many of the features of north-east Dublin into his books. In his novel "O'Donoghue" he devotes a chapter to Clontarf in which the Bull Island features. In another of his works "That Boy of Norcotts" he introduces the Green Lanes of Clontarf.

The celebrated poet Charles Lucas lived for some time at a house known as Pennyville, at the end of the present Fairview Avenue. He was personal physician to Lord Charlemont, and like Charlemont, he totally supported the Irish Parliament, but was opposed to Catholic relief and emancipation.

Jane Barlow, a poet and writer of the late 19th and early 20th centuries, was born in Clontarf. She later lived in Ballyhoy Cottage on the Howth Road in Raheny, which is today known as Raheny House (a retirement home). Here she was regularly visited by her fellow poet and novelist Kathryn Tynan. Jane's main subject matter in her prolific career was Irish peasant life.

James Joyce, perhaps Dublin's most famous writer, in his youth lived for a while on Richmond Road, Fairview, and later resided on Inverness Road (off Phillipsburg Avenue). Joyce was a frequent visitor to Clontarf and loved to stroll on the Bull Wall and the seafront promenade. Joyce himself traced his first inspiration as a writer to the effects a nubile young girl had on him, on Dollymount Strand in 1898.

The Irish language writer, Seosamh Mac Gríanna, who was born in Rinn na Féiriste Co Donegal in January 1900 and was trained as a national school teacher, lived in Clontarf for some years in the 1950's. He lived in a little cottage (once a St. Anne's Park Gate House) called Lilyvale (formerly Seatown House) on the Seafront, the city side of Watermill Road. Something of a nomad, a wayward character who became somewhat "disturbed", Mac Gríanna, who had opposed the Free State in the Civil War was, in August 1922 imprisoned for fifteen months. In the late 1920's he gave up teaching to concentrate full time on writing. In the Clontarf locality he was affectionately known as "the professor" as "butts" and for good measure as "Joe Feilini"! Without a regular income he lived very frugally in Clontarf and was lucky to have some benevolent friends. He penned some of our best known Irish books including "Filí gan Iomrá", "An Gradh agus an Ghruaim" and "Mo Bhealach Féin". He also did a considerable amount of translation work.

Fluent Irish writer and speaker Breandán Mac Raois was a Clontarf resident. He was born in Belfast and was taught Irish by the Christian Brothers. Many will recall his voice from his contributions to umpteen historical radio programmes. A prolific Irish writer who lived in Clontarf and someone who was well acquainted with Seosamh Mac Griana (see above) was Pronsias Mac an Bhéatha a fluent Irish speaker whose birthplace was Belfast but came to Dublin at a young age. A civil servant who lived in Clontarf for more than thirty years he wrote eleven books all in the Irish language. He is, perhaps, best remembered for his biography of James Connolly ("Tart na Cora") and for his once regular column in the (now defunct) Evening Press newspaper.

The Clontarf area was/is home to a host of Irish authors including C.M. Ceallachán, P. Breatnach, A. Mac Neil, P. O'Conluain, C. O'Coigligh, M. O'Súilleabhán, F. O'Rioín, L. Mac Uistin and S. O'Ciosáin.

Novelist, short story writer, dramatist, children's author and fellow of the Royal Society of Literature, Roddy Doyle resides in Clontarf. Best known for his Barrytown trilogy of novels, all of which have been made into films (with the "Commitments" also adapted for stage), he won the Man Booker Prize in 1993 for his brilliant novel "Paddy Clarke" Ha Ha Ha". He was also awarded the Irish Pen Award in 2009.

Hugh Mackle author of "County Dublin you may not know, 100 rambles through Dublin" and a number of other guide books lived in Clontarf as did distinguished author and historian professor Owen Dudley Edwards. Another Clontarf resident was professor Niall O'Dónaill renowned for his massive Irish - English Dictionary which is generally accepted as the standard Irish - English Dictionary. Clontarf residents Canon F.W.R Knowles (mentioned above) and Muriel Mc Ivor published little booklets concerning Clontarf and in more recent times locals Val Lynch and Claire Gogarty published books on Clontarf's history.

One time compiler of "Dubliner's Diary", a pioneering social column in Dublin's once biggest selling evening newspaper "The Evening Press", Terry O'Sullivan (real name Tomás O'Faolain) and his writer journalist daughter Nuala O'Faolain lived in Clontarf. Terry was originally a teacher and later a lieutenant in the army and came to live in Clontarf in the mid 1950's.

The Westmeath born disabled author-poet Christopher Nolan came to live in Clontarf for sometime in order to be close to the services offered by the Clontarf based Central Remedial Clinic.

The outstanding Irish scholar and writer of the 1950's Donncha O'Cheileachair M.A. was on the staff of Belgrove Boys' School in Clontarf. His best-known work is the famous book of Irish short stories "Bullaí Mhartain" which he compiled with his sister Síle. From Cúl Aodh in west County Cork, Donnacha was an authority on the Irish dialect from that area and was highly respected, and often consulted by Irish scholars and writers of his era. Indeed he collaborated with many writers in compiling their works. Notable in this area was his help in compiling De Bhaldraithe's famous "An Doinneanach" the biography of another famous 'dictionary man'. Patrick Dinneen. Donnacha would surely have produced many more valuable contributions to Irish literature were he not to die at a young age in 1960.

Áine Cannon who was for many years principal of Belgrove Girls Senior School in Clontarf, wrote the little primary school book "Dosaen Scéal". She complied a work on the saints of Ireland as well as a book on the poet Antaine Raifteirí. She also edited a book of essays by various authors, on the famous 19th century Archbishop of Tuam Dr. John McHale.

John McGahern the well-known novelist and short story writer taught for a number of years in Belgrove Senior Boys' School. Several of his works are familiar including "The Barracks" (1962), "The Dark" (1965), and "High Ground" (1985). Among the many awards he won for literature was the prestigious American-Irish Foundations Literary Award in 1985. But the most famous novel by the County Leitrim born John will always be - especially for those who are familiar with Belgrove School - "The Leavetaking" published in 1974. He was dismissed from his teaching post in Belgrove for moral reasons and in "The Leavetaking" he gives a restrained reaction to what must have been a hurtful experience. In the book Belgrove school is thinly disguised as St. Christopher's. Essentially autobiographical, it is an analytical work full of lonely countryside memories. He was a victim of the eternal argument - should private affairs effect your public position?

A prolific writer who was also on the staff of Belgrove Senior Boys school, Vincent O'Donovan, won the Listowel Writers' Week award four times - with two plays and three short stories. One of his award-winning short stories "A Light Upon The Water" was adapted and presented on B.B.C. radio as a play. He published two collections of poems - "Fantasia" and "Kittiwake". His poems betray the keen eye of the acute observer. His writing has a touching lyrical style - very perceptive with real, descriptive and beautiful images.

Others

The distinguished actor Barry Fitzgerald was born on Vernon Avenue, Clontarf in 1888, as William Joseph Shields. He was educated at Merchant Taylor's School. He joined the Civil Service in 1911. He started his acting career with Kincora Players. He played at the Abbey Theatre from 1916 to 1929 in his spare time. He adopted the stage name Barry Fitzgerald to avoid "complications with his job in the Civil Service!" However he resigned this job in 1929 to become a full time actor. He really came to prominence in 1934 when touring the United States. New York critics led by George Jean Nathan voted him best character actor of the year for his performance as Fluther Good in "The Plough and the Stars". He also won brilliant reviews for his role as captain Jacky Boyle in "Juno and the Paycock". He lived in the United States from 1936 touring until 1937 when he went to Hollywood where he remained for over twenty years. He appeared in numerous films and won an Oscar for his portrayal of Father Fitzgibbon in the film "Going My Way" which also starred Bing Crosby. In fact he was nominated twice for an Oscar for the same role in this blockbuster film - best actor and best supporting actor. This was the first and only time this happened in Oscar history as the rules were subsequently changed to prevent it happening again. Apparently Barry based the character, Father Fitzgibbon, on Father Patrick Hayden who came as a curate to Clontarf in 1892 and for a time was acting P.P. in the ailing years of Archdeacon O'Neill's administration in the Clontarf parish. Barry also played in the celebrated classic film "The Quiet Man" alongside John Wayne and Maureen O'Hara. The film, directed by John Ford, was recorded in the west of Ireland mainly in the grounds of Ashford Castle, Cong, County Mayo. Barry's brother, Arthur, also achieved much fame at the Abbey Theatre and played a minor role in "The Quiet Man". Barry Fitzgerald loved, when time allowed, to spend some summer weeks sailing in Dublin Bay. He never married and returned to Ireland in 1959. He died in a Dublin hospital on January 4th, 1961. He was a member of the Church of Ireland and he had a National Funeral from St Patrick's Cathedral, Dublin.

One of the world's greatest musicians, Handel, came to Dublin on November the 18th,1741, on the invitation of the Lord Deputy, the Duke of Devonshire. He gave his first Dublin concert on December the 23rd, 1741 in the "Musickhall" Fisamble Street. On April the 12th, 1742 came the world premiere of his "Messiah", at the same venue. Handel, born in Halle in 1685 and composer of the "Hallelujah Chorus",stayed in Dublin for nine months. During that time he spent many days at Clontarf Castle which still houses a piano on which he played numerous musical pieces.

For a few years in the 1850's William Dargan lived in Maryville House (near today's St. Paul's College) the lands of which became part of St. Anne's Park. He was involved in the construction of the Howth Road (see chapter 9) but is best remembered as Ireland's greatest railway engineer. He constructed Ireland's first railway line - the Dublin-Kingstown (Dún Laoghaire) line which opened in 1834, and was responsible for constructing hundreds of miles of railway in Ireland. A philanthropist many and varied were his other interests including involvement in the opening of the National Gallery of Ireland in 1864, where in its grounds there stands a bronze statue of Dargan.

Although born in County Sligo, film director and author Neil Jordan spent most of his early life, living in Clontarf and was educated in Belgrove N.S. and St. Paul's College. Jordon, a rumpled figure with a deceptively east-going manner, first came to public notice as a dramatist and in 1976 his collection of short stories "Night in Tunisia" was published - falling somewhat short of the masterpiece it was first thought to be. A number of his works were featured on B.B.C. Radio and on R.T.E Radio and Television. However he became an acclaimed and highly successful novelist with "The Past" (1980) and "The Dream of a Beast". Turning to film making, Jordon proved he has imaginative flair, with "Angel" (which he wrote and directed), "The Company of Wolves" and "Mona Lisa". Another film based on the early 1920's in Irish politics and in particular on Michael Collins got mixed reviews. Jordan's detractors say that his early work tends to be somewhat prurient. He is internationally acclaimed as a very talented writer and director. He now lives in Bray, Co. Wicklow.

The singer Bernadette Greavy - a contralto - born of a Dublin mother and Roscommon father, was reared in Clontarf. Used to stages all over the world, nothing appeals to her more than a walk along the Bull Wall. The best loved Dublin comedian, Maureen Potter is another celebrated Clontarfite who lived on Vernon Drive. Maureen, a legend of more than fifty years in Irish show business, warmed the hearts of generations of Dubliners with her own inimitable brand of spontaneous comedy, in pantomine and in cabaret. She and her script writer (for her) husband Lt. Col. John O'Leary are buried in the last new grave to be opened in the Old Clontarf cemetery on Castle Avenue. Peadar Kearney, who composed our National Anthem "Amhrán na bhFiann", was a Clontarfite, as was the man who officially translated the Anthem into Irish, Liam O'Rinn. Actress May Ollis, lived in Clontarf. She played many leading roles on stage, in films and in radio plays. She will probably be best remembered for her role as Mrs. Rita Nolan in the R.T.E series "Tolka Row". She also made a number of appearances in the series "Glenroe". The former governor of the Central Bank Tomás Ó Cófaigh whose signature appeared on all our banknotes lived in Clontarf for many years.

A famous 'religious name' associated with Clontarf is that of Matt Talbot "The Servant of God". His parents, Charles Talbot a dock labourer and Elizabeth Bagnall, were married in St. John the Baptist Catholic Church in Clontarf on September 16th 1853 - the service and ceremony being performed by Fr. Edward Kennedy C.C. They lived at nearby number 2 Rutland Street (a place now part of Clontarf Park) after the marriage. But when Matthew, their second child, was born they moved to 13 Aldborough Court.

No community or parish in Ireland would be the "complete package" without a good G.A.A. heritage! And Clontarf is not found wanting in G.A.A circles! Early G.A.A. stalwarts in Clontarf (mentioned already in this chapter) were Séan O'Donavon, Jim Boland and Harry Boland. A former president of the G.A.A. Doctor J.S. Stuart lived in Clontarf for some time and a long time resident was Séan Ó Síochain who was General Secretary (and later Director General) of the G.A.A. for 15 years.

Former R.T.E. Gaelic Games pundit Mick Dunne (mentioned below) resided in Clontarf as did the "Mayo captain" of 1950-51 Séan Flanagan (mentioned earlier). Three members of the very successful Dublin Senior Football team of the 1970's were Clontarf residents -Tony Hanahoe, Gay O'Driscoll and surely one of Dublin's greatest ever mid-fielders Brian Mullins. Brian played as a juvenile with Clontarf G.A.A. Club and as an adult with St.Vincent's Club. Of that "folk-heroes" team too, Pat Gogarty attended Belgrove Boys School. The team's manager Kevin Heffernan (or 'Heffo') resided locally, on the St. Anne's Park section of the Howth Road. Hanahoe was captain on two of three occasions Dublin won the All-Ireland Senior Football Championship (and the Sam Maguire Cup) in the 1970's. He was also part of Heffernan's management team for a few years and for a time Dublin player manager. In soccer circles long time secretary of the Irish Amateur Football League and general soccer administrator, Noel Kennelly resides in Clontarf as did former Irish senior international player Paddy Ambrose. In the world of Rugby Football the celebrated Brian O'Driscoll who captained the Irish senior team for many years and in 2014 became the world's most capped senior rugby international in test matches and ended his career with 141 Caps, is a Clontarfite as is international player Cian Healey.

Legendary golfer Christy O'Connor, whose career stretches over many decades has resided in Clontarf since he accepted an invitation to join the Royal Dublin's Golf Club at Dollymount in April 1959, as the club's professional. An honoury member of that August club since 1972, "himself" (as O'Connor is affectingly known) has trailed a golfing blaze of achievements on golfing greens around the world which are remarkable by any yardstick. In so doing he has stylishly brought much honour and acclaim to himself, his club, his country and indeed to the game of golf itself. He has long been one of Ireland's greatest sporting ambassador's. In a golfing lifetime of outstanding achievements, glorious victories and a number of golfing 'firsts' on the Irish, European, American and general world golf stages, his achievements include winning the first golfing four figure prize in Europe (£1,000 in The Swallow - Penfold tournament in 1955), 10 Irish professional championships, 10 appearances on Ryder Cup teams, (the last in 1973). master Golfer twice, P.G.A.A Match Play Champion and winner of the world's biggest golf prize at the time, £25,000 for his John Player Classic win in 1970. He also dominated the international Seniors Tour for many years. And in 1958 with Harry Bradshaw he won the Canada (later world) cup. As the guy on the 19th hole might say "follow that"!

There was and is quite a Clontarf representation on our airwaves - mainly on R.T.E. radio and television. Newsreader of yesteryear David Timlin was a Clontarfite as was Gerry Ryan, of (particular) R.T.E. radio 2 fame. Well known in the broadcasting world are Joe Duffy, Marty Whelan, Pat "the hat" Igoldsby, the late R.T.E. sports correspondent Mick Dunne and his newsreader daughter Eileen Dunne, Mark Cagney and Ian Dempsey all of whom resided in or are happily residing in Clontarf. Two more recent Clontarf names on the airwaves are sports broadcaster Damien O'Meara and celebrity "gossip girl" Siobhan O'Connor. And Public relations/communications guru and journalist Terry Prone hails from Clontarf.

The Infamous Sham Squire

One of the most obnoxious and distasteful characters ever to inflict his presence on Clontarf or indeed any part of Dublin, was the notorious Francis Higgins, the 'Sham Squire'. Higgins, for a while, lived at the seafront end of Strandville Avenue. Born in a Dublin cellar in 1746 he had a somewhat deprived childhood and became successively a messenger-boy, a shoe black, and a pot boy in a porter house in Fishamble Street. He somehow, learned to read and write and, in fact, became such an accomplished penman, that he got a job as a scrivener. From then on his whole life revolved around seducing, procuring and informing.

Using his talent as a script writer of considerable style, he forged documents proclaiming himself owner of a large estate of land. He also got a fine government job with the revenue commissioners. Using these documents he procured marriage to Mary Ann Archer, the daughter of a well to do Catholic merchant, with social ambitions. Very soon Mary Ann realised she was married to nothing more than 'a lout with a leer' so she left him and had him prosecuted for fraud. At his trial in 1767 it was Judge Robinson who gave him his nickname when he contemptuously remarked that 'thy Shame Squire is guilty of great duplicity'. The name stuck and Higgins got a £5 fine and a year in jail for fraud. During the few weeks sentence he did serve, he married his jailer's daughter. On his release he was up to his old tricks again. He began selling smuggled tea to unsuspecting grocers. Then he informed the revenue commissioners who raided the premises, seized the tea and imposed heavy fines. He gathered rewards for trapping victims but quarrelled with his accomplices, breached the peace, and got another year in jail. Again released early, he made a fortune through wheeling and dealing in the gambling houses of Dublin. After threatening the owner of the 'Freeman's Journal' with prosecution regarding the repayment of a loan, Higgins was sold the journal for a quarter of its value. He used the newspaper as an organ of government propaganda, thereby supporting a corrupt administration in the last troubled years of the eighteenth century, and attacked those who fought for reform. He was rewarded with various offices such as Coroner of Dublin in 1784, and later, Under Sheriff of the County of Dublin. Dubliners did notice his lifestyle not least his carry on as a pimp. The editor of the "Dublin Evening Post", John Magee ridiculed him in his paper referring to him as a "Just Ass of the Peace", and named an illegal gambling house owned by Higgins. But the Sham Squire, aided by the notorious John Toler (later Lord Chief Justice Norbury or the 'hanging judge') took court action against Magee and cleared his name. Higgins, with his accumulated wealth, became virtually a genuine squire. He lived in a mansion on St. Stephen's Green and was a bosom pal of the reigning Chief Justice, Lord Clonmel. Higgins died suddenly on the 19th of January, 1802 at the age of fifty six. He was buried in Kilbarrack cemetery under a large monument costing the then rather extravagant sum of £30. A hypocrite even after death, he left much of his fortune, largely collected by wangling and swindling, to charity.

The Sham Squire's career and his burial place were largely forgotten when sixty four years after his death Dr. William J. Fitzpatrick published in 1866 "The Sham Squire and the Informers of 1798" and in it pinpointed Higgins as the man who betrayed Lord Edward Fitzgerald, one of the leaders of the United Irishmen's rebellion in 1798. He also betrayed the Sheares brothers Henry and John, both United Irishmen. It transpired that Higgins received the £1,000 reward for the capture of Fitzgerald as well as a £300 pension per year. When this secret was revealed a group of outraged Dubliners marched to Kilbarrack cemetery to posthumously administer justice to the traitor. They completely destroyed the sepulchre, generally defaced the grave and carving a pike and gallows left the message "Here lies the monster Higgins, Lord Edward's informer".

Harry Boland	George Colley	Oscar Traynor
Micheal Collins	Sean Loftus	Bram Stoker
William Carleton	Barry Fitzgerald	Sean O Siochain

Neil Jordan    Peadar Kearney    Nuala O'Faolain

Brian Mullins    Christy O'Connor    Brian O'Driscoll

Maureen Potter    Roddy Doyle    Gerry Ryan

CHAPTER ELEVEN

Schools in Clontarf

One of the earliest references to education in Clontarf is an 1834 account which states. very briefly, that the area had "two daily schools, one supported by subscription, and the other by a collection of the Roman Catholic Church. Samuel Lewis in his famous 1837 work says: "In the old (Clontarf) chapel is a male and female school, supported by the interest of accumulated receipts at charity sermons, amounting to £700, and of a bequest of £500 by Mr.Carey. The average number of children is 100. The parochial school, to which Mr. Vernon has given a house, rent free, is supported by subscription."

Clontarf Royal Charter School, Clontarf Road.

The Clontarf Royal Charter School was one of about forty such schools throughout Ireland. They were part and parcel of the Reformation - a method of trying to entice Catholic children to Protestantism. The schools were the brainchild of a group of Irish 'nobility, gentry and clergy', who met early in the 18th century and formed a society named "The Incorporated Society for the Promoting of English Protestant Schools in Ireland" to promote and establish parochial day schools, for the instruction of poor children in the English language, and the principles of Christian religion. In 1733 King George II granted a Royal Charter for the incorporation of this society. The charter noted that in Ireland "there are great tracts of land almost entirely inhabited by papists. . . the erecting of English Protestant schools in those places is absolutely necessary for their conversion . . . and that they may be instructed in the English language"

It was a direct result of this charter, that the Clontarf Charter School came into existence. The King's representative, Lord Harrington, laid the foundation stone for the building in 1748. The school opened in 1749 to cater for 100 boys, although many of the other schools catered for girls also. The building became something of a Clontarf landmark, a famous Palladian style historical building with its dome colonnade and cupola. It was situated on the seafront, a little on the city side of the present Strandville Avenue. The building was still standing early in the 20th century. In the Charter Schools, generally, children of both sexes were "dieted, clothed and instructed free of expense". In the early 1800's the schools had, in all, 1,500 boys and 1,050 girls on the roll. An infirmary to accommodate sick children from all the charter schools was added to the Clontarf School in 1794.

In the Clontarf school the boys were taught the "three R's" as well as basic trade skills in such as agriculture, knitting, spinning and gardening to which they might become apprentices. For a time children found begging in Clontarf could be lawfully committed to the school. The school crest consisted of a plough, a spade, a spinning wheel and a bible open to the line "the poor have the gospel preached to them". Between February and November, 1787, numbers in the Clontarf Royal Charter Strand School fluctuated between 77 and 32. On a particular day in that year an account read:

"A great number of the children are small. Several look about seven or eight years old. Many look delicate. 57, work at spinning cotton. They are confined within doors and stand at least seven hours a day at the spinning wheels." Generally, the Charter Schools generated national hostility and provoked even more serious religious differences, in a country already quite strained with such troubles. Due to falling numbers in attendance and some unfavourable reports the Irish Education enquiry caused the Charter Schools to close after 1825. By all accounts the last headmaster in the Clontarf school, Mr. Wesley, didn't have the best of reputations. The school and its ten acres of land were rented to the headmaster at £50 so he was dependant on the labour of pupils to achieve a more substantial income. By 1830 just about all the controversial Charter Schools were discontinued and the Clontarf School closed in 1831. But the society itself continued to exist and later the Clontarf Charter School building was turned into a bathing establishment and called Kingscourt House, or Mansion, with hot and cold sea water baths open to the public and run by the proprietor Mr. Brierly. In this he was probably the first Clontarfite to formally 'harness' the sea for bathing and cash in on the natural amenity. But people, such as the writer Frances Gerard, complained about Brierly's baths and 'the disreputable bathing machines and the curious habiliments of the bathing women who have been known to whip up a stout gentleman, carry him far out to sea, dip him three times, and bring him back, helpless as a child". So the house was suppressed as a bathing establishment, being an outrage to common decency and the Board of the Incorporated School Society let the ground and premises to tenants for £100 per year. Later Kingscourt House or a house on its site came to be nicknamed 'Informers' House' as it was apparently used to house informers (especially in the Fenian era) to whom the government afforded protection.

Mount Temple Comprehensive School, Malahide Road.

After the suppression of the Charter School, the Incorporated Society for Promoting English Protestant Schools in Ireland had a Commercial School in Aungier Street - of which the famous Dublin writer George Bernard Shaw was a pupil. This school was closed at the end of the 19th century, but the Governors felt it was essential to have a boys secondary school in north Dublin. Accordingly, they acquired premises in Mountjoy Square in 1896 and appointed the Rev. William Anderson as the first headmaster of the new Mountjoy School. The Governors Collegiate boy's school had been moved from Santry to Portarlington but in 1902 they closed this school and established Mountjoy School as their new Boy's Collegiate School.

The grounds of the old Charter School, off Strandville Avenue, were used by Mountjoy School as playing fields up to 1948. In 1948 the Governors purchased Mount Temple Mansion (built in 1862) and 20 acres of land between the Malahide and Howth Roads, the city side of Clontarf Golf Club grounds. This was originally the Bradshaw Estate and Clontarf Golf Club had its grounds and clubhouse here before becoming established in Donnycarney House. A large school building programme was begun and, on completion of the first block, the school was transferred from Mountjoy Square in September 1949 and the new buildings were formerly opened in 1950. Additions and extensions since then, and ever increasing enrolments have made the school one of the biggest mixed secondary schools on the north side of Dublin, with many of its pupils coming from the Clontarf catchment area. Four of Mount Temple's most famous pupils are the members of the U2 band who rose to international fame in the early 1980's. They are Paul Hewson (Bono), Dave Evans (the Edge), Larry Mullen and Adam Clayton.

The Hibernian Marine School, Seafield Road (East).

The original Hibernian Marine School - the 'nursery for the support, education and training of the orphans and children of Marines' in order to help them make a career at sea - was opened in a house in Ringsend in 1766. However, they had outgrown these premises by 1770 and the Governors of the Hibernian Marine Society took out a lease on a plot of land on Sir John Rogerson's Quay, to build a new premises to replace their Ringsend School. This new Hibernian Marine School cost £6,000 to build - a cost which was defrayed by Parliament - and was opened in 1773. The school Governors obtained a Royal Charter from George III two years later. In 1872 the interior of the main block was burnt out and, using temporary accommodation, the Governors again looked around for a congenial site for a new school. Their search finally led them to Clontarf where they built a magnificent building. The new building, which was to become another Clontarf landmark for many years, was opened by the Lord Lieutenant, Earl Dudley, on the 8th of June, 1904. The school became part of the social and cultural life of the Clontarf region. Local memories recall an anti-aircraft gun on the school grounds during World War Two. Over the years historical and social developments within the country led to a number of changes and amendments in the running of the school. It graduated from a primary to a secondary school, providing full education from ten years of age to leaving Certificate or Matriculation, and traditionally being a boarding school it opened to day pupils. The spirit and traditions of the Hibernian Marine School, fostered by successive generations, managers, pupils and teachers is probably best summed up in the school motto which read. "Accipe quae peragenda prius" - "attend to what must first be done". The school building on Seafield Road East, on part of the site now occupied by the Seacourt housing estate, was demolished in 1972.

Greenlanes School, Seafield Avenue.

This is Clontarf's Church of Ireland primary school. The lovely and romantic name heralds from the 19th century, when Greenlanes was the name of the townland around part of Seafield Road. A school is mentioned in the 1854 Church of Ireland records and in 1879 it is recorded that forty pupils attended the school. The old school was situated on Seafield Road where the sexton's house and parochial hall stood, opposite Belgrove Boys School. In 1894 the National Board of Education received Greenlanes School into its list of registered schools. A new school was built in 1952 in a private secluded site among hedgerows just off Seafield Avenue. A typically country style school, it was formally opened in 1952 by the Minister of Education, Mr. S. Moylan, after a blessing and thanksgiving service was conducted by the Church of Ireland Archbishop of Dublin, Most Rev. Dr. A. Bartan. Canon Neligan, who produced a souvenir booklet documenting the history of the school, wrote: "When a school is not only efficient but happy, that is the mark of real success and such had been the achievement of Greenlanes School". It was once the largest Church of Ireland national school in the Republic - with five classrooms and over two hundred children in the late 1950's. Population shifts and the dwindling Church of Ireland community in the Clontarf area has caused the numbers attending the school to fluctuate. However no longer exclusively Protestant it is a thriving school and maintains a fine education record.

Clontarf Presbyterian School, Howth Road.

Situated beside the Presbyterian Church at the junction of the Howth Road with the seafront road near Fairview is Clontarf Presbyterian school or 'Howth Road School'. It was built in 1890, then consisting of just one classroom. In 1892 it became a two teacher school. In 1894 three extra classrooms were added and in 1910 a separate boys school was constructed. Later the school divided into three separate schools - infants, girls and boys. This triad was reduced in 1950 to two

- an infants' school and a mixed school. Then in 1971 these two were amalgamated into one school. Another addition to the school was made in 1971 when a teachers' room was added and the whole school was renovated and modernised by the minister Mr. McKillen at a cost of £15,000. The reconstructed and refurbished school was officially re-opened on the 19th February, 1971 by Right Rev. Dr. Haire the Moderator of the General Assembly of the Presbyterian Church of Ireland. An industrious little school it is not exclusively Presbyterian, and has up-to date equipment and teaching aids. The school has educated pupils from Fairview, Killester, Marino, Donnycarney, Coolock and Raheny as well as Clontarf.

St Paul's College, Sybil Hill.
In 1732 the Vernons of Clontarf Castle sold about forty acres of land to a man named Fade. He built a Georgian style house there. The house - built of good materials, with excellent workmanship and showing splendid if restrained taste - he named Sybil Hill (sometimes written Sybyl Hill or Sable Hill). Later Mr. John Barlow owned Sybil Hill. In 1878 his sons sold their interests to Sir Arthur Guinness. By inheritance the last (Guinness) person to live there was retired Protestant Bishop of Meath, Archbishop Plunkett. On his death in 1947 his son sold Sybil Hill and its accompanying land acres to Fr. O'Doherty of the Vincentian Order. Sybil Hill House was first established as St. Paul's secondary school in 1950 when four priests of the order - Fathers Moran, Mullan, McMarrow and O'Hanrahon - moved into the house. For its first two years the school was based in Sybil Hill House. Just twenty-two boys enrolled in the beginning. A preparatory school was opened in 1951 (and closed later). In 1952 the original school building (today's college) was completed and in October of that year it was officially opened and blessed by His Grace Archbishop McQuaid of Dublin. In 1958 it extended to include the gymnasium and chapel. Today the old house serves as a retirement home for Vincentians. In 1969, on joining the 'free education scheme' the school immediately broadened its scope and influence by attracting ever increasing numbers of pupils. An expansive building programme was undertaken to cater, as the size of the school doubled. The last phase of expansion included the building of a fine swimming pool (now closed) in 1973. As well as enhancing school facilities, this pool was a very much appreciated local amenity. St Paul's always kept local needs in mind by providing many facilities for use by local communities in the form of leisure activities, evening courses, meeting rooms for various groups, summer school facilities and the once famous local teenage disco known as 'The Grove'. The Grove, originally organised in Belgrove Soccer Club Mount Prospect Avenue back in 1967 has an

endearing indelible spot in the hearts so many Clontarfites and Dubliners in general - see chapter thirteen below.

The school provides academic courses second to none, being especially aware of the emphasis on technology in the modern world. The college caters for the full spectrum of sporting activities, of which rugby, perhaps, attracts most attention. Realising that a school today cannot operate in isolation from the home, the college has a full time Chaplain who is constantly visiting students' homes to foster a spirit of mutual goodwill between home and school. Thus, set in the historic Sybil Hill part of St. Anne's Estate, St. Paul's College, with close on 1,000 students, is one of the country's biggest secondary boys' schools. The school motto "Gestis Censere" (roughly translated means "by your deeds you are known") directs the pupils to realise that their actions show their character.

Holy Faith Convent, Belgrove Road.
The Holy Faith Order first came to Clontarf on the invitation of the then parish priest of Clontarf Archdeacon O'Neill. Their original house or convent (and still today's convent) is the building on the Clontarf Road immediately the city side of St. John the Baptist Catholic Church. It had originally being bought by a former Clontarf Parish Priest, Fr James Callanan in 1843 from his own resources. On his death in 1846 his sister sold the building to the Royal Irish Constabulary and it served as a regular police barrack until about 1888. In 1890 the Holy Faith sisters acquired the property and on September 22nd of that year they opened the building officially as the Convent of Our Lady Star of the Sea - admitting three girls and a boy as their first pupils. The school was to be a girls school with a boy Juniorate attached.

By 1902 the sisters found it necessary to add seven new classrooms to the original building as they catered for more and more pupils. As expansion continued and as they planned for a totally new school in the future the sisters purchased surrounding grounds and numbers 178 to 182 Clontarf Road (formerly Rostrevor Terrace), as well as number one Belgrove Road formerly known as "Shanahans Garage". (178-182 Clontarf Road continued to be used as a primary school until 2004 when the sisters decided to close it. These houses are now used by retired members of the Holy Faith Order).

After detailed planning, building of the present Holy Faith Secondary school began on the Feast of the Little Flower, October 3rd 1950. By September, 1953 the new classrooms were completed. On October 2nd, 1953 the Feast of the Holy Angels the new Secondary School was formerly opened and blessed by the Archbishop of Dublin J.C. McQuaid, D.D. Since then the Holy Faith Convent (a day school) has expanded still further and has always been a leading girls secondary school in the north city area. Year after year, in the best Holy Faith tradition, the school produces well educated classes to obtain outstanding results at Leaving Certificate level.

Clontarf Traffic School for Children, Clontarf Road.
Clontarf had what was surely the most unique 'school' in the country. Certainly a school with a difference, it was called Clontarf Traffic School and its purpose was to teach children, in a practical and real way, the rules of the road. Indeed it could be said that it taught them survival in Dublin's traffic jungle. The school was regarded as an asset and indeed as an essential ingredient of the educational system. The school was situated between the Alfie Byrne Road and the Clontarf Road close to the Dublin-Belfast railway line. It was first constructed in 1972 at a cost of £42,000. It consisted of a traffic complex complete with a maze of roads, road signs, one way systems, pedestrian crossings and roundabouts. The children learned through the use of special cars and bicycles provided, how to use the road safely. The school had video and film rooms also where road safety films and slides were shown. It was most suitable for children between the ages of seven and twelve who were usually taken by their schools and expertly tutored by specially trained Garda officers. About 20,000 children a year availed of the facility. The school certainly made a valuable contribution to road safety in Dublin. The facility no longer exists and its site is now occupied by all weather football training facilities.

Clontarf National Schools, Vernon Avenue.
If you travel down Vernon Avenue towards the seafront, Clontarf male and female schools were on your right just past Vernon Gardens. The site later became the Holy Faith Convents hockey pitch and sports field. It is now owned by a building company. The schools were built at the height of the Great Famine in 1846/47. The funds for erecting the schools were via 'grants from the commissioners (of education) and local sources'. The schools were officially opened in November, 1847. Thus, they operated under the old Board of National Education set up in 1831 with the famous letter of the Chief Secretary for Ireland E.G. Stanley as its 'Charter'. There is no record of the schools ever being called anything except 'Clontarf National Schools' and the location is always described as Greenlanes Townland, Clontarf Parish, Coolock Barony, North Dublin Poor Law Union and Clontarf East Ward Electoral division. Records of the schools from the beginning still exist in the form of roll books, inspectors observation record books, suggestion books, school register books and daily report books.

From these records, it is apparent that Clontarf schools differed little from those throughout the country. The classrooms themselves were somewhat small - being designed with economy in mind to be just capable of accommodating the local children. The pupils attending brought their own books and the schools offered the full range of curriculum subjects then taught - spelling, reading, writing, geography, grammar, geometry, arithmetic, book-keeping and for girls only, needlework. Clontarf schools opened from 9.30am until 3.00pm in winter and 9.30a.m to 5.00p.m in the summer. The boys and girls schools were separate from the beginning. The chief obstacle which obstructed the academic work of the school was poor attendance. Nationally about 65% of children did not attend school. Those who did attend had a short school life - from about six or seven years of age until twelve - and only about 40% were present on any one day. The figures for Clontarf schools appear to be roughly in line with the National figures. Compulsory attendance was then deemed unworkable in a rural society - and Clontarf was to be very much a rural society for many decades yet. Eventually, in 1892, attendance at school between the ages of six and fourteen was made compulsory, although pupils could have part-time work between eleven and fourteen years of age.

Much social history can be gleaned from examining the schools' record books. For example in the 1860's the address of most of the pupils attending the boys' school were the older long established Clontarf 'hamlets' of Clontarf Sheds, Greenlanes, Conquer Hill, Danespark, Chapel Lane, Ruthland Place and Fortview Avenue. Occupations listed for parents are a far cry from the business executive-civil servant-professional style occupations of today's Clontarfites. Fathers' listed livelihoods were in the main, 'carman', 'sailor', 'blacksmith', 'fisherman', 'labourer', 'gardener', 'coastguard', 'porter', 'servant', 'ploughman', 'huckster', 'carpenter', 'coachman', 'carter', 'farmer', and 'tailor', with the odd policeman, doctor and shop-keeper. Occupations listed for mothers are mainly 'charwoman', 'washerwoman', 'cook', and 'dairy woman'.

In the same period pupils were struck off the school roll after being absent for thirteen consecutive weeks. (This remained the case up to April 1908, when a pupil's name was deleted from the class roll after an absence of four consecutive weeks or twenty school days.) A reason or excuse was recorded by the school to account for a child's absenteeism and a random sample from the boys' roll makes most interesting reading: 'getting fishing bait for his father', 'apprenticed to a carpenter . . . to a smith . . . to a builder. . . to a gunmaker', 'fishing', 'drawing sand', 'gone to England (or America)', 'taking care of the house (or child)' - 'mother working', 'herding cows', 'going on messages', 'gathering cockles to sell', 'salmon fishing', 'gone to sea', 'herding sheep', 'hired', 'serving milk', 'driving a horse', and simply 'gone to service'. The more lucky ones are recorded as 'gone to college', 'gone to a classical school' or 'appointed a school monitor'. Sadly youth mortality seems to have been very much a common occurrence as the word 'died' makes a regular appearance. Some 'choice' reasons are also listed such as 'dismissed' or 'idling at home!'.

After 1870, Clontarf schools in common with all national schools, operated under the 'Results System'. This system tried to encourage greater efficiency by basing fees paid to teachers on the result of an annual examination by an inspector on children who had attended on a fixed number of occasions. The fees often amounted to a substantial portion of the teacher's total pay. In 1875 the average Irish National Teachers annual income from all sources was £53-6-0. In 1900 the 'Results System' was replaced by the 'Revised Programme'. This brought many changes to the system but the major one was that, from then on classes above the level of infants were to be organised in six 'standards'. In 1899 school records show that in Clontarf boys school the salary of the principal teacher was £13-6-0 per quarter and that of the assistant was £18-0-0 - salaries were paid on March 31st, June 30th, September 30th and December 31st. In 1900 a monitor (or pupil-teacher) was paid £1-5-0 per quarter. In addition there was a yearly payment of a Residential Capitation Grant. Under this (in 1907) the principal received £15-0-0 and the assistant £3-5-0. Incidentally the teachers were burdened with rather cumbersome restrictions on their personal freedom. They could not participate in politics - even attend a political meeting. They could not live on a licensed premises. They were forbidden from supplementing their income by engaging in any business which 'was likely to impair their efficiency'. They were totally under the control of their clergyman managers who could appoint or dismiss them, without consultation with the National Board of Education. As well as the meagre salaries, already quoted, the rules required sixty pupils on the register in order to employ one trained assistant. But one need only check Clontarf Schools' roll books to verify the fact that individual teachers had to cope with classes far in excess of 60 pupils. This situation continued for long decades after 1900 and a chat with any retired teachers from that era will validate this as a fact. It is interesting to note the return of the use of the Irish language to the school roll books, with the setting up of a native government in the 1920's.

Clontarf National Schools 'grew up' under the incumbent parish priest, the amiable Canon Rooney who did so much to provide the huge parish with sufficient schools and churches. In his "Short History of Dublin Parishes" Rev. N. Donnelly states that "in 1901 a new lease for the male and female national schools on Vernon Avenue was secured". This was a perpetuation of the lease arranged by Canon Rooney and the then P.P. Archdeacon O'Neill was also fortunate to accept £2,000 from the local Miss Allingham to 'enlarge, improve and fully equip the schools'. The schools operated until 1940 on the Vernon Avenue premises and were served by a mixed variety of teachers, some of whom incurred the wrath of visiting inspectors who left many positive and quite a few negative comments in written form on school record books. In some cases the inspectors themselves may not have been above reproach. As in many cases throughout the country, they tended to ignore the problems within the schools- especially overcrowding and irregularity of pupil attendance. Also, due to lack of facilities, and indeed for financial considerations, many teachers were untrained. People with bad memories of their national school days tend to proportion the blame entirely on the particular teacher they had. This certainly was justifiable in some instances but in many cases due recognition is not given to the relentless pressure exerted on teachers, by the inspectorate. This together with the other problems listed meant teachers were often quite frustrated. Also one cannot fail to recount the fact that with some, to quote the poet Oliver Goldsmith *'the love they bore to learning was in fault'.*

Belgrove Schools are Born.

Canon James Dempsey, who was Parish Priest of Clontarf from 1923-1936, came to realise, that Clontarf National Schools were becoming somewhat dilapidated and were straining to cope with the increasing Clontarf population. The Vernon Avenue site didn't really lend itself to proper development as it lacked space, being somewhat hemmed in. The Canon looked around for an alternative site and, before his death in 1936, he secured the purchase of Belgrove House and a few acres of ground on Seafield Road West. Little did he know that this purchase was to usher in a new National School era in the Clontarf area. A very ordinary set of schools were to be transformed into a quite excellent learning institution. Ironically, a clause in the purchase agreement stated that a school was not to be erected on the property. This clause was later circumvented by the school managers. Before detailing the progress of St. John the Baptist's Girls' and Boys' (Belgrove) schools we will first take a brief look at the history of the house that was to replace the old schools on Vernon Avenue and give its name to a new school.

Belgrove House Seafield Road (St. John's House).

Samuel Lewis in his 1837 "Topographical Dictionary of Ireland" lists among the 'handsome seats and pleasant villas' of Clontarf that of R. Simpson at Belgrove. The last family to reside in Bellgrove (the Second 'I' was dropped over the years) House and estate, and the family always associated with it were the Dolan's. The

Dolan family originated in Welshetown near Clogerhead, in County Louth. It is not clear when the Dolan's acquired the Belgrove estate in Clontarf, but their Clontarf interests date back as far as 1859 when a John Dolan rented Woodpark estate on Vernon Avenue. The family then lived in north County Dublin. The last Dolan 'landlord' in Belgrove, and the one affectionately recalled by older Clontarfites was Dominic Dolan. (see chapter nine above). He lived in Donnycarney before moving to Clontarf. In Thom's directories of the 1870's he is listed as a 'haymerchant' with a business in Townsend Street and later in Bolton Street. He became involved in the wholesale pharmaceutical business and later in the importation of oil. When the giant Anglo-American Esso oil company began operations in Ireland they bought his interests and he became their first Irish manager. He may have been the first Dolan to live in Belgrove House with its regular farm-yard which had become quite dilapidated at the turn on the 20th century. He built the block of eight large red brick houses on Castle Avenue, which stand between Kincora Road and Seafield Road, a speculative venture which left him in permanent financial trouble. He lived in the Seafield Road end house - St. Dominic's - while Belgrove was being renovated and extended. Dominic was a man who liked to live up to the 'big house' image, and is fondly remembered by locals being chauffeured around in his horse drawn trap by his driver John Moffit. In his "Old Clontarf" Canon Knowles recalls Dominic Dolan: "On the opposite side of the road was the big house of Mr. Dolan with its fine yard gates and very high wall and main entrance. I remember Mr. Dolan going to Dublin in a truly splendid round trap drawn by a big glossy horse. . . I think Mr. Dolan favoured what we children called a 'half-tall hat' and had bushy side-whiskers".

Dominic Dolan died in the early 1930's and his spinster daughter Mary Jane lived in the house for a number of years after his death. Another daughter (Dominic had a large family) was an Irish Sister of Charity, Sister Joseph Dolores. She was for many years Reverend Mother in the well known Merrion School for the Blind in south Dublin and also spent a considerable time on the missions. As an aged nun she paid a nostalgic return visit to Belgrove House in the early 1970's and fondly pointed our her bedroom in the old building, while accurately recounting childhood memories of her homestead. The house itself faced south and there was a driveway from the cottage at the west end of the present girls' school. (This gatehouse is still there but is in private ownership). The 'tradesmens' entrance was where the present main gates are on Seafield Road. Just west of these gates stood a complex of mews, stables and out-houses. They later served for a while as a Social Club for domestic girls, C.B.S.I., Girl Guides and for a short lived Catholic Sea Scout Troop. Two fairly large rectangular fields covered the area on which the boys' school complex now stands. Looking from Belgrove House the field nearest Seafield Road was an orchard with a high wall encircling it. Later it became a hockey pitch used by the Holy Faith Convent. It was in a lovely sylvan setting being surrounded by trees, with camogie and cricket also played there. The other field had clusters of trees and was used for grazing animals. South of today's girls' school a local tennis club was started in the mid 1950's. The club played tennis, and ran dances in the east part of Belgrove House. The tennis lasted only a few seasons as the grass courts were ploughed up by a workman due to a misinterpretation of orders.

From 1940 until 1971 the house (renamed St. John's House) served as a school and as St. John the Baptist Parish Hall. Then Mr. Jim Nolan and local priest Fr. Menton set up a management committee to organise the affairs of the house. Its facilities were used by a plethora of parish and other clubs, societies and organisations with the then Eastern Health Board being the anchor tenant for many years after 1972. Later it became the home of Clontarf G.A.A. club which is dealt with below in chapter thirteen.

Origin of Name Belgrove.
One can only speculate as to the origin of the name Belgrove. It could be an Anglo-French combination meaning beautiful (belle) wood (grove). Belgrove may also be a French family or place name. Or it could be adopted from the well known Belgrove Square in London. Indeed the Welling area of London has a Bellegrove Road and a Belle Grove Close and there is a Belgrove Street in London W.C.I. This then was the building to which the old Clontarf National School were transferred from Vernon Avenue in 1940. £10,000 was spent converting the premises into a school house and the official opening took place on 27th of May, 1940. The title of the schools was changed from Clontarf National Schools to St. John The Baptist National Schools. But this name - although the official one - never really became popular as from day one the new schools inherited the original name of the building - 'Belgrove' - as its adopted name. This name has become colloquially and intimately identified with the schools ever since. Indeed it has given the schools a particular individuality and a specific character being a somewhat sweet sounding romantic name with 'airs and graces' that seem enticing and the type of name a great institution would possess! The schools thus intimately known as Belgrove were born and have since then earned for Clontarf a place and reputation in Irish primary school education that is equal to any throughout the country.

Existing school records tell us that there were 424 pupils on roll on the official opening day of the schools. 331 of these pupils were under the principal of the girls' school, Miss Áine Scott with a staff of five assistant teachers and the remainder - 93 boys were under the boys' school principal Mr. Gerry Ryle who had one assistant teacher. The boys' school, then just a senior school, only had boys from 3rd class onwards, as the girls school taught the boys from infants up to second class - as had been the case in the Old Vernon Avenue Schools.

Since that opening day in 1940 Belgrove schools have been very successful in turning out well educated and competent pupils who cherish traditional Christian values and are more than prepared for the second level system. Any analysis of the origin of the success of Belgrove schools will invariably go back to the arrival of two principal teachers to the schools in the early 1940's. These were Miss Áine Cannon M.A.H.D.E. and Mr. Micheál Kelleher M.A.H.D.E. Both were responsible for nurturing the schools along by carefully building up competent teaching staffs and it is both their names that will always be particularly recalled when past pupils ramble down the nostalgic avenues off Memory Lane in recounting their days in the old 'Alma Mater'. Both differed in style but their basic aims, goals and emphasis were similar and it is from them that modern Belgrove dates. And the standards they set continue to prove very difficult to match, never mind surpass. Both principal teachers came to Belgrove with the much sought 'highly efficient' teaching award. Miss Cannon, originally from Kiltimagh in Co. Mayo, taught in Marlborough Street School before she came to Belgrove as Principal of the girls' school in 1943. Mr. Kelleher, who was born in Macroom, Co. Cork, taught in Brunswick Street School and later in Glasnevin Model Schools before he arrived in Belgrove, as Principal of the boys' school in 1944. Both appear to have been well chosen for the task of establishing efficient Clontarf Schools. This, they both achieved, with considerable organisation with foresight and planning, proper discipline, and genuine honest-to-God work. The end product was well run schools which produced well taught pupils. Both principals were totally committed to their work - no outside interest deflected them from their dedication to the progress of Belgrove Schools.

Gradually as parents in Clontarf and its environs saw the results being achieved in Belgrove Schools they were grateful to have their children educated there. As the fame of the schools spread the numbers increased rapidly and by 1956 the Belgrove roll books had swelled to include 700 boys and 600 girls. As early as 1953 it was clear that the old Belgrove House could no longer cope with such massive numbers. Teachers were holding their classes all over the grounds - in the mews, sharing rooms, in corridors, in makeshift huts, ect. In 1954 a new nine room boys' school was built at a cost of £48,000 beside Belgrove House - this was opened in 1955 and became the Junior Boys' School. In 1963 eight more rooms were added to the boys' school (in fact two of the original nine were knocked down and ten erected) and opened in 1964. This became the Senior Boys' School block (both boys' schools were partly rebuilt, extended and refurbished in 2012). By this time the boys' school was no longer a senior school only as it enrolled its boys from infants on. It moved from Belgrove House altogether and the house became a girls' school only. On January 1st, 1964 both schools divided into two in a major reorganisation making a total of four schools on the Belgrove complex, each with a separate principal teacher. Mr. Kelleher became principal of the new Senior Boys' School catering for 3rd to 6th classes and Mr. Richard Motherway became the first principal of the Junior Boys' School which catered for reception infants to second class. Miss Cannon was principal of the Senior Girls' School which accommodated pupils from 2nd to 6th class and Mrs. Sheila McCarthy became the first principal teacher of the new Infant Girls' School which had classes from reception infants to first class. The girls remained in the old building until 1971 when their present new and modern schools were opened by the Archbishop of Dublin Dr. Dermot Ryan (the classes had been gradually filtering to the new complex since 1969).

The old Belgrove House had never really been a success as a school and always had problems with heating, lighting and general conditions as well as the odd rodent! The numbers attending the four schools reached a climax in the early to mid 1970's when close to 2,000 children attended Belgrove. But contrary to popular opinion there never was a conscious decision to build up and create a 'big and great' Belgrove. It happened as a result of two factors(i) the results achieved by the teaching staffs attracted more and more pupils, (ii) the numbers flowed to the schools as the population of Clontarf exploded in the 1950's and 1960's. But there was no myth or mystique surrounding the achievements in Belgrove. Hard working teachers achieved the required results. Belgrove particularly shone in the cut-throat scholarship era. All they won - and there were many - were won in open competition. Early scholarships were means tested and Belgrove boys' first winner was Jim Doyle. Retired teachers now recall that in winning a scholarship, competition was so keen that standards were practically of an intermediate certificate level - including algebra and the parsing and analysing of complex sentences in both English and Irish. In one particular year Belgrove won no less than twenty four scholarships. The boys' school then had a 'scholarship class' and Mr. T. Desmond Millett became mainly associated with its success. (He later joined the priesthood as a late vocation.) In short the yardstick of the day was good results and Belgrove produced these each year without fail.

In the 1950's the local St Paul's College secondary school was opened and since then many of Belgrove's boys' attend there. But over the years Belgrove pupils have also gone to O'Connell's Schools, St. Joseph's Fairview and Belvedere

College. They have also attended secondary schools all over the country - many on valuable scholarships - such as Clongowes Wood College, Castleknock, Rockwell, Gormanstown, St. Peters (Wexford) and St. Brendan's (Killarney). Most of the girls attend the local Holy Faith Convent, Clontarf. The schools have always provided the full range of primary school subjects as well as many extra activities, including music, elocution, French, dancing, drama, basketball and swimming. The schools hold regular concerts and pupils are taken on many school outings. No aspect of our native culture has ever been neglected in Belgrove - especially the Irish language and our Gaelic games. The Catholic faith has traditionally been passed on with a good moral training for children preparing for life, but in the ever changing attitude and overall climate in the field of religion Belgrove can be regarded as inclusively accommodating to non Catholic religions and traditions.

Belgrove has always been fortunate to have the support of wonderful parents who have always been deeply interested in their children's education and very eager for them to achieve competent standards. They always co-operated magnificently with the teachers and work of the school in all its aspects. Indeed even before the era of pre-school it was obvious that children attending Belgrove Schools from the Clontarf catchment area were "book friendly" and had been "read to".

Belgrove, as an educational establishment, has always set, achieved and maintained high standards. Situated within the boundaries of St. John The Baptist Parish, the schools are supported by all three Clontarf parishes, now operating as one Parish under an overall "moderator" parish priest. The schools serve a catchment area that includes Clontarf and her hinterland. Pupils attend Belgrove for various reasons. For locals it is practical and sensible to send their children to the local schools. Secondly, because of its reputation as an excellent academy of learning, Belgrove is simply a very attractive school - one might say that the legacy of excellent results in the Corporation scholarship era lives on. (Of course today's Belgrove delivers competently educated children in its very best tradition and this is a strong consideration for parents anxious for their children to achieve high standards.) Also parents who are themselves former Begrovians harbour tremendous affection 'an oul grá', for and affinity to their old 'Alma Mater'. They have first hand knowledge of its reputation and tradition and like to return their offspring to Belgrove even if they themselves no longer reside in Clontarf. You might say "once a Belgrovian, always a Belgrovian"

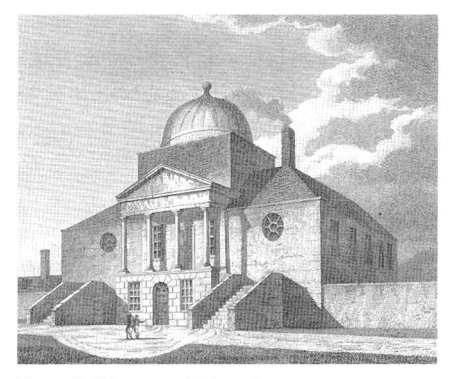

Royal Charter School

Mount Temple Comprehensive School

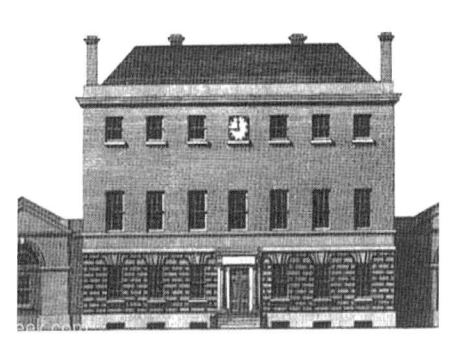

Hibernian Marine School

Church of Ireland School / Hall

St Pauls College

Holy Faith Convent

Belgrove House

Belgrove Boys School

Belgrove Junior Boys School Crest

Belgrove Group 1941

John McGahern, former teacher at Belgrove Boys School

Old Steel Staircase at Belgrove House

CHAPTER TWELVE

Health Service in Clontarf

The National Health Service (Executive) centre covering and serving the Clontarf area is in the Civic Offices, Ballymun, Dublin 9. Clontarf's own Health Clinic is on Vernon Avenue at its junction with Sybil Hill Road, and on the site of the original gate house entrance to the former Wood Park (dairying) estate.
A few hundred yards further along Sybil Hill Road (which has a Raheny Dublin 5 postal address) is the KARE Dublin City (North Bay) citizens information, advice and advocacy centre opened back in 1965.

The Central Remedial Clinic, Vernon Avenue.
The Central Remedial Clinic (C.R.C.) was founded in 1951 by Lady Valerie Goulding and Miss Kathleen O'Rourke. It began as a non-residential unit born in the realisation of a need for aftercare service for victims crippled by poliomyelitis after the great Polio Epidemic which struck Ireland in the 1940's and 50s. These two ladies, with little or no money but a reservoir of determination set out to establish an organisation that was to considerably influence the development of physical medicine and rehabilitation in Ireland. Miss O'Rourke concentrated on physiotherapy while Lady Goulding built up a collection of voluntary car drivers to bring patients to and from their classes. Their first premises was a small flat in Pembroke Street but in 1954 the fund-raising efforts of Lady Goulding enabled them to move their 'hospital' to an old Georgian house called Prospect Hall in Goatstown where the clinic was able to expand and extend its range of services. Additional professional staff were employed, a school was established, a hydrotherapy pool provided and finally a sheltered Workshop Programme was initiated for the severely physically handicapped. Needless to say there was an endless struggle to meet capital and development needs and the mainstay of the financial income was realised from the operation of a very successful Football Pools Lottery. Lady Goulding's own efforts for, and devotion to, the clinic fired the imagination of many people and her appeals for aid produced a very positive response from just about every section of the community.
By the mid 1960's lack of space was hampering any further extension of the Clinic's work and plans were drawn up for the erection of a new unit incorporating all the existing services and allowing for the establishment of much needed new ones. After consultations with Government Departments and the National Rehabilitation Board, the present Remedial Clinic site at Vernon

Avenue, Clontarf was purchased in 1965, in conjunction with the Irish Wheelchair Association. Much fund raising was needed to raise the half a million pounds needed to build the magnificent specially designed clinic we know today. It was officially opened in October 1968 and present at the opening was the late Eamon De Valera, President of Ireland. Since then the Clinic - a deceptively large complex - has achieved international recognition for its work in Medical Rehabilitation and the uniqueness of its integrated services. The Clinic is a frequent host to major International conferences. Clontarf's non-residential rehabilitation centre for the physically handicapped has five main departments, each working in close co-operation with the others. They are (1) a physiotherapy department, (2) an occupational therapy department, (3) a primary school, (4) a sheltered workshop and (5) a day centre. The C.R.C. also has a micro electronics resource centre to develop computer aids for handicapped children, which has opened up a new life for so many handicapped people. In all hundreds of patients from all over the country are treated on a regular basis at the clinic. It employs one hundred disabled adults in its own workshop which specializes in commercial printing and the production of beautiful top quality hand-made lampshades. The Central Remedial Clinic has its own transport fleet consisting mainly of mini buses. The canteen in the clinic serves hundreds of meals a day. A number of sports clubs operate within the complex. The annual day to day running costs of the C.R.C. are huge, a good portion of which comes from voluntary sources. In addition, voluntary funds are the mainstay of support for its research and development work. Volunteers play a vital role in the general running of the complex especially in the areas of fund raising, catering and transport. The board of governors are extremely grateful for the constant support of the general public. The authorities are also indebted to those who use the facility of the clinic's swimming pool - including many local schools, local swimming clubs and private groups.

The main building of the clinic complex is named the "Penny Ansley Memorial Building" in acknowledgment of the generous support the Ansley family contributed to the whole rehabilitation project. Penny died tragically with her son in a motor accident. Her father George, a long time friend of Lady Goulding, later had one of the clinic extensions dedicated to him.

Lady Valerie's Goulding, an English woman, was the daughter of the late Viscount Monckton of Benchley who was King Edward VIII's confident and lawyer during the 1936 abdication crisis. Lady Valerie was taken out of school to act as her father's secretary and messenger to ensure total secrecy during the abdication period. She attended all the meetings between her father and the King as they sought some way to avoid abdication. In the process she came to know

Mrs. Wallis Simpson also. She acted as courier for her father's very frequent correspondence with the Prime Minister Stanley Baldwin. Coming to Ireland Lady Valerie married businessman Basil Goulding. In 1968 she was honoured by the National University of Ireland with a Doctorate of Law in appreciation of her contribution to the development of rehabilitation in Ireland. Later she was appointed as a senator. In July 1985, after thirty four years as the C.R.C. driving force she retired although she remained a member of the Board of Governors of the C.R.C. Today's clinic is a credit to her lifelong fund raising drives of which the legendary Jimmy Saville walks, begun in 1968, were perhaps the most successful. Clontarf's all male Holly and Ivy Club (formed in 1966) played a major role in these walks. Lady Goulding was succeeded as chairman of the board of governors by her son Hamilton Goulding. A bronze head of Lady Goulding was unveiled in her honour at the Clinic in March 1987, and children and adults with physical conditions such as cerebral palsy, spina bifida, and muscular dystrophy will long thank her for her pioneering work in providing services such as clinical assessment, physiotherapy, occupational therapy, social work, psychological help, training development and day activity options for them.

The Incorporated Orthopedic Hospital of Ireland, Castle Avenue.
The Incorporated Orthopedic Hospital of Ireland, now known as Clontarf Hospital, came into existence at a period when poverty and destitution lay like a weal on this country. As the inevitable result of bad food (and not much of it), of miserable housing conditions and of widespread unemployment, children were the first to suffer. Crippled children were a common sight in Dublin those days, suffering from diseases of the spine, rickets, bone deformities and various other weaknesses that were the outcome of malnutrition. The Orthopedic Hospital grew out of the need to alleviate the pain and misery that resulted from these distressing ailments.
The hospital was born in 1876, in the private house of surgeon Doctor Robert Lafayette Swan at Usher's Island, (on Dublin Quays) when he started his work with four children as patients. He saw the need for an urgent crusade to establish a centre to treat the many children in misery from Orthopedic complaints. Dr. Swan was a skilful and successful surgeon whose career became one of splendid service to his native Dublin, and the country generally. He treated cases of club foot and other congenial deformities as well as spinal afflictions and hip disease. Orthopedic surgery had a special interest for him and his works as an author in this area were highly valued by his contemporaries in that field. He was elected President of the Royal College of Surgeons in acknowledgement of his good work. As more and more children came to him for treatment, Dr. Swan, with the

aid of his good friend Mr. Journeux, moved the hospital to more pretentious premises in Great Brunswick Street (now Pease Street) where it remained until 1902, when it was moved once again to spacious accommodation made available by the Board of Works at 22 Upper Merrion Street. Dr. Swan often took the children on holidays to his new private residence at Delaforde in Templeogue - then a faraway place in the country. He died in 1916, having lived to observe his group of four grow to an average of eighty patients. The hospital, then entirely dependent on voluntary subscriptions, was essentially devoted to the treatment of children with deformities and was the only one of its kind in Ireland.

On 29th June, 1941 the hospital moved from Upper Merrion Street to 'Blackheath House' Castle Avenue Clontarf, the former residence of the Black family built in 1872. The wall of one of the stairways still has a stained glass depiction of the Black family's Coat of Arms. A hospital report of that year records the event. "In 1940 an ideal site was discovered at 'Blackheath' Castle Avenue, Clontarf. This was a splendid country mansion, built of stone throughout. It contained forty-five rooms and faced due south on ground sloping gently down towards Dublin Bay - with a clear view of the Dublin mountains. It stood on six and a half acres of its own ground, with a splendid screen of timber to the north and east acting as a wind-break against our worst winds. The reception rooms formed large wards, with windows down close to the floors - acting almost as open-air wards" A new hospital of 120 beds was established here with up to date hospital wards and facilities, staff quarters and containing ample accommodation in the grounds for further expansion. The entire hospital (patients, staff and equipment) was moved on that June day in 1941 from Upper Merrion Street to Clontarf without incident. Indeed the 'cavalcade' arrived at Castle Avenue two hours ahead of schedule!

Shortly the number of child-patients reached one hundred and thirty two and while the hospital had a fully recognised national school since 1911 it now employed three full-time teachers to ensure that children who might have to spend two or three years in 'undeserved imprisonment' would not be academically two or three years behind their companions on returning home. Down through the years the hospital has cared for children from all over Ireland suffering from deformities of the hips, legs, feet, ect., in a cultivated atmosphere of care and affection. The case history of one particular patient demonstrates the happy environment fostered in the hospital.

A lady who had been a patient in the hospital in Merrion Street sixty years earlier and was then living in Portland, Oregan U.S.A. came to Ireland for a holiday in June, 1974. While here she paid nostalgic visits to places of childhood memories - her old home, local church and school and the Orthopedic Hospital. On returning to the U.S.A. she wrote back to the hospital authorities as follows: "I had become ill with polio and was admitted to the Orthopedic Hospital. My personal memories are of Dr. Haughton (one of the hospital's original and well known doctor-surgeons) who cared for me while at the hospital. He certainly performed surgical miracles for me making it possible for me to live a very normal life. From time to time I have needed some minor corrective surgery on my left foot and each time my doctor has commented on the wonderful care I had way back then when the treatment of polio was comparatively new. One orthopaedist I know mentioned that he had spent some time as a student at the Orthopedic Hospital in Dublin, and praised it highly. I took a masters degree in Social Science and in my work with children and their families I am constantly reminded how important it is to a child to have warm, loving and caring adults during the growing up years. "I remember with great affection the adults I knew at the Orthopedic Hospital and although unaware of it at the time this influence on me has remained a vital force throughout the years."

The role of the hospital has changed slightly in the past twenty years or so. As surgeons can now, thankfully, diagnose at birth many of the diseases which in the past necessitated a long term stay in hospital, children can be treated immediately and most of those who in the past would have to be hospitalised can now be treated as out-patients. This progress meant that the number of children resident in the hospital decreased greatly. Thus the Orthopedic Hospital authorities, being aware of the severe shortage of beds for adults in the major city hospitals, offered accommodation for eighty-four post-operative rehabilitation cases. This offer was immediately accepted by the Minister of Health. The hospital admitted its first adult patients on April 4th, 1972 and since then has received many patients from most of the large Dublin city hospitals. In 1976 the President of Ireland, Cearbhall O'Dálaigh, honoured the hospital by attending its centenary celebrations.

In the early 1990's plans were put in place to move the wards from the main house to a newly built fit for purpose hospital facility adjoining the old Blackheath House which still houses the Administration Departments of the hospital. The new hospital building was completed in 2009. The hospital consists of 5 wards, Blackheath Ward, Gracefield Ward, Vernon Ward, Kincora Ward and Swan Ward. The wards were called after local places in the Clontarf area with Swan ward being called after Dr. Robert Lafette Swan the surgeon who founded the original hospital. Today's Incorporated Orthopedic Hospital also comprises of a beautiful gymnasium for rehabilitation in the Physiotherapy Department, an X-ray dept for the hospital patients and for referrals from Local General Practitioners, an Occupational Therapy Department a Social Work Department and Pharmacy Dept.

The hospital entrance is now on Blackheath Park off Castle Avenue beside the little laneway named Blackheath Grove the original entrance to the Black residence. There are surviving memories of Mrs. (Gibson) Black careering in the laneway in her pony or donkey drawn trap! Landscaped gardens feature in a large and open hospital entrance. The hospital continues to specialise in Orthopedic rehabilitation but has extended its service over recent years to further rehabilitation of older persons while it also provides a respite bed service to the local communities. Beds are also allocated to the north Dublin City Hospitals (the Mater Miseracordae and Beaumont Hospitals) as interim care rehabilitation beds. The Incorporated Orthopedic Hospital of Ireland began operating as "Clontarf Hospital"and was officially opened in June 2010.

The Irish Wheelchair Association, Blackheath Drive
In 1965 Lady Goulding of the Central Remedial Clinic and Father Leo Close (the first wheelchair user in the world be ordained a priest and the real driving force in the establishing of the I.W.A.) of the Irish Wheelchair Association jointly purchased a site from Doctor O'Sullivan of Verville Retreat. The site, known as 'The Plotfield' was eight acres in extent. The Irish Wheelchair Association was then less than five years old and their aim was to bring wheelchair users into the mainstream of society - a task many cynical observers at the time regarded as 'well-meaning day-dreaming'. In 1967 the Association built a simple cedarwood building which was to become the Association's centre of activities (and head quarters). The building named Áras Chuchulain, on Blackheath Drive, was officially opened by the Minister for Health, Séan Flanagan, on 21st May, 1968. At the time the Wheelchair Association had two branches, one in Limerick and one in Galway and had a total membership of less than two hundred. Originally the Clontarf premises was meant to be a hostel where physically disabled young people would have a suitable place to live while at the same time receiving training for appropriate employment. However, the dedicated leaders of the project, led by the Association's first Chief Executive Officer, Phillip O'Meachair, decided that the sad situation of wheelchair users and physically handicapped people was a social problem extending beyond employment and one that demanded a community response. Accordingly they expanded their aims and now the Association has branches spread all over the country and its membership has grown to many thousands.

In 1981 Charles J. Haughey dug the first sod for a very ambitious Activity Centre and Sports Complex. Completed at a cost of £100,000 the magnificent building provides a sports and recreational hall for local groups and the Activity Centre is a most purposeful community resource in Clontarf enjoying a large input of local volunteer support. The Irish Wheelchair Association members themselves have a very thriving sports club and regularly compete at local, national and international level in table tennis, basketball, field and track events, swimming, sailing, bowls, archery and snooker. Many local groups over the years have supported the Association by hiring and using the Sports Hall. The Wheelchair Association is indebted to all for their ongoing support. Overall the I.W.A. provides high quality services to people with physical and sensory disabilities to help them lead regular independent lives in their own communities. The range of services and programmes offered at the Clontarf Centre include a Resource and Outreach Centre, Independent Living Units, Assisted Living Services, wheelchair sales, rentals and repairs, a gymnasium, the Carmel Fallon Holiday Centre and the aforementioned Sports Hall.

Verville Retreat, Vernon Avenue.
The austere even mysterious mansion on Vernon Avenue known as Verville Retreat has been a psychiatric hospital since 1857, later catering for patients suffering from Alzheimer's. From outside the building looks a cold silent and severe residence. But when one tours the interior of the establishment nothing could be further from the truth. It provides a homely, pleasant, relaxed and comfortable residence for fifty-five female patients. The institution was first opened by Colonel Lynch, an English army officer and doctor who served most of his army career in India. A Mr. O'Sullivan acquired the estate in 1916 and extended it to include local estates known as Oakley and Woodpark. Its grounds formerly included the sites of the local Central Remedial Clinic, the Irish Wheelchair Association premises and Hampton housing estate. The building is very much of the 'old world' setting. The original house is perhaps the oldest building in Clontarf - its semi circular windows representing the Queen Anne style of architecture (see Hollybrook Park chapter nine). Many extensions were somewhat haphazardly added to the old house giving a building of varying levels - with steps 'all over' the premises. In time the fully private hospital came to be very capably run by the very helpful Doctor M. O'Sullivan a daughter of the man who built up the estate. The hospital has very spacious units for its inmates and has its own laundry and a lovely little oratory chapel. The name 'Verville' is derived from a combination of Vernon from Vernon Avenue and Villa for the big house. The estate was originally named 'Fairville'.
(This was the account of Verville Retreat we published back in 1987. The institution is now closed for a number of years and the building derelict with, as noted earlier, Verville Court apartments occupying most of its grounds)

Nursing Homes

Clontarf has two large nursing homes or retirement homes for the elderly. One is Nazareth House home opened in 1970 by the Poor Sisters of Nazareth on the Malahide Road beside the Casino. The other is the Sacred Heart Home on Sybil Hill Road opposite St Pauls College. It was opened in 1971 and is run by the Little Sisters of the Poor. Two smaller Nursing homes in Clontarf are Laverna home on Haddon Road and the Clontarf Nursing Home on the Clontarf Road near Fairview.

Clontarf Community Affairs

Clontarf Residents Association

Clontarf residents have a very vibrant, watchful and active association, which concerns itself with all environmental matters relating to the Clontarf area as well as social problems. The problems that mainly concern the Residents Association are crime, vandalism and employment for school leavers. Environmental problems are many and include traffic problems, public transport, recreational facilities, pollution, noise and general litter problems including derelict sites and unkempt buildings. Bur perhaps the association has spent more time on the problem of planning permission - or lack of it - than on any other single issue. The Residents Association has lodged countless planning appeals with the relevant authorities with a view of keeping Clontarf safe, clean and full of her old character and heritage. The more outstanding successes in this area concern Dublin Bay itself. The Residents Association were loud, active and strong in playing their part in preventing ninety-four acres of inner Dublin Bay, opposite Clontarf and Dollymount, (and 2,000 acres of the bay in all) from being filled in and developed by Dublin Port and Docks Board to include an oil refinery in Dublin Bay, as a result of the infamous 'studies' plan in 1972. Ten years later probably their greatest fight began against the quite unbelievable proposals to store 100,000 tons of liquid petroleum gas under Dublin Bay putting 60,000 lives at risk in the event of a serious accident in the storage caverns and thus leaving Clontarf in a situation almost akin to sitting on a time bomb. On December 12th, 1984 preservationists were jubilant when their appeal against the 'storage in the bay' was upheld by an Bord Pleanála. On both issues (which were the legacy of Clontarf's geographical position by sea) Clontarf Residents Association must be commended for their swift and vigorous action. In both cases their objections centred around general concern for the locality and its residents in the areas of (1) General environmental (2) The danger of water and air pollution and, in the case of the gas caverns, well founded general safety worries, (3) Fear for the future of the Bull Island and its flora and fauna, (4) The threat to the value of property in the vicinity. These concerns came to the fore once again when in 1999 the Dublin Port and Docks board proposed to reclaim 52 acres right in the eye of Clontarf bay. Again this ridiculous proposal was vehemently and successfully opposed by Clontarf residents association, this time spearheaded by an "ad hoc" group called Dublin Bay Watch.

Clontarf Community Festival

Clontarf Community Festival was held in August each year, and became a two weeks event. The idea of a festival was developed back in 1979 when a week end of activities was organised to raise funds in aid of suffering people in Kampuchea, India. Later the festival broadened to embrace the entire community in Clontarf and bring them together in a close atmosphere of co-operation. During the festival a series of activities were organised to generate and foster community pride, togetherness and enthusiasm. Seminars and discussion groups helped make people aware of local, national and third world social problems. All proceeds raised for the duration of the festival went straight to various third world relief projects. The roster of activities for the two weeks each year were colourful and varied with events for all age groups. Competitions and exhibitions were organised by all sports clubs in the area - tennis, golf, Gaelic games, squash, soccer, swimming, badminton and table tennis. Other events included dart competitions, pub quizzes, draughts tournaments and bridge competitions. Fashion shows were held as well as a fair and a car treasure hunt. But the two most popular events each year tended to be the locally based ten kilometre race and the 'Lark in the (St. Anne's) Park' music marathon.

The festival grew bigger and raised more funds each year. For this, each year's festival organisers - all voluntary groups or individuals - must be given the highest praise. All the activities took place at various centres around the locality and the many sponsors of various events must also be highly commended for their unfailing annual generous help. Each year the festival committee produced a very worthwhile and well edited magazine - which became something of a Clontarf annual. But the real success of the Clontarf festival was due to the patronage and support the many activities received from the Clontarf public. Changing circumstances, have led to a much shorter festival and in recent times the Clontarf Festival - known as the Viking Festival - takes place over one weekend in June every year.

Éigse agus Pobal Chluain Tarbh.

A little 'oasis' for the Irish language has always existed in Clontarf. Little tell-tale signs are positive proof of this - such as private houses named with Gaelic names, the many parents who sent and send their children for a summer spell to a Gaeltacht area and the increasing number of people who seek a full time education "tré gaeilge" for their offspring. Indeed if one speaks in the first national language in social company in Clontarf, invariably some member of the company will be only too willing and able to respond. 'Pobail Chluain Tarbh' was set up in 1972 to provide the Irish speaking community of Clontarf with an opportunity to come together on a regular basis by organising Irish language events. Since 1980 'Pobail' run an Éigse Irish language week each year. This week is a well organised and most enjoyable time with various activities for all ages. The aim of the week is to introduce Irish to the people of Clontarf and encourage them to use it as often as possible. The week is a light hearted affair where bilingualism is accepted for those whose 'blás' has somewhat rusted! Events include question time, concerts, céilis, record recitals, chess, Gaelic games, orienteering as well as lectures and discussion groups. The efforts of 'Pobail Chluain Tarbh' in organising the annual Éigse are encouraged and assisted by Bord na Gaeilge and Comhdáil Násiunta na Gaeilge. Radio na Gaeltachta also takes a keen interest in the Éigse. Pobail Chluain Tarbh organises Irish language classes, a book club, nature walks and a weekly coffee morning, all 'tré gaeilge'.

Clontarf Community Information Centre

For a number of years starting in July, 1975, Clontarf's local Community Information Centre, situated on Churchgate Avenue, provided comprehensive information on subjects such as taxation, consumer services, housing, social welfare, redundancy and family law. The centre kept a constant updated filing system to ensure the accuracy of the information imparted by the staff who ran the centre. Confidentiality in all matters was guaranteed by the Voluntary staff picked from various community organisations. The KARE Centre (mentioned above) now fulfills this role.

Clontarf Garda Station

The 77th report (1908-09) to the commissioners of public works in Ireland stated that new barracks planned for Clontarf would accommodate thirty four constables and six sergeants and would replace barracks rented at Ballybough and Clontarf. The 78th report (1909-10) recorded that "the new police barracks and station at Strandville Avenue have been completed and occupied and the barracks at Fairview and Clontarf surrendered". The new building was of 9,500 square feet, two stories with upper dormitories and Georgian in style. The Dublin Metropolitan Police (D.M.P) were the Dublin Police at the time. The original entrance to the now Garda Síochána Station was directly from Strandville avenue. The barracks were accompanied by a ballcourt (handball alley) which, interestingly, was a common feature in Royal Irish Constanbulary (R.I.C) stations at the time.

Scouts in Clontarf.
In 1907 Lord Robert Stevenson Smythe Baden-Powell founded the Scout Movement. His theories for the boy scouts were first tested on Brownsea Island off the south coast of England. Lord Baden-Powell became chief scout of the World Scout Movement. Twenty years later, in 1927, the Catholic Boy Scouts of Ireland were started by Father Tom Farrell. On the 13th November, 1931 the 66th St. John's Unit, Clontarf, Catholic Boy Scouts of Ireland were founded. The first scout master was William Breen of Seaview Avenue. The Unit took an active part in the Eucharistic Congress held in Dublin in June, 1932. The Unit received a new flag from the Cassidy family in 1937, which was used until 1978 and is now on display in the main hall in the scouts' Den. In 1956 - the Unit's 25th anniversary - it formed its first Cub Pack. In 1977 the Unit took part in the Golden Jubilee Celebrations of the C.B.S.I. in Mount Mellery. In that year also St. John's Unit had the distinction of forming the first C.B.S.I. Beaver Colony in Ireland, as well as a mixed Venture group. Forty seven years after partaking in the Eucharistic Congress, the St. John's Unit was very much involved in Pope John Paul II's Irish visit in 1979. In the days prior to the visit they showed the general public around the papal altar in the Phoenix Park. During the Mass celebrated by Pope John Paul II some of the leaders were positioned near the altar. In 1972 a fund-raising committee was set up to raise the capital necessary to build a new scouts' Den. This ambition was realised just in time for the Unit's own Golden Jubilee year, 1981. The Den, on Brian Boru Street, was formally opened on November 15th, 1981, by Mr. George Colley T.D. The Unit caters for about two hundred members. St. Anthony's Clontarf 92nd Scout Unit, formed in 1967, have their Den at Castle Grove. It is worth pondering for a moment over the organisation, aims and works of the scouts. Many of us dismiss a child in the familiar scouts' uniform as 'one of them' and generally fail to appreciate the very positive contribution the Scout Units make to each child's welfare and consequently to society in general. The scouts' motto is 'Bí Ullamh' (be ready or prepared). The divisions within each unit are (1) Beavor Colony for 6-8 year olds, (2) Cub Pack for 8-10 year olds, (3) Scout Troops for 11-15 year olds and Venture Groups for boys and girls from 16-19 years old. Scouts are organised on regional and parish basis and much of their outdoor training activities involves

camping and self catering. The general aims and objectives of the scout movement are to help in the proper guidance and training of young people. The scout is directed and moulded to develop spiritually, intellectually, physically, socially and culturally to play a proper and useful role in society. And of course, in modern times, girls and boys participate.

The 5th Port of Dublin Sea Scouts, Dollymount.
The Dollymount 5th Port Sea Scouts are attached to the Scout Association of Ireland and are thus inter-denominational and non-political. The first sea scout headquarters was erected on the Bull Island by special permission and charter from the Dublin Port and Docks Board in 1912 and with improvements, alterations and additions has remained in use ever since. The headquarters beside the Bull Island cottages, has always been known as the 'Crow's Nest'.
The first organised sea scout troop on the Bull Island was started by H.M. Coastguards in 1920. This lasted only a few years. In 1933 the 2nd Port of Dublin Sea Scouts were formed on the Island. This troop was very successfully run and enjoyed many victories in the various scouting events. Due to a change of policy in 1948 their troop was disbanded and in September, 1949 the present 5th Port of Dublin Sea Scouts was founded and has continued to flourish over the years. The troop, which accommodates youths up to twenty years of age, caters for about three hundred members each week, and its badge is the universally recognised 'Fleur-Di-Lis' with the Viking Helmet as the 5th Port's own special insignia. As well as the normal scouting tests and requirements the troop engage themselves in many aquatic pursuits, especially rowing, canoeing and sailing.
The 5th Port Sea Scouts, Dollymount, is regarded as one of the leading troops in the entire association. Over the years, all the major trophies open to them have been won by the troop. In particular, winning the Sir William Fry cup for seamanship and the Irish Shipping trophy for all round swimming ability were special occasions for the troops. Another outstanding achievement for the troop was the gaining of two medals for gallantry. Indeed the group have numerous rescues to their credit. The troop has been represented at most of the world's international scout Jamborees and in 1975, in Norway, eight members of the 5th Port Scouts were attached to Troop Two which went on to win the award for best troop attending the Jamboree. The troop provides a First Aid service from their base, to the public, all year round. They also keep the life-buoys along the Bull Wall in order by regular checking. A most useful service provided by the 5th Port Scouts is a weekly litter patrol - summer and winter - to keep Dollymount Strand clean and tidy. The troop's annual camp is a moving one. They start at the source of one of the country's biggest rivers and follow its course to the sea.

Since 1968 the Scout Association's sister movement, the Irish Girl Guides, have also used the 'Crow's Nest' as a base for their activities.

Public Transport in Clontarf.

The Trams.

The question of the feasibility of laying down a tramway system in Dublin came before the Corporation in 1861. The city engineer at the time, Mr. Neville, suggested that an experimental line be laid down between the city centre and Clontarf. Nothing came of this suggestion and it was 1880 before the first tram service began between the city and Dollymount. The trams, at first, came only as far as Annesley Bridge. These early trams were pulled by a team of horses, with a 'tip' horse to help at inclines such as Newcomen Bridge. The first trams had no organised stops, rather the driver halted the tram when signalled to do so. Clontarf had a tramshed or stable on the site of the present day bus garage. It is basically the same building as clearly evidenced by looking at the (old) side and back walls. The rest of the building was given a modern brick frontage in the 1970's. The first section of this track to be electrified was the between Dollymount and Annesley Bridge and the first electric tram ran on it on November the 11th, 1897. On March 19th, 1899 the rest of the Clontarf line to the city centre (Nelson's Pillar) was electrified. This was the first electric tramline from any suburb to the city centre. (The very first electric tram in Dublin ran in 1896 on the Dublin Southern Districts Tramway Company line between Haddington Road and Dalkey. A power station operated from Shelbourne Road for this line.) Clontarf tramshed was extended to include a new power station which remained in operation until 1906 when the powerful Ringsend station was opened. The Clontarf line was a pioneer in both Ireland and Britain for the use of high tension electric current on overhead wires, with substations.

The route from the city centre to Clontarf was operated by the staff of Dublin United Tramways Company. In 1898 the "Clontarf and Hill of Howth Tramshed Company Ltd." was established and an agreement was made with the D.U.T.C. to run trams from the city to Howth. The D.U.C.T. drivers and conductors would be in charge from the city as far as Dollymount - which was called 'the junction'. From there the staff of C & H.H.T.C. staff would take over. But two great obstacles had to be overcome before a line could be laid to Howth. One was the fierce opposition of the Great Northern Railway Company who had a railway line to Howth themselves. The other was the strict conditions laid down by Lord Ardilaun of St. Anne's. These included free access for himself to the foreshore and to his private rifle range, non interference with the free flow of the Naniken

River and that only a single track be laid along the St. Anne's section of the tramline. In fact it turned out that the section from Mount Prospect Avenue to the Whip o Water had just a single track. The Clontarf-Howth line eventually opened in July 1900 with power from a D.U.C.T. generator at Clontarf. It ran via Blackbanks and Sutton - the C & H.H.T.C. had their tramsheds at Blackbanks. Despite the fact that the section mentioned above - with only one line - caused some congestion, a smooth, fast and efficient service resulted.

The trams, or 'galleons of the street' as the poet 'A E' (George Russel) called them, were surely part of what was Dublin 'in the rare oul times'. They were objects of genuine interest and love for generations of Dubliners. The trams became part of the social life of the then smaller and more close knit community. The service from the city centre to Clontarf and Howth established a reputation for being excellent and frequent. Indeed affairs were of a 'personal' variety as staff and passengers were generally on first name terms. As well as ferrying people the trams offered a freight service also - including two from Howth carrying sand and fish!

Trams had no upper saloon covers and ladies who opted to travel in the upper deck were considered 'bold and daring'. Indeed 'decency boards' were fitted to spare ladies alighting the steps from any would be Peeping Toms downstairs! Regular stopping places were now marked by poles with a white centre section and tickets were of different colours and were punched. Before route numbers were adopted route signs were operated. The Dollymount daytime sign was a green shield and at night two green lights were used. When route numbers came into operation Dollymount became route 30 and Howth route 31.

In the days before the promenade was built along the seafront in Clontarf a ride on the open upper deck of a tram in harsh weather was something of an endurance test. As only a low sea wall separated the tramline from the waves of the sea, storms, especially in winter, aided by Clontarf's notorious south easterly gales, very often washed over the wall and choked the tramtracks with sand. This caused endless delays and hold ups. Another problem was that of flooding along the seafront - especially at the seafront end of the Malahide and Howth Roads and (before the new tunnel was built) at the mouth of the Hollybrook River. A special 'ferry' or 'supermarine' tram was built by the D.U.C.T. to overcome this problem. This was a single decker with its floor about four feet above the rails with the engine suitably mounted to escape being flooded and put out of action. The nostalgia of this 'steps up' tram lives on. The trams undoubtedly greatly helped entice people to come to live in Clontarf. Like places such as Rathmines, Pembroke and Donnybrook on the south side of the city, a wave of middle class 'emigrants' came to Clontarf and built the many fine residences which made the area fashionable.

For a time the trams were the fastest vehicles on the road. Their first serious competitors were the early buses - in hindsight it can be stated that the arrival of the internal combustion engine ended the era of the tram. The big advantages the buses had were their speed and manoeuvrability. The buses could struggle round all the developing streets in Clontarf's hinterland - and indeed played a part in 'opening up' that same hinterland - while the tram was stuck to its track. Thus people who might have to walk a mile or more to a tramstop found the bus much more convenient. Open competition developed (which lasted until C.I.E was formed on 1st January, 1945) in which buses literally beat trams to the stops to 'grab' passengers first, leaving many trams to run empty. In 1925 Dublin's first official bus route - City Centre to Killester via Clontarf - was established. (It was a single decker number 43). In 1939 the route 30 trams to Dollymount were replaced by double decker buses. Clontarf was for many years served by C.I.E. city bus service route number 44A later replaced by the familiar 130 buses. The last trams along the Clontarf seafront were on the Howth line and these were finally withdrawn in March 1941. July 1949 saw the last trams leave all city streets. In 1959 the Hill of Howth trams were eventually replaced by single decker number 88 buses. Today the old tramline lies buried beneath Clontarf Road and with it memories of days that have been, but the Clontarf area is served by the Clontarf Road Station on the electrified Dart System.

Great Northern Railway - Clontarf Station.

In the years leading up to 1840 plans were drawn up for the Dublin-Drogheda railway line (part of the Great Northern Trunk railway) to be laid. The original plans envisaged the line leaving O'Connell Street (then Sackville Street) going on to the Customs House Docks and proceeding across the North Lotts (the land reclaimed or being reclaimed from the Sea around the mouth of the Tolka) to Clontarf Sheds. Then it was to swing back inland over the then green fields until it crossed the Howth Road, close to where All Saints Church stands today. However, objections and objectors sprang up everywhere leading to much controversy. In Clontarf the residents objected to the line, with its timber and iron viaduct, crossing the bay, as it would ruin the view and end Clontarf's days as a scenic bathing resort. The residents even had Daniel O'Connell state their case at Corporation level. In the end they were successful and aiding and abetting their cause was Sir Benjamin Lee Guinness who staunchly refused to have the railway line encroach in any way on his St. Anne's estate. The end result was the Belfast line being laid where we have it today.

On Monday October 12th, 1840 construction of the Clontarf railway embankment began with the section that runs parallel to today's Hollybrook Grove. The Raheny section was completed in 1841. The director of operations for the entire work was Sir John McNeill. The familiar Clontarf landmark known as the 'Stone Arch', 'Double Arch' or 'Skew' bridge which crossed the Clontarf Road was constructed in 1843 and was at the time regarded as an engineering triumph for McNeill. The building of the embankment from the Tolka to Clontarf paved the way for the reclamation of the area now known as Fairview Park. The bridge and embankment destroyed the 'fair view' out along the coast from Fairview and the embankment blocked access to the once popular strand at Clontarf/Fairview. The entire embankment - built laboriously by horse and hand - was completed by the end of 1843. In May 1844 the line from Dublin to Drogheda was formally opened and launched into service. Ironically, in its very first year of service, the embankment had to withstand its most severe test. The great storm which literally washed away Clontarf Island on October 9th, 1844, really tested the endurance of the line and the skew bridge. Both came through unscathed. Between 1844 and 1850 a station operated at Clontarf. By 1849 eleven trains served Clontarf daily. In 1897 on the site known as Black Quarry (on the Howth Road) Clontarf railway station proper was built, and finally opened in 1898 by the Great Northern Railway Company. No doubt this was in recognition of the fact that Clontarf was now a fast expanding suburb. The station, known simply as 'Clontarf Halt', passed most of its life as a quiet suburban station. But on the night of December the 8th, 1954 after a day of incessant rain and strong wind the railway bridge spanning the Tolka River at East Wall Road was swept away and the Tolka river burst its banks. This blocked access to Amiens Street Station and overnight the quiet Clontarf station became a major rail terminal, all trains from the north being routed there. For the next few weeks more passengers passed along Clontarf's single wooden platform than it had witnessed in its life span until then. On January 5th, 1955 the rushing and busy schedule at Clontarf ended as the railway bridge over the Tolka was again erected and trains once more were able to use Amiens Street. Clontarf Railway Station resumed its peaceful suburban life - but not for long. On September the 2nd, 1956 the 11.10p.m., train from Howth to Amiens Street stopped at Clontarf. This was to be the last train to use the station as the next day September 3rd, 1956 the station was closed down permanently.

One historic stop at Clontarf took place during the 1916 Easter Rising. As food in the Clontarf area was running out and fresh supplies were not coming through due to the breakdown of services during the Rising a heavily laden food train arrived at Clontarf Station from Belfast carrying generous supplies of bread, flour, bacon and many other varieties of food. The gesture from the people of

Belfast was much appreciated by Clontarfites. Today's number ninety four Howth Road, beside the railway bridge, was the station building, complete with ticket office and waiting room. The adjoining number ninety six was the station master's residence. The little green gate, just on the city side of number ninety four was the entrance that led to the station platform.

Hackney Service in old Clontarf.

The "Dublin Public Carriage Fares and Bye-Laws" (1905) booklet gives us exact details of the operation of stands or stations for hackney carriages, cabriolets, and state carriages in Clontarf at the turn of the century. Coaches, charabanks as well as horse/pony/donkey and cart/trap were also used. The hackneys were all horse drawn. There was three stands for Hackney Carriages in Clontarf. One was at the Seafront end of the Malahide Road (where a taxi rank still exists today). The rules for drivers and their carriages using this stand or rank were "The stop is a hazard for eight carriages. Carriages must range close by the footway at Marino, and on the same side of the road; first horses facing the bay. The horses on this hazard to keep clear of the crossing at the Crescent." The second stand or station was at the seafront at Vernon Avenue and its regulations were: "The stand is a hazard for four carriages. Carriages are to range about four feet from the sea wall at Vernon Avenue; first horse's head to be in line with the electric pole opposite the public house 'The Sheds' - horses facing Dublin." The third stand was at the Bull Wall. The conditions governing the use of this rank were: The stand is a hazard for four carriages. Carriages are to range close to the sea wall at the entrance to Bull Wall (Howth side); First horse's head to be two yards from the round stone at entrance - horses facing Dublin. These stands are to be filled by carmen residing in this district or else from the main stand at Lower Sheriff Street."

Clontarf's Licensed Premises.

In the public houses of Clontarf you can encounter Dublin wit and banter as well as its wisdom - on top of excellent beer and spirits! My own observation of Dublin wit as experienced in Clontarf is that its key is very often the way it is delivered - relative to the context or situation. Secondly it's the fact that it is delivered spontaneously that makes Dublin wit so funny... its' like many a boxer's tale of woe after a fight. . . he never saw the punch coming but felt it afterwards. For a good cross section of public opinion you need not bother passing Clontarf's inns. Sport of course ranks high on the agenda. And when one observes the friendly mingling of representatives of various sports in an establishment like the Sheds one wonders about often expressed sentiments as regards the various codes ability to co-exist. Pride of place is given to the beloved boys in Blue and Navy - the Dubs, Dublin senior footballers and also their hurling counterparts. Needless to say one encounters the odd tall story - especially in sporting circles - like the one related to me regarding a soccer match played on a soccer pitch where Clontarf Park is today. (I refuse to name either Queens Park or Corinthians!) I hope the story is true! The tale recalls a certain bus driver many years ago who couldn't get time off to play for his team in a very important match. Whether by accident or design he just happened to be passing the seafront at Clontarf during the course of the match, and stopped the bus at a vantage point to check on proceedings in the game. Is so occurred that a crucial moment had arrived in the game - his team, a goal down with time against them, were awarded a penalty. Being the regular penalty taker for the team our driver couldn't stand idly by (or at least sit behind the steering wheel of a bus!) Grabbing his boots - which he always kept handy - he abandoned bus and passengers and appeared on the field to take the crucial kick . . . For the record he missed, but what the irate passengers and his employers had to say I never did find out!

Bram Stoker Hotel, Clontarf Road.
A record exists of a licensed premises and restaurant on this site being purchased by a Mr. John Flanagan in February 1899. Later, adopting the name Fingal House from the old North Dublin district of that name and owned by the Bresnan family it earned quite a reputation for itself as an upmarket restaurant and guest house with a full bar licence. The hostelry which became Clontarf Court Hotel is built on a site beside Fingal Avenue once known as "Fingal". Today it operates as the Bram Stoker Hotel.

Harry Byrnes Public House, Howth Road.
An Inn has existed here since 1809 and it became one of two official coach depots when the Howth Holyhead mail service began in 1814. It had livery stables, a forge and its own well - which is now encased within the pub. In 1855 Thomas Carolan leased the premises (from Lord Howth) and in his little Clontarf booklet Canon Knowles tells us it was known as "Carolans on the Hill" when that part of the Howth Road was still open country. It opened its doors at six a.m. to cater for country carmen making their long slow journey from country outposts to Dublin city markets. In 1906 John Deneefe became its owner and later, in 1947, one of his barmen - Harry Byrne - bought it for £22,000. Since then it has been known as Harry Byrne's although its official name is Hollybrook House. The premises is still run by the Byrne family. Bram Stoker was known to have "sunk a black or two" on the premises as indeed was Oscar Wilde, although Wilde's

tipple may have been a more refined 'gin and supplement'!
In his poem "Pub -Crawl" Vincent Caprani has a word about Byrnes!

"Or opposite end of Richmond Road,
The widow Meagher's and Gaelic code,
Or Kelly's Cole's or other pubs.
Where they all booh Kerry and cheer the Dubs,
Or further on the road to Howth,
That other inn of happy note,
Harry Byrne's of noble fame,
And echoes of Bram Stoker's name."

Clontarf Castle Hotel, Castle Avenue.
Clontarf Castle is dealt with in chapter four above.

Gilbert and Wrights, Hollybrook Park.
The original Hollybrook House building that stood on this site can be dated to 1812. But the edifice mainly associated with the place was the Hollybrook Hotel which was for many years the only residential hotel in Clontarf. It was owned by the Bresnan family, mentioned above as the owners of Fingal House. It was a most comfortable quiet hotel within a short bus ride of Dublin city centre. The hotel was a very popular choice of venue for wedding receptions and a host of other social functions. The bar, lounge and restaurant operating there today trade under the name of Gilbert and Wright.

Pebble Beach, Conquer Hill Road.
   It the heart of Conquer Hill the Pebble Beach Bar and Lounge was originally Verlings grocery and butcher shop. The actual pub licence dates from the mid 1950's and it was thus named by the first publican to operate the premises as a public house - Tim Kinsella - after a golf course in California. As the years went by it was operated in turn by Leo Fitzgerald, Tom Maguire, Michael Grace, Kelly and Gleeson and presently by the Grainger family.

The Sheds, Clontarf Road.
Records from 1719 suggest that a property in the Sheds fishing village (see chapter one above) called "The Sign of the Ship" may have been an alehouse later known as "The sign of the Star and Garter" Today's premises, called after that colloquial and most romantic name "The Sheds" was first opened in 1845 by James Gerard Mooney - who went on to form the large chain of "Mooney" pubs. A Patrick Powell is listed as running the pub in 1915 and later the Cullen family from whom

Peter Connolly purchased the premises in 1927. Since then it has been operated by the Connolly family. It is sometimes mistakenly thought that The Sheds assumed that name from the local Tram Sheds, but it in fact predates the trams. The famous author James Joyce who loved to stroll along the seafront and the Bull Wall is known to have patronised the place.

The Yacht, Clontarf Road.
The premises known as The Yacht was once the grocery shop and public house of Thomas Carolan who acquired it in 1861 (see Harry Byrnes above). In 1937 the McAuley family became proprietors who in turn sold it to Michael Tobin in 1947. The Tobin family operated the business until 2003 when they sold it to the present licensee, Eamon O'Malley.

Clontarf Baths.

The beloved - especially of swimmers - little establishment known as Clontarf Baths and Assembly Rooms (for social meetings and events) was originally constructed in 1880. In the year 1886, two years after the founding of Clontarf Swimming Club, Mr. W.L. Freeman who resided on Beechfield Lane (which is now Oulton Road) formed a private company, bought and reconstructed the baths to specifically suit the needs of Clontarf Swimming Club. Mr. Freeman was himself a member of the club. Basically a simple structure, the Baths had a huge wall down the middle segregating the ladies' and the gentlemen sections. There were also facilities for hot sea- water baths and shallows for children and beginners. Mr. Freeman was president of Clontarf Swimming Club for three years, 1916-1919. Mr. W.J. Jameson of Balmoral Lodge, Castle Avenue, who was president of Clontarf Swimming Club for many years prior to Mr. Freeman's election in 1916 was vice-chairman of the private company formed by Mr. Freeman.

Clontarf Baths was in no way associated with the infamous Brierlys Baths alluded to in Chapter Eleven, above!

Maggie and Auld Craddock.
In his well known little booklet "Old Clontarf" Canon F.W.R. Knowles has a nostalgic few lines on the baths from his childhood memories of about 1913. I quote directly: "The Clontarf baths was originally owned by a private company, it was a concrete Island in the sea approached by a bridge of concrete, steel and wood. No doubt its concrete piers gave it great strength as it had to withstand the battering of fierce south-easterly gales and high tides. . . The Baths had not only the usual plunge baths but also hot sea-water baths. The bridge crossed an

enormous concrete seawater storage tank from which a big vertical boiler and pumps were supplied, in fact with its steam engine the baths was most impressive. But an electric motor replaced the steam engine and finally the whole hot bath system was scrapped. The big storage tanks were filled with sand by means of an old ship's derrick and mast hosting a big bracket. . .The Baths had strictly segregated bathing . . . The ladies' bath was presided over by an old woman called Maggie, she was hot bath attendant, masseuse, cleaner and lifeguard. But on one occasion an emergency arose, a Belgian woman was drowning and Maggie's only contribution to the rescue was to walk down the long diving board and drop a lifebuoy into the water a good sixty feet from the drowning Belgian!. . . I remember seeing some ladies in mobcaps and calico nightdresses bobbing up and down at the long rope. They could do little else dressed as they were. There were nuns from the local convent. . . The men's baths were presided over by a fearsome individual like Captain Kettle, he ran the cash desk, stoked the boiler and had a rooted antipathy to small boys. He was generally known as 'Ould Craddock'. Once a retired fishing smack, by name 'Irish Mollie' broke from her moorings in a gale, almost got into the men's bath and then went through the bridge. If the Baths were not the better of it, poor Mollie was not either."

Trendy Times

A new company, Clontarf Baths Ltd., bought the premises for £800 from Mr. Freeman's company in 1945. Mr. Freeman could no longer maintain his interests in the Baths but sold only when he was given assurances that the new owners (eight businessmen who were all members of various swimming clubs) were bona fide and stipulated that the premises would be kept as a swimming pool for the north Dublin area. The first chairman of this new private company was Mr. Warden. He immediately removed the cumbersome and space consuming centre wall giving a larger unified swimming area. In hindsight we can deduce that the ending of 'segregation' marked the beginning of more 'trendy' times and the bikini was just around the corner! The hot sea baths were also discounted as they were proving uneconomical mainly due to the constant rising of the price of fuel. In an eye catching advertising brochure for the re-opening of the 'new baths' in 1945, the public were lured to Clontarf 'the spot in the sun' to enjoy - 'the finest bathing facilities in Ireland', 'frequently changed water', the south facing structure which is a sun pocket unsurpassed anywhere in Dublin' and 'coaching facilities for all swimming standards'. A hot water bath (while in operation) could be had for 2 shillings (10p) and a plunge for 4d (2p). Those were the days!

Annual Grant

The new company soon found itself in debt, and asked Dublin Corporation to take over the baths. But a wary and wise corporation offered them an annual grant instead (based on the running costs for a year). It is under this system that the Baths operated for many years. The entire establishment consisted of a sizable swimming pool with dressing rooms and showers. It had a little green patch railed off on each side of the entrance with ample parking facilities in the adjoining lay-by. A vibrant amenity the Baths hosted many swimming races and galas and for many years a most popular Christmas morning swim.

In the mid 1980's long-time pool attendant, Mr. Joseph Rooney, talked fondly of the baths. "The water is drained and the pool cleaned out" he says "according to the swim load." And with a twinkle in his eye he adds "them corporation officials are glad to give an annual grant towards the upkeep and general running costs of the Baths. They realise what a valuable amenity the pool is - one they themselves would have to provide otherwise." Clontarf Baths has been the home of the illustrious Clontarf Swimming Club since the club's infancy. Many other swimming clubs - some extinct, some still thriving have histories based in the Baths. Among these are (Men's Clubs) - Civil Service Swimming Club, North Dublin Swimming Club and O'Connell Schools Boys' Club and (Ladies' Clubs') - Clontarf Ladies, Atlanta, Dominican Past Pupils, Republican Ladies and Civil Service Ladies. The Baths finally closed in 1996 and became something of an eyesore on the Clontarf promenade. Several planning applications to develop the site were rejected by an Bord Pleanála. Finally, in 2012 restoration plans to reincarnate the Baths to former prominence with extra facilities were approved by an Bord Pleanála. The Application plans came from the Clontarf Baths and Assembly Rooms Company Ltd after an agreement with Clontarf's Swimming Club. And of course all of us who have in the past "taken the plunge" in the "briny Baths" hope the venue will once again be reopened to offer its services to future generations.

Clontarf's Blue Lagoon.

A scheme of proposals for the development of the Bull Island and the 'Crab Lake' expanse of water between it and the mainland known as the 'Blue Lagoon' or 'Marine Lake' project was first put forward in 1929. Between then and the 1950's the plans were resurrected on several occasions and would most likely have been adopted were it not for the bureaucratic bungling between the many public bodies involved. The project eventually became something of a joke and a dream, and was finally abandoned forever. The basic idea of the project was to transform the Dollymount and Sutton coastal area into one of the finest seaside recreational centres in Europe. It certainly would have fundamentally transformed the whole image and aspect of Clontarf and as a result today's Clontarf would have developed into a much different place. The whole idea was first mooted when a number of interested parties felt that the natural playground of Dollymount could be greatly enhanced if the tidal area between the Bull Island and the mainland were enclosed by means of two dams or embankments - one at the present Bull Bridge, the other between the Bull Island and Sutton Strand. These would be provided with locks and sluices for connection with the open sea. This area, together with the Island itself, would provide 1,000 acres of a 'marine lake site' for development as a 'Coney Island' or a 'Monte Carlo'. There would be a constant depth of seven feet of water in the actual water area - although in the central shallow section of the channel, 300,000 cubic yards of silt would have to be removed. The entire area was to be surrounded by a nine mile long road forty feet wide and six feet above spring tide, providing a lovely seaboard drive.

Airport on Bull Island.
The site then would provide a three and a half mile long marine lake replacing the unsightly and barren (at low tide) coastline from Dollymount to Sutton, and would have the Bull Island complimenting it. It was to become an unrivalled aquatic pleasure ground with a delightful marine drive which would considerably enhance Dublin's attractions. Indeed the whole project was regarded as the basis for a municipal and national asset of immeasurable value. The amenities planned were many and varied. The area was to become a national regatta and aquatic sports arena. It would provide rowing facilities and cater for motor boat, swimming and sailing clubs. The magnificent and permanent marine lake would be available and suitable for every variety of aquatics. Facilities would be provided for boat houses with grandstands and car parks for regatta events. There was even mention of developing a national stadium on the site. The plans also included the provision of an aerodrome on the Bull Island and the lagoon itself would act as a seaplane base.

It was intended that much of the effort would be directed towards attracting tourists, but also the citizens of Dublin were to be adequately catered for. One hundred acres at the Bull Wall end of the Island were to be reserved for development as a pleasure park complete with a fun fair and a children's playground and adequate public recreational ground. There were to be a number of safe bathing beaches for residents and visitors. Plans were included for a marine garden, an aquarium and the impounding barriers at each end would accommodate pedestrians and cyclists as well as motor traffic. In fact the coastal road was to become part of a continuous coastal drive from Fairview through Clontarf, Sutton and Portmarnock to Malahide.

Attraction.
A central alluring feature of the proposals was the infinitesimal cost involved. The entire scheme was estimated to cost a mere £60,000. This, reduced to terms of an annual levy on the ratepayers of Dublin and Howth, meant an increase of a single halfpenny on the Poor Law valuation - which was indeed regarded as the 'mere bagatelle' it was. Furthermore a further attraction lay in the amount of short and long term employment the project would create. The construction, maintenance, administration and day to day running of the centre would keep many a Dubliner off the dole queue while the commercially minded would find the centre as attractive as the pleasure seekers.

Objections.
The golf clubs on the Bull Island were not too happy with the proposals especially the Royal Dublin Club whose club house would have to be moved to a central position on the links. Bird lovers were worried at the disturbance of many species of birds visiting the Island - although provision was made for a bird sanctuary to be retained on the northern end of the Island. There were worries also as to the effect on existing sewage arrangements. Fears were expressed as to the effect the embankments would have on the scouring action of the tide which keeps the Liffey mouth open - which took so long to sort out in past generations. But perhaps the most widespread fear was the threat of a permanent unpleasant odour if the green seaweed Ulva Latuca (or sea lettuce) became established in the lagoon. Other places had been scourged by this odour caused by the decomposition of this seaplant when its growth became uncontrollable. In the early 1950's a miniature marine lake was created in the lagoon as an experimental station to ascertain the conditions under which the plant grows. This was to be as far as the project advanced. In any case the many public authorities involved - the Government, Dublin Port and Docks Board, the North Dublin Rural District Council, Howth Urban District Council and the local residents - never organised themselves to form a central committee to take charge of the entire project. And so ended the 'Bue Lagoon' development.

Clontarf Lead Mine.

Clontarf once had its very own lead mine. The entrance to the seaward shaft of the mine was a cylinder-shaped stone tower on the city side of where Clontarf Baths stand today. The position of the tower is now occupied by a seaside shelter. The mine extended under the sea floor as well as inland and another shaft of the mine was opened in the present day O'Connell schools G.A.A. grounds on Clontarf Road. Many authorities state that the mine was opened and worked many occasions since the reign of King James I (1603-25). In 1756 proper mining began at the seaward shaft of the Clontarf mine and developed into extensive works. But the sea constantly frustrated the work and engineers never overcome the problem of regular tidal overflows. Insufficient timbering was also a problem. In 1837 all mining activity ceased permanently in the Clontarf mine. Many experts have argued since that this particular spot in Clontarf actually has rich deposits of lead ore and that the early mining carried out was really only work on an outcrop. In the "Natural History of Dublin" (1772) we can read that the Clontarf lead mine was opened in 1768, about 80 yards from the shore. Fourteen tons of ore were raised yielding a little silver ore and 12cwt. of lead per ton. The pits were only five fathoms deep and filled at every high tide. A report on the metallic mines of Leinster dated November 1st, 1827 states that a new shaft was opened at Clontarf in 1809. This shaft reached eight fathoms and contained a vein of galena and blande two feet wide.

Clontarf's Rivers

The Clontarf district is drained by two rivers.

(1) The Hollybrook River.
The Hollybrook river rises close to Wad Bridge on the Ballymun Road. It was once known as the Wad or Wadda river. (Close to its source it flows through an area that once formed a townland called Wad. This townland is recalled in Wadelai Road and Wadelai Gardens. Another Ballymun/Glasnevin old townland name at the source of the Hollybrook - Stormstown - is commemorated by Stormanstown Road.) Emerging from under Wad Bridge, the Hollybrook runs in an easterly direction, then south east into Artane under Doyle's Bridge on Beaumont Road. It continues south through Thorndale and under Donnycarney Bridge (once Scurlogue's Bridge) on the Malahide Road. It flows though part of Clontarf Golf Club's links then heads in a south westerly direction - parallel with the Dublin Belfast railway line for a short distance - and crosses under the Howth

Road close to Gilbert and Wrights bar and lounge. From there its 'home strait' takes it slightly east, then south to where it enters the sea by means of a tunnel under the Clontarf Road at Strandville Avenue. Practically the entire course of the Hollybrook river is now coulverted.

(2) The Naniken River.
Sometimes this name is spelt Nannikeen but its correct name is 'Abhann-na-gCian' a name adopted from the Cianacht sept or clan of ancient times. The Naniken originates in the Beaumont area and enters the sea at Naniken Bridge on the James Larkin Road. On its route it crosses the Malahide Road at Artane Bridge and the Howth Road at Ballyhoy Bridge and the rest of its course is a leisurely one through St. Anne's Park. It was for a time known as the Ballyhoy stream and its point of entry to the sea at one time marked the Dublin city boundary line.

Crab Lake.

The narrow ribbon of sea which flows between Dollymount and the North Bull Island was originally known as Raheny Lake but was later renamed Crab Lake Water or Crab Lough and gave rise to the term 'lakeview' in the area. The Bull Bridge (originally Crab Lake Bridge) spans this stretch of water to join the Bull Wall with the mainland. It is fed by three rivers - the Naniken, the Santry and a stream which joins it at the Whip O Water. The name Crab Lake also applied to the waterlogged ground towards the seafront between today's Conquer Hill Road and Seapark Drive. On early maps this ground was marked as 'Brick Kilns' just east of Clontarf Herring Sheds. Apparently much brick clay was removed from the spot leaving pits (or 'dumps' to the children) which led to water lodging and the formation of a swamp. It was not fully reclaimed until 1950 and in later years was part of Davitt's dairyland. Crab Lake is listed in old Dublin directories as the name of a townland. The area has been built upon in recent years as an extension to the eastern end of Kincora Road and creating Kincora Court houses. The artificial lake formed by the Ardilaun's in St. Anne's Park, by damming the Naniken river, is also often erroneously referred to as Crab Lake.

Central Remedial Clinic

Old Orthopedic Hospital

Verville Retreat

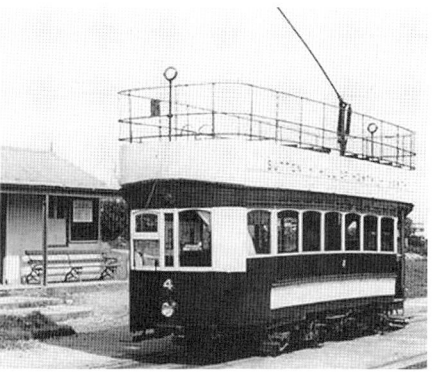

A Tram

Site of Old Railway Station

Clontarf Baths

Harry Byrnes Pub

Old Hollybrook Hotel

The Pebble Beach

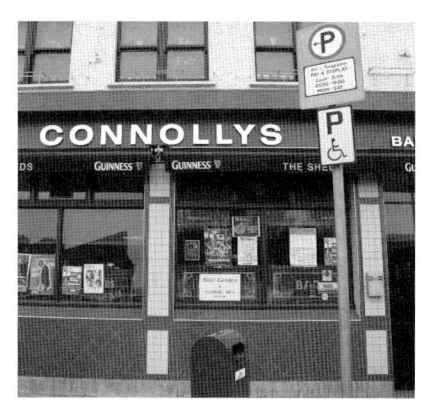

The Sheds Public House

The Yacht Pub

Dollymount House

CHAPTER THIRTEEN

The Sports Clubs of Clontarf

*"When the Great Scorer comes
To write against your name
He writes, not if you won or lost,
But how you played the game."* **Anonymous**

The cornucopia of sporting clubs which thrive in Clontarf speak volumes for the sensible and healthy attitude Clontarfites have towards the value of sport. The whole spectrum of sporting activities is catered for - and over the decades the locality has produced the gladiators capable of adapting to any new sport introduced to the vicinity. Indeed the great variety of sports clubs in the area has played a large part in urging people to choose Clontarf as their address. The clubs, over the years, also helped an ever enlarging community to become mutually acquainted and thus played their part in making Clontarf the mature suburb it is today. It is almost impossible to include data on all the sporting clubs in a study such as this so we will mainly concentrate on the bigger clubs. This is not to suggest that the smaller clubs such as the Clontarf Archery Club, various Bowling Clubs, the Basketball clubs, the Table Tennis clubs, Clontarf Hockey club, and Clontarf Pigeon Racing club, do not greatly contribute to the social and sporting life of Clontarf. And the strides forward made by Clontarf in the Community Games field, in all its aspects, must be greatly commended especially as all its activities are youth centred.

Gaelic Football in Clontarf

Brian Boru Gaelic Football Club

Gaelic Football came to Clontarf with the formation of the Brian Boru Club in 1919. The club was first organised by a group of Tipperary men who worked for the L.M.S. Shipping company (later British Railways). At a committee meeting of 21st October, 1919 they decided to affiliate to the County Board. They did much of their early training with the O'Tooles Club who dominated Dublin football in the 1920's. (O'Tooles were based in Dublin's north inner city).

When Clontarf G.A.A. "Old Timers" reminisce about those early years they will recall that the club grew up in the era of the War of Independence, the Black and Tans troubles and the Civil War. They trained alongside such O'Toole all time greats as the McDonnell's and the Synnotts. Rooted in the political activities of the time the Brian Boru Club became very Clontarf centered and acquired their own playing field, the Brian Boru football ground adjoining the then B&I playing pitches - part of the site which is now covered by Chelsea Gardens housing estate beside the old Danes Park. Indeed the club was ahead of its time in that it had its own club house and its own Brian Boru band. The club house was situated on the Vernon Avenue end of the present Churchgate Avenue (then Chapel Lane) and was used mainly as a social centre - for playing cards or simply 'chatting'. The senior team acquitted themselves admirably on the field of play against some of the most powerful clubs in Dublin football - the Geraldines, Kickhams, St. Mary's and the previously mentioned O'Tooles. The Club won the Dublin Junior football championship in 1930. Clontarf family names that will always be associated with the 'Brian Boru's' include the Stewards, the Farrells, the Yeates, the Bruens, the Cadwells, the Dorans and the Brennans.

The Brian Boru's were always a very enthusiastic club with their players traditionally 'able to look after themselves'. Perhaps too much pride and passion became associated with their play and this led to their downfall. In August, 1931 the club received a three month suspension as a result of 'incidents in a match against St. Mary's played at Croke Park'. Then in 1941, after a particular match against Sean McDermott's, played at Coolock, the wrath of Dublin G.A.A. Officialdom fell heavily on the Brian Borus and immortalized them in Dublin G.A.A. folklore by suspending them from the Gaelic Athletic Association for life. The banning edict had two stipulations in particular (i) The name Brian Boru could never again be used as the name of a Dublin G.A.A. club and (ii) Certain players (mentioned by name)could never be involved in the affairs of any Dublin G.A.A. club again. The clubs well known secretary at the time was Joe Yeates.

The 'life sentence' on Clontarf Gaelic Football was later remitted to a ten years ban and in the 1950/51 season the club was allowed back into the mainstream of Dublin G.A.A. affairs - but under the new name of Clontarf G.A.A. Club. Now the affairs of the club were looked after by Paddy O'Kelly and the secretary Michael Brennan. (Michael's father Joe Brennan, originally a Kildare man, was county board delegate at the time of the initial ban. The Brennans lived on Bull Island.) However the ten year gap had taken its toll and Gaelic football had lost much of its impetus in Clontarf. The new club found the problem of dwindling numbers too much of a handicap and after only a few years once again went into 'liquidation'. The reality was that only a handful of families in the Conquer Hill area were keeping the Gaelic tradition alive in the vicinity and their supply of youthful material was just about exhausted. The tragedy was that the club ceased to function just before the post war (world war two) population explosion 'hit' Clontarf - and although the club revived again briefly, in the mid 1950's it finally disbanded altogether in 1957. Had the club been kept alive, today's club would have its own playing field and ample room on which to build an adequate clubhouse. Over the years the 'Brian Boru's' and 'Clontarf' wore various strips - including (their original strip) a white jersey with a shamrock emblem, a black and amber jersey and a maroon jersey with a blue or purple collar Surviving members of the "old Clontarf G.A.A. club" kept up the tradition of holding a re-union dinner get together every year, until their numbers melted away.

Clontarf G.A.A. Club.

During the swinging 1960's when the Beatles captured the hearts of teenagers around the globe. . . when the then Cassius Clay danced around and tormented Sonny Liston and a succession of later opponents . . .when the motor car came to the countryside in general . . . and the world seemed young, bright and gay, Clontarf G.A.A. Club was growing up. The new club (which is really Clontarf's fourth G.A.A. club) was founded at a meeting on Tuesday April 11th, 1961 in Belgrove School. First initiated as a hurling club it concentrated its early efforts on juvenile teams with football being quickly added to its itinerary. The club rapidly matured and expanded to be in a position, in 1967, to field its first adult team in the Dublin Junior League Championship. In 1973 the club achieved Intermediate status and with typical Clontarf dedication and commitment reached the Senior ranks in 1979. Another milestone was reached in 1985 when the club contested its first ever Dublin senior championship county final.

Those 'founding fathers' back in 1961 include names synonymous with the club's progress in succeeding years - Gerry O'Connor who presided over the inaugural meeting, Tim Moore, Joe Glacken, and Michael Gleeson. Belgrove School has, ever since, been the club's nursery. The then boys' school principal Michael Kellegher as well as teachers Fergus O'Kennedy (who through repeated exhortations to his fellow gaels was mainly responsible for the formation of the club)and Frank O'Dea also attended that first meeting and from then on there has been no shortage of enthusiastic and dedicated teachers willing to work for the club and give pride of place to Gaelic Games within the school. Now catering for male and female juveniles and adults at most levels of gaelic games playing activities the membership of the club is large. Hurling had been 'lost' for a number of years but was revived in 1981 in the same year that camogie was established in the club, In 1986, the clubs silver jubilee year, the executive committee of the club laid ambitious plans to provide the club with the facilities of a clubhouse. After major fundraising – including the legendry "marches" in conjunction with Donnacha O'Dulaing of R.T.E. - the clubhouse project reached fruition with its official opening in 1998. The building – with many ancillary amenities – is in fact a beautifully restored, converted and renovated Belgrove House (see chapter eleven above). The clubhouse surely gives Clontarf G.A.A. Club stability and permanance. As the club's image has always been that of a community club rather than an isolated G.A.A. Club, the facilities the clubhouse provides helped complete its integration with the entire Clontarf community.

Clontarf teams, in their familiar red jerseys with white trimmings play their home matches on the well manicured swards of St. Anne's Park with superbly developed playing pitches. And auguring well for the future is the vibrant thriving "nursery" with coaching mainly conducted in playing fields operated in partnership with St. Paul's College. Over the years Clontarf G.A.A club has been represented at various levels including county level in football hurling, camogie and ladies football. The "biggies" to date must be Noel Mc Caffrey his son Jack Mc Caffrey and Jim Ronayne. Noel is the holder of a National League Medal and a Football G.A.A. All Star Award. Jim and Jack hold All Ireland Senior football medals and Jack, in 2013 was named young footballer of the year. Jim, Jack and Martin Doran also hold National Football League medals. Noel was also the first clubman to wear the green of Leinster winning a Railway Cup Medal in 1986. Deceased former chairman Bill Ronayne (Jim's father) was involved with All Ireland winning minor teams in 1982 and 1984. Present clubman Mick Bohan has been part of the Dublin Senior football management body for some time. Over the years the club has also produced some fine referees of whom former chairman, Aidan Sheills is probably best known, Former chairman, the late John Joy, is commemorated by the John Joy Cup which is competed for annually in Dublin Junior Football circles.

Clontarf G.A.A. Club had and continues to have a myriad of volunteer workers who made and keep it the respected club it is today.

"Like as the waves make towards the pebbled shore,
So do our minutes hasten to the end:
Each changing place with that which goes before,
In sequent toil all forwards do contend." **Shakespeare**

Clontarf G.A.A Club will long hail and salute the history made by two of its sometime players, albeit in the Rugby Code! A remarkable and unique double records that Brian O'Driscoll as captain (see chapter 10 above) in 2009 led the Irish Senior Mens team to Grand Slam glory. Fiona Coughlan followed suit in 2013 when again as captain she led the Irish Senior Womens team to the grand slam. We all salute their playing skills and leadership qualities.

SCOIL UÍ Chonaill G.A.A. CLUB.

The Christian Brothers of O'Connell primary and secondary schools North Richmond Street, in Dublin's inner city, began their association with the parish of Clontarf in October, 1931. Unable to provide adequate sporting facilities for their ever increasing number of pupils in the environs of the school complex, they leased playing fields on the Clontarf Road - opposite Clontarf Baths. (The original lease was due to terminate in March, 1989). Since 1931 pupils attending O'Connell's Schools have benefited immensely by almost daily use of the playing grounds, during school terms, for Gaelic football and hurling as well as many other field sports.

In the years after 1931, it came to the notice of the school authorities that when boys had finished their studies in O'Connell schools they were very often lost to Gaelic games as Dublin G.A.A. clubs in those days - strange as it may seem - tended to reject all would be members except the players of quality. Consequently in 1950 Brother Scully (then the school principal) with the help of a number of enthusiastic parents (especially Dominick Bohan) established Scoil UÍConnail G.A.A. club. The aims of the club were (1) To give both pupils and past pupils of the schools the opportunity of playing Gaelic games under the auspices of the Dublin County Board - both within and outside the school environment. (2) To give its members of all ages the opportunity of achieving and maintaining physical fitness and a healthy lifestyle. (3) To develop the character and discipline associated with team games. (4) To enable the members to continue their association with O'Connell schools. (5) To meet with people of like interests and (6) To build up a circle of friends and companions. These ideals, which were established by the clubs founding fathers, hold good to this day.

In 1963 the Christian Brothers acquired an "inland" extra lot of two and a half acres, to extend their Clontarf ground, in exchange for a one acre building site fronting the Clontarf Road. A vital additional aspect of this transaction was the acquiring of a new lease on the entire premises for 250 years, thus firmly consolidating the school and club's base in Clontarf. Now, with this long-term foothold on the grounds, the club soon commenced development work to modernise the facilities. The whole plot was drained and levelled and a new pavilion constructed which included showers and extensive changing facilities. While this work was been carried out (it was completed in August 1965) the club had the use of Fingallians G.A.A. club facilities in Swords for its activities. Since then modern and comfortable facilities have been provided in the form of dressing rooms, a large bar and a function room.

Since its foundation in 1950 "Scoil"(as the club is intimately known) has greatly expanded to cater for most age levels in football, hurling, camogie and ladies football. While many competitions have been won by different teams over the years, pride of place must go to the two Dublin senior football county championships won in 1983 and in 1986.

Membership of the club is still almost exclusively confined to present and past pupils of O'Connell schools who reside in all parts of Dublin, including Clontarf. Perhaps the greatest tribute one can pay to the many tireless volunteer workers who do the backroom work in the day to day running of the affairs of the club is to record that today's vibrant Scoil UÍ Chonaill operates so smoothly while at the disadvantage of having its playing premises at quite a distance from its mother house and nursery. While the input of club members and officials to Dublin G.A.A. wider circles has been considerable two of the more prominent names are Tony Hempenstall and Robbie Kellegher. Hempenstall was, in October 1986, named as a member of the Dublin senior football team three man management body. He had a previous term as a selector. Robbie Kellegher was the effective and stylish left full back on the very successful Dublin senior football team of the seventies and also represented Leinster on Railway Cup teams. He was also part of a triumvirate who managed the Dublin senior team in 1985/86. Liam Egan is another 'Scoil' player to wear the blue of Dublin. Club member Tommy Naughton is a former manager of the Dublin Senior hurling team.

Soccer in Clontarf.

The Clontarf district is the proverbial hive of soccer activity with a number of clubs operating in Junior soccer circles.

Belgrove F.C. used to be Clontarf's "bigwig" in soccer terms. In its formative years Belgrove was known as Killester Unknowns. Their first colours were a strip of yellow jerseys but these were laid aside when the club purchased a blue set from the ailing Haverty Rangers. Belgrove played their soccer on St. Anne's Park up to 1958 when they moved to new premises on Mount Prospect Avenue which was the site of Eason's old sports grounds. In Eason's time the tradition of a disco was born in the clubhouse and thus became the (now former) Grove disco when Belgrove moved in. A fire in 1975 caused the disco to move to nearby St. Paul's College. The club's facilities were the envy of many League of Ireland clubs encompassing an excellent playing surface, floodlights and top class social facilities in their clubhouse. The hallmark of the club always was admirable all round organisation which paid rich dividends in the form of honours won. Their first trophy win was the A.U.L. Division3 league title in 1948-49 and the highlight probably their win over Virginians in the F.A.I. Junior Cup Final in the 1956/57 season. In 1998 the club celebrated its 50th birthday. The club played in division one of the Leinster Senior League and the League of Ireland "B".

If trophies are the yardstick of a successful club then Oulton founded in 1965, are the 'leaders' of the "pack". Strongly associated with the local 'Sheds' tavern they managed, at one time or another, to win all the major trophies within the League including the Amateur Cup in 1980, and the Leinster Junior Cup in 1984.

With Belgrove F.C. and Oulton F.C no longer on the Clontarf scene the biggest club in the area is now Clontarf F.C. a club that fields teams from under 8 to adult/senior.

'Mr. Amateur League' himself, Noel Kennelly (referred to in chapter ten) first became secretary of the Amateur League in 1967. and served as secretary of the F.A.I. coaching committee as well as holding a number of minor offices within the organisation. A very 'organised' secretary Noel insured that discipline and order prevailed within the League. He is an expert on the laws of soccer and always presented excellent ideas on the future development of the game in this country.

Clontarf Rugby Football Club

"In times of peace and times of war
Through times of joy and hopes and fears
As constant as the northern star
Our flag has flown, a hundred years."

Clontarf Rugby Football Club, which has always sported Clontarf's traditional colours of red and blue, was founded in 1876 and celebrated its centenary in 1976. The clubs first playing fields were on Vernon Avenue. This ground was rented annually for £3 from a certain Monsieur George who was a horse buyer for the French army. The club was first established as a Junior club and indeed was known locally as the "Junior Club". After a few seasons at Vernon Avenue the club established itself on a ground beside Clontarf Yacht and Boat Club - where the C.I.E. bus depot stands today. This venue was complete with club rooms including dressing rooms. In 1892 the club moved again, this time to facilities used by Clontarf Cricket Club on the Howth Road, close to the seafront. In 1896 the club settled into its present base on Castle Avenue. The first pavilion was at the southern boundary not far from the entrance gate in the Stiles Lane. In those early years Clontarf, due to its Junior status, lost many players to the bigger senior clubs - including Jack Roche, A.K. Wallis, Tommy Thornhill and George Walmsley all of whom went on to win international caps. In 1900 Clontarf had its first success on the playing field when they beat G.P.O. by 4 points to 3 to win the Junior League. This paved the way for the club to join the ranks of senior clubs which it did for the 1902-03 season. In 1908 the club erected a new pavilion on the Castle Avenue grounds which by now sported three playing pitches. The pavilion meant that players could have a 'luxury' such as a cup of tea after a match. This pavilion was to be altered, enlarged and improved many times in the future - in 1923,1956 and 1962.

Since the initial success in 1900 the club has won many competitions at various levels. But biggest achievement award goes to the clubs 1st team that brought the Leinster Senior Cup to Clontarf for the first and only time in 1936 when they beat Blackrock by 16 points to 8 in the final. This feat was matched when in 2014 the club won its first ever All Ireland Senior League Title. Over the years Clontarf has had many of its players selected to play at interprovincial level and on various other representative teams. Fourteen Clontarf players have achieved international caps for Ireland - C.P. Stuart, S.E. Polden, H.S.T. Cormac, G.J. Morgan, D.J. Langan, F.G. Moran, B. Mullin, P. Lawlor, J. Fortune, F. Ennis, B. Jackman, F. Dunlea, J. Downey and C. Healy. The club has also given the I.R.F.U. and its Leinster Branch a host of administrators who have made notable contributions in various aspects of policy and development. An outstanding Clontarf player, Frank O'Driscoll, never got a full international cap but played for the touring Irish side led by Tom Kiernan in Argentina in the 1960's.

Clontarf Rugby Club held its first Annual Dinner in the Wicklow Hotel on April 30th, 1887. From its early years the club had close connections with Clontarf Yacht and Boat Club and Clontarf Swimming Club. All three clubs had many common members. Clontarf club had an interval from 1914 to 1918 during the first world war, but it restarted again in 1919. Clontarf has earned a reputation as being one of the most difficult clubs to beat in cup competition. Always a great social club, in 1952 they became the first Irish Rugby Club to tour France. Since 1886 the grounds at Castle Avenue have been occupied jointly by Clontarf Cricket Club in the summer and the Rugby Club in the winter. Indeed both clubs share the honour of being the second oldest club in the area - pre dated only by the Yacht and Boat Club. Grounds and pavilion problems, and other matters common to both clubs, have been dealt with by a joint committee since 1908. In 1947 the late Mr. J.G. Oulton (who served terms as President of both clubs) offered the two clubs the opportunity of purchasing further ground close to Castle Avenue and also acquiring, on a long lease, the present Cricket ground which was then used variously as a tennis club (Lido Club), a hockey ground and for allotments. The Cricket and Rugby Clubs quickly availed of Mr. Oulton's offer. In May 1982 the pavilion was badly gutted by fire. The two clubs took the opportunity to look again at their own situation in the old 'arrangements'. A new agreement was reached after much soul searching regarding the use of the grounds and the overall development of the entire premises. As a result each club was made 'independent' with its own ground invested in the clubs separately. A new common agreement in the area of social facilities was also reached, and a major pavilion redevelopment project launched.

The entrance gate at Castle Avenue (built and opened in 1924) is a memorial to Charles Killingly a one time secretary and treasurer of the club. For many years before the "professional era" it was traditional for the Irish international Rugby squad to have a final workout on the Clontarf grounds on the eve of their departure, via Dublin airport, to various international venues. Clontarf Rugby Club operates a thriving and expanding juvenile section.

Golf Clubs.

The Royal Dublin Golf Club, Dollymount.
The Royal Dublin golf links on the North Bull Island Dollymount has narrow fairways and its variety of holes is not great. It cannot be regarded as a plush course being in the 'backyard' of dockland. However, now well into its second century, and taking into account its traditions, achievements, general reputation and all round high standards it must be regarded as a course of international standing. The celebrated club was born at a meeting on May 5th, 1885, at number 15 Grafton Street. The meeting was called by an enthusiast named John Lumsden who hailed from Banffshire in Scotland and came to Ireland in 1867 as a banker. That meeting inaugurated the club as the Dublin Golf Club and its members soon secured a new playing course, complete with a little pavilion, in the Phoenix Park at a place then known as the 'Bents'. (Lumsden and some friends had first played on a course in the Phoenix Park close to the grounds of the Phoenix Cricket Club). Thus the club was established only four years after Ireland's first golf club - Belfast - had been started in 1881. Lumsden himself became Dublin Golf Club's first captain.

Although a very successful start was made in the Phoenix Park the club moved to a course at Sutton in 1886 where it remained for three years. Then in 1889 the club obtained permission from Colonel E. Vernon of Clontarf Castle and from Dublin Port and Docks Board to lay out a new course and erect a little clubhouse hut on the North Bull Island. The 'new' club opened up in March 1889 and has remained on the Bull Island to this day. It flourished from the beginning - despite the fact that Sunday players had to 'enter discreetly' due to the fact that Mr. Vernon disagreed with Sunday golf. In 1891 the Dublin Golf Club accepted the option - granted by Queen Victoria - of becoming the Royal Dublin Golf Club.

At the time the Duke of Connaught, commander in chief of British forces in Ireland, was a member of the club. The aforementioned little clubhouse was the old single storey pavilion - which had come from the Phoenix Park - and was erected close to the Bull Wall. This was extended in 1890 and again in 1893. In 1903 the club bought 2,072 acres of Island land from Colonel Vernon. In 1904 the club erected a new clubhouse on this land. It was "a two-storey" wooden building with brick, chimney stacks and a red tiled roof. This building was added to in 1909. On September 5th, 1914 following the outbreak of World War I the club's grounds - in common with the rest of the Island - were commandeered by the British Army for military training. When returned after the war the course was practically unrecognisable. The greens and the general layout was a total mess and the clubhouse itself, which was used as an Officer's quarters, was in a very dilapidated condition. The army paid the club £10,000 in compensation which was spent in giving the clubhouse a total overhaul and redecorating it. The golf course was redesigned by Mr. E.S. Colt.

In 1943 came the club's greatest disaster. On the night of August 2nd the much beloved clubhouse was burned to the ground. No lives were lost but everything was totally destroyed including most of the clubs records. Wartime (Second World War) difficulties together with the possibility of the Irish Tourist Board going ahead with the 'Blue Lagoon' (see chapter twelve) project delayed the immediate replacement of the clubhouse. In the meantime temporary buildings were erected and finally on October 2nd 1954 Taoiseach, John A. Costello officially opened the new clubhouse building. This is today's Royal Dublin premises but extensions and alterations were carried out in 1962, 1965, 1974, 1981, 1983 and 1985.

Almost from the beginning the Royal Dublin Golf Club has been established as one of Ireland's most renowned link courses. From the very early years the club has hosted all the major Irish events on numerous occasions - the Irish Amateur Open Championship, the Irish Professional Open Championship, The Irish Championship and the Irish Women's Championship. Over the years the course has witnessed the play of the golfing world's greatest stars, amateur and professional - especially during its years as host to the revitalised Carroll's Irish Open in the 1980's. In 1985 the club proudly celebrated its centenary and marked the occasion with a beautifully produced book on the history of the club. The club colours are dark green and dark navy with a yellow stripe.

St.Annes Golf Club, Dollymount.

Nesting among the sand dunes on the northern end of the Bull Island is St. Anne's Golf Club, loveliest of homely clubs. The club came into existence on

July 1st, 1921 when permission was sought by and granted to a group of Clontarf and Dollymount residents to play golf on a course of their own on the Bull Island. This permission came from the Royal Dublin Golf Club who in 1904 had achieved exclusive rights to play golf over the entire Bull Island. During the reconstruction of the Royal Dublin Golf course, after its occupation by British troops during World War I, these residents had begun to play golf on part of the Bull Island now occupied by St. Anne's. On getting 'the franchise' from Royal Dublin the name St. Anne's was adopted by the group - from the local St. Anne's estate. It was not until October 24th, 1929 that a formal lease for the exclusive right to play golf was granted by the trustees of Royal Dublin to St. Anne's for a term of twenty years from November 1st, 1926. The annual rent was £500. The clubs first president was J.P. Cullen, the first honoury secretary was Mr. T. Murray and the first club captain was Mr. M. Davitt. The club's colours are red, green and blue and the crest sports a hare, a sky lark and the old Dublin three castles insigne.

St Anne's original clubhouse stood close to the site where the Interpretative centre stands today. At first it was a little more than a hut which improved in stages to become a more spacious building. In pre Causeway Road days an old gravel track-road led across the Island from the Bull Wall inside the outer ridge of sand dunes to the clubhouse. When the Causeway Road was built it 'ploughed' through what was then the ninth green of St. Anne's. In March, 1974 the club built a new clubhouse on is present site. At the time the clubs committee had considerable difficulty in convincing various interested parties that the new clubhouse was in keeping with the 'T' shaped building originally sanctioned in July, 1972. The clubhouse was accused of being guilty of 'encroachment' and the building they erected, it was alleged, was much more 'prominent' in its sitting and form of construction that the design first approved would have been. Allegations were also made that the present roadway to the clubhouse was constructed through the sand dunes without consulting the parks superintendent. The clubhouse was gutted by a severe fire in 1982 but has been rebuilt into a most comfortable '19th hole' overlooking the entire course.

The original lease was renewed as it became due and the club is presently operating on a ninety year lease from Dublin Corporation. This lease was drawn up in 1971. First opening as a nine hole course the club has long since become a full eighteen hole course. The second nine hole area is mainly reclaimed land adjacent to the original nine holes. In their reclamation work the club had to overcome the dilemma of the danger of damaging some of the ecological heritage present. In this they were closely monitored by the Bull Island Conservation Committee.

By far the clubs most famous member and character was a man bearing a famous name - the late Michael Collins. A founder, and life long member of the club. Collins had become a father figure by the time of his death in 1981. At various times he was greenkeeper, stewart and barman at the clubhouse. Older members of the club clearly remember Michael draughting water from Blackbands to the old clubhouse with a horse and cart. A man of many tales he often related the occasion his famous name had him arrested. Apparently in the early 1920's Michael used to collect his pay-packet in a shop (later O'Grady's) close to the Bull Wall. A sharp eyed British Officer on a visit to the shop spotted a brown envelope marked 'Michael Collins'. He and a few colleagues lay in hiding for the 'biggie' to collect the envelope. When Collins showed up they instantly arrested him convinced it was the real man of 1921 Treaty fame for whom every British Officer in Ireland was looking. After considerable questioning he was released.

Clontarf Golf Club, Malahide Road.
Clontarf Golf Club on the Malahide Road was officially established at a meeting held in Clontarf town hall on January 22nd, 1912. It was founded to provide playing facilities for many everyday golfers who couldn't be accommodated in the existing clubs in the vicinity. At that inaugural meeting a decision was taken that membership would consist of 'residents' (people who lived locally) and 'non-residents' (those outside the Clontarf area). From the beginning the club had lady associate members. Clontarf Golf club was the first club in Ireland to provide five day members. In the early years there was no golf on Sundays.

The club course and first clubhouse was originally situated on the Bradshaw estate which adjoined the present links. Today's clubhouse, once known as Donnycarney House, was first built in 1781 by Robert Carroll proprietor of Donnycarney Quarries. There is no record of a previous building on the site. In 1853 Alex Thom (of the Dublin postal directory firm) came into ownership of the house. He is reputed to have employed the renowned Irish architect of the Victorian period - John Skipton Mulvany - to remodel the entire house. He died in 1879 and Sir Arthur Porter (master of the Rolls) acquired the property. He was in residence until Clontarf Golf Club officially took over in 1922. In its teething years Clontarf Golf Club was nurtured along by early and founding members who gave outstanding contributions to the development of the club. Names such as Rev. J.L. Morrow, Senator James Moran, Geo Booker, Tom Carson and Harry Crawford will always be fondly and admirably recalled whenever members discuss the history of the club.

On the competitive front Clontarf Golf Club is the leading winner of the Barton Cup - having won it nine times. Five club members have won the Lumsden Cup.

One of the club's star players is a lady, Elaine Bradshaw, who won the Irish Ladies Close Championship on three occasions. Elaine also represented Ireland in international golfing competition on nine occasions.

Swimming

Clontarf Swimming Club.

How old is swimming? As old as man himself? As old as the sea? If you lived in ancient or even old Clontarf how would you rate your chances of being an accomplished swimmer? I think they would be excellent. But please don't misunderstand. I'm talking about surviving, living, the quality of your life - not about winning swimming championships! Living in a precinct such as Clontarf, the smell of brine would be in the nostrils from birth. Much of your food might have to be eked from the sea and you might also 'be involved in trade' with passing ships. You also would learn to protect your surrounds and as the enemy always came from sea - remember the Firblogs. . . the Tuatha De Danann. . . the Vikings. . . and the Norman's. . . you would have to patrol your sea line. Thus whether you found yourself at sea, trying to coax a livelihood from her or protecting your terrain in a vessel that might not be straight from the Harland and Wolff, the ability to swim would be good for the nerves! Even if you never had occasion to take to sea, would her physical presence, as the natural boundary, not be a challenge - does man not always strive to conquer, or at least come to a 'working relationship' with his environment? Then, as the quality of life in Clontarf changed dramatically down through the years surely your natural tendency would be to see the nearby mass of water in a new light . . . to use the sea for recreation and pleasure. To harness her for sporting purposes.

Whether or not Clontarf's Swimming Club, came to be spawned in this manner we do not know but the Club was founded in 1884 and its growth and development since then is legendary. Thus like the only three clubs that predate it in Clontarf (Yacht and Boat, Rugby and Cricket Clubs) the Swimming Club has witnessed the first and last of Dublin's Horse Trams, the coming and passing of the Electric Trams, has lived through the age of the Diesel and has ushered in the ultra modern Dart rapid train system! Only two swimming clubs in the entire country predate Clontarf - Dublin Swimming Club founded in 1880 and Sandycove Swimming Club founded in 1882. Clontarf Swimming Club is in fact ten years older than the L.B.I.A.S.A. and the I.A.S.A. itself, both of which were formed in 1894.

Clontarf's reputation as a successful club over the years became respected among swimming enthusiasts almost worldwide. The club achieved a reputation as a great social club - embracing all the best of good fellowship - at home and abroad.

Being blessed with a succession of excellent club secretaries who organised quite brilliant tours abroad the club became a great ambassador for Irish swimming and came to be in very popular demand. And their competitive record in Britain and all over continental Europe is an enviable one. Another great feat achieved by the club was the fact that they hosted a number of outstanding swimming Galas over the years. A ladies section to the club was organised as early as 1917. And the club always had a thriving under age section also. The big, competitive and prestigious club celebrated its centenary in 1984, the highlight of which were an excellent centenary banquet and dance, an exceptional exhibition of club photographs (from club files and members' private collections) and the creation of a magnificent presidential chain of office - made entirely from the gold medals won by many former champions. Nowadays the club is not so prominent, but many changes have taken place in the field of swimming not least being the arrival of the indoor heated swimming pool (Clontarf being an outdoor club all its life) while the game of water polo itself declined drastically in its appeal and popularity.

Based at Clontarf Baths since its early years the club, in 1908, became affiliated to the I.A.S.A. and in that same year came its first success when the Leinster Junior Water Polo League was won with A.J. Cullen as Captain. In 1910 the Club became a senior club. The club's early meetings appear to have been held in Greenlanes National School - then on Seafield Road. In its first years many of the club's races were held at 7 a.m! This explains the club's emblem - a sunburst, or the rising sun as perceived by those early morning enthusiasts. A shamrock was added to the crest when J.S, Brady won the club's first Irish Swimming Championship - the 220 yards race in 1913. In that same year T.H. Corrigan also won the Irish 440 yards championship. In 1928 the club won the Leinster Senior Water Polo League for the first time - with a team captained by E.J. (Ned) Lightfood who also played international Rugby for Ireland and was later an Irish Rugby selector. In 1936 the club won the 'blue riband' of Leinster Water Polo, the Senior Cup for the first time and in 1938 captured the All Ireland Senior Water Polo Cup.

In its illustrious past, connoisseurs of Irish Swimming records know that the achievements of Clontarf Swimming Club are unlikely ever to be equalled by any other swimming club never mind surpassed. In terms of ability to win - (at all levels including all-Ireland level) - the club is certainly Clontarf's most outstanding sports club. In the late 1930's and early 1940's in a quite extraordinary run of success Clontarf literally reigned supreme in Irish Swimming circles. Success came at swimming and water polo at all levels and a long list of Leinster and Irish squad championships and water polo championships wins stand to Clontarf's credit as well as a plethora of individual events won.

Since A.J. Cullen was first 'capped' for Ireland in 1913 the club has produced a string of water polo internationals including quite a few who had the honour of captaining their country. The club was also represented by two players - J.S. Brady and S. Barrett - on the first Irish Water Polo team to take part in the Olympic Games, in Paris in 1924. Countless club members played interprovincially, and a litany of club members went on to become very respected officials in the Leinster Branch of the I.A.S.A. The club's last 'great' water polo side was the all-conquering team of the 1950's. Overall it is fair to comment that Clontarf club produced brilliant water polo teams rather than top class individual swimmers. But there were many exceptions to that of course, particularly the club's star of star's R.N. (Richie) Case. Richie, from the well known swimming family, was a phenomenon in the water. He was Clontarf's sailfish. Being superb at every distance in every style he, one time or another, held every Irish swimming record and amassed a cornucopia of national titles. He had no serious rival in Irish swimming while at his peak. He was Clontarf club champion for no less than sixteen consecutive years and in one year (1936) he won all of the Irish freestyle men's championships. Michael Kelly from the Clontarf Club became Ireland's first ever representative in the European Swimming Championships when he competed at Budapest Hungary in 1958.

Other swimming Clubs.

The North Dublin Swimming Club also had its headquarters at Clontarf Baths. Founded in 1929 the club affiliated to the I.A.S.A. in 1936 and has also built up a formidable record of aquatic achievements since then.

Clontarf Cormorants indoor swimming club operated from St. Paul's College swimming pool for many years. They have an impressive record of dedication and achievement and regularly took many awards in Dublin, Leinster and Irish Championships. They have also sent competitors to compete at Olympic games level. With about one hundred members they did much of their training as early as seven o'clock in the morning. Alas, St. Paul's swimming pool is no more.

Clontarf Yacht and Boat Club.

Clontarf's 'mother' club and one of the east coast's oldest clubs, is Clontarf Yacht and Boat Club. It was founded on March 1st, 1875 by John Sullivan, a member of a publishing firm, who became its first Commodore. In that year Sullivan, acting on behalf of Clontarf Yacht and Boat Club, took out a yearly tenancy of the premises known as 'Belvedere' on Clontarf Road, which has ever since been the clubhouse of the Yacht and Boat Club. 'Belvedere' was then described as 'a country style house' and had once been the home of Captain Henry Thompson an inspector of constabulary. Later the house became identified with the well known Dublin family of Gardiner.

The last private occupant of the house was a merchant named Charles Heaviside. The ground landlord Colonel J.E. Vernon granted the club a long lease on the premises and it also had the support of Sir Arthur Edward Guinness (later Lord Ardilaun). In its first year the club had eight members. Sailing and Boating were the predominant motives that brought the initial members together. However dances were held regularly for many years and outings undertaken. Chess and draughts were played in the clubhouse and before long the billiard room was opened.

'Belvedere' itself and its function rooms have been altered and renovated many times since 1875 but still retains its original character. The club colours are the red and blue of Clontarf and while records show that the club's early regattas were dominated by rowing events the club now undertakes the regular (and full) annual programme of events common to thriving Yacht and Boat clubs. The club is a vibrant club with a club spirit all of its own. It maintains a close liaison with the Clontarf area and with many of the district's other sporting clubs. Its original members were of the upper class Clontarf variety and many were members of Clontarf Cricket, and Swimming clubs also. Being now well into its second century the club members have a tremendous tradition of know-how with regard to seafaring matters. They have a mine of experience and technical expertise in sailing and are most competent as competitors, administrators and as race organisers.

Junior sailing has always featured in the club's activities but was only formally organised in the 1960's when a Cadet section was established - with six 'Measle' boats. The cadets now sail many varieties of boats and many cadets have, over the years, passed the Irish Yachting Association's three stages scheme of badges. Quite a few, indeed, have qualified as instructors. The Clontarf Yacht and Boat Club can certainly be proud of the success and achievements of its cadets. The Albatross used to be the clubs logo but in 1982 it was dropped in favour of the Clontarf Bull.

Clontarf Cricket Club.
Clontarf Cricket Club, like the Rugby Club was established in 1876. The club's first ground was at the seafront end of the Howth Road - where they were joined in 1892 by their ever since 'sister' club Clontarf Rugby Club. In 1896 both clubs moved to the present grounds on Castle Avenue. Initially the club was founded as a Junior Club fielding just one team. In 1898 Clontarf Cricket Club won its first trophy when beating Old St. Mary's by an innings in the Junior Cup final. However the club had a somewhat low profile until after the turn of the 20th century. In 1908 the club was promoted to senior status. Like the Rugby club, the Cricket Club ceased to operate during World War 1 from 1914 to 1918. In 1926 the club won the Leinster Senior League for the first time. These successes have been repeated many times since then together with a myriad of other honours at all levels. The club's first international player was S.H. Crawford in 1903. Over the years a succession of Clontarf players have achieved international caps down to the recent years which saw players like L. Podge Hughes, Enda A. McDermott and Gerry A. Kirwan 'capped'. The list includes G.J. Morgan who played both international Rugby and Cricket for his country. The club also has a long list of players who gained interprovincial and other representatives honours. In 1938 N.C. Mahony played for Leinster v Ulster in July while in August he played for Munster v Leinster. This was a most unusual distinction, to play for and against the same province in the same year. As well as players Clontarf has given many capable officials to Irish Cricket who have made very positive contributions to the progress of Irish Cricket The cricket ground was for long years used for the playing of Rugby also but since 1958 this practice has ceased. Since then Clontarf's ground has been developed into just about the finest cricket ground in Ireland and indeed is now the country's premier international cricket ground. Many international teams have played there (since the club hosted its first international in 1964) including Scotland, Holland, Denmark, Switzerland, Australia, India and the West Indies. Since 1981 the club has adopted the practice of producing fine programmes for home matches.

In 1940 ladies cricket was inaugurated and Clontarf quickly entered competition in this area. In the following years Mary Coffey became arguably Ireland's finest ever lady cricketer. The club's ladies section 'died' in the early 1960's but was 'resurrected' in the mid 1970's and now thrives once again. In 1985 the club won the Marigold Cup (the Leinster Womens Cricket Union's Senior Cup) for the first time. The club also has a very well organised juvenile section.

Tennis.

Clontarf Lawn Tennis Club.

Clontarf Lawn Tennis Club began its life in 1887 with just one court and a shed in a field at the rear of number 45 St. Lawrence Road. Just one year later the club moved to a site on the seafront opposite Clontarf Baths and established a new pavilion with seven courts. This site was acquired from Mr. T. Stuart of Beechfield House. From the beginning the club provided for family membership but the number of lady members must have been ever increasing because in 1895 the all male committee decided to add a ladies dressing room to the pavilion. The committee organised regular 'smoking concerts' and dances in Clontarf town hall to meet the expenses of running the club. The first patrons of the club were Lord Ardilaun of St. Anne's and Colonel Vernon of Clontarf Castle. The tennis courts were kept in good playing order by regular rolling with a donkey drawn water ballast roller - but the maintenance of the donkey caused a number of understandable problems!

In the early years the club celebrated the 'At Home' each July. A marquee was erected and a band hired to supply music. This custom ended with the outbreak of the first world war. Indeed the same war caused the suspension of inter club competitions with a consequent drop in the standard of tennis played at the club. In 1931 the club courts were moved 'inland' to their present position off Oulton Road and the ground on the seafront was developed for housing. In 1937 the club celebrated its golden jubilee amid a rising standard of tennis within the club. In 1942 Clontarf Tennis Club won Class I of the Dublin Lawn Tennis Council's League and in 1943 won the Class II League. Today Clontarf has floodlit hard courts catering for an ever increasing number of players. The club suffered a severe setback in May 1982 when the clubhouse was destroyed by fire. But a new clubhouse was opened for Christmas 1984. The club celebrated its centenary in 1987.

Clontarf Church of Ireland Lawn Tennis Club.

Clontarf Church of Ireland Lawn Tennis Club on Seafield Road West was founded in March 1935. The club took over the playing grounds behind St. John The Baptist Church of Ireland after the old Beechfield Lawn Tennis Club was dissolved. The club has always been the centre of social activities for the younger members of the parish community during the summer months. The club competes annually in the Dublin Lawn Tennis Council's Leagues. In 1955 a hard court was laid which was a great asset in wet weather. Nowadays, of course, all courts are all weather courts.

Clontarf Cycling Club

Clontarf cycling club was founded in 2013 and operates from Clontarf G.A.A club premises on Seafield Road. A thriving club, fully registered with the Irish Cycling Federation, it is one of the country's biggest clubs and among its members is that one time doyen of Irish cycling, Sean Kelly.

Clontarf GAA Clubhouse

Noel (left) & Jack McCaffrey

Jim Ronayne (right) in action for Dublin

Belgrove Boys School Team 1961

Joy as Clontarf FC win Matt O Leary Cup 2012

Clontarf Rugby Club Open Day

Royal Dublin Golf Clubhouse

St Annes Golf Club Clubhouse

Clontarf Golf Clubhouse

Action from Clontarf Swimming Club's Annual Sea Race

Clontarf Yacht & Boat Club

Clontarf Tennis Club

APPENDIXES

1. From "The Dublin Directory" 1870.
CLONTARF AND DOLLYMOUNT (Clontarf Township).

Clontarf, a maritime parish and extensive village in Coolock barony, Dublin County, three miles E.N.E. from the General Post Office, Dublin, comprising an area of 1,190 acres, of which 38 occupy the village and sheds in Clontarf. Population of parish 2,682. It is a memorable place in Irish history, as the scene of a great battle fought by King Brian Boromh, or Boru, on Good Friday, 1014, that put an end to the Danish power in Ireland, the details of which are variously and diffusively narrated by the native historians, and form, it is said, the subject of Gray's ode to the "Fatal Sisters". There are extensive and profitable oyster beds off the sheds. The central portion is a street that runs from the shore inland to the gate of the castle, but the greater and more diversified part faces the strand in continuous rows or clusters of houses, besides numerous small cottages, suited to sea bathers, that line the green lanes and avenues of the village. The castle of Clontarf, one of the first within the English pale, was taken down in 1835, and the present mansion, with a Norman tower, erected thereon. A handsome Church has been recently built. The Roman Catholic Chapel is a large and handsome structure. There is a Widow's Alms House, a Parochial and Roman Catholic Free school, and County and District Constabulary Police Station. It is much frequented in summer for sea bathing. The Drogheda railway skirts the village, near Marino Crescent. Near Dollymount, at the further extremity of Clontarf strand, is an extensive causeway or break-water, called the "Bull Wall," erected by the Ballast Board, with a view of deepening the channel between it and the lighthouse on Poolbeg Wall. It extends upwards of one and a half miles in a S.S.E. direction.

2. From "The Dublin Directory" 1910.
CLONTARF AND DOLLYMOUNT.

Amalgamated with the City of Dublin by Act of Parliament, 1900.

Clontarf, a maritime parish and formerly a township in Coolock barony, Dublin County, three miles E.N.E. from the General Post Office, Dublin comprising an area of 1,289 acres, of which 33 are occupied by the "sheds" of Clontarf. It is a memorable place in Irish History, as the scene of a great battle fought by King Brian Boromh, or Boru, on Good Friday, 1014, that put an end to the Danish power in Ireland, the details of which are variously and diffusively narrated by the native historians, and form, it is said, the subject of Gray's ode to the "Fatal Sisters." The High road skirts the strand, and off it branch many important roads and avenues, which are lined with villas and houses. The green lanes of Clontarf are justly celebrated for their sylvan beauty; along them are situated many fine residences. The castle of Clontarf, one of the first within the English pale, was taken down in 1835, and the present mansion, with a Norman tower, erected thereon. A fine Town Hall was erected in 1894, and enlarged 1898. There is a handsome Church of Ireland Church and Presbyterian and Methodist Churches. The Roman Catholic Church is a large and handsome structure. There are Parochial, Presbyterian and Roman Catholic Free Schools, and others, under the National Board. The O'Brien Institution, situated on the Malahide Road, is for Roman Catholic Orphans. There are also two District Stations. It is much frequented in summer for sea bathing, and is well provided for as regards recreation, as the Royal Golf Club Links are at Dollymount and there is also good cricket and tennis clubs, and a yacht club. A commodious station of the Great Northern Railway Line has been erected near the Howth Road. The tramway in the district is electrically equipped, a very fine power station being erected in the grounds of the tramway Depot, everything in connection with the installation being of the newest and most approved type. There is also an Electric Tram road from Clontarf to Howth. Near Dollymount, at the further extremity of Clontarf Strand, is an extensive causeway or break-water, called the "Bull Wall". It extends upwards of one and a half miles in S.S.E. direction. A tram car starts from Sackville Street every five minutes. There are 3 Post Offices in the District, 2 of them being also Postal Telegraphs Offices.

3. From Porter's Guide and Directory for North County Dublin 1912. CLONTARF, DOLLYMOUNT AND FAIRVIEW.

Incorporated with the City of Dublin by Act of Parliament, 1900. It is about two and a half miles from the General Post Office. It occupies a memorable place in Irish history as the spot where Brian Boroimh, King of Ireland, defeated the Danes and drove them into the sea. It is also the spot where the great national meeting of Irishmen under the presidency of Daniel O'Connell was suppressed in 1843. It is a favourite residential district with Dublin citizens, and is considered a remarkably healthy neighbourhood. Considerable improvements and developments have been made, and are now in progress. The formation of a new park, now rapidly approaching completion, will add to the numerous advantages of Clontarf as a health resort. The streets are all admirably arranged, and contain many well-built houses and terraces, while the whole neighbourhood abounds in the most delightful walks. The views from the sea-front are of the most surpassing beauty. There are several important, educational institutions, Primary and National Schools, and Catholic, Protestant, Presbyterian and Methodist

Churches. There is an excellent Golf Club, under the professional management of Mr. Tom Hood. It has several convenient places, public baths and a coastguard station. There is a railway station on the Great Northern Railway system, and an excellent electric tram service leaving Nelson's Pillar every five minutes.

4. Address of King Brian Boru to his Army prior to the Battle of Clontarf Good Friday 1014.

(These are the traditional line attributed to the venerable Monarch by William Kenealy)

Stand ye now for Erin's glory! Stand ye now for Erin's cause!
Long ye've groaned beneath the rigour of the Northmen's savage laws.
What though brothers league against us? What, though myriads be the foe?
Victory will be more honoured in the myriad's overthrow.

Proud Connacians! Oft we've wrangled in our pretty feuds of yore;
Now we fight against the robber Dane upon our native shore;
May our hearts unite in friendship, as our blood in one red tide,
While we crush their mail-clad legions, and annihilate their pride!

Brave Eugenians! Erin triumphs in the sight she sees to-day
Desmond's homesteads all deserted for the muster and the fray!
Cluan's vale and Galtee's summit send their bravest and their best-
May such hearts be theirs for ever, for the freedom of the West!

Chiefs and Kerns of Dalcassia! Brothers of my past career,
Oft we've trodden on the pirate-flag that flaunts before us here;
You remember Inniscattery, how we bounded on the foe,
As the torrent of the mountain bursts upon the plain below!

They have razed our proudest castles - spoiled the Temples of the Lord -
Burnt to dust the sacred relics - put the peaceful to the sword-
Desecrated all things holy - as they soon may do again,
If their power to-day we smite not - if to-day we be not men!

On this day the God-man suffered - look upon the sacred sign-
May we conquer 'neath its shadow, as of old did Constantine!
May the heathen tribe of Odin fade before it like a dream,
And the triumph of this glorious day in future annals gleam!

God of heaven, bless our banner - nerve our sinews for the strife!
Fight we now for all that's holy - for our altars, land, and life-
For red vengeance on the spoiler, whom the blazing temples trace-
For the honour of our maidens and the glory of our race!

Should I fall before the foeman, 'tis the death I seek to-day;
Should ten thousand daggers pierce me, bear my body not away.
Till this day of days be over - till the field is fought and won-
Then the holy Mass be chanted, and the funeral rites be done

Men of Erin! Men of Erin! Grasp the battle-axe and spear!
Chase these Northern wolves before you like a herd of frightened deer!
Burst their ranks, like bolts from heaven! Down on the heathen crew,
For the glory of the Crucified, and Erin's glory too!

5. A Song of Defeat

Lines 9-31 of Stephen Gwynn's fine poem "A Song of Defeat" deals with the Battle of Clontarf

I call to your mind today,
Out of the mists of the past,
Many a hull and many a mast,
Black in the bight of the bay,
Over against Ben Eadair:
And the lip of the ebbing tideway all
Red with the life of the Gael and the Gall,
And the Danes in a headlong slaughter sent;
And the woman of Eire keening
For Brian, slain in his tent.

Mother, O grey, sad mother,
Love with the troubled eyes,
For whom I marshal today
The sad and splendid array,
Calling the lost to arise,

As some queen's courier unbidden
Might fetch her gems to the sun,
Praising the glory and glow
Of all that was hers to show -
Eire, love Brian well,
For Brian fought, and he won:
God! That was long ago!

6. Brien the Brave.
" Remember the glories of Brien the brave,
Tho the days of the hero are o er;
Tho lost to Mononia and cold in the grave,
He returns to Kincora no more!

That star of the field, which so often has pour d
its beam on the battle is set;
But enough of the glory remains on each sword
To light as to victory yet!

Mononia! when nature embellished the tint
Of thy fields and thy mountains so fair
Did she ever intend that a tyrant should print
The footsteps of slavery there?
No, freedom! whose smile we shall never resign,
Go, tell our invaders the Danes,
That 'tis sweeter to bleed for an age at thy shrine,
Than to sleep but one moment in chains!

Forget not our wounded companion who stood
in the day of distress by our side,
While the moss of the valley grew red with their blood,
They stirred not but conquered and died!
The sun that now blesses our arms with his light;
Saw them fall upon Ossory s plain!
Oh! let him not blush when he leaves us tonight,
To find that they fell there in vain.

7. Suppression of 1843 "Monster Meeting".
("Minutes and details of a (special) meeting (at 10.00a.m.) on the 7th of October, 1843 at the office of the Privy Council with order of equal date to engross a

production forbidding attendance at a meeting (Daniel O'Connell's proposed monster meeting) in Clontarf on the 8th of October.")

"The Board having met, according to special summons, for the consideration of a Draft of a Proclamation cautioning all persons at Clontarf on Sunday the 8th day of October instant, for the alleged purpose of petitioning for a Repeal of the Legislative Union between Great Britain and Ireland. The said Draft was accordingly considered and, after amendment, read, agreed to and signed, as also an order for engrossing and sealing the same."

The Lord High Chancellor of Ireland was to issue a warrant under the Great Seal of Ireland putting the Privy Council's decision into effect. Present at the meeting in the Privy Council Chamber were His Excellency Thomas Philip, Earl de Gray, Lord Lieutenant, The Lord Chancellor, Lord Eliot, the Earl of Donoughmore, the Master of the Rolls, Lt. Gen. Sir E. Blakeney, the Recorder, Mr Shaw, the Attourney General Mr Smith and the Solicitor General, Mr Greene.

(8). Captain Weldon's hand written account of the escape of James Stephens.
"A narrative of the escape of Jas Stephens. Amongst the many startling events that took place at that period of the history of our land which was comprised in the great Fenian movement perhaps the most startling and romantic was the memorable and almost miraculous escape of the Head Centre of the I.R.B. Jas Stephens. As many accounts of that now historic exploit have found their way into print both in this country and that greater Ireland beyond the Atlantic viz, America. Perhaps a round unvarnished tale of the departure from Dublin will not be unacceptable to our readers. The leave-taking from Her Majesty's Hotel at Richmond. I have nothing to add to that with which our Irish Public are already familiar. Same with subsequent hiding. My narrative begins with the early days of the month of March 1866. When with John Flood, an old friend and townsman of mine and here I may state as fine a specimen of Irish manhood as need be seen and his friend Colonel Kelly of the United States Army with whom I had no previous acquaintance. I made arrangements to take Stephens and themselves to a port in the North of France. For the benefit of those who may not have had recollection of those stormy days I may mention that at that period of which I am giving an account the whole available forces of the Crown of these Islands were concentrated upon one object and that object was the capture of the redoubtable Jas Stephens added to which there was a reward of £3,000 upon his head. So that the taking of his body alive out of Ireland was a task of no small magnitude more especially as the whole line of quays both North and South were placarded with this tempting offer of £3,000 to any one who could give such

information as would lead to the capture; so that the sailors who manned the vessels that left the port were and not unnaturally on the alert as to strangers taking passengers in any of their vessels mostly coasting colliers. That being the class of vessel which I commanded and owned at the time. The brigantine "Concord" of Dublin of about 200 tons burden. I may here state that the usual number of my crew were six men and a boy. In consequence of my passengers in order to avoid suspicion I discharged a corresponding number of my crew including my chief mate. Which now only left me two men and the boy and nautically speaking the three duffers. Now it is a notorious fact that at this time there were two Revenue cutters stationed at the mouth of the River to board and search any suspicious craft outward bound. For eight of nine days after our arrangement we were detained in the Liffey waiting for a favourable wind. In the meantime making such preparations necessary for such a perilous undertaking. I was caused an additional anxiety on the 11th by hearing from a pilot who had taken out a vessel that day. He said he was obliged to heave to in the Bay. Where a search of over an hour was made by Her Majesty's Officials and not an inch of the ship but was overhauled and every man on board questioned. After hearing this all but cheerful news from the pilot who little thought what an interest I had in this yarn. I went to my cabin to think. I leave my readers to imagine what my thoughts were if they are so minded. On the 12th I had my vessel hauled out in the River ready to start and on Tuesday evening the 13th I was at the steps opposite Boyd's Chemical Works by appointment. Where my three adventurers stepped into my boat and I rowed them on board as quickly as possible. We cast off our moorings and had the vessel hauled over the North side of the river to make sail. With the wind North East and Kelly, Flood and Stephens working manfully at the winch. We had considerable delay to the want of nautical skill of my three adventurers. It was 1.30 a.m. when we hailed the Revenue cutter to know the time of course this was to avoid suspicion. At first we feared she should board us but she passed up River merely asking "What ship?" I answered "Concord of Dublin for Cardiff." We had to run the gauntlet of two cutters in the Bay but we sailed gaily and innocently between them without notice. Shaped a Southerly course we passed the Mugland off Dalkey and afterwards Bray Head, which showed out remarkably beautiful in the moonlight. At this time we were going free with every stitch of canvas we could carry with a fresh N.E. breeze. By daylight we were off Wicklow Head when the wind died away and changed to the S.E. which was a head wind. The course we were steering was S.E. and we were keeping close to the land to gain all the advantage of the ebb tide which had about two hours to go. You may imagine especially those with nautical knowledge that we were unpleasantly close to a nasty lee shore. However we beat against it as far as Arklow Bay where we had to put in to avoid the flowing tide. About mid-day the wind increased and I saw we were going to have a very bad night as the sky gave to the experienced eye all the indications of a storm from the South. My position was now truly a bad one. With the prospect of a gale right in our teeth a dangerous shore under our lee, and two Revenue cutters in Dublin Bay. About 2 p.m. I hastily consulted with my passengers as to the desirability of putting down our helm and making a course for some other port in Scotland. After a short time they agreed and down went the helm as we squared our yards making to the Northward, thus avoiding Dublin Bay by running over the Kish Bank. Which in itself as I have no need to inform nautical people was a risk of no small magnitude in the breeze that was blowing at the time. Slow sailing craft as we were we went eleven knots; the wind still increasing. I was now making the Mid Channel as it was not prudent to keep close to the Irish land. There was also every likelihood of the wind becoming more Easterly which afterwards turned out to be the case. It was now blowing half a gale but I carried ever stitch till 10 p.m. when I took all my light canvas. This was most fortunate for about eleven o'clock we were struck with a very heavy squall which under small sail was like being almost under water. I may mention here that a sunken reef runs out from this headland for about two and a half miles and the end of it at that time was marked a buoy and this was last the object I wanted to fetch. With the aid of the flowing tide and the increased sail I was in great hopes of weathering. It was a very narrow strait and when passing it one could have thrown a biscuit at the buoy. Shortly after passing this range of rocks, a steamer came in sight and so overstrained were my nerves that I took her for one of H.M's gunboats in pursuit of us. There is not much to be wondered at the nature of my charge required me to be at the wheel almost all the time since we left the Quays in Dublin. The prolongation at the disagreeable weather had the effect of almost driving me mad. Flood, Kelly, and Stephens had provided themselves each with a six chamber revolver. This warlike preparation I am glad to state was unnecessary as the steamer before mentioned turned out to be the Derry boat from Liverpool with goods and passengers. We now shortened sail and eased the vessel of her strain. When we entered the North Channel the sea became heavier and owing to the narrowness of the Channel at the place and the tide running very rapidly was setting us fast to leeward. I now saw it was useless to remain at sea for every hour our position was becoming more dangerous. Night coming on our vessel labouring and straining in a heavy sea and a nasty rocky shore on our lee. I made up my mind reluctantly to run for Belfast Lough. I may say that at this time we got so far leeward we could hardly weather the Copelands so that absolutely there was nothing for us but the Lough and the sound of Donaghadee. To all the hopes of fetching Scotland that night had to be abandoned. At two o'clock on the 16th March I ordered the yard to be squared and run for Belfast Lough where I let go my anchor right opposite the Coast Guard Station in White House Roadstead as dusk was setting in. At five o'clock next morning I weighed anchor with a fair wind and stood down the Lough. I had not however proceeded more than a few miles on my voyage, when off the Copeland Island the stand of the vessel's wheel carried away. The vessel's head immediately swung round and faced up the Lough again. This caused a considerable delay as purchases had to be rigged as temporary steering gear. However we managed to get the vessel's head round and ran her before the wire again. It was a strong breeze from the South East and once more shaped a course for Irvine. And more luck went against us for as we stood more easterly the wind headed us again and I decided to try for Ardrossan as we were able to be to windward of our course for the port. When at eight o'clock that night we were arriving around in the Harbour. Watching a good opportunity I landed my three passengers at a landing place opposite a hotel named the Eglington. I found the water knee deep and carried my three passengers or adventurers one by one ashore. Our leave-taking was very brief; merely a firm shake hands on my part and a wish for their safe departure from the British Isles. On theirs a profound expression of gratitude and that was the last I ever saw of the gallant old chief and his intrepid companions, one of whom as I mentioned before was an old personal friend of mine."

(A further page of Captain Weldon's account has, unfortunately, been mislaid over the years.)

9. Addendum.

Clontarf's familiar and decorative green promenade (see chapters one and nine above) stretches from the twin arched railway bridge in Fairview to the landmark Bull Island Bridge (see chapter six above), with the sea waves forever coming and going alongside. The promenade came into being when a seawall was built followed by an outer sea wall in 1932-34. The area between the two walls was infilled and completed in the mid 1960's. The promenade was then landscaped. When the tide is out the wreck of one of the barges used in the infilling work - somewhat akin to a ribcage - can be seen opposite the Strandville Road/Hollybrook Road area. A stroll along "the prom" allows you to view some Clontarf landmarks often forgotten as well as affording the walker a panoramic view of Dublin Port, Dublin Bay and the Dublin and Wicklow Mountains.

As you begin your walk (northwards), at the Alfie Byrne Road, you see the seat named after the said former Lord Mayor just a few yards from "The sails" a wind sculpture by Eamon O'Doherty erected in the Dublin Millennium year of 1988. As you progress the sea, with all its mysteries manifestations and moods, is your constant companion. And you also have the company of six information boards detailing the battle of Clontarf and events sourounding the battle. The boards also offer very interesting nuggets of data on numerous local items of interest. You can view the two familiar ESB Chimneys (now unemployed!) and the huge gastries, countless buildings and containers that are the heart of port activities That severe bleak grey cold look that once stared back at you is now happily camouflaged by the green trees and shrubs that have been coaxed to grow around the port area facing Clontarf. Soon you pass the derelict site of the once proud Clontarf baths and the "Green Lump" that is the pumping Station opposite the seafront end of Vernon Avenue. All along the seaside shelters are familiar and becoming familiar is the Maoi Sculpture (close to the pumping station). This giant Sculpture was presented to the City of Dublin by the Chilean government in 2004. Chile and Ireland are especially linked because of Ambrosio O'Higgins and later his son Bernardo who were instrumental in Chile gaining full independence (from Spain) in 1817/18. The sculpture itself comes from Easter Island (Rapa Nui), famous for these massive carved statues, the legacy of "neolithic" people of unknown origins. The Chilean Island lies some 6000 kilometres west of Chile.

Opposite the Yacht and Boat Club is "the slipway" long established as a spot for easing boats in and out of the sea. Gazing seawards from here you can see the North and South Bull Walls with their respective lighthouses - the North Bull (just beyond the Réalt na Mara" monument) and the Poolbeg lighthouse. You can observe the large ferry, cargo and cruise ships gliding in and out of the port.

On the south side of the bay you can see Clontarf's twin town of Dun Laoghaire nestling close to the Dublin and Wicklow Mountains. All along the promenade is the very well laid and convenient cycle track or lane. (See also chapter one above).

....

Standing sentinel at the seafront end of Conquer Hill Road is an old electric (ESB) transformer dating back to the days of the trams. Now an old relic, a curiosity, it was nicknamed the "Silver Pole" but is nowadays attired more in black!

....

A plaque in a house on Kincora Road records the fact that Austrian theoretical physicist Erwin Schrodinger lived there from 1939-1956. He was invited to Ireland by the then Taoiseach Eamon De Valera and appointed a senior professor at the newly opened Dublin Institute of Advanced Studies. He became an Irish Citizen in 1945 and while in Ireland he published seven books and some 75 articles on the philosophy of science and generally on the natural sciences.

....

Matters cultural are well catered for in Clontarf. Clontarf tourism, formed in 2013, now incorporates the old Clontarf Heritage Society and the well established Stoker Dracula Gothic Organisation (itself set up in 1991). As well as operating a Failte Ireland visitor information Centre, Clontarf Tourism organises historical and sightseeing walks and tours as well as providing Stoker Dracula and historical talks, film shows and documentaries which can be taken to schools, clubs and other venues. The very atmospheric, comfortable and homely Viking Theatre opened at the Sheds Public House in November 2011 and has reawakened interest in the theatre and drama in Clontarf with ongoing professional presentations and management. Clontarf Historical Society dates back to 1988 and annually provides a most interesting series of lectures.

Comhaltas Ceoltoirí Chuain Tarbh (CCT) is one of the oldest traditional music organisations in Ireland. CCT has been involved in traditional instrument teaching, the development and promotion of Irish traditional music and encouraging musical groups and ceilí bands of all ages on Dublin's northside since its foundation in 1963.

....

If you happen to take a stroll in the quiet Clontarf cul-de-sac that is Kincora Park you might wonder why a colourful flag flies outside one particular building. The flag is that of the Republic of Cuba with its familiar blue and white stripes and lone star embedded in a red triangle. You are in fact passing the Cuban Embassy in Dublin.

AN FOCAL DEIRIDH
Did you know that on the 19th of January 1785 Wicklowman Richard Crosby made the first successful manned flight in Ireland? He crossed from Ranelagh Gardens on Dublin's southside to Clontarf in a hydrogen balloon !!!

View of Clontarf Promenade

The Sails on Promenade

Clontarf Village

Maoi Sculpture

Schrodinger Plaque

ESB Transformer at Seafront on Conquer Hill Road

10. Clontarf Shops of Yore

Jimmy Harrisons Newsagents

Curleys Butchers Clontarf Rd

Noones of Conquer Hill Rd

Vernon Stores, Vernon Avenue

And a Baymount House Memory

> **BAYMOUNT HOUSE BOARDING SCHOOL,
> NEAR DOLLYMOUNT, CLONTARF, DUBLIN.**
> *Under the Direction of Mr. KEILY.*
>
> IN this Establishment, young Gentlemen are expeditiously prepared for Business, College, or any other pursuit in life. Religious instruction is under the care of a resident Catholic Clergyman, who received his Education in France. Health is promoted by parental kindness, spacious and well ventilated dormitories and study rooms, a cheerful and delightful situation, pure air, *Sea Bathing;* and the Demesne affords an extensive range for exercise.
>
> No Summer Vacation is given, and the Terms will be found more moderate than those of any other respectable Establishment in the Kingdom.
>
> *Freeman's Journal, July 20th, 1833*